For nearly thirty years, the artists that passed through the gates of Disney Animation, and even non-artists like myself, were influenced by the craft, skill, wisdom, writings and sketches of Walt Stanchfield.
—Roy Disney

Walt was a kind of Mark Twain for us at Disney. He always taught with humor and skill. You learned to see the world through his eyes. I remember him one day encouraging us to leap into our drawings with boldness and confidence, "Don't be afraid to make a mistake. We all have 10,000 bad drawings in us so the sooner you get them out the better!" Sitting in Walt's class was as much a psychology course as it was a drawing class. One couldn't help walk away with your mind and soul a little more open than when you entered.
—Glen Keane, Walt Disney Animation Studios

Walt Stanchfield's classes and writings were little distillations of the man: quirky, strongly stated in a genial voice, and brimming with a lifetime of sharp observations about story telling and graphic communication. Whether he drew with a ball point pen or painted with a brush dipped in his coffee cup, he got to the essence of things and was eager to share what he learned with his eager disciples, myself among them. He was grizzled and he was great and proof that there was more than one Walt at the Disney Studio that could inspire a legion of artists.
—John Musker, Walt Disney Animation Studios

Walt Stanchfield was one of Disney Animation's national treasures. His classes and notes have inspired countless animation artists, and his approach to drawing of caricature over reality, feeling over rote accuracy, and communication over photographic reproduction gets to the heart of what great animation is all about. Huzzah to Don Hahn for putting it all together for us!
—Eric Goldberg, Walt Disney Animation Studios

During the Animation Renaissance of the 1990s, one of the Walt Disney Studio's best kept secrets was Walt Stanchfield. Once a week after work, this aged but agile figure jumped from drawing board to drawing board, patiently teaching us the principles behind the high baroque style of Walt Disney Animation drawing. Being in a room with Walt made you feel what it must have been like to have been taught by Don Graham. Having one of your life drawings be good enough to be reproduced in one of his little homemade weekly bulletins was akin to getting a Distinguished Service medal! Senior animators vied with trainees for that distinction.
—Tom Sito, Animator/Filmmaker/Author of Drawing The Line: The Untold Story of the Animation Unions from Bosko to Bart Simpson

This exciting collection of master classes by the great teacher Walt Stanchfield is destined to become a classic on the order of Kimon Nicolaides' exploration of the drawing process. Stanchfield (1919–2000) inspired several generations of Disney animators and those of us outside the studio fortunate enough to happen upon dog-eared copies of his conversational notes, which we passed around like Leonardo's Codex Leicester. Stanchfield beautifully communicates the essence and joy of expressing ideas through the graphic line and accumulating a visual vocabulary. Drawn to Life is a treasure trove of cogent, valuable information for students, teachers and anyone who loves to draw.
—John Canemaker, NYU professor and Academy Award®-winning animation filmmaker

Walt Stanchfield, in his own unique way, taught so many of us about drawing, caricature, motion, acting, and animation. Most important to me was how Walt made you apply what you had observed in his life drawing class to your animation. Disney Animation is based on real life, and in that regard Walt Stanchfield's philosophy echoed Walt Disney's: "We cannot caricature and animate anything convincingly until we study the real thing first."
—Andreas Deja, Walt Disney Animation Studios

Walt Stanchfield's renewed emphasis on draftsmanship at the Disney Studios transformed the seemingly moribund art of animation. His students were part of a renaissance with The Little Mermaid and Who Framed Roger Rabbit, a renaissance that continues with films ranging from The Iron Giant to Lilo and Stitch to Wall-E.
—Charles Solomon, Animation Historian

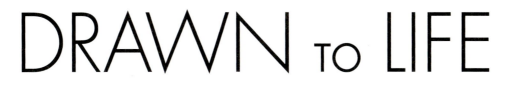

DRAWN to LIFE

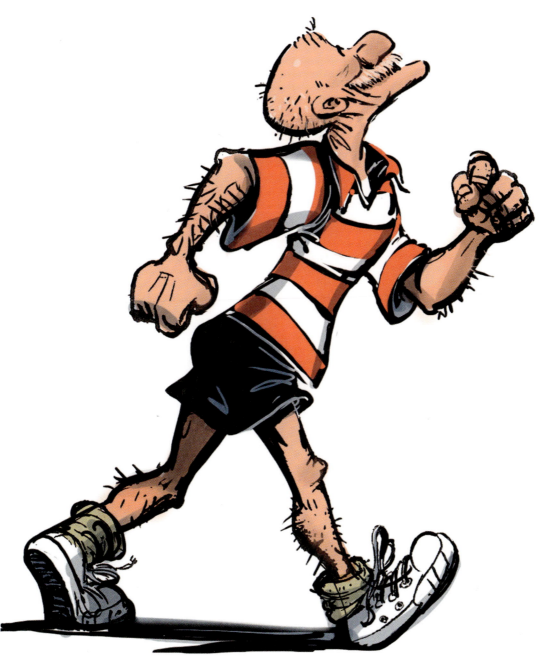

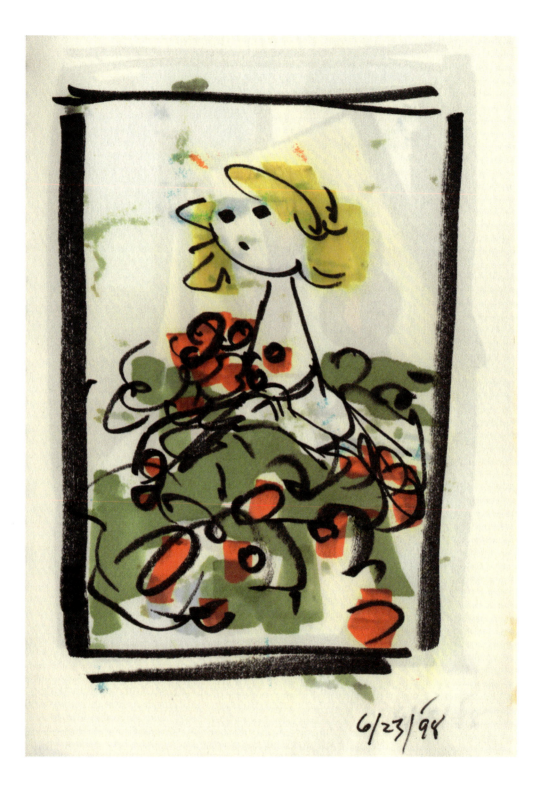

6/23/98

DRAWN to LIFE

20 GOLDEN YEARS OF DISNEY MASTER CLASSES

Walt Stanchfield

Edited by Don Hahn

AMSTERDAM • BOSTON • HEIDELBERG • LONDON
NEW YORK • OXFORD • PARIS • SAN DIEGO
SAN FRANCISCO • SINGAPORE • SYDNEY • TOKYO

Focal Press is an imprint of Elsevier

Focal Press is an imprint of Elsevier
30 Corporate Drive, Suite 400, Burlington, MA 01803, USA
Linacre House, Jordan Hill, Oxford OX2 8DP, UK

Library of Congress Cataloging-in-Publication Data
Application submitted

British Library Cataloguing-in-Publication Data
A catalogue record for this book is available from the British Library.

ISBN: 978-0-240-81096-6

For information on all Focal Press publications
visit our website at www.elsevierdirect.com

11 12 5 4

Printed in Canada

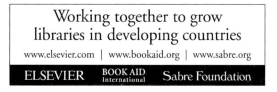

Working together to grow
libraries in developing countries

www.elsevier.com | www.bookaid.org | www.sabre.org

ELSEVIER   BOOK AID
            International   Sabre Foundation

Dedicated with love to Dee

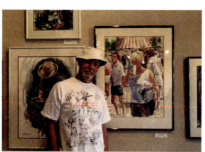
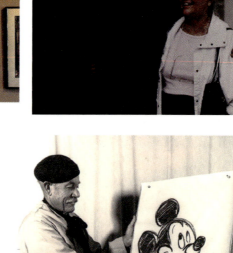
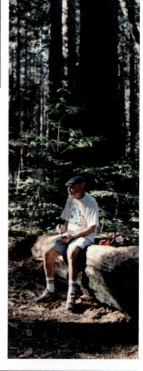
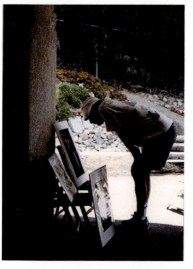
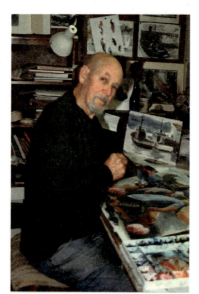
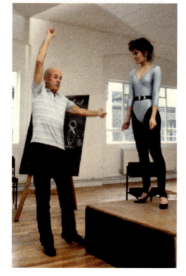
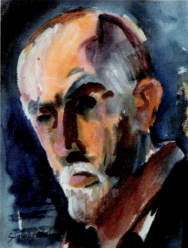

It is management's wish that the "Disney tradition" be revitalized and maintained. The tradition, as we see it, reflects the desires and aspirations of Walt, who, when alive strove to bring animation to a highly developed art. In attempting to recapture the quality attained in former years, we need but refer to the letter Walt wrote to Don Graham in 1935. It expresses the needs of the animation artist and the means he felt were necessary to develop and fulfill those needs.

Walt not only encouraged his employees to better themselves by bringing teachers and lecturers to the studio but he demanded constant improvement. We don't have Walt with us today but we do have the great heritage of animation he left, plus the facilities and the talent with which to uphold that heritage and, to risk hopefully sacrilege improve on it.

Never the less, there will be an attempt to reinstate the learning atmosphere that once permeated this studio. There will be various classes, conducted by numerous instructors. There will be suggested reading and film study; discussion on action analysis and its application to our media.

There will be no attempt to return to any particular era of the past, but to incorporate a composite of all the great accomplishments of the past into a future product that we can all be proud of.

Stan Hulseth 2/10/81

Contents

Creativity   235

Thinking   305

Credits   400

Foreword

Once in a lifetime, a truly exceptional teacher crosses your path and changes your life forever. To me and to many, many of my colleagues in the arts, Walt Stanchfield was that teacher.

Part painter, part poet, part musician, part tennis bum, part eccentric savant, part wise professor, Walt inspired a generation of young artists not only with his vast understanding of the animator's craft, but also his ability to teach that craft and share his enthusiasm for a life in the arts.

Born in 1919 in Los Angeles, Walt began his career in animation in 1937, right out of high school, at the Charles Mintz Studio. He served in the U.S. Navy, then joined the Walter Lantz Studio prior to his lengthy tenure at The Walt Disney Studios. There he worked on every full-length animated feature between *The Adventures of Ichabod and Mr. Toad* (1949) and *The Great Mouse Detective* (1986).

Walt's writing started in the 1970s, when veteran animators at the Disney Studio were at the end of their illustrious careers and new talent was pouring into the studio. Frank Thomas and Ollie Johnston turned to writing their iconic book *The Illusion of Life* and Stanchfield focused on establishing a training program for new animators with veteran animator and director Eric Larson. Walt held regular weekly drawing classes and lectures for the crew. Among the young talent: Brad Bird, John Lasseter, Don Bluth, Joe Ranft, John Musker, Ron Clements, Glen Keane, Andreas Deja, Mark Henn, and so many others.

By the mid 1980s Walt started weekly gesture drawing classes for the entire studio. At the end of each class, he grabbed a few drawings that inspired or challenged him, then pasted them up with his typewritten commentary as a handout for everyone in the class. These weekly lecture notes along with his early writing for the animation training program are the basis for this first-time publication of his complete and prolific work.

In late 1987, I asked Walt to come to London to train the crew on *Who Framed Roger Rabbit*. The artists led by legendary director Richard Williams would crowd around him on the vacant third floor of the Edwardian factory building that was our studio. They would hang on his every word and absorb every line of his drawings. When it came time to pose, we had a leggy supermodel dressed up like Jessica, but Walt was the one who moved like her and helped us see what made her beautiful and sexy.

Walt's writing became the bible of animation for a very young enthusiastic crew of artists that would eventually create films like *The Little Mermaid*, *The Lion King*, *Aladdin*, and *Beauty and the Beast*. Because of Walt's informal approach to these notes, many of the drawings included here are a generation or two away from the artist's original. This photocopied style is very much in keeping with Walt's casual, conversational style of teaching.

The text herein has largely been left alone, as written by Walt. His conversational style is so completely accessible to the artist, it seemed wrong to formalize or edit his voice out of the material in any way. Parts of the text are very heavy with animation terms and technique, but remain as written because they apply to the art of drawing in any medium. Topics appear in no particular order and the sections are meant to be browsed as either instant inspiration, or week-long immersion into any array of subjects. The random nature of topics is also a signature of Walt's personality and approach. He saw life as a unified experience. Drawings inspired paintings, which inspired poetry, which inspired architecture, which inspired travel, which inspired tennis — all connected parts of an artist's life experience.

Drawn to Life is one of the strongest primers on animation ever written. The material spares no detail on the craft of animation, but also digs deep into the artistic roots of the medium. We get a chance to see Walt grow personally as an artist over the span of 20 years represented in these two books. It's a journey that takes him from admired production artist, to technical teacher, to beloved philosopher.

Walt's affect on his students extended way beyond the drawing board. It's not just that he drew better than everyone else, or taught better than everyone else — I admired Walt so much because he seemed to live better than everyone else. When he was not drawing, he was playing guitar, writing poetry, tending his vegetable garden, or making baskets in the style of the Chumash Indians. He was never without a pen and would often color his drawings by dipping a brush into his cup of coffee at breakfast. The drawings were always loose, improvisational, impressionistic and alive, just like their creator.

He passed away in the year 2000 leaving behind a thousand pages of lecture notes and a generation of magnificent animators. With thanks to Dee Stanchfield, Focal Press and The Walt Disney Studios, and special thanks to my co-editors, Connie Thompson and Maggie Gisel, it is with great pleasure that the genius of Walt Stanchfield is now available to you in the pages of *Drawn to Life*.

Don Hahn

Acknowledgements

EDITED BY:
Don Hahn

CO-EDITORS:
Maggie Gisel
Connie Thompson

EDITORIAL CONSULTANT:
Dee Stanchfield

EDITORIAL STAFF:
Kathy Emerson
Christopher Gaida
Josh Gladstone
Kent Gordon
Charles Hayes
Fumi Kitahara
Tracey Miller-Zarneke
Stephanie Van Boxtel

BUSINESS AFFAIRS:
Kevin Breen

FOCAL PRESS/ELSEVIER:
Jane Dashevsky
Paul Gottehrer
Amanda Guest
Georgia Kennedy
Chris Simpson
Katy Spencer
Anais Wheeler

DESIGNED BY:
Joanne Blank
Dennis Schaefer

WALT DISNEY PUBLISHING CLEARANCES:
Margaret Adamic

ADDITIONAL CLEARANCES:
Ashley Petry

DISNEY ANIMATION RESEARCH LIBRARY:
Fox Carney
Doug Engalla
Ann Hansen
Kristen McCormick
Lella Smith
Jackie Vasquez
Mary Walsh
Patrick White

ARTIST RESEARCH AND LOCATION:
Chantal Bumgarner
Ginger Chen
Tenny Chonin
Howard Green
Tiffany Herrington
Bill Matthews
Robert Tiemans
Pamela Thompson

TRANSCRIPTIONS:
Patti Conklin
Kathleen Grey
Rhiannon Hume

INITIAL DESIGN CONCEPTS:
Kris Taft Miller

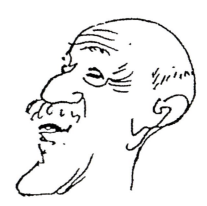

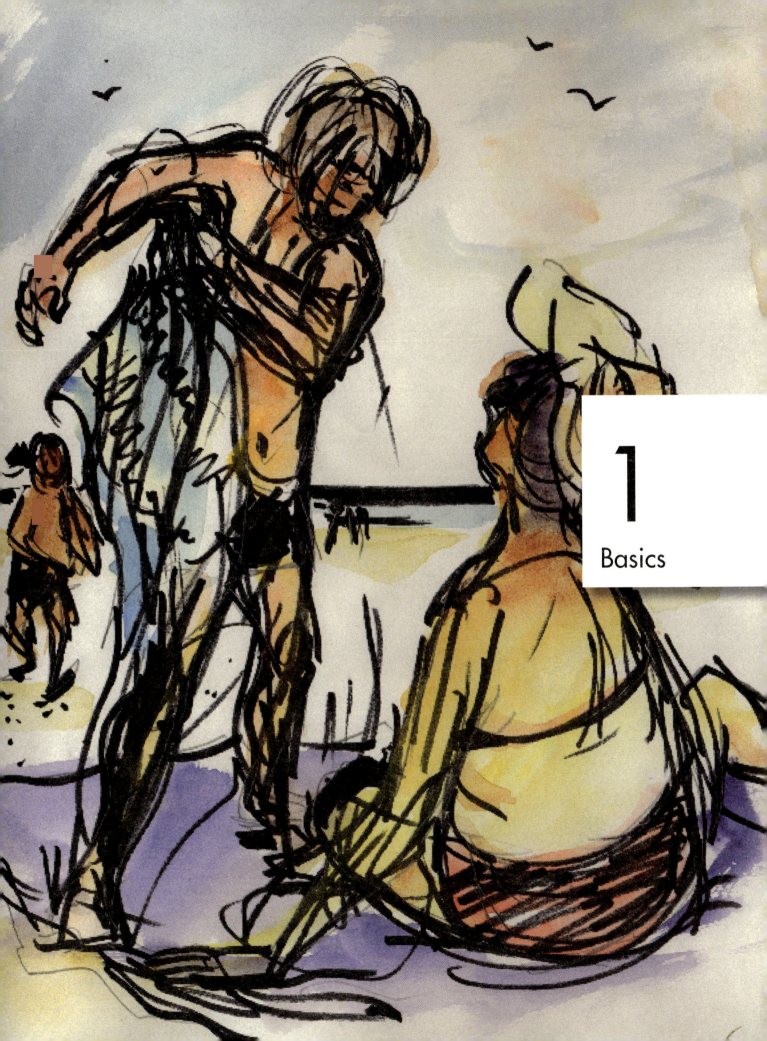

1

Basics

1 Enthusiasm

Having been brought out of retirement for the fourth time, I have been trying to impart some of the drawing know how I have gathered in these past years. (I started at Mintz's Cartoon studio on September 13, 1937). I have incorporated the weekly "handout" which I think works better than lectures. They allow me to more thoroughly express the salient points that come to mind. Also they do not interfere with the already too brief time we have to draw from the model. What's more, they are "collectables" that, in the future, may be reviewed when the need arises.

These handouts allow me to delve deep into my experiences and observations and come up with something that may be of help to you. I have concentrated on gesture drawing because that is one of the foundations of good animation. Necessary to good gesture drawing are acting, caricature, anatomy, body language, perspective, etc., so from time to time these topics are isolated and discussed.

At times I even play the "guru" and deliver a sermon of a positive thinking nature. I approach the subject cautiously for I realize each person's background is different and sometimes deeply meaningful in terms of lifestyle and psychological undergirding. But psychology there is, and it cannot and should not be ignored. *Your mental and emotional processes are you.*

Your mental and emotional processes are what motivates you and without motivation you would accomplish nothing. And without enthusiasm, motivation would atrophy before you could make a quick sketch. Your mind is like a projector — whatever you choose to put into it is what will be seen on the screen (the choice is yours and yours alone). The switch is motivation and the electricity (power) that keeps the whole show moving along is enthusiasm.

Wally "Famous" Amos; the chocolate chip cookie man, in his inspiring book, *The Power in You* said, "Enthusiasm is the mainspring of the mind which urges one to put knowledge into action." In his book he put key thoughts into boxes (which reminds me of a jewel in a setting) like these on the next pages

2 Principles of Animation

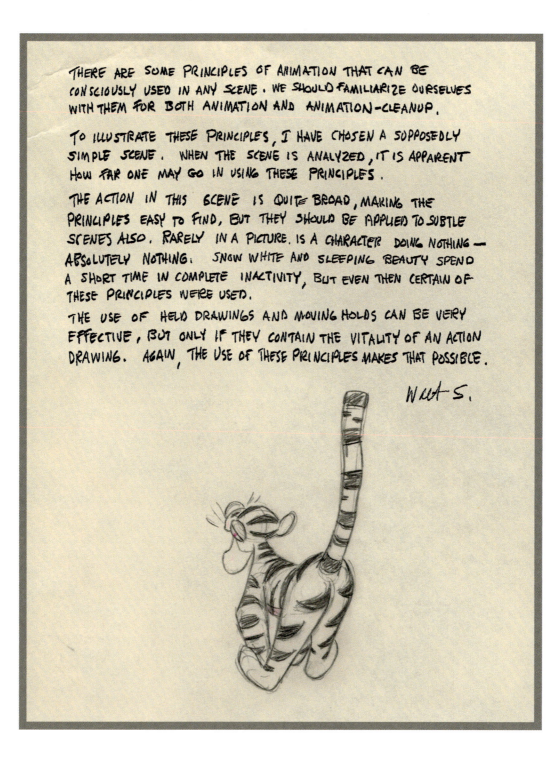

THERE ARE SOME PRINCIPLES OF ANIMATION THAT CAN BE CONSCIOUSLY USED IN ANY SCENE. WE SHOULD FAMILIARIZE OURSELVES WITH THEM FOR BOTH ANIMATION AND ANIMATION-CLEANUP.

TO ILLUSTRATE THESE PRINCIPLES, I HAVE CHOSEN A SUPPOSEDLY SIMPLE SCENE. WHEN THE SCENE IS ANALYZED, IT IS APPARENT HOW FAR ONE MAY GO IN USING THESE PRINCIPLES.

THE ACTION IN THIS SCENE IS QUITE BROAD, MAKING THE PRINCIPLES EASY TO FIND, BUT THEY SHOULD BE APPLIED TO SUBTLE SCENES ALSO. RARELY IN A PICTURE. IS A CHARACTER DOING NOTHING — ABSOLUTELY NOTHING. SNOW WHITE AND SLEEPING BEAUTY SPEND A SHORT TIME IN COMPLETE INACTIVITY, BUT EVEN THEN CERTAIN OF THESE PRINCIPLES WERE USED.

THE USE OF HELD DRAWINGS AND MOVING HOLDS CAN BE VERY EFFECTIVE, BUT ONLY IF THEY CONTAIN THE VITALITY OF AN ACTION DRAWING. AGAIN, THE USE OF THESE PRINCIPLES MAKES THAT POSSIBLE.

Walt S.

HERE IS A LIST OF THINGS (PRINCIPLES) THAT APPEAR IN THESE DRAWINGS, MOST OF WHICH SHOULD APPEAR IN ALL SCENES, FOR THEY COMPRISE THE BASIS FOR FULL ANIMATION.

POSE AND MOOD
SHADE AND FORM
ANATOMY
MODEL OR CHARACTER
WEIGHT
LINE AND SILHOUETTE
ACTION AND REACTION
PERSPECTIVE
DIRECTION
TENSION

PLANES
SOLIDITY
ARCS
SQUASH AND STRETCH
BEAT AND RYTHEM
DEPTH AND VOLUME
OVERLAP AND FOLLOW THRU
TIMING
WORKING FROM EXTREME TO EXTREME

STRAIGHTS AND CURVES
PRIMARY AND SECONDARY ACTION
STAGING AND COMPOSITION
ANTICIPATION
CARICATURE
DETAILS
TEXTURE
SIMPLIFICATION
POSITIVE AND NEGATIVE SHAPES

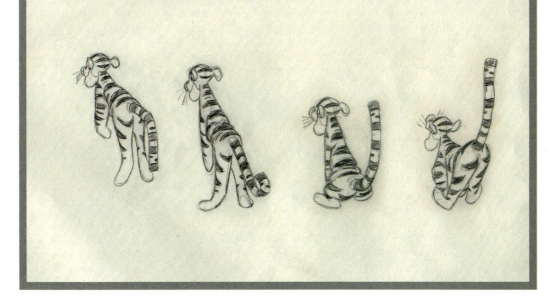

THE PURPOSE OF STUDYING AND ANALYZING A SCENE LIKE THIS IS TO ACQUAINT ONESELF WITH THE POSSIBILITIES IN THE USE OF THE PRINCIPLES OF ANIMATION. I HAVE LISTED 28 PRINCIPLES, THOUGH THERE WELL MAY BE MORE AT FIRST THESE WILL HAVE TO BE USED CONSCIOUSLY, THEN HOPEFULLY IN TIME WILL BECOME SECOND NATURE. THESE ARE THE TOOLS OF ANIMATION AND SHOULD BE INCORPORATED WHENEVER POSSIBLE.

SOME OF THEM ARE ACCIDENTALLY STUMBLED UPON WHILE ANIMATING IN AN EMOTIONAL SPURT, BUT WHEN THE EMOTIONS ARE LAK, KNOWING THESE PRINCIPLES WILL ENABLE THE ARTIST TO ANIMATE HIS SCENE INTELLECTUALLY, LOGICALLY AND ARTISTICALLY AS WELL AS EMOTIONALLY.

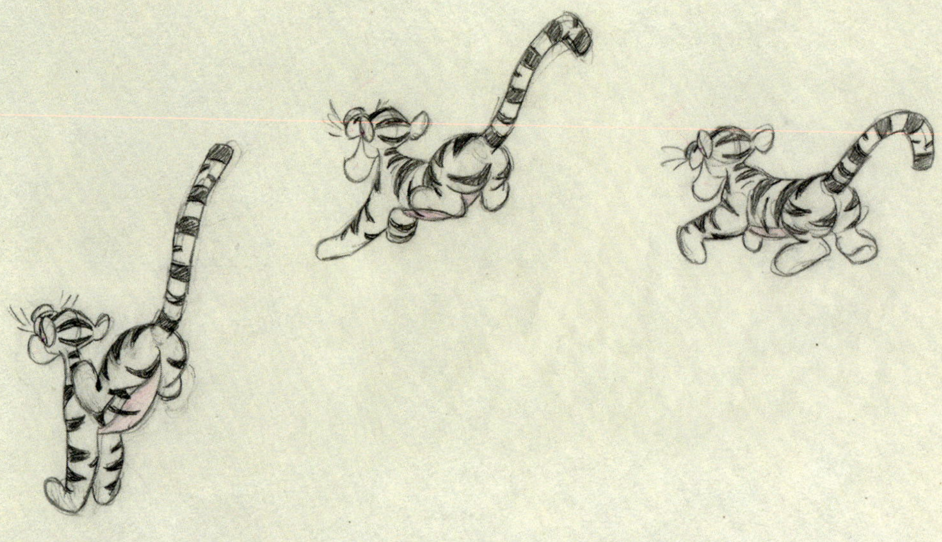

AN EXAMPLE OF THE OBSERVATIONS THAT MIGHT BE MADE BY FLIPPING AND STUDYING JUST THESE TWO DRAWINGS. BY SHIFTING YOUR EYES FROM ONE DRAWING TO THE OTHER YOU CAN SEE THESE THINGS HAPPENING. WATCH THE NEGATIVE SHAPES CHANGE ALSO.

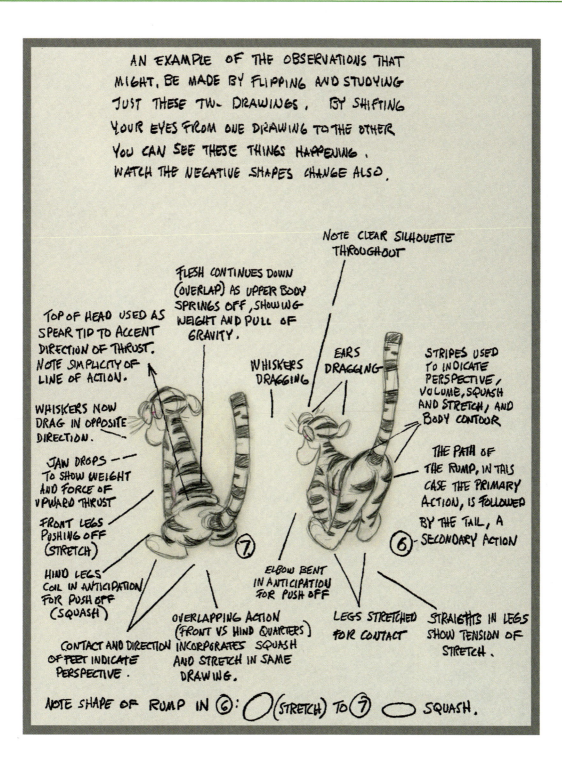

NOTE CLEAR SILHOUETTE THROUGHOUT

FLESH CONTINUES DOWN (OVERLAP) AS UPPER BODY SPRINGS OFF, SHOWING WEIGHT AND PULL OF GRAVITY.

TOP OF HEAD USED AS SPEAR TIP TO ACCENT DIRECTION OF THRUST. NOTE SIMPLICITY OF LINE OF ACTION.

WHISKERS DRAGGING

EARS DRAGGING

STRIPES USED TO INDICATE PERSPECTIVE, VOLUME, SQUASH AND STRETCH, AND BODY CONTOUR

WHISKERS NOW DRAG IN OPPOSITE DIRECTION.

JAW DROPS — TO SHOW WEIGHT AND FORCE OF UPWARD THRUST

THE PATH OF THE RUMP, IN THIS CASE THE PRIMARY ACTION, IS FOLLOWED BY THE TAIL, A SECONDARY ACTION

FRONT LEGS PUSHING OFF (STRETCH)

HIND LEGS COIL IN ANTICIPATION FOR PUSH OFF (SQUASH)

ELBOW BENT IN ANTICIPATION FOR PUSH OFF

LEGS STRETCHED FOR CONTACT

STRAIGHTS IN LEGS SHOW TENSION OF STRETCH.

CONTACT AND DIRECTION OF FEET INDICATE PERSPECTIVE.

OVERLAPPING ACTION (FRONT VS HIND QUARTERS) INCORPORATES SQUASH AND STRETCH IN SAME DRAWING.

NOTE SHAPE OF RUMP IN ⑥: ◯ (STRETCH) TO ⑦ ⬭ SQUASH.

... TO CONTINUE ALONG THIS LINE OF INVESTIGATION...

THIS DRAWING WOULD BE CALLED THE "PUSH OFF". NOTE THAT EVERY LINE AND SHAPE ON THE DRAWING HELPS THE UPWARD THRUST. EVEN THE TAIL, WHICH IS STILL FOLLOWING THE PATH SET UP FOR IT BY ITS PRIMARY FORCE, THE RUMP, HELPS BY WAY OF CONTRAST AND FOLLOW THROUGH. PICK ANY SHAPE ON THE FIGURE AND COMPARE IT TO DRAWING ⑥ ON THE PRECEDING PAGE NOTE HOW EACH SHAPE CHANGES TO ENHANCE THE OVERALL SHAPE AND ACTION : THE NECK, THE CHEST, THE LEGS, THE BACK, ETC.

EVEN THOUGH THIS IS JUST ONE DRAWING, THERE IS NO DOUBT ABOUT THE ACTION THAT IS TAKING PLACE IN THIS PART OF THE SCENE. THIS SHOULD BE TRUE OF ANY DRAWING IN ANY SCENE.

ON THIS ONE DRAWING YOU WILL FIND MOST OF THE PRINCIPLES OF GOOD ANIMATION DRAWING:

POSE AND MOOD
SHAPE AND FORM
ANATOMY
MODEL AND CHARACTER
WEIGHT
LINE AND SILHOUETTE
PERSPECTIVE
DIRECTION
TENSION
PLANES
SOLIDITY
SQUASH AND STRETCH
OVERLAP AND FOLLOW THROUGH
PRIMARY AND SECONDARY ACTION
NEGATIVE AND POSITIVE SHAPES
SIMPLICITY
TEXTURE
SIMPLIFICATION

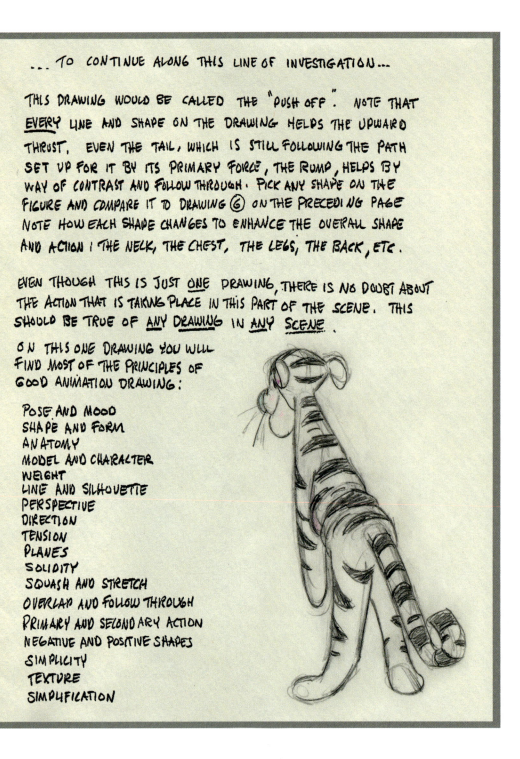

3 Consider Anatomy Alone

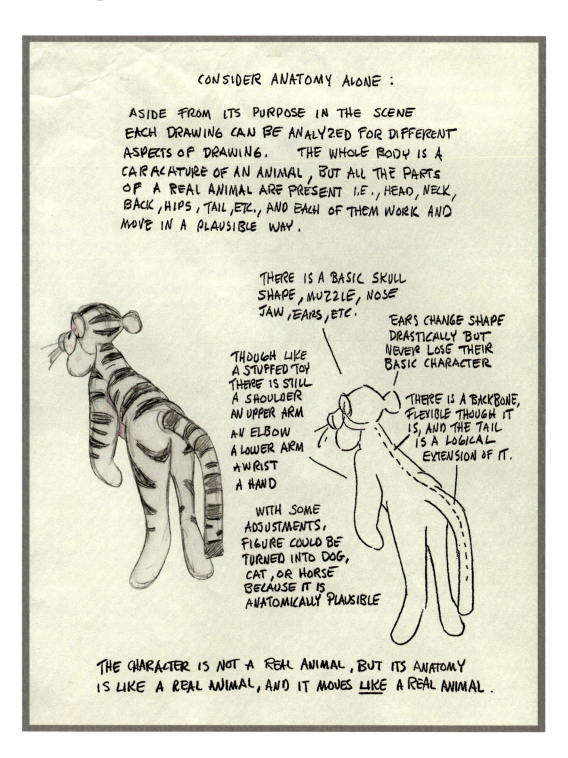

CONSIDER ANATOMY ALONE:

ASIDE FROM ITS PURPOSE IN THE SCENE EACH DRAWING CAN BE ANALYZED FOR DIFFERENT ASPECTS OF DRAWING.   THE WHOLE BODY IS A CARACATURE OF AN ANIMAL, BUT ALL THE PARTS OF A REAL ANIMAL ARE PRESENT I.E., HEAD, NECK, BACK, HIPS, TAIL, ETC., AND EACH OF THEM WORK AND MOVE IN A PLAUSIBLE WAY.

THERE IS A BASIC SKULL SHAPE, MUZZLE, NOSE JAW, EARS, ETC.

EARS CHANGE SHAPE DRASTICALLY BUT NEVER LOSE THEIR BASIC CHARACTER

THOUGH LIKE A STUFFED TOY THERE IS STILL A SHOULDER AN UPPER ARM AN ELBOW A LOWER ARM A WRIST A HAND

THERE IS A BACKBONE, FLEXIBLE THOUGH IT IS, AND THE TAIL IS A LOGICAL EXTENSION OF IT.

WITH SOME ADJUSTMENTS, FIGURE COULD BE TURNED INTO DOG, CAT, OR HORSE BECAUSE IT IS ANATOMICALLY PLAUSIBLE

THE CHARACTER IS NOT A REAL ANIMAL, BUT ITS ANATOMY IS LIKE A REAL ANIMAL, AND IT MOVES LIKE A REAL ANIMAL.

4 Anatomy Continued

ANATOMY, OF COURSE IS ESSENTIAL TO ANY DRAWING WHETHER IT HAS A DIRECT REFERENCE TO NATURE OR IS COMPLETELY IMAGINARY. THOUGH A CHARACTER AND/OR ITS ACTION MAY BE GREATLY EXAGGERATED OR CARACATURED, ANATOMY IN A SENSE REMAINS FAIRLY CONSTANT. AN ELBOW IS AN ELBOW AND ONLY BENDS IN A CERTAIN WAY, AND HAS ITS LIMITATIONS. LIBERTIES MAY BE TAKEN BUT THE "REALITY" OF EVEN A CARTOON MUST BE KEPT OR IT WILL LOSE PLAUSIBILITY OR CREDULITY. IT IS NOT AN EASY THING TO CONVERT ONE'S KNOWLEDGE OF STRUCTURAL ANATOMY TO THE CARTOON MEDIUM.

IT HAS BEEN SAID THAT THE LOCATION OF A JOINT IS MORE IMPORTANT THAN THE JOINT ITSELF. FOR INSTANCE IF AN ARM SHAPE HAS BEEN ESTABLISHED, IT CANNOT HAVE AN ELBOW BEND IN AN IMPROBABLE PLACE, NO MATTER HOW WELL THE ELBOW IS DRAWN. COMPARE TIGAR'S ARM TO THAT OF A REAL TIGER.

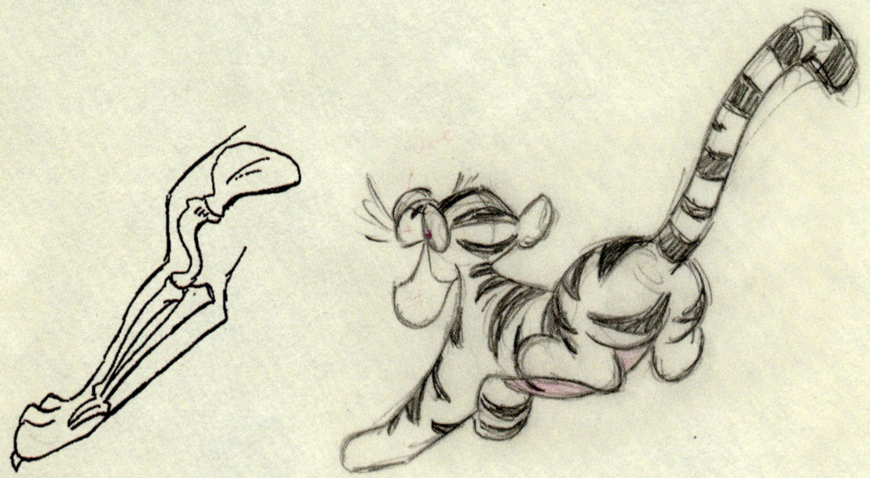

5 Consider Weight

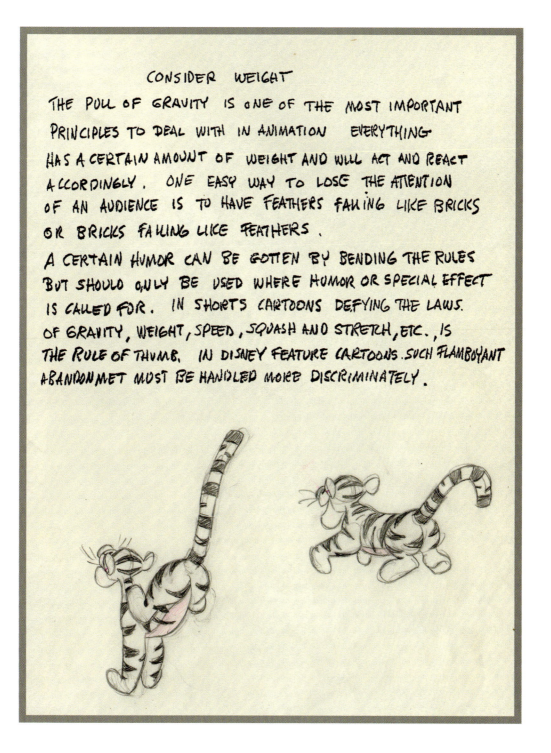

CONSIDER WEIGHT

THE PULL OF GRAVITY IS ONE OF THE MOST IMPORTANT PRINCIPLES TO DEAL WITH IN ANIMATION. EVERYTHING HAS A CERTAIN AMOUNT OF WEIGHT AND WILL ACT AND REACT ACCORDINGLY. ONE EASY WAY TO LOSE THE ATTENTION OF AN AUDIENCE IS TO HAVE FEATHERS FALLING LIKE BRICKS OR BRICKS FALLING LIKE FEATHERS.

A CERTAIN HUMOR CAN BE GOTTEN BY BENDING THE RULES BUT SHOULD ONLY BE USED WHERE HUMOR OR SPECIAL EFFECT IS CALLED FOR. IN SHORTS CARTOONS DEFYING THE LAWS OF GRAVITY, WEIGHT, SPEED, SQUASH AND STRETCH, ETC., IS THE RULE OF THUMB. IN DISNEY FEATURE CARTOONS SUCH FLAMBOYANT ABANDONMET MUST BE HANDLED MORE DISCRIMINATELY.

6 Squash and Stretch — 1

Hardly any action will happen without squash and stretch. Sometimes it will be quite broad and obvious, and at other times so subtle that it will be felt rather than seen. Here is an example of squash and stretch, where the anticipation drawing is also the stretch drawing. Notice in the center drawing both squash and stretch occur at the same time. The body is squashed while the arms are stretched to their limits. The last drawing is also a stretch drawing but not as violent as the first.

Notice how the animator directs your attention to the object of the move. In the first drawing there is a strong triangular shape, with lots of tension set up, narrowing right down to the briefcase handle. The grabbing attitude of the right hand, the open stance of the body, and the strong eye contact all help. Notice here how everything has been pulled away from the line of vision, allowing the look to be unobstructed. In the second drawing, the triangle has squashed and nearly dissipated itself in the contact. Work your eyes from drawing to drawing and watch this happen.

Notice, too, how the animator has opened up the negative areas in the anticipation or "preparation for the action" drawing, and the sudden diminishing or disappearing of them in the "action proper." Then normal negative areas are reestablished in the "termination of the action."

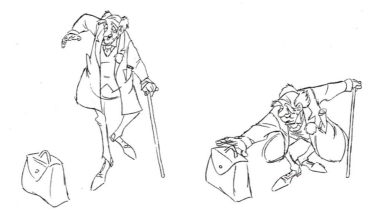

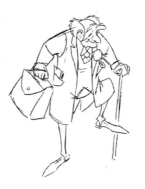

7 Squash and Stretch — II

Squash and stretch can be very broad, or it may be very subtle. In the Disney features, subtlety has been developed to a high degree. The type of story, the liberal use of dialog, and the close-up has made this imperative. We capitalize on the use of squash and stretch in the face. For instance, the eyes, opening wide for surprise or fear (stretch), partly closed from the cheek action during a smile (slight squash), or squeezed into slits from anger or suspicion, or strain (squash).

Nothing moves independently. If the mouth is active as in dialog, everything on the face is going to react and move accordingly. Smile broadly in a mirror and observe. The upper lip area squashes up toward the nose, while at the same time stretches out into the cheek area. Notice how it changes shape yet still retains its volume. The upper lip action causes the nostrils to spread. The cheeks spread outward and upward. This causes the bottom lids of the eyes to raise up over the bottom part of the eyeball, causing the eye to appear to squash.

All this cheek flesh raising up clashes with the temple flesh which doesn't want to go anywhere because it is less fleshy and is attached to something more solid. The result is a set of tiny wrinkles next to the eyes on the temple.

Even the ears and sideburns react, even the neck and collar, and to an infinitesimal degree, the cloth on the upper chest. To carry the point this far in animation may prove to be impractical, but it was mentioned for observation's sake and to emphasize the fact that nothing moves independently in full animation. All the parts of a drawing are related, just as all drawing in a scene is related to all other drawing.

The cleanup person must be aware of how much squash and stretch the animator has used and where he has used it. While going through the scene to acquaint himself with it, it might be good to make notes on the drawings such as "squash here" etc., lest in perfunctorily cleaning up the scene he over look it.

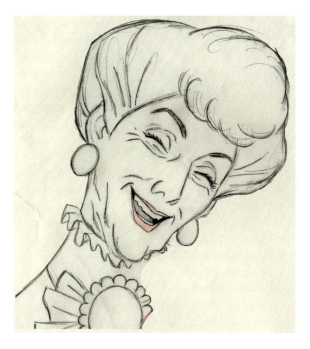

8 Stretch and Squash — III

Stretch and squash is one of the most used principles in animation. The lack of it can make a scene seem lifeless. The over use of it has not yet occurred.

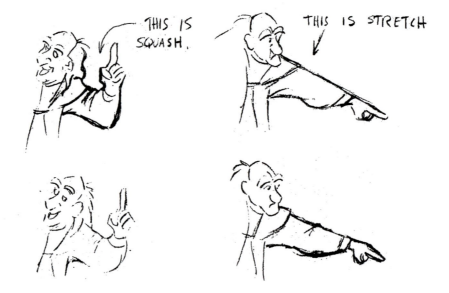

Same action with less emphasis on squash and stretch. Move your eyes back and forth to observe which has the stronger impact.

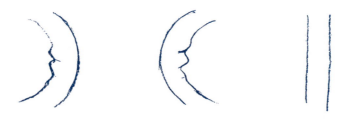

The principle of stretch and squash can be used whenever an object bends or straightens. Look for ways to use it. It can mean the difference between animating an object or just moving it.

9 Line and Silhouette

Line, of course, is what we must use to delineate our drawings. Silhouette is a test of whether or not the lines have successfully depicted the pose.

To draw a shape with a single line with no shading or texture means we must tell the whole story with line alone. The line has to explain the action, as well as what is happening to the structure as it performs that action — what is beneath the clothing or the fur or the skin.

A line drawing may have all the necessary parts and props but not pass the silhouette test. This simply means the drawing should have been staged to read more clearly, even if it were to be completely blacked in.

A "line" drawing actually is a "shape" drawing, as the silhouette test shows. One does not animate lines, but shapes. Lines merely make it possible to depict shapes and to convert those shapes into squashes and stretches, lateral and foreshortened drawings, straights and curves, etc.

A variety of lines will add to a shape's interest and persuasiveness. For instance, curved against straight, short against long, heavy against fine.

A judicious use of thick and thin will add texture to the drawing and further the illusion of third dimension — heavy lines to imply shadows; thicker lines to suggest eyelashes in contrast to the delicate line of the eye orb. Thick lines on parts closest to the viewer tend to make them seem closer, again adding to the much desired third dimensional effect.

The term "touchup" originated on 101 Dalmatians. In an attempt to retain the spontaneous qualities of the animation ruffs, the drawings were merely shorn of superfluous action and construction lines. Also the backgrounds had a Xeroxed line drawing placed over them, simulating the line drawings of the animation. It was a successful marriage of animation and background.

For the time being, we have of necessity gone back to cleaning up the drawings, but are still attempting to retain the spontaneous qualities of the animators' drawings. Although cleanup usually implies a slick drawing with faultless line quality, it certainly should still have the looseness and pliability of the original, plus the solidity of a well-constructed drawing. In the end, there is no such thing as an animated drawing as opposed to a cleanup drawing; they are one and the same and should be treated so.

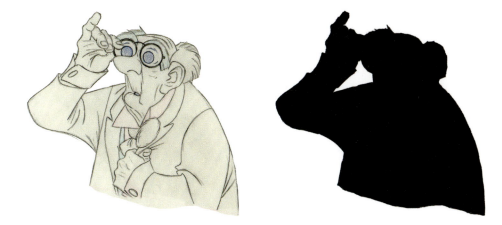

10 Basic Shapes versus Details

Here is a series of three animation drawings broken down into their simplest elements. Basically, simple shapes are what the animator uses in animating a character. When these basic shapes are "working," then the detail may be added. Most detail such as hair, wrinkles, clothing, etc., can be used to enhance the main action.

In cleanup, the assistant animator must be able to spot the basic shapes and their movements in spite of any details that might tend to camouflage them. Once he has found the essence of the pose or action, the details will nearly take care of themselves; that is, the main action will dictate or suggest the detail action.

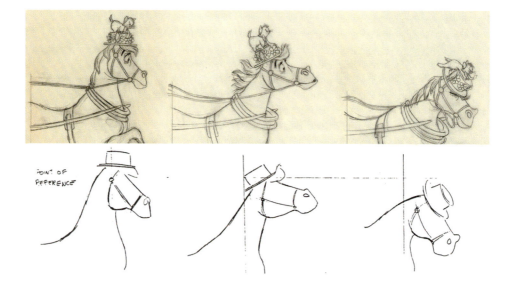

11 Using Basic Shapes as Aid in Difficult Drawings

There is no substitute for good drawing. The logical approach to good drawing is to rely on basic shapes. Most of the problems that come up are when a character or a piece of that character moves far enough so it cannot be inbetweened — it has to be actually drawn. All of a sudden here is a hand that has to be drawn…from scratch! No model! No hand ever got into that position, or an ear, or a tail, or hair. The extremes were easy poses to draw but the inbetweens are impossible.

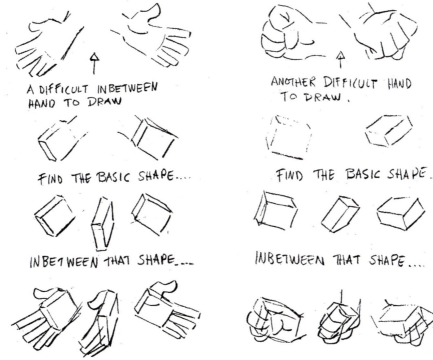

A DIFFICULT INBETWEEN HAND TO DRAW

FIND THE BASIC SHAPE....

INBETWEEN THAT SHAPE....

AND ADD THE DETAILS

ANOTHER DIFFICULT HAND TO DRAW.

FIND THE BASIC SHAPE.

INBETWEEN THAT SHAPE....

AND ADD DETAILS

12 Simplify Where Possible

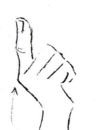

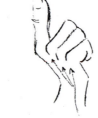

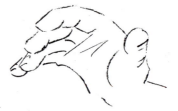

THIS KNUCKLE
EXPLAINS ...

..WHAT THESE
DON'T HAVE TO .

IN A CLOSE UP 3 SECTIONED
FINGERS , AND SOME DETAIL
IN HAND MAY BE DESIRABLE .

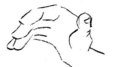

IN A MEDIUM OR LONG SHOT
2 SECTIONED FINGERS WILL DO,
PLUS LESS DETAIL .

USING A MULTITUDE OF
WRINKLES ONLY COMPLICATES
THE DRAWING AND MAKES
BREAKDOWN AND INBETWEEN
HARDER .

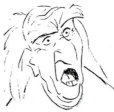

AN EXCESS OF WRINKLES ON A
FACE INCREASES THE POSSIBILITY
OF JITTERS, ON THE CHARACTER
AND THE INBETWEENER ...

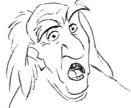

THE SIMPLE APPROACH IS CLEARER,
AS EFFECTIVE AND MUCH
EASIER TO HANDLE .

THE SIMPLER DRAWING IS
EASIER TO HANDLE AND EASIER
TO "READ" AT A GLANCE .

13 Straights and Curves

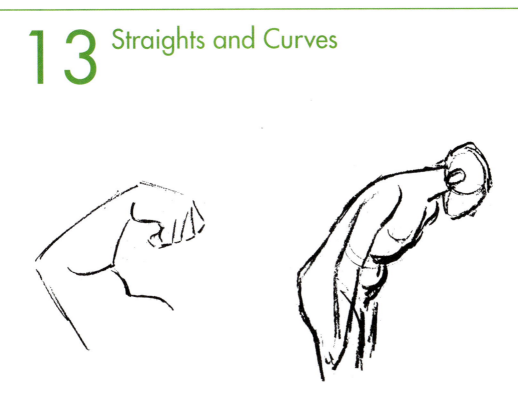

Usually the part of the body that is curved is the muscular or fleshy part that bends or folds inward. The straight is usually the boney part, which stretches or pulls tight when a bend takes place. Keeping this in mind will help determine the straights and curves on a character while in a normal or relaxed pose.

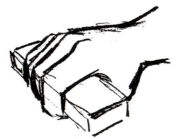

THE REVERSE WOULD BE TRUE
WHEN THE FLESHY PART IS
AGAINST SOMETHING RIGID . . .

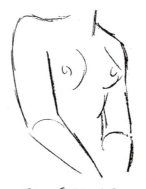

TWO FLESHY PARTS
PRESSING TOGETHER
WILL CAUSE A STRAIGHT

14 Overlap, Follow-through, and Drag

WATCH FOR OVERLAP AND FOLLOW-THROUGH ON PARTS OF THE BODY. TO FIND IT, DETERMINE THE PRIMARY ACTION AND ANYTHING ATTACHED, IF FLEXIBLE, WILL HAVE AN OVERLAPPING ACTION.

FOR INSTANCE A FOOT DOES NOT JUST INBETWEEN WHEN LEAVING THE GROUND.....

..... THE ANKLE (PRIMARY ACTION) LEADS WHILE THE TOES COMPLETE THEIR ACTION, THEN FOLLOW THRU

PRINCIPLE FOR CHANGING DIRECTION CAN BE APPLIED TO ANYTHING FLEXIBLE

CONNECTION TO PRIMARY ACTION (A) CHANGES DIRECTION FIRST. MIDDLE SECTION FOLLOW (B). TIP, DEPENDING ON LENGTH AND FLEXIBILITY, CONTINUES ITS COURSE OF ACTION TILL INTERRUPTED BY PULL OF MAIN BODY (A & B).

HAIR, EARS, TAIL, COAT TAIL, SKIRT....

STUDY ACTION WITH STRIP OF THIN PAPER

TO KEEP HAIR, COAT TAILS, DRESS HEMS, ETC, SOFT OR FLEXIBLE — DRAG SLIGHTLY AT BEGINNING OF MOVE OR AT INCREASE WITHIN MOVE OR AT END OF MOVE (OVER-LAP) OR AT CHANGE OF DIRECTION (SEE ABOVE)

APPENDAGES "DRAG" UNTIL THE PRIMARY ACTION CHANGES DIRECTION, THEN WHEN THEIR "SECONDARY ACTION" IS SPENT, OVERLAP, FOLLOW-THROUGH + DRAG.

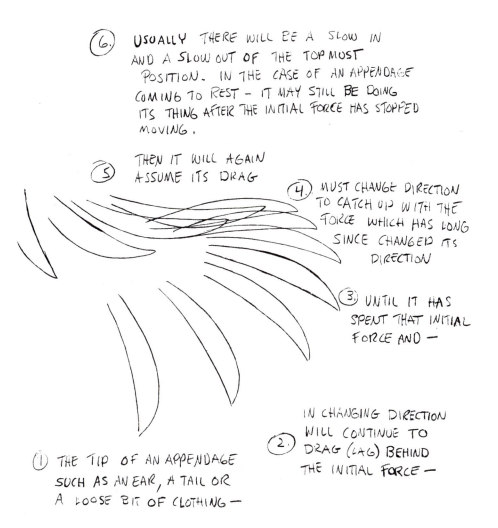

6. USUALLY THERE WILL BE A SLOW IN AND A SLOW OUT OF THE TOP MOST POSITION. IN THE CASE OF AN APPENDAGE COMING TO REST — IT MAY STILL BE DOING ITS THING AFTER THE INITIAL FORCE HAS STOPPED MOVING.

5. THEN IT WILL AGAIN ASSUME ITS DRAG

4. MUST CHANGE DIRECTION TO CATCH UP WITH THE FORCE WHICH HAS LONG SINCE CHANGED ITS DIRECTION

3. UNTIL IT HAS SPENT THAT INITIAL FORCE AND —

2. IN CHANGING DIRECTION WILL CONTINUE TO DRAG (LAG) BEHIND THE INITIAL FORCE —

1. THE TIP OF AN APPENDAGE SUCH AS AN EAR, A TAIL OR A LOOSE BIT OF CLOTHING —

15 Eyes

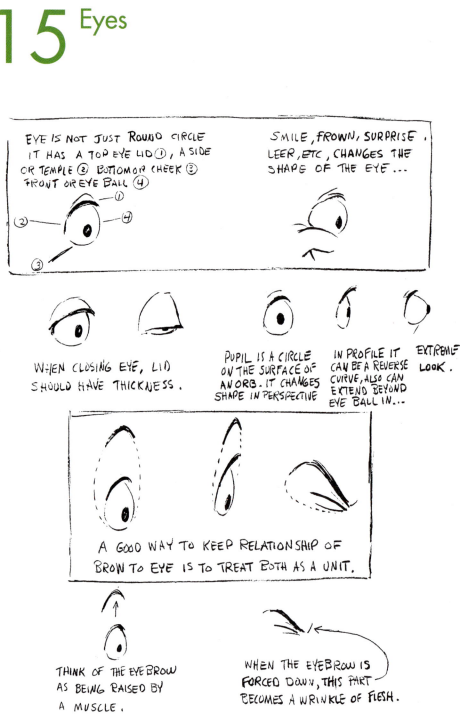

EYE IS NOT JUST ROUND CIRCLE
IT HAS A TOP EYE LID ①, A SIDE
OR TEMPLE ② BOTTOM OR CHEEK ③
FRONT OR EYE BALL ④

SMILE, FROWN, SURPRISE,
LEER, ETC, CHANGES THE
SHAPE OF THE EYE...

WHEN CLOSING EYE, LID
SHOULD HAVE THICKNESS.

PUPIL IS A CIRCLE
ON THE SURFACE OF
AN ORB. IT CHANGES
SHAPE IN PERSPECTIVE

IN PROFILE IT
CAN BE A REVERSE
CURVE, ALSO CAN
EXTEND BEYOND
EYE BALL IN...

EXTREME
LOOK.

A GOOD WAY TO KEEP RELATIONSHIP OF
BROW TO EYE IS TO TREAT BOTH AS A UNIT.

THINK OF THE EYEBROW
AS BEING RAISED BY
A MUSCLE.

WHEN THE EYEBROW IS
FORCED DOWN, THIS PART
BECOMES A WRINKLE OF FLESH.

16 Avoiding Tangent Lines

AVOID MORE THAN 2 LINES INTERSECTING

DO THIS INSTEAD

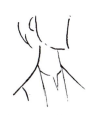

TANGENT COULD OCCUR WHERE VEST, SHIRT AND NECK LINES MEET

SLIGHT ADJUSTMENT WOULD CREATE DEPTH AND DEFINE SHAPES BETTER

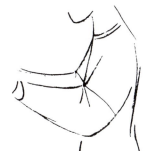
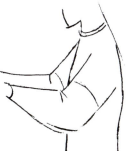

NOTICE TANGENT AT NECK— COLLAR-ARM-CHEST AREA, ALSO AT CHEST-ARM-SLEEVE- WRINKLE .....

SLIGHT ADJUSTMENT MAKES MORE READABLE DRAWING

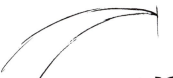

ANOTHER KIND OF TANGENT. IF THIS IS DESIRED LENGTH

DRAW SO IT WILL BE PAINTED TO THE TIP.

17 Some Simple Rules of Perspective

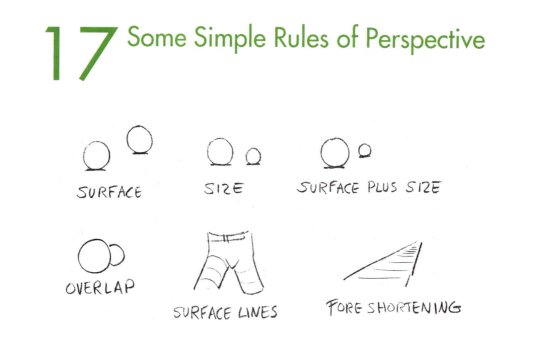

SURFACE   SIZE   SURFACE PLUS SIZE

OVERLAP   SURFACE LINES   FORE SHORTENING

18 Some Ways to Create Space and Depth

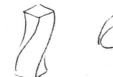

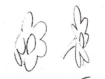

TWISTING   CUPPING + OVERLAP   FLOWER STRAIGHT ON APPEARS FLAT   TWISTING IT CREATES DEPTH

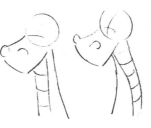

HAND STRAIGHT ON APPEARS FLAT   TWISTING IT, ADDING OVERLAP CREATES DEPTH   ETC.

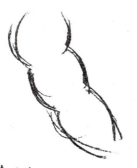 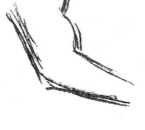

AVOID MONOTONOUS
SHAPES

RATHER USE STRAIGHTS
AGAINST CURVES

AVOID STATIC
REPETITIONS

VARY THE SHAPES
EITHER IN SIZE, SHAPE,
OR DIRECTION.

AVOID PARALLELS

VARY SHAPE

AVOID EVENESS IN HAIRS,
FEATHERS, FINGERS, ETC.

VARY THEM IN SIZE,
SHAPE, DIRECTION OR
DISTANCE APART.

19   Some Principles of Drawing

Again, in our model sketching sessions we naturally employ our efforts to drawing the model, but our attention is directed not so much to copying or getting a photographic likeness but rather to studying and capturing the essence of the poses. Our goal is to be able to apply the principles we learn to our animation drawings — whether we are animating, cleaning up, or inbetweening. Some of the main things we should be concentrating on are the basic principles of squash and stretch, balance and weight distribution, and how these things work for us in animation. Copying the model without this awareness would be like copying a novel to learn how to write novels.

In every move a figure (human or cartoon) makes its adjustments in the various parts of groups of parts to pull off the move. Usually a preparation of anticipation precedes the move and more than likely involves a squash, plus the distribution of weight to intensify the thrust of the move. The move or action itself usually is a stretch. But even in an extreme squash drawing, some parts have to stretch to get into that position.

The principles involved are simple and obvious and are applicable to any action. If the body leans forward to grasp some object with its outstretched hand — there must be stretch, and there must be an adjustment in weight distribution such as counterbalancing with the opposite arm, and placing one foot closer to the object than the other to keep the body balanced. There are other things that will contribute to the reach also. Eye contact with the object funnels the attention to the reason for the action; keeping the path between the hand and the object and the eyes and the object clear of any obstruction, opening the hand in anticipation for the grasp. Timing, which we can't depict in a sketch, is also important. It will be different for delicately picking up the object as opposed to seizing it in a broad sweep of the arm, plus of course the continual redistribution of weight, and the choice of which part of the move will be reserved for the extreme, extreme.

So our real goal in studying a model is to draw not bones and muscle and insignificant details but rather squash and stretch and weight distribution, plus — just to keep life interesting — composition, shape and form, perspective, line and silhouette, tension, plans, and negative and positive shapes, to mention a few.

The point is if we go at drawing from the standpoint of anatomy or model we are less likely to achieve the expression we are after, whereas if we work out some symbols for squash and stretch and apply them to anatomy, we can achieve our sought after gesture — then bring it onto model, along with other refinements later. Milt Kahl and Ollie Johnston could animate with all those refinements, but let's face it we are not that far along (as yet). If we are talking cleanup or inbetween we still have to start with the gesture before getting involved in the details of model and line and color separations; things that are important but only *after* the storytelling gestures have been taken care of.

Simply put, a straight line is the symbol for a stretch, and a bent or folded line is the symbol for a squash. So whether the action is a broad stretch of the arm and body, or a subtle stretch on a face caused by a smile or an open mouth — the symbols are applied to the anatomy to put these ideas over.

Time should be set aside for the practice of sketching with these symbols. I do not mean merely drawing with straight and curved lines per se, but rather to modify the anatomy to encompass these principles in drawings that are flexible enough to mold into the desired gestural needs. This flexibility should be encouraged and nurtured. To sketch in a rigid fashion discourages adjustments and improvements. "Hey, I just drew a great arm — it may be in the wrong place, but it's such a great arm — I'll just alter the rest of the figure to fit *it*."

The goal is to find the essence of the gesture and make all the parts of the body contribute to and enhance that gesture.

There once was an artist who sketched
So a career in the arts he thus fetched
He studied in class
But oh my, and alas
When his drawings weren't good he was wretched

A Milt Kahl example of anticipation (preparation) and stretch.

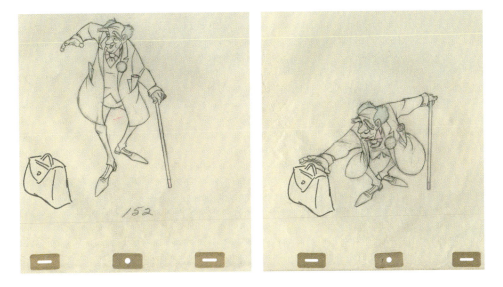

Inanimate characters also stretch and squash.

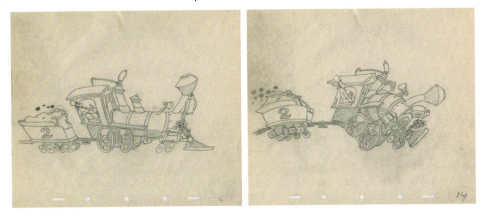

An example of the observations that might be made by flipping and studying just these two drawings. By shifting your eyes from one drawing to the other you can see these things happening. Watch the negative shapes change also.

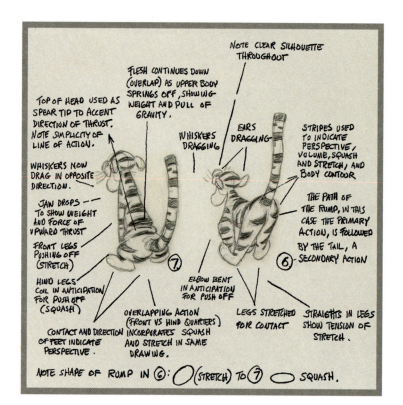

20   Great Performance or Just a Drawing?

   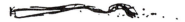

Anatomy of a match and a burnt match.

If you had to draw a burnt match would you say to yourself, "Okay, this is the anatomy of a match." No, you would say, "This is a match whose anatomy has been burnt and twisted into an agonizing shape." A shape that hurts deeply if I imagine myself being in that state. If I *feel* what has happened to that match has happened also to me — then this is the feeling that I have to draw, to portray.

One night we had Lalla posing for us in our gesture class. She is an excellent model who acts out little one-pose dramas. One student was making a beautiful drawing of a pose that was similar to the burnt match, but his drawing looked like a woman in repose, rather than in mental and physical agony. I said, "Yours is a nice drawing but that pose is a Kathe Kollwitz situation." He said, "Who is Kathe

Kollwitz?" She was a Prussian artist who grew up in a period of much conflict. She lived in Germany during Hitler's rise to power, and depicted the tragedies and sufferings of the period.

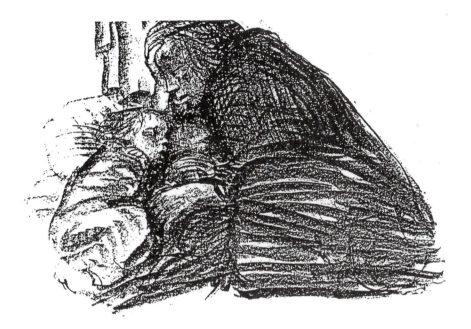

This is a well-constructed drawing. It has all the parts and they are put together beautifully, but that is not what you see when you look at the drawing. What you *see* is fear and hunger and despair, and you feel this, plus pity, revulsion, and anger. All gestures are not quite that dramatic but all gestures are certainly more than their parts.

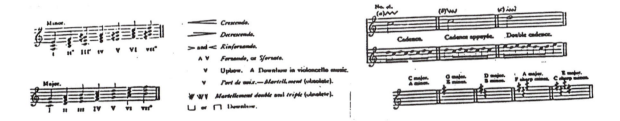

These may be some of the parts to your favorite music but they mean nothing until they are put together and performed in a manner that brings out their meaning. Likewise the parts of the figure must be put together in a manner that will portray or caricature the meaning of the pose. Otherwise it will be just a drawing. What a horrible fate — to be *just* a drawing.

Do this experiment — get a wooden match and look at it. That represents your model or character in animation. Then light it and let it burn half way. Now it represents your model or character in gesture. It has been transformed from the anatomical match into a burnt match. The illustration ends here because a match can't act, but a model on paper or a character in a film can act; that is if you, the artist, will transform them into meaningful gestures. Here are some animation drawings that have transcended the anatomy and model of the characters. They are good drawings but not *just drawings.*

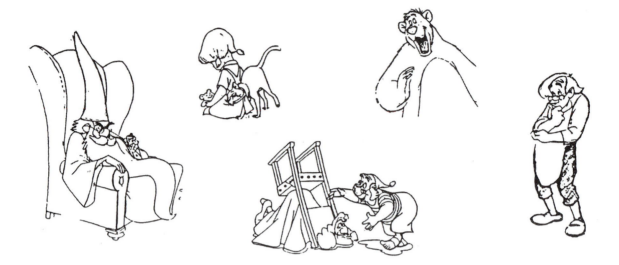

21 Drawing Calories

Lots of people are calorie conscious these days. So why not artists too. Calories, as applied to food, refer to its heat-producing or energy value. This simply means that the foods we eat both maintain the body and supply the energy needed to carry out our daily chores. It takes just so many calories to keep a person vigorous in mind and body. There are charts available that indicate the caloric values of the various foods and drinks. So why not a calorie chart for drawings. Here's a suggested chart. Let's say it takes around 2,000 drawing calories to make a healthy, vigorous drawing.

Squash and stretch	500
Anatomy	300
Angles	300
Straight against curved line	300
Gesture	750
Overlap	500*
Diminishing size	500*
Surface lines	500*
Fore shortening	300*
Surface	400*

Calories with asterisk are from the Rules of Perspective chart.

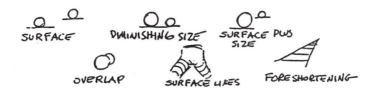

Wow, did I go over 2,000 mark! About 4,350. But not to worry. When I prepare for a competitive tennis match, I overload my body with burnable calories to ensure lots of stamina. And I tell you it is almost like cheating. After an hour or two of intense exercise, the 30-year-olds I play with are panting, and I have energy to burn. So, let's make our drawings the kind that have energy to burn — not tired looking, but perky and expressive. They should shout out to the viewer, "I have gone all out on this pose, held nothing back, with no fear of pooping out. I have given it all I've got, but with energy left over for many more to come." Knowledge is the thing it takes to plan the course but energy is the thing it takes to make it all happen. So, watch those calories.

Here are some high-energy drawings. Study them for their use of the above listed calories.

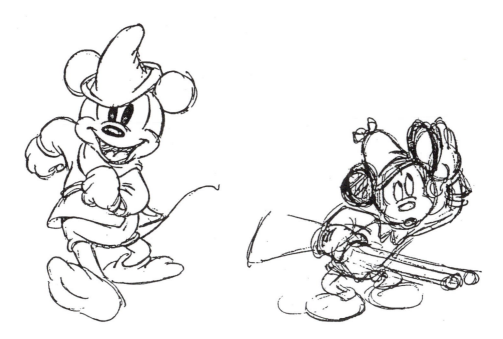

22 Sketching

Don't be afraid to sketch in public places such as museums, parks, restaurants, etc. And don't let wind, rain, cold, or heat deter you — those conditions sometimes yield the best sketching. Let someone else drive when traveling so you can draw. Capturing a scene while moving at high speed will sharpen your eye. But also take time to do a more detailed sketch. First draw a rectangle and work within that to force yourself to make a composition — relating one thing to another and to the borders. If you feel a need for toning the sketches, use cross hatch or carry a couple of gray felt tip pens. Get in the habit of using a pen. It is much more direct and does not rub off like a soft pencil. Sketch at home too. Never sit in front of the TV without a sketchpad on your lap. Sketch faces, figures, and stage settings. If your dog or cat is lying on the floor nearby, sketch them. Sports events are especially fun to sketch — boxing matches, football games, etc.

You may shun landscapes — saying that you are interested only in figures or cartoons, but trees, mountains, rivers, and clouds have gestures that can be beneficial for analyzing action. Mountains stand erect, lean, lie down, sprawl, and spill out onto valleys in alluvial forms. Trees loom, twist in agonized or humorous gestures; they stand erect, stretch, and lean; some are tired, some perky; some bear fruit or flower, which in itself is a gesture. Even the atmosphere of a landscape has a (spatial) gesture.

Vehicles have gestures of their own. Some cars seem to slink along, some move proudly. Some are raised way up on springs — like they're holding up their skirts so they can cross a stream. Special equipment like skip-loaders, semis, derricks, and delivery trucks all seem to be doing their own thing. They're as different from each other as a farmer is from an office worker or a military man is from a hobo. Don't sketch vehicles as if you were doing a Ford ad — go for their personalities, their gesture. Sketching isn't only fun, but it will also help you master those blank sheets of paper you are going to be spending the rest of your life battling.

People usually do what they are in the habit of doing. That may seem like an obvious thing to say, but it is significant in a number of ways. Arguing in its *favor*, it is a comfortable way of living. There are a minimum of decisions that require attention, and hopefully the things you are in the habit of doing and the manner in which you do them are compatible with your idea of the "ideal" life. And if you're studying to be a concert pianist or a rock band drummer or a pro tennis player, you had better submit to some rigorous habit forming — such as hours and hours of practice.

Arguments against forming daily habits that guide you through life without having to make any new choices are quite numerous. The old adage "use it or lose it" is applicable here. If one has formed pretty solid days worth of habits that carry him through the days and months and years — he is going to grow smaller and smaller as age sets and the more habitual he is the sooner age will set in.

Someone said, "Change will help keep the balance sheets in order," or something like that. We are not talking change for the sake of change — but for improvement — for expanding the consciousness, for an ever fresh and open-minded attitude to your piece of the universe. Habits are a blessing when they relieve us of the burden of having to relearn everything we do every day. But if they lead us down the narrowing road of complacency, they become a drag.

That great teacher and the great guy, T. Hee, told his students to be like a sponge — soak up all the knowledge and information you can. Never allow yourself to get into a self-satisfied or complacent state. He advised never to drive home from work by the same streets twice. Take alternate routes — observe the new houses, trees, gardens, etc., and do not just drive by them — look at them, see them. When walking along a sidewalk, look into the store windows, not just a glance, but a good look, to see what's there — the set up, the merchandise, the signs. Sketch it in the mind's eye. Observe passersby. Notice their walks, their postures, their rhythms, look for their history on their faces. Observe,

observe, observe. And of course there is no better way to observe than to carry a sketchbook with you wherever you go.

Whether your heart is set on the fine arts or on animation, quick sketching is the shortest route to training yourself for capturing those spontaneous gestures and poses that are so essential to good drawing. Break one of your bad habits today. Which one? The habit of not sketching.

Also relative to drawing is the sharpening of your sense of dramatics and humor and of science and psychology. What are your reading habits? If they are narrow and limited, make a determined effort to expand them. Read a book on acting. Read a mystery; read a book on the life of Pissarro. Have a few books of *The New Yorker* cartoons in your library. Read Van Gogh's *Dear Theo*. Read a few self-improvement books. Call 244-2816 once in a while.

Listen to some jazz, some symphony, a string quintet, and some country music. Stop everything and just listen. There are some delightful Irish and Scottish recordings. Feel the leaves of a sycamore tree, a wad of cotton, a piece of sandpaper. Pick up a stone from the beach or from the mountains and fondle it. See if it has a message for you. Notice its color and texture — imagine doing an abstract painting of it, or actually do it. Sharpen your senses in all ways. Life will open up its vistas of adventure and courage and venturesomeness. Then when you make a sketch you will feel an authoritative confidence flow into it. It will have the rhythms of the music you have heard, the drama of the books you have read, and the tactile influence of all the things you have touched.

Sounds like a dream? No way! You have been given all these things, these possibilities, and for the small price of a few new habits ... who knows?

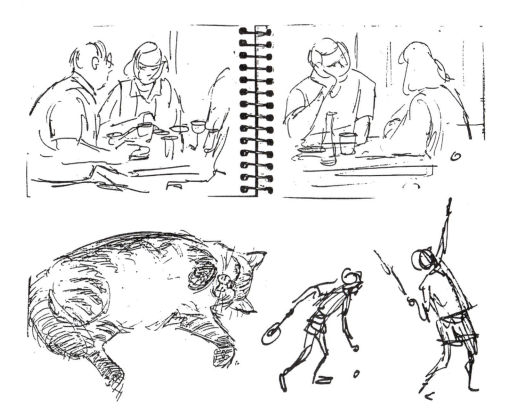

23 Animation and Sketching

Animation! This is your main concern — this is the vehicle in which you have chosen to express yourself. A whole list of "tools" are required: drawing, timing, phasing, action, acting, pantomime, staging, imagination, observation, interpretation, logic, caricature, creativity, clarity, empathy, etc., a mind-boggling array of prerequisites. Rest at ease. You were born with all of them. Some of them may need a little sharpening, others may need to be awakened from a deep sleep, but they are as much a part of you as arms, legs, eyes, kidneys, hemoglobin, speech, etc. Reading and observing are two emancipators of the dormant areas of the mind. Read the classics, biographies, humor, mysteries, and comic books. Observe, observe, observe. Be like a sponge — suck up everything you can lay your eyes on. Look for the unusual, the common, characters, situations, compositions, and attitudes and study shapes, features, personalities, activities, details, etc.

Carry a sketchbook — a cheap one so you won't worry about wasting a page. Sketch in the underground, while watching television, in pubs, at horse shows. Draw constantly. Interest in life will grow. Ability to solve drawing problems will be sharpened. Creative juices will surge. Healing fluids will flow throughout your body. An eagerness for life and experience and growth will crowd out all feelings of ennui and disinterest. If you go on a trip, whether long or short, let your sketchbook take preference over your camera. You'll find yourself looking and *seeing* more than ever before. You will find yourself searching out new things to see, new places to visit, and more varieties of people to "capture" in your sketchbook — your ever growing sketchbook. It will become your diary. Think of it as a graphic autobiography. A unique account of your personal observations of your all too brief journey on this planet.

Where are you going to get all this energy, you ask? Realize that the human body is like a dynamo, it is an energy-producing machine. The more you use up its energy, the more it produces. A work-related pastime like sketching is a positive activity. It is an activation. Inactivity, especially in your chosen field; is a negative. Negativity is heavy, cumbersome, debilitating, unproductive, and totally to be avoided. Take a positive step today. Buy a sketchbook and a pen (more permanent than pencil) and make a little rectangle on the page and fill it with a simple composition. Identify it and/or date it and feel good about it. Do not think or speak negatively about it. If it is not as satisfying a start as you would have liked, do not be critical — that is where you are — face it. Just turn the page and start another. All those faculties that are required to make a more satisfying sketch are being awakened — even now — as you search for a new subject and begin to sketch. No one else in the universe would have drawn it quite like you. If you think you would like to do better make another, and another, and another. Keep the first ones. Watch the growth of both your facility and your interest. Put an end to limiting yourself by drawing nothing but torsos in a life drawing class (do I exaggerate?) activate the potential crannies of the mind.

There is a law in the Christian religion that says (I paraphrase) if you can believe, so shall it come to pass. You can break a civil law but you cannot break a spiritual law. You have to be careful of your thoughts. Once you start one of the spiritual or mental laws working, all sorts of things begin happening behind the scenes to implement its fulfillment. So if you want to be able to draw well, start a sketchbook and get a good law working for you.

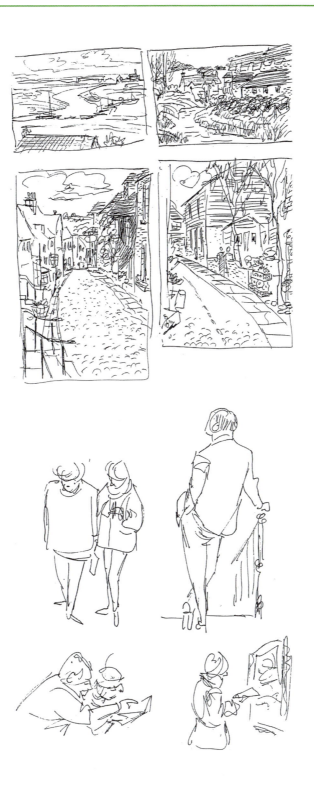

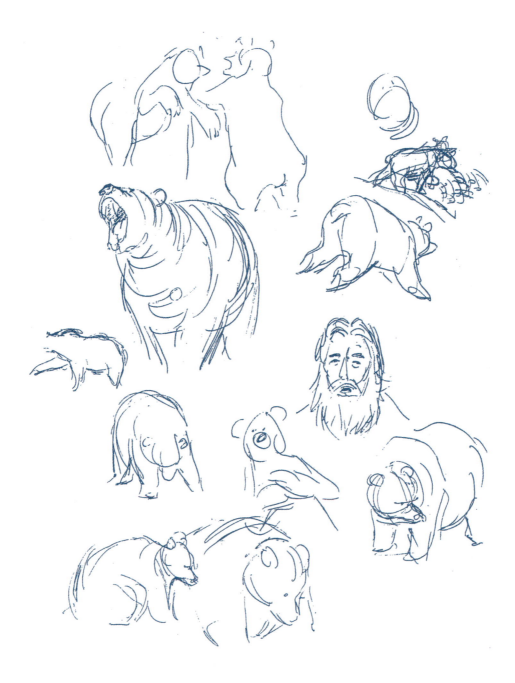

24 Simplicity for the Sake of Clarity

Ian Steele, our Tuesday night model, said a very significant thing to me after the session. He said after holding a pose for some minutes he no longer had that fresh, intense feeling for the pose that he had when he first assumed it. That is something that happens in all phases of life. First love is so strong and exhilarating after 30 years of marriage that feeling diminishes (or is gone). The first bite of some delicious food tastes so vivid — after munching on it for half an hour, the taste almost disappears. Likewise the artist, when he first gets an inspiration or tackles a pose in an action analysis class sees the pose, is struck by its clarity and its expressiveness, then after working on it for a while that first impression is gone and with it goes any chance of capturing it on paper. That's the reason we should learn to get that first impression down right away — while it's fresh, while it's still in that first impression stage — before it starts to fade.

Any of you who have studied Zen will be familiar with the practice of seeing everything anew constantly. You don't dig up the past and use it to make judgments on the present — everything is new, there is only now, this moment, so each moment has that first impression newness. Applied to drawing each moment reveals the pose as if you had just seen it for the first time. Every stroke you make with the pencil is like a knife-edge that carves out the pose as if it were the first time you ever saw it.

The reason I keep harping on "forget the detail" for this particular type of study is that the detail doesn't buy you anything at this stage of the drawing. Doodling with detail will cause you to lose that first impression. The time to study bone structure and muscles is in anatomy class or at home with a good book on anatomy. In an action analysis class a rough circle is all you need to locate and suggest a knee or an elbow or a wrist. Two lines is all you need to locate and suggest the various parts of the arms and legs — preferably one of them straight and the other curved. The straight one is used on the stretch side and the curved one used on the squash side.

When I say locate and suggest, that is exactly what and all you need. What you are drawing is a *pose* not *parts*. The simplest kind of suggestion is the surest way to a good drawing.

I have xeroxed a little series of drawings from *The Illusion of Life* to show how an extremely simple sketch can express so much and thereby be a perfect basis for the final drawings. Notice how the hands and feet were not ignored in the sketches. As a matter of fact they are a dominant element of the poses.

Keep it simple and expressive.

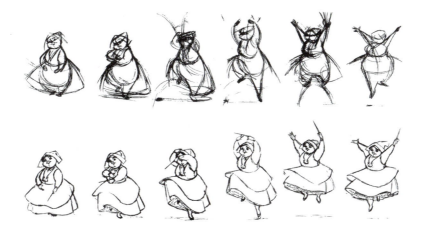

25 Construction Observations Useful in Animation

Humans, most animals, and to a degree cartoon characters are constructed on a solid-flexible, solid-flexible basis:

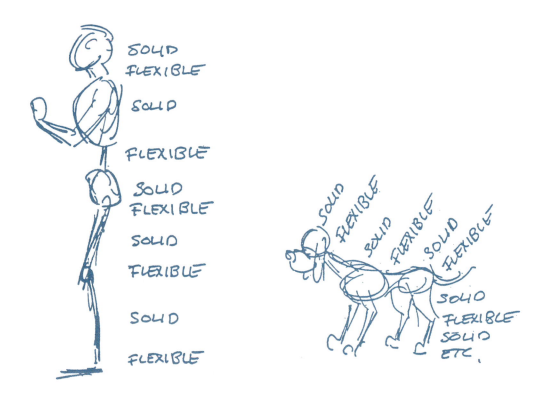

A cartoon character is more flexile, but the principle of solid-flexible is applicable because all the same parts are there — they are merely caricatured.

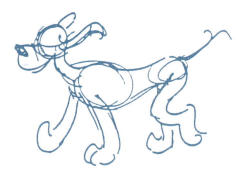

The solid and flexible parts of a character's head can be used to great advantage in animation; for instance in dialog or in an open mouth stretch:

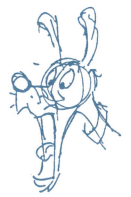

The stretch will mean more if you can first give some sense of the normal; for instance if you first show the dog in his normal pose, then squashed it for anticipation:

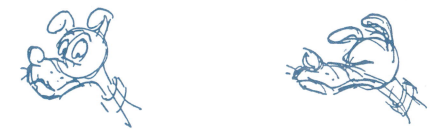

Then the audience really feels the stretch when it comes. For the sake of illustration, say you start with a stretch drawing, the impact will not be as great. As a matter of fact if the viewer is not familiar with the character, he might think that the wide-open mouth is his norm. That may be stretching the point a little but it illustrates a valuable principle of animation: squash and stretch.

Even though considering the skull part of the head to be the solid, that doesn't mean the surface features need to be frozen to that shape. An expression where the eyes open wide and the jaw drops can send the eyebrows sky high on the brow. The lines under the eyes can drop way down below normal, pulled down by the jaw action. This happens nearly every time something is stretched. You might say, nothing ever happens without influencing something else. The closer the "something else" is to the primary action, the more it will be influenced. For instance let's take a row of lines:

| | | | | | |

And pull the one on the right to the right:

| | | | | | | |

In searching out ways to use the principles of animation such as squash and stretch, one should think of animating an object or character rather than merely moving it. Even in your mind's eye, there is a difference between looking at an action as opposed to seeing an action, or in other words, watching an action as opposed to experiencing an action. In the book *Inner Tennis* the author speaks about "riding the ball." It is a psychological think — it causes one to think of taking part in the hitting of the ball and in its flight — as opposed to just hitting the ball and letting it go anywhere it pleases. These are all just different ways of saying, in true Zen fashion, animate the action as if you were it.

26 The Opposing Force

Many of you who were adventurous enough to experiment with the cylinders last session were very successful. I noticed a very marked improvement in several artists' work. Now, I'd like to suggest you concentrate, at least for a portion of the meeting, on combining the cylinders with the solid-flexible concept.

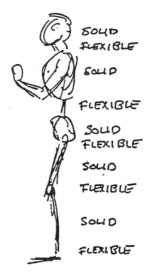

The solid-flex thing is the basis for all the angles that portray the various actions, moods, and expressions that we are called upon to draw. Each section has a limited, yet unique movement to perform. Those movements are the means through which we express all of our body communications. Try to relate some incident in your life, or mimic someone else's with your neck in a brace and your hands tied behind your back. You would make up for it by bending at the waist and the knees. You would make the whole upper part of your body do what your head normally does, and the bending of your knees take the place of hand gestures.

In addition to these readable, "communicate-able" movements of the solid-flex portions of the body, we use an accent motion called "opposing force." That motion is preceded by what we call anticipation. Every move we make has those two elements, sometimes almost imperceptibly subtle, and sometimes wildly exaggerated.

Here is an example of an opposing force. Bernard starts out in a part squash pose, then opens his arms outward and his head upward — all in opposing directions. (Note the tangent of the tail and hand in the first and second drawing — not good)

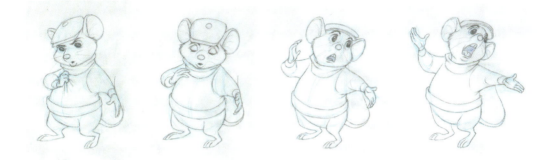

Another example where Ollie Johnston worked Rufus' lower jaw against his scarf for an opposing force.

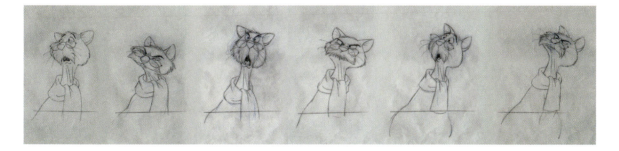

Here's a less subtle example. Notice how hand and pot go up while the head and left shoulder lower:

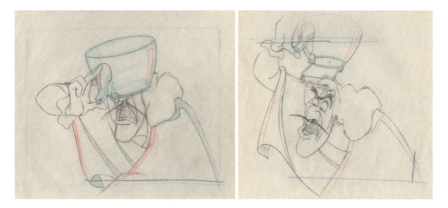

Another — quite exaggerated yet very delicate:

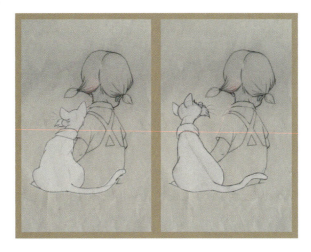

Another:

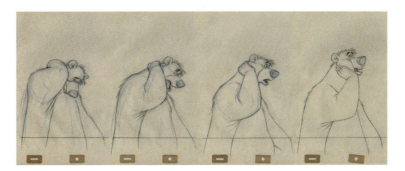

And yet another:

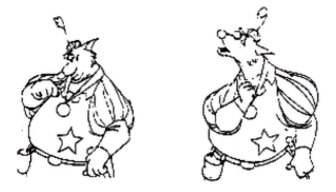

These are all gestures we use in different degrees during our daily living. Slightly, in ordinary circumstances, more exaggerated when mimicking or telling a story, and greatly magnified when animating. Go back over these examples and study how the solid-flex parts of the body were employed to execute those movements. Work your eyes from drawing to drawing observing the use of angle against angle, squash against stretch, and close proximity to openness.

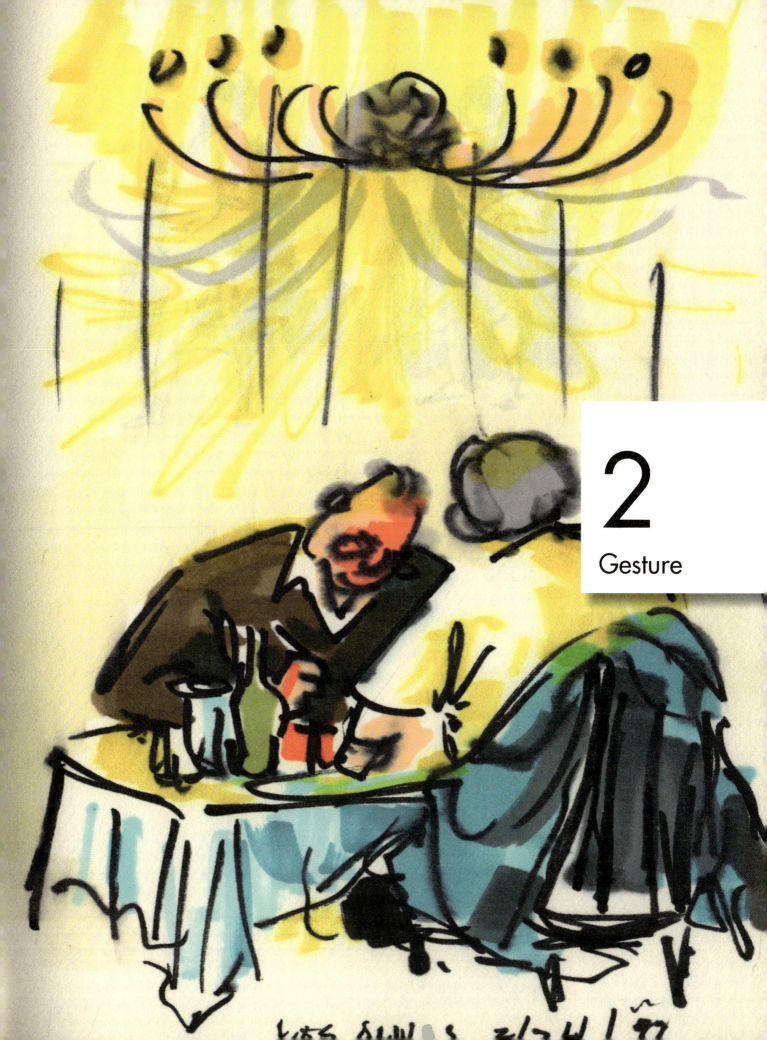

2

Gesture

27 Anatomy vs. Gesture

We, who are essentially cartoonists by trade, do not use rendering and are rarely called upon to draw a nude figure. Our interest is in the gesture, which is the vehicle used in fitting a character into the role it is called upon to act out. We have drawn variously, dogs, mice, owls, elephants, cats, people, etc., each distinct character with distinct bodily shapes and bodily gestures. So to approach a model with the idea of copying a human figure plus its clothing could be called a waste of time. Our interest is in seeing the differences in each personality and their individualistic gestures and, like a good caricaturist, capture the essence of those differences. When we review the cast of characters in our past films we realize the need to place these individual characteristics with the proper character and to be consistent in their depiction. Holmes' actions had to be different and distinct from Dawson's, or their personalities would become a blur. Mickey Mouse had his own personality and his own movements and gestures, which were consistent with his body structure and the personality given him. Goofy, a hundred-fold different in all ways from Mickey, was Goofy because of the same principles used in different ways. There are really only a few principles of drawing but an infinite number of personality traits and gestures. To "hole in" after learning the body structures is to miss the excitement and the satisfaction of using that information to tell the story of life through the nuances of gesture.

We should be taking advantage of the variety of subjects in our sketching sessions. This one has a large midsection with a receding chin. His body tapers down to tiny ankles that seem incongruously inadequate to carry the weight. This one is chunky, even muscular, but dainty in movement — even graceful. This one seems to act out his gestures so that we almost feel his mind working. Should we keep these things in mind rather than deltoids, ulnas, and the seven heads tall syndrome? As Robert Henri said: "seeing into the *realities* — beyond the surfaces of the subject."

We must be emotional about our subject whether it has to do with serious matters or with humor. We cannot back off from our emotions — if we do the result will be a mere anatomical reproduction.

A drawing or a scene is not final when a material representation has been made; it is final when a sensitive depiction of an emotion has been made. The significance is not in the story alone, but in the illustration that makes that story come alive. Yes, there is anatomy, form, construction, model, and two or three lines of etceteras, but only as far as those things are expressive of the story.

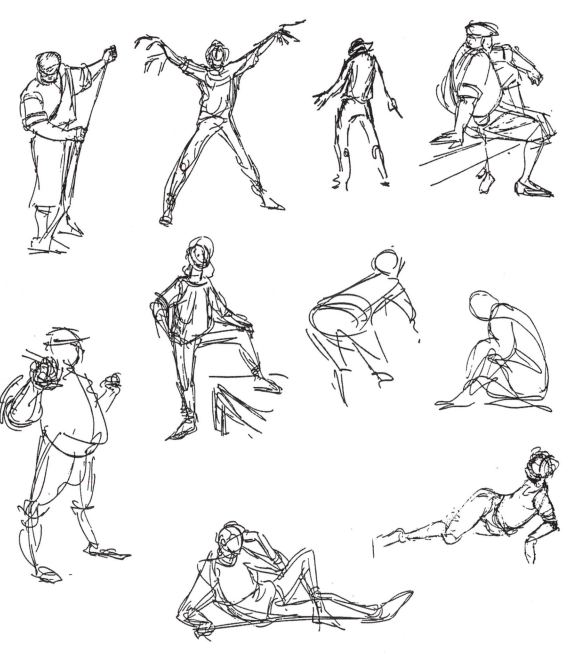

28 Mental and Physical Preparation

I would be amiss if, in this visit with you, I didn't mention mental attitude or physical well being, along with some possible means of acquiring and/or maintaining it. Much recent research has proven the benefits of pursuing such a program.

All of us have experienced periods of diminished energy and depression. It's possible to have one or both of them creep upon us so slowly that we are unaware of the change, and there we are, dragging our (mental and physical) feet. Over a period of time we may even come to believe that this is the way life is supposed to be. You've heard people when asked "How are you?" They answer "okay," meaning of course, not bad enough to say "lousy," and not good enough to say "terrific."

If I was selling this program of physical and mental betterment for money, I would do it on a money-back guarantee basis, because I am confident that a little physical and mental gymnastics are necessary for an artist's well being.

Each one has to find his or her approach. If you are involved in a sport, and do it fairly often, that may be all you need. If not, perhaps some simple aerobics will do the trick.

I personally have settled for 25 or 30 minutes of stretching and aerobics each morning, plus (when at home) at least one hour of competitive tennis (singles) every day. This, plus hikes on the beach or in the hills have kept me fairly physically fit. So at 68 I am still quite active.

As for food, I am not over zealous about what I put in my body, but I am very careful to get enough of the foods that will rebuild the worn down parts and to maintain the parts that are working well. That in itself takes a little special attention. But in the long run it is worth it.

As for mental hygiene, again it must be a personal choice and one that helps keep everything in perspective. It may be through the use of religious devotionals, a philosophy or yoga, or Zen. Whatever it is, it should serve to activate the "juices" and to stir up the desire to improve yourself — to reach beyond yourself — beyond where you are now. It has to make you want to express yourself (your self), to create.

You must create. The injunction of life is to create or perish. Good physical and mental conditioning are necessary to do this. Remember this: The creative energy that created the *universe*, created you, and its creative power is in you now, motivating you, urging you on — always in the direction of creative expression. I have a formula: "Impression minus expression equals depression." This is especially applicable to artists. We have trained ourselves to be impressed (aware) of all the things around us, and in the natural course of our lives those impressions cry out to be expressed — on paper, on canvas, in music, in poetry, in an animated film.

So shape up!

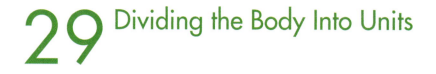 Dividing the Body Into Units

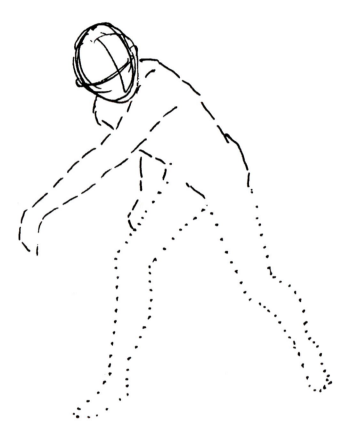

One way to keep continuity of parts in your sketches is to divide the body into two or three units. While sketching in unit #1 see unit #2 clearly in your peripheral vision and even, in a lesser degree the third unit. Then while sketching unit #2, keep the third unit clearly in mind plus the unit you have just sketched in. The idea is that the whole pose must be kept constantly in mind — no going off and drawing a head or an arm as something separate, but rather as parts of a whole. The relationship of the shoulders, elbows, hands, etc., and especially the foot on which the weight of the body is on, must be "mapped" out or planned ahead so that the essence of the pose is not lost — or in regard to the weight, the whole drawing be off balance. Let the mind and the eyes constantly scan the pose so as not to lose sight of the first impression — which was the fresh, vivid view of the whole gesture before you get involved in drawing the parts.

All too often in sketching, while not seeing the whole figure (the figure as a whole, that is), it is possible to end up with a delightful drawing, but which is at variance with the pose or gesture. It is fine when doodling to start out with nothing in mind — somewhere on the paper — and end up with a present-able drawing with a gesture of its own (but not yours). But when striving for a predetermined gesture, a measure of discipline is necessary. You not only must capture what is needed but perhaps even push it a little further. In cartooning (animation) we often push the gestures so far they become a caricature. With this kind of discipline under your belt even your doodles will be more meaningful.

You might liken drawing to playing a musical instrument — especially one like a horn or a stringed instrument where you have to manipulate your highly disciplined lips or fingers to produce a tone. The music (in drawing the pose) must be reproduced perfectly or something is lost (most likely the audience). Jazz improvisation is more like doodling except that it is produced within a certain structure, rhythm, harmony, key, style, etc., so even here, there is discipline. Any of you who play a musical instrument will know that you have to use your peripheral vision to look ahead a measure or two to keep any kind of continuity going. The rhythm would falter musically if the notes were read one at a time, likewise in drawing, the pose must be captured with a continuity of form — a looking ahead to tie all the parts into a rhythmical and faithful express of the pose.

30 Dimensional Drawing

The ability to see in third dimension is fairly near the top of the list of requirements for the animator, assistant animator, and the inbetweener. Most of us come by this knowledge only after years of observation and practice. Some years ago, a simple little drawing book was given to me by its author, Bruce McIntyre. He had devised a sort of shorthand art course that he taught to young children and the results were amazing. His whole premise was built on six rules of perspective and an involved use of directional symbols.

The perspective rules are simply this:

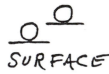
SURFACE

SIZE

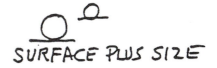
SURFACE PLUS SIZE

OVERLAP

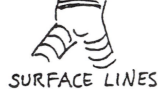
SURFACE LINES

FORESHORTENING

The first two rules, I think, are a preparation for the third one — surface plus size, a rule that is very usable in animation. For instance when working on a scene with a layout like this:

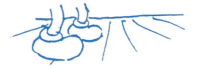

A character standing on that plane would have two feet fitted to that surface, creating not only a stable stance but also a third dimensional.

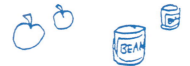

Any props such as apples, cans, bowls, etc., as seen below.

The overlap rule is very important to all phases of drawing, especially when the illusion of third dimension is desirable.

Here is an outlandishly simple example where the whole head area is in front of the shoulders and in the next drawing there is a complete reversal. In the first drawing, note how definite the overlap is depicted: the fingers in front of the jaw, the thumb behind and the left thumb in front of the elbow, the fingers behind. Being definite with overlap helps the drawing "read" clearly.

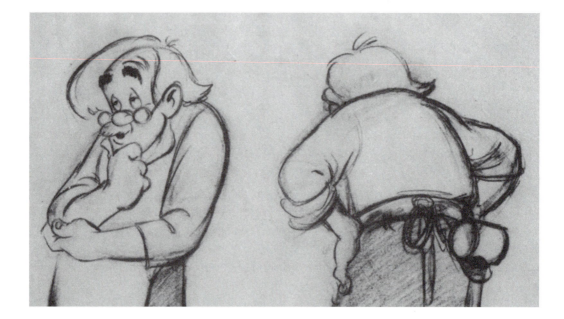

One of the worst traps that catch us unawares is when overlap and tangent gang up on us. A simple example is two mountain shapes drawn with no overlap that automatically creates a tangent and destroys any illusion of depth whatsoever:

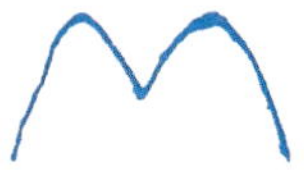

The-simple solution to this problem is to add overlap

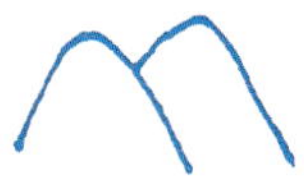

making it very clear which hill is in front of the other. Then if you force the perspective by adding surface plus size to the drawing it will be more definite and read much faster.

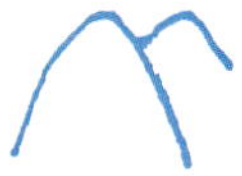

The importance and usefulness of the surface lines rule can only be hinted at. In a rendered drawing or painting, the artist has untold nuances of color, shading, and rendering to emphasize the depth — the animator has only line. Plus, of course the rules of perspective. As for surface lines, there are usually very few in a line drawing. When using a cigar with its surface lines (the band) the importance of using them for direction and depth can easily be seen:

There are few areas on cartoon bodies that can be used like the cigar band. If none at all, the two objects would look like each other only one smaller than the other.

So the artist must use whatever suggests itself. A sleeve for instance

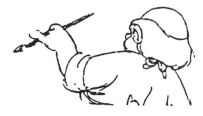

or a pant cuff

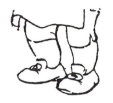

or a belt, collar, hemline, pattern on the material, or wrinkles in cloth:

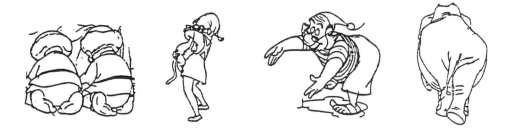

In the case of heads, the basic structure has to serve as a *surface line*. For instance, the eye, nose, and mouth lines are unseen but implied and depicted by the placement of the eyes and mouth and the direction they take when the head is tilted:

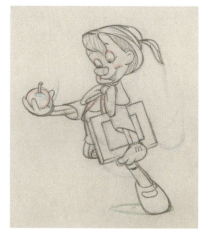

Along with these "unseen" surface lines, there is *overlap* such as (in this case) the hair, first being seen somewhat behind the forehead then reversing to be in front of the forehead in the second drawing. The ear employs another rule: *foreshortening*. The other rules such as *surface plus size* and *perspective* would have come into play had the head turned to the side:

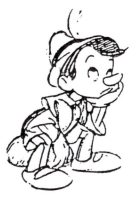

Although the other ear is not seen so it cannot be compared with the one that is seen, it will have grown in size as the head turns the ear toward you and closer to you, thereby giving even a better illusion of depth in motion than you would get from seeing a still drawing or the two ears:

That increase in size plus a change in shape (angle) plus following an arc (as if the ear were orbiting the outside of a sphere like the head would give a maximum third dimensional effect).

The last rule of perspective is *foreshortening*, which is none other than Italian perspective in a simplified form. It is used extensively in animation by simply drawing things larger in the foreground than those of like size in the background. For instance, on a head "forced perspective" is used in drawing the eyes, eyebrows, etc.

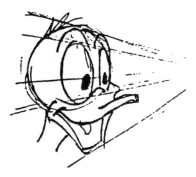

It is the kind of perspective you would get when using a wide-angle lens on a camera. The difference is that the photograph appears distorted and unreal. In the cartoon it is acceptable, partly because we can adjust the whole drawing and make it plausible. It is defying reality but in a logical way. Using logic in animation is a powerful tool. That is how we can use such extreme action and pull it off as believable.

Tangents are the enemy of the illusion of depth and to be avoided at all cost. Tangents occur when two or more lines converge

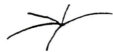

or when one line ends at some point then seems to continue on at another point.

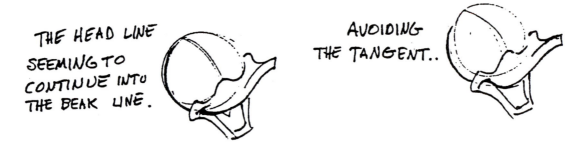

THE HEAD LINE SEEMING TO CONTINUE INTO THE BEAK LINE.

AVOIDING THE TANGENT..

Here is an obvious instance of tangent trouble and a simple solution wherein a great deal of depth and clarity is achieved.

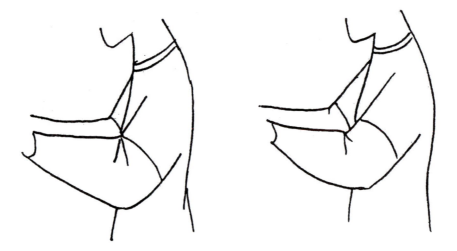

If you can arrange it so all of the rules of perspective are used in one drawing, you will have the maximum third dimension possible in a line drawing.

The directional symbols mentioned above were simple arrows pointing in a number of directions. Each arrow and its direction had a code number. Their use was related to the manner in which Bruce taught drawing. I had never involved myself with his use of directional symbols, but the principle of it completely captivated me. It has influenced every drawing and painting I've made since. This principle has made me conscious of the fact that *everything* is pointing in some direction: pointing away from us, or sideways to us, or three-quarters up at a certain angle, straight at us or slightly to the left or right or down. Most often these directional lines coincide with perspective lines and have a common vanishing point. In the case of drawing a figure, the line directions are not random but have to do with the pose or action. To be conscious of the direction that arms and legs and fingers, etc., are pointing is the key to the third dimensional drawing. It is the thing that reveals to us the six rules of perspective; for instance, if in drawing the legs of a character you find one pointing toward you and the other pointing away:

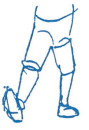

You know that the *surface lines* will be dictated by those directions and also *surface plus size* will influence the placement and size of the feet, and *overlap* will be necessary to show the right leg is in front of the left leg. *Foreshortening* will be subtle but the left leg will diminish in size as it recedes from hip to ankle:

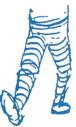

Difficult foreshortening in a pose can be more easily handled if one is aware of which direction the object is pointing; for instance, if there is a figure bending over toward you, which is a difficult view. The problem can best be conquered by the awareness of what is happening. To you it looks like this:

From the side it would be a much more drawable view.

However, merely being aware of the side view will help you pick the rules of perspective that are needed to conquer this foreshortening dilemma.

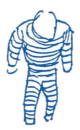

The surface lines of the chest and stomach will be almost circular; the arms, held slightly back will have a less circular surface line; and one leg forward and one back will require opposite surface lines. The leg on the right would diminish slightly in size as it goes away from you while the other increases, employing the *foreshortening* rule. The head in front of the chest applies the *overlap* rule, while the rule of *surface plus size* is employed in the feet. True, these things (rules) are present all around us, so, so what? The what is being aware of them as a positive aid in drawing, allowing you to progress directly to the pose, rather than rely on a lot of doodling, pencil manipulation, and haphazard accidentals.

If you wanted to play Mozart music on the piano, you would not doodle on the piano hoping some day to come across something that sounded like Mozart. No, first you would study the rules — the rudiments of music — and then with a little practice you could bring Mozart to life. Drawing is no different.

There is another approach to drawing the figure that may seem a bit bizarre at first, but is worth your consideration. It is especially helpful when working out a difficult foreshortening problem. This method merely employs pipes as parts of the body.

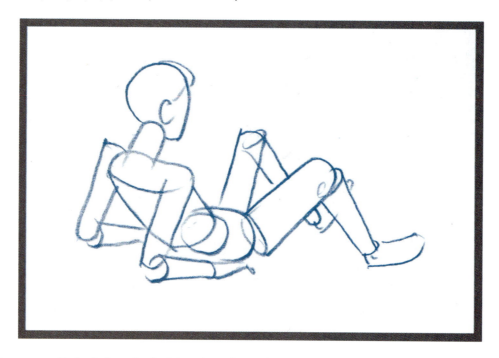

This system will also help with all of the other rules such as *surface lines*, *surface plus size*, and *overlap*.

31 The Value of an Action/Gesture Analysis Study

It is a personal pleasure to have watched the progress you have made in the evening drawing sessions. I think it is time to remind you that the ability to be aware of the various gestures, emotions, and general body language, and the ability to capture them in a drawing is a vital step in becoming a good animator. You should realize that those beautiful, expressive gesture drawings you have been making are the very backbone of a scene of animated action. Of course, along with this, there must be the ability to incorporate acting, timing, and all those myriad details like squash and stretch, anticipation, interpretation of dialog, etc. So in addition to the gesture sketching, lectures, films, and discussions with knowledgeable co-workers, I recommend that you study the *Art of Animation* by Don Graham and the lectures by Eric Larson. If you don't have a copy of either, see Bill Matthews or myself and we will see that a copy is made available. This is not to suggest that any one or two sources of information will transform you suddenly into a master, but certainly the process of learning is ongoing and we have to remain active in our search.

In the past Walt Disney and Don Graham made some important discoveries through an intense search for the then new art form of animation. We can't go back to that original mode of discovery but we can avail ourselves of the findings, the knowledge, and wisdom that has been documented. That nucleus of artists from forty or fifty years ago was no more talented than this class. They had to go to art school to learn to draw, they had to read, study, and search; they had to discover for themselves what they had to offer. They too had to devote a major part of their lives to harness that great creative energy.

Our efforts here in the gesture analysis class are one of the necessary areas of study that inches us closer to our goal. Read what Eric Larson says in his chapter on caricature:

Since we are challenged to put "drawings that live" on the screen, our animated characters, human, animal or inanimate, must be sincere and governed by believable traits and mannerisms. They are linear drawings made alive by the animator through his imaginative analysis of thought processes, emotions, and actions.

And in the same chapter:

All our great characters (Pinocchio, Bambi, Snow White and the Seven Dwarfs, Mickey, etc.) have been the result of the successful caricature of reality, and our knowledge and use of reality has been gained from an analysis and application of that which we have observed, read about, been told about, discussed, and perhaps even dreamed about. It is the sum total of all this that will make our linear characters entertaining and have meaningful, harmonic relationships with the audience.

Don Graham, in his book *The Art of Animation*, speaks of those early attempts to study action and gesture analysis. Here is a quote from his chapter "Analysis of Action":

If, now, the human figure could be drawn not just frozen in an action pose but as a caricature of the action idea, a new understanding of drawing was inevitable.

Early animators were familiar with action and loved it. They could clearly visualize a jump, a run, and a throw because they had experienced such actions physically. Once the action was visualized, the trouble of drawing the action had been greatly reduced.

I submit that even though a person is not athletically inclined, there is a muscular sense that allows him to experience muscular action within his mind or imagination. This is called kinetics or kinesthesia, the perception or motion. You can see people using it while watching a ball game or a murder mystery. They'll yell "Throw the ball!" and up goes their throwing arm. When someone is shot in a movie, there is often a physical reaction. If the picture is vivid enough, there could even be pain. I'll never forget a shooting in the cowboy picture, *Shane*. The blast from the gun knocked the victim from a boardwalk. The whole audience jumped a foot. Sometimes while watching or sketching a boxing match, I notice one of the boxers drop his guard and my arm muscles twitch as I go for the opening.

Through this sense, the animator creates the limitless actions and gestures he is called upon to draw. And this is the thing we are striving to develop here in our action/gesture analysis class.

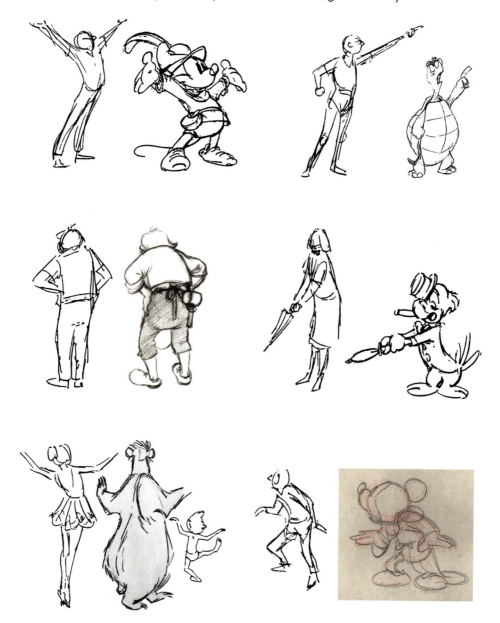

Some "fabricated" quick sketches to suggest how the study of poses and gestures can and will help in solving animation drawing problems.

32 Using a Simple (But Logical) Approach to Drapery

The draped figure will be one of the many problems that will follow you like a heel fly throughout your career. The best thing for you to do (to keep your sanity) is strive to handle it in the simplest way possible. This is not to suggest simplicity is easy — just less frustrating. Think of the character as the star of the scene, and the garment as a subordinate actor chosen to make the star look good. The director of a stage play does not have to plan action for drapery, what the actor does will take care of it. But you as an animator must do just that. You have to act out the character's role, plus the costume's, which should be done in such a way as to compliment the action of the actor.

It is important, also, to drape a figure to emphasize the type of character portrayed. Is it a woman or a man? Is it a neat person or a slob? Is the dress formal or casual? Is it supposed to flatter the actor or make it look ridiculous?

A clear understanding of drapery plus a general understanding of the types of garment construction would be helpful. There is a book called *The Complete Book of Fashion Illustration* by Sharon Lee Tate and Mona Shafer Edwards (Harper & Row, publishers), which gives a very helpful view of drawing the figure with clothes on. I recommend it.

Glenn Vilppu has made videotape on drapery wherein he simplifies it very succinctly. He has broken down the folds of cloth into seven basic categories, which should help you to make logical what often appears to be haphazard.

Category No. 1 he calls the "pipe fold." It occurs when cloth hangs from just one point.

Category No. 2 is when cloth hangs from two points causing a "diaper fold."

Category No. 3 happens when a hinging bit of cloth is allowed to fold up on the floor as the cloth is lowered at an angle. This is called the "zigzag fold."

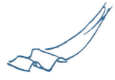

Category No. 4 is a "spiral fold." This results from cloth as it wraps around shapes such as arms, legs, or other parts of the body.

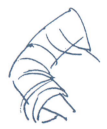

Category No. 5 is the "half-lock fold," which manifests itself at the knee when the leg is bent and also at the elbow when the arm is bent. When the knee or elbow is bent to more extremes there occurs what Glenn calls the "complete-lock fold."

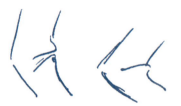

Category No. 6 is the "falling fold." This will develop when some hanging cloth is allowed to bunch up on some surface.

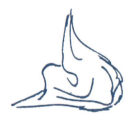

And finally, category No. 7 is the "inert fold." This is the only fold that seems to have no potential for energy, it just lies there, inactive.

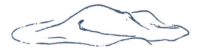

Being aware of these somewhat simple categories of folds will help you interpret what happens to drapery under certain conditions. Also, the more complex actions and poses will cause those categories to overlap and produce a hybrid fold, which, without the benefit of knowing the origin of the contributing folds, might prove to be slightly bewildering.

So when you see a fold that is hard to categorize, with the help of this list, you can search out its origins and, lo, erudition shall prevail. Identifying the types of folds will be harder when drawing from the model, for natural drapery doesn't always just lay it all out in simple terms.

However, when drawing on your own, such as in animation, you can use more simplified forms of drapery — those that match the action or enhance the pose. With the help of Vilppu's list of folds it will be easier to spot and identify such problem areas as you are forming your "first impression."

It might also help to develop a vocabulary of "drapery action terms" such as hang, suspend, dangle, swing freely, be pendent, adhere to, sag, revolve around, drape, incline, bend, droop, descend, incline, sway, dip, settle, plunge, drag, trail, hang over, drape over, envelope, wrap, adorn, and enshroud. Each of these terms suggests an individualized action that helps get you involved in what is happening to the drapery. It is good to be aware of the vast number of possibilities that are always present—especially if you are academy award winning scene conscious.

Here are three extreme drawings by Milt Kahl. They show how directly he went at drawing the figure and they demonstrate how, in spite of using folds in the girl's skirt, it is basically treated as a shape. Glance from one drawing to another and observe how the overlap on the skirt embellishes the action.

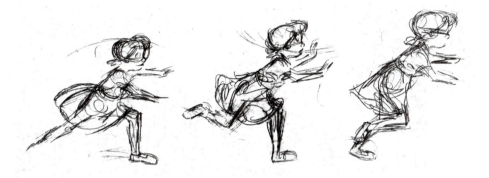

33 Drapery — Its Role in Drawing

Drawing from a model with clothing or costume can be a real challenge. Wrinkles, folds, seams, belts, pleats, ruffles, and shirring all seem so important and at times, downright overwhelming. Their importance cannot be denied, but their reason for being there and looking the way they do must be carefully considered lest we find ourselves drawing lines, lumps, pieces of cloth, and incidental paraphernalia rather than a human presenting us with a gesture to draw, who is incidentally wearing some clothes or a costume.

For our purposes, the clothed figure suits our needs — forces us to the brink of our drawing capabilities. Our job as animators (layout, story, etc.) is to be surrogate actors for our cartoon characters who will be wearing countless kinds of costumes. Let's face it, clothes cannot act. If clothes seem to act it is because the body underneath is acting (posing or gesturing). The clothes will react in a like manner and will even enhance the gesture. But if the drawing has not captured the gesture, all the manipulation of wrinkles, lumps, bulges, folds, seams, and superficial incidentals one can dream up will not bring off the drawing. A real solid, expressive, sparkly drawing is one where the clothing is doing what the body is causing it to do.

Reasons! Reasons! Reasons! Always look for logical reasons for the shapes of the clothing or drapery — and the reason will always be found in the bodily gestures.

It helps to mentally take the clothing apart to see how it is constructed; for instance, a sleeve — how big around is the shoulder opening, how is it attached to the bodice, does it taper, does the shoulder seam attach at or below the shoulder? Ward Kimball's great observation is very apropos here. He said if he could take something apart and put it back together again, he could draw it.

For the sake of studying the figure for animation, lines of clothing should not be sketched in just for an impression — they should be logical. If you were to use that drawing in a scene, those drapery lines would have to animate as a secondary action with the primary action being the body itself.

Here are some beautiful examples of how the clothing can be handled in a simple way, yet be effective in complimenting the action.

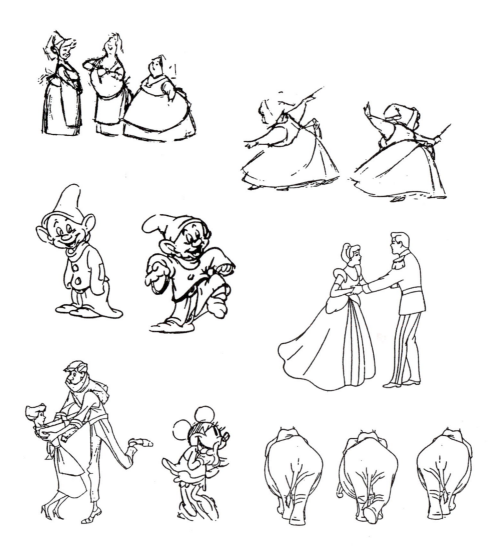

34 The Seriousness of Head Sketching/ A New Phrase: "Body Syntax"

Try to keep from getting too serious while head sketching. After all, you are in the cartoon business and most of the Disney characters are somewhat comical, and if not comical, then at least they are caricatures of serious beings. Usually when a person takes himself too seriously he is in our eyes a "comedian." He is ripe for caricature. So if cartoons are not somewhat caricatures of reality they may be taken too seriously and lose that special spark of humor. Very few, if any, of the animators I've known found drawing easy. One of Ollie Johnston's sayings, "It ain't easy," became a studio quip. Drawing funny cartoons was and is a serious business. It seems like the funniest scenes were the ones that were "sweat over" most. They were serious matters that required the animator to never forget (in all his groping and mental anguish) that the result he was after was to make the audience smile.

Yes, try to keep from getting too serious while head sketching. Museums and living rooms are full of serious portraits that are just dying to be retouched with a little humor. But, of course, portraits were not invented to make people smile — cartoons were. If you think the world is all so serious, you should be a historian or a philosopher, but if you desire to bring a little humor into the lives of those humor-hungry people "out there," then be a cartoonist and be serious about losing some of that seriousness.

There is an insistent tendency to look at the model in a serious, even detached way almost as if it were a still life devoid of feeling and personality. We look at the model to pick a starting point; we draw it. We look back to see if we did it right and make a few more dabs at it to reassure ourselves. We look up for another line to add — perhaps connected to the first one, perhaps somewhere else in some unrelated area. We look down, sketch in the new line tentatively, reinforce it, after another look at the model, with several swipes of the pen. The gesture goes unrecognized. The more unrelated lines that get pat down, the farther from our grasp goes the gesture.

Imagine yourself drawing a simple shape like a circle or a square. Do you see yourself sketching a bit here or there, going over what you have done, then on to another section, seeing only those small sections of line you are putting down. No! Of course not. You see a circle and the size you want to make it and in as few lines as possible — wham! Down it goes. A human body is more complicated, granted, but the act of drawing its gesture is much the same. You must see the whole, and wham! (over a longer period of time, of course), down it goes. You have hardly looked at the details. They influence and enhance the pose (gesture) but are somewhat incidental to it. The model could strike the same pose while wearing any number of different outfits. If it is outfits you are interested in, invest in a Sears catalog. If it is gesture you are interested in, then look beyond those extraneous, sometimes gesture-destroying details.

I love to read. I love the way authors put their words together. I love syntax. I love the way the words reveal the plot and the personalities of the protagonists that carry me along in the plot. But if I'm not careful, I get caught up in admiring the details and how the story is told, getting behind in what the story is about. We have been having some terrific models whose "details" (body syntax) are fascinating to the point of distraction. It seems like the more interesting the details, the more difficult it is to see the simplicity of the gesture. So, as it takes a special effort on my part to read for the story, so it is with most of us — we have to make a special effort to draw for the gesture.

Imagine yourself as a pilot landing a plane. Some weird phenomenon has blotted out all but a tiny detail of the field. MAYDAY! MAYDAY! You need the whole field so you can make a good judgment of the situation. If you try to put down on that little detail it might be a section way at the end of the runway, two feet from the fence. Okay, the same with drawing — you need the whole body (the field) to keep your judgment of the gesture true.

Earlier I mentioned body syntax. That's a phrase worth coining. The non-grammatical meaning of syntax is "connected system or order; orderly arrangement." What is a pose or gesture but an orderly arrangement of body parts to display a mood, demeanor, attitude, mannerism, expression, or emotion. The phrase "orderly arrangement" (body syntax) is worth ruminating over. An orderly arrangement or body parts − — I love it. Even the sentence places arrangement before parts.

I apologize for the over-abundance of text from here on. Because drawing is largely mental I am trying to reason along these lines. Once the physical faculties of manipulating a pen or pencil to one's satisfaction is conquered, that side of drawing is taken care of and from there on it is mental. It is then the ability to analyze, imagine; to caricature, to assemble, and organize all the separate elements of storytelling into one drawing or into a series of drawings (animation). As we have come to realize since Dr. Betty Edwards, drawing is a right brain activity. The left brain is a serious namer of things, while the right brain uses all that seriousness for some creative purpose. The left and right sides of the brain are the "odd couple" of the cerebral community — the right side is the slightly less serious of the two.

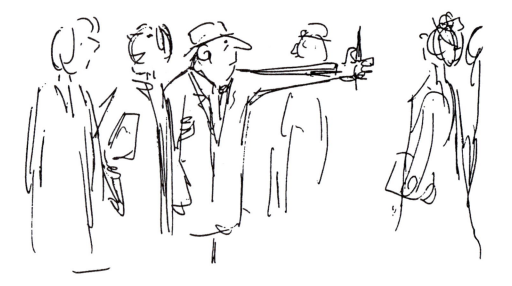

"He can't draw but he likes to size people up."

35 The Head in Gesture

We have spent some months now sketching the figure with special emphasis on gesture. In my estimation it has been a rewarding experience. I have stressed its inclusion at all parts of the body including the hands and feet because they are such an important part of any pose or gesture. No parts of the body have been isolated as more important than any other simply because body language entails all of the parts. An exception to that rule occurs in animation where close-ups or waist shots are featured. Because of this, it behooves us to spend some time in a study of heads and the upper torso. The emphasis should still be on gesture, and as we did with the rail figure, ignore the details as much as possible. A very simple symbol for the head shape, eyes, nose, and mouth will suffice to "nail down" the gesture or expression. We are all at different stages of drawing ability, so some may feel it unnecessary to start with such simple shapes. If so, try to treat it like a refresher course and spend a little time at it.

Basically, the head from a front view is an egg shape, and from the side it is two egg shapes (see the following illustrations). This is an oversimplification, but is useful in laying out the first stages of a drawing. Head shapes vary in many ways and once an individual's variances are discovered, they can be exploited to acquire a likeness or if desired, carry them farther into caricature. A person's real head and feature shapes cannot really be known until we have seen that person from different angles and in different moods and circumstances such as laughter, anger, fear, clowning, seriousness, strain, etc.

In animation most needs have been built on the circle. Cheeks have been added or mouse ears or duckbills have been added and suddenly there is a universally appealing character. I said suddenly, but the truth of the matter is, many months of intensive search and experimentation have preceded the final acceptance of most character models. Some, such as Mickey Mouse and Donald Duck, have continually evolved their entire lifetime. Because many characters are built somewhat on the same basic formula, great care must be taken to retain the subtleties that distinguish one from another. Animation allows the characters to be freely caricatured in action but though the shapes are stretched and squashed to unbelievable limits, they must be recognizable as that character at all times. A good model is one that has shapes that can be animated into various poses and expressions without losing its character. The general shape of the head and its individual features must be established in its normal state first so that squashes and stretches will be recognized as such. In other words, a thoroughly recognizable norm will serve to emphasize any deviation; giving added punch and authority to special expressions. On the other hand, since we have already enjoined the audience to suspend their disbelief in such beings as talking mice and temperamental ducks, it is important to sustain this newly created plausibility by keeping the characters consistent. Studying the model and people in general with this in mind gives us purpose and hopefully the added incentive to do so.

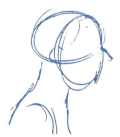 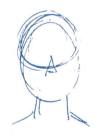 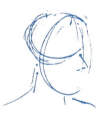

Profile — Two ovals.   Front on — A circle and an oval.   3/4 View — Oval and modified oval.

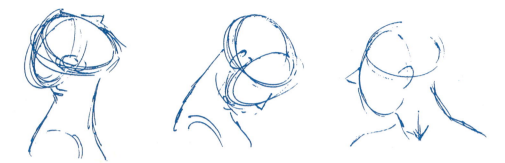

Approximate limitations of looking up and down and sideways using neck.

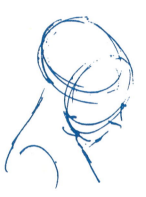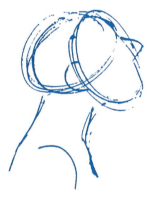

Looking up and down not using neck.

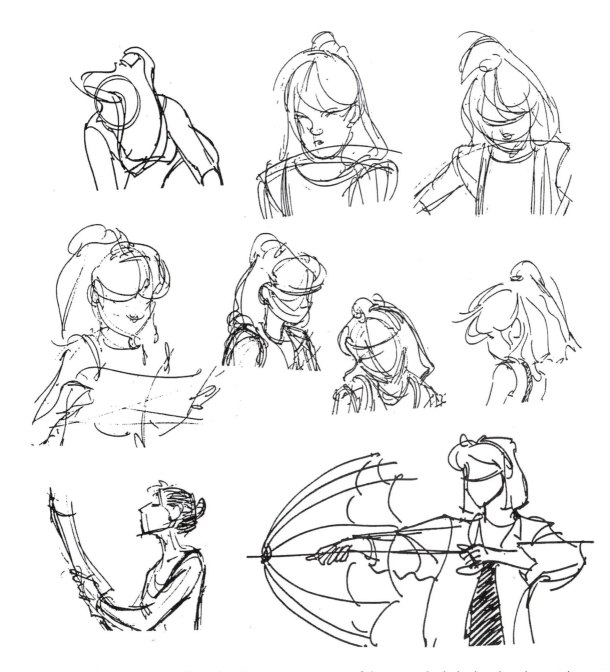

   Some of your drawings from the class are suggestive of the way I think the head studies might go. They are simple enough to allow the express to beam through, not weighted down with tons of ostentatious falderal.

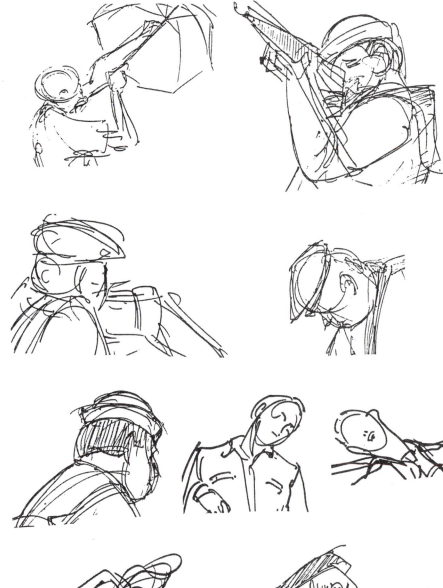

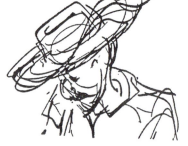

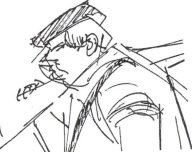

36 From the Living Model to the Living Gesture

A scene of animation is more or less a series of gesture drawings. The difference is that an animator's drawing is likely to have some things in it that are not associated with still drawings. For instance, an animation drawing might have some overlapping action, some drag, some squash and stretch, and a stance that may be off balance, or a view that one would avoid or adjust in a still drawing. But basically the extremes in a scene of animation are gestural drawings created to fit the needs of the story.

In the case of using live action as a basis for animation, the animator soon learns that tracings of photostats will not suffice. Here is where his ability to understand and draw gestures really hits pay dirt. I have seen scenes where photostats had been practically traced, and the scene was lifeless. One of the reasons for this is that live action actors do not move from extreme to extreme as animated characters do. Studying live action clips will reveal that many actors mince through their parts like a cloud changing shapes in a breezy sky. Often actors are used whose gestures are broad and crisp, making the animator's job much easier.

So I guess what I'm driving at is the importance of studying a live model for gesture, and of realizing that the extremes used in animation should have the same care of investigation and thoroughness as the study drawings. That is why I continually suggest (implore) that you do not attempt to copy the model, but rather capture and draw the gesture.

Somewhere I read "Whenever a photograph contains the principles and disciplines of the artist, the better it will be; but the more a drawing looks like a photograph, the worse it will be." Also, and I paraphrase: draw verbs, not nouns. A noun is a thing that can be named; a verb is that thing given the breath of life.

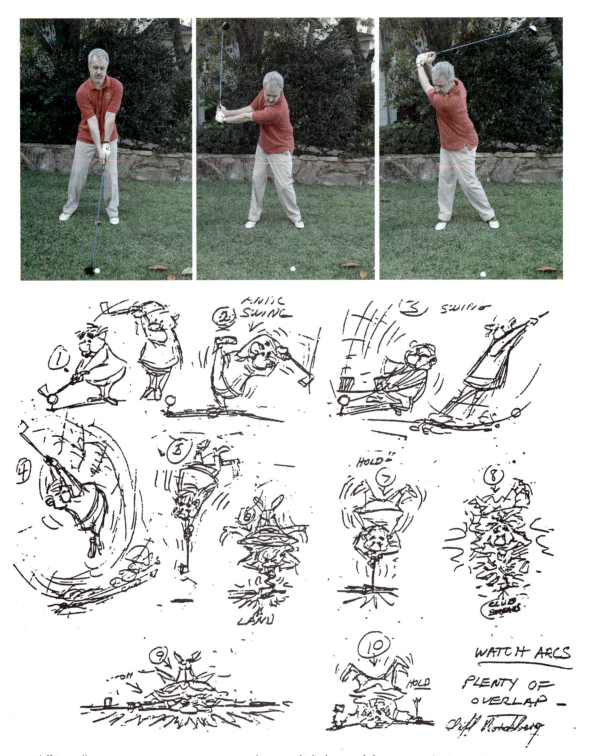

Cliff Nordberg was a master at carrying things a little beyond the camera's viewpoint.

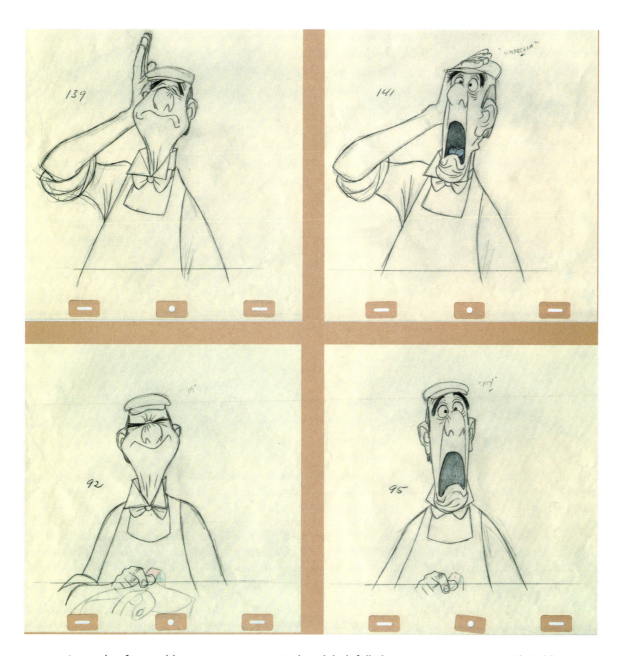

A couple of typical human gestures carried to delightfully humorous extremes — Milt Kahl

37 A Little More on Heads

Rather than tackling a head drawing with its down-the-road-to-destruction details, try approaching it by some simple basic shapes. Talk to yourself (it helps to talk your way through a drawing because ordinarily we don't carry very many fancy descriptive terms in our everyday vocabulary), and if we follow just the simple things we can describe, we'll have less trouble. For instance, for the animator a few words like "structure," "angle," "squash," and "stretch" will carry us pretty far into any drawing. Okay (this is still you talking to yourself) the head structure is basically this shape:

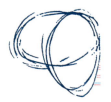

This particular head is tilted 3/4 to the left and is facing 3/4 to the front, and since this is a 3/4 view of the upper oval—it will now be half way between an oval and a circle:
Not this,

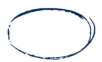

or this,

but this,

so I get something like this:

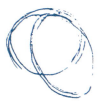

I see because the head is tilted to the left (observers left) that the left side of the neck is going to be squashed while the right side will be stretched:

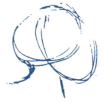

Now I need some shoulders to stabilize what I've drawn. Because I know that the neck merges into the spine in the back and into the chest in the front (I will hook up my mental computer for a side view — ah, there it is).

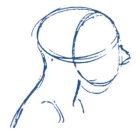

I will now add the shoulders with that in mind.

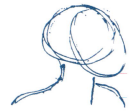

making sure to connect the neck gracefully to the shoulder on the left, and connecting the other shoulder with a nice strong angle to give it a third dimensional look, because I know that this

puts the neck in front of the shoulder better than this,

or this,

or this,

or this,

or this.

The hair is quite a dominant feature on this person and since the head is tilted that way I see that the hair reacts somewhat like the neck, so I'll draw a squash on the left side and a stretch on the other:

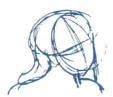

I want to make sure I'm being clear (and simple) about the hair, and though on the model it sort of goes this way and that — I must be logical. So I will simply drape the hair over the shoulder on the squash side and let the hair stretch down past the right shoulder, and oh yes, making sure I use that principle of perspective (one object in front of another to create depth) by getting a good angle on the meeting place of the hair and shoulder.

This,

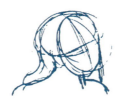

rather than this,

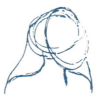

or this,

or this.

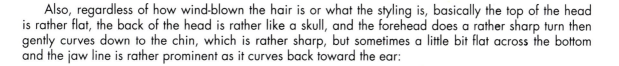

Also, regardless of how wind-blown the hair is or what the styling is, basically the top of the head is rather flat, the back of the head is rather like a skull, and the forehead does a rather sharp turn then gently curves down to the chin, which is rather sharp, but sometimes a little bit flat across the bottom and the jaw line is rather prominent as it curves back toward the ear:

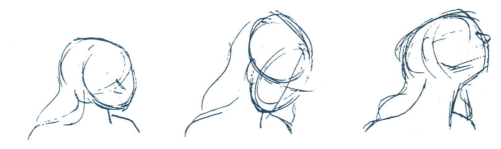

So now I have just used up my four-word drawing "starter vocabulary" and so far it feels pretty solid. Now, I don't know about you (you're still talking to yourself) but I think this is a good start, and I think it might be time to add a nose and a couple of eyes, but of course not until I've gotten some simple shapes in mind — something like what I've done so far:

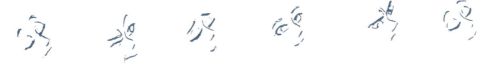

I think it's pretty safe, if not essential, to think of the head as basically two oval shapes. Those shapes automatically suggest a kind of flat plane on the top of the head, plus that bump at the back of the head; a flatness for the face and a chin. It even helps locate a place for the ear:

From the front, a circle for the top portion of the head and the oval for the facial area again automatically suggest a temple, the narrow facial area, and a chin:

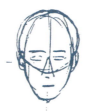

If these are thought of as *the basic head*, then from there one can deviate for the cartoon or the caricature look. You may want to go as far as to suggest the head takes on one of these shapes

as some of the characters of our former pictures have done. But hidden in all the myriad poses and gestures of the various characters are those basic shapes plus the creative use of those four basic words: structure, angle, squash, and stretch.

Next are a few of the characters from Disney features and shorts. They are all built on some basic head shape or shapes, after which the details such as their features are added. The shapes are flexible, that is "animateable," but never so flexible as to take on the shape or personality of some other character. The skull is usually pretty solid, while the rest of the head parts do the squashing and stretching. It's pretty hard to go wrong if you handle the basics correctly. It's the same in any activity — the basics have to be learned first, then, and only then, may the details be added to complete the creative act.

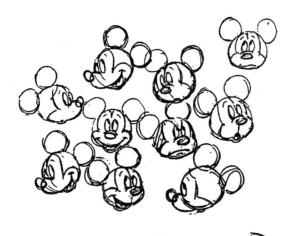

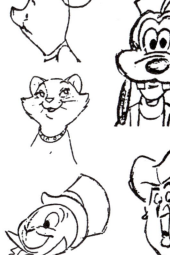

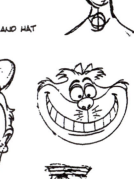

START WITH
SIMPLE SHAPE

ADD FORM
LINES AND NOSE

NOW THE EYE

NOW THE COLLAR AND HAT

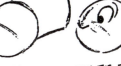

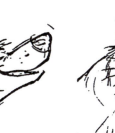

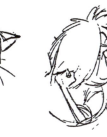

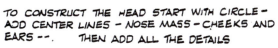

TO CONSTRUCT THE HEAD START WITH CIRCLE -
ADD CENTER LINES - NOSE MASS - CHEEKS AND
EARS -- .   THEN ADD ALL THE DETAILS

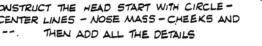

38   Feeling the Pose

I repeatedly harp on feeling the pose rather than merely looking at it. By only looking at it, you have to keep looking at it repeatedly as you copy the parts. In feeling the pose you actually picture yourself as doing the pose. If you have to, stand up, put down your drawing board, and assume the pose. Feel which muscles pull or contract to get which stretch or squash. Feel where the weight falls, what is entailed to keep your balance. Feel the psychological attitude it imparts, i.e., if the head is drooped, does it evoke a sad or disappointed feeling; if the head is held high, do you feel proud or haughty or reverent — or what? So with the whole body impose some kind of attitude on it. Then you have that pose locked into your mind and can summon it up at will by simply seeing it in your mind and assuming that attitude. As a matter of fact you can see it from any vantage point — you could even do some mental levitation and look down on it from above.

Contrast that approach with the slow and ponderous neck-tiring process of looking at the model, noticing the angle of the upper arm, looking back to the paper and sketching in the upper arm, then looking at the model to see what the lower arm is doing, then back to the paper to sketch that in, then back to the model to search out the next thing to draw, then back to the paper to see if what you have already drawn will give you a clue to what to add next, and so on, etc.

The "feeling the pose" method is of great help during live sketching where you have an awkward view of the model, say, a view where one leg and one arm are hidden from your view. With the live model the pose is somewhat clear because there are dozens of telltale indications of what is going on, but these illusive indications are difficult to capture in a line drawing. However, if you lock into the pose, you can make the necessary adjustments required to clarify it. After all, in animation you would have to do that. You go to great lengths to get everything out in the open to make your pose "readable" — so why not in a practice session. I'm sure you all know how to fantasize so put it to use in drawing. If you can lock into the pose you can also fantasize the pose into useful variations, which sounds a little like animating.

39 The Pose Is an Extreme

While animating, you have the advantage of flipping the drawing you are working on with the previous extreme, to develop the full effect of an action:

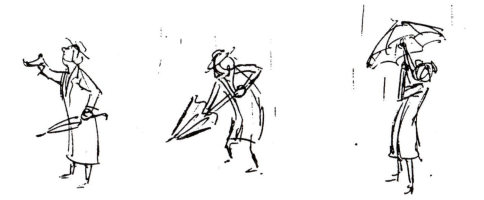

(Glance back and forth from one drawing to another and you get the effect.) This effect of motion lays open to view the main, or primary, action. Everything else becomes a secondary action in some degree or another. An animator never allows a secondary action to take precedence over the primary action. You might think of the primary action as the center of interest while all other actions diminish in concentric rings of importance:

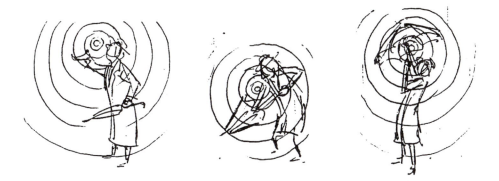

If the viewer's eye is pulled to some activity somewhere far from the center of interest then this becomes a conflict of interest, and the viewer has to fight his way along the story, instead of being swept along a well-focused, well-planned, easy-to-read action.

While sketching from a model there is a tendency to think of the pose as a still life. For the sake of animation study, think of the pose rather as a part (or extreme) of an action. You have no previous extreme to flip from but you do have that sense of motion to give you the feel of what the body went through to get to that pose. This helps you to establish the center of interest and to feature or stress the important action. In our class, time and again there has been a pose where the model, having brought a prop, has built a pose around the prop; for instance, opening an umbrella. Last week, 5 minutes into the sketching, there were, out of 17 drawings, only 3 or 4 umbrellas sketched in.

The "first impression" should have been "woman opening umbrella." The center of interest! There should have been an overwhelming obsession to produce a drawing that says "woman opening an umbrella."

Even after accepting the fact of the center of interest, the battle has just begun, and the shortest route to victory is the use of all the rules of drawing: perspective, tension, angles, rhythm, squash and stretch, etc. Every single line should support the theme and help accent the thrust of the action. The feeling of motion, that is the building up of physical action to reach that climax of the pose, can be conjured up mentally and will serve as a previous animation extreme to "flip" from to reach a dynamic extreme drawing — one that says, for instance, "woman opening umbrella."

But whatever the prop or whatever the action, there is a story to be told, and a prop definitely suggests a theme. A story sketch man usually has only one drawing to describe a scene — he must choose one that will illustrate the story point. If an umbrella is involved, you can be sure he will construct a sketch featuring an umbrella. The story men and the director could care less about how much the story sketch man knows about anatomy or detail drawing, as long as the story point is getting across.

There comes a time in an author's career when he transcends the obsession to get the proper amount of verbs and adjectives and prepositions into a sentence and concentrates on telling his story in an interesting, absorbing, stimulating, arresting, striking, attractive, appealing, and entertaining way.

The artist (animator), (you) have the same raison d'être.

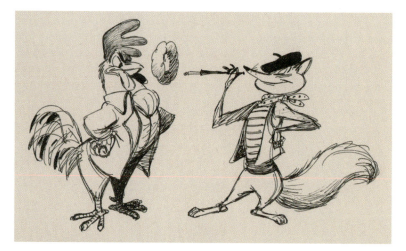

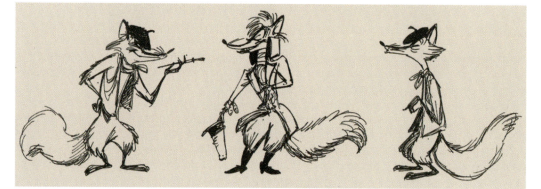

40 Pose and Mood

The ability to animate is akin to the ability to act. Animation is, in effect, acting on paper. This doesn't mean an animator must be able to act well on stage or before a camera, but that he must certainly be sensitive to poses and gestures that portray the various moods and emotions that story telling demands. After all, any poses that are chosen for the different phases of an action must serve the function of telling the story in a convincing and entertaining manner.

The animator must portray the character's actions and reactions, their wildest feelings, and their subtlest moods. Whether the character is animal, human, or an inanimate object, the action must be caricatured beyond what might have been done in live action, although never beyond the limits of good taste.

Drapery too must be caricatured, and though it may have to be handled independently, it must not work independently. That is, it must relate to the action, or if not moving, must relate to the pose.

Posing for mood or character may be enhanced by the use of symbols (see the chapter Symbols for Poses). Study the model sheet on the next page for Madame Medusa from *The Rescuers*. She is constantly in contorted poses that form diagonals and twisted spirals, her fingers are restless and tense, her arms form triangles and warped spares. The shape from her hips to her knock knees, to her feet, form an hour glass — something you'll find on the belly of any female black widow spider.

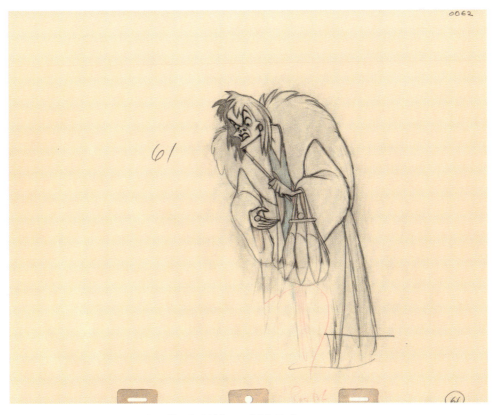

Cruella de Vil from *101 Dalmations*.

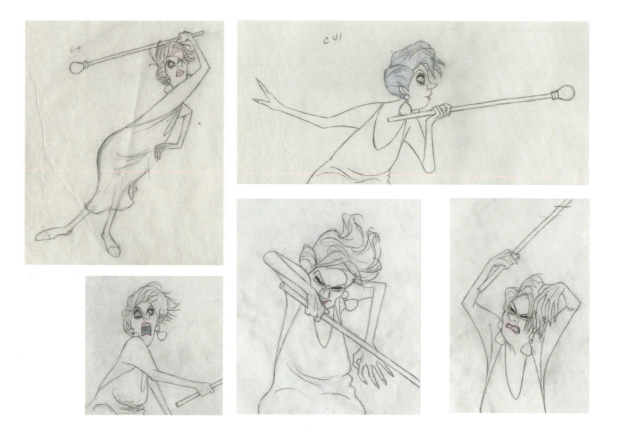

Study Madame Medusa from *The Rescuers*. Restlessness is in her very character, diagonals are her very structure.

The movement from one pose to another is also important. Certainly, a person in a serene mood will not move jerkily or menacingly. Likewise a person whose life is in danger will not waltz from one dungeon window to another to see if the man with the axe has arrived.

Once a mood has been established, it must be maintained until there is reason for it to change, and when the mood does change, it must be definite. An audience likes to be held in suspense in a murder mystery, but it doesn't like the insecure feeling of not knowing a character's mood. As a matter of fact, they are flattered when they can detect moods or even anticipate them. In music, most people like a definite beat. They know what's coming, they know what to expect, and they can count on it. Take away the beat, they feel unstable. In cartoons, especially feature cartoons, take away the mood or the "beat," and in its place go instability, plus unlikelihood, plus incredibility.

Alice in Wonderland thrived on sporadic mood changes. Alice is constantly thrown off balance, but the audience isn't, because they know these changes are in themselves the very humor the story is telling.

41 Pose and Mood Plus Timing and Phrasing and Texture

Poses in a scene accomplish more than just the mood or dramatics: they also create extremes. Animating a scene by extremes (as opposed to animating straight ahead) makes it easier to time the action by use of timing charts. These charts are put on each extreme, making it possible for the follow-up crew to complete the breakdowns and inbetweens according to the animator's concept. The timing charts are also a record of how the scene was animated, so if any timing changes are necessary they can be made by merely adjusting the charts and then new drawings are made accordingly.

Don Graham in his chapter on reality (from the unpublished *Art of Animation*) called the extreme "a story-telling drawing," and that by making this drawing more expressive; the intervening action could be suggested rather than delineated. He also suggested "posed" animation is like watching a hummingbird darting from flower to flower. The rest periods when the bird is hovering in midair or when it is poised with its beak buried in a flower are the poses we *have* to see. The intervening action can be mere blurs, but the essence of the action will be clear.

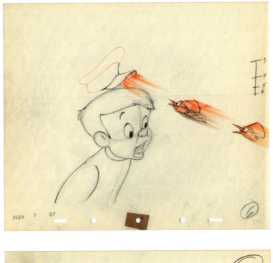

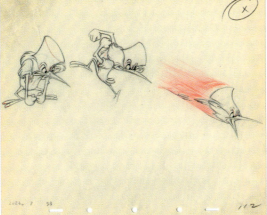

Discrimination of course must be used in the use of blurs. Certainly, characters like Taran and Eilonwy (*Black Cauldron*) are not going to move fast enough to cause blur. But still, in their case, the premise holds true that the extremes are the most important drawings and should be the most expressive. Good, crisp timing will make blurs unnecessary.

Phrasing is another aspect of animating with extremes. People and animals tend to move in idiosyncratic phrases. They move-pose, gesture-pose, anticipate, move-pose, etc. Different species have phrased movements that are peculiar to that species. Speech is delivered in phrases. We say ten words and pause or five words and pause, etc. Some people rattle on until they run out of breath and then pause. John Lounsbery and I once ran a whole picture reel of *Peter Pan* with just one line of repeating dialog. It was amazing the number of scenes the dialog synced to.

Phrasing, as Eric Larson pointed out in his paper "Getting It on The Screen," brings an action or an attitude to life, which makes it interesting and believable. Phrasing can also be thought of as a beat or rhythm. All of life has a rhythm: some days are full of staccato beats; others are so slow they seem to contain nothing but long holds. A day can be charted like a scene of animation: there are accents like extremes, moments of decision making like anticipations, and slow-ins and slow-outs.

Some people *act* and can make their own rhythm, others *react* and their rhythms are determined by chance. In animation there can be no chance — rhythm must be created consciously.

The pose that best portrays the mood of a scene can be thought of as an extreme–extreme. That drawing will usually be the one taken from the storyboard. It is only natural that one drawing in a scene will be the most extreme. That extreme–extreme should be reserved for the pose that stresses the storytelling aspect of that scene. Usually in a line of dialog one or two words will be emphasized for dramatic impact or to stress their meaning.

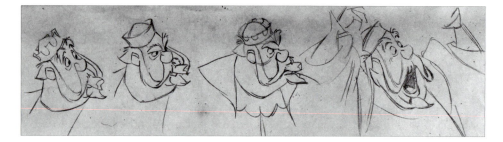

Those stressed words suggest to the animator where and how to time the action, which drawing is to be the anticipatory one, the extreme one, or the extreme–extreme one. If several words are spoken closely together, one extreme may take care of them by means of phrasing. There might be thirty words spoken in a scene but only six extreme drawings.

Groups of words that form phrases are chosen, which not only simplifies the animation, but it also makes it easier to emphasize the important words. The dialog might even suggest a different phrasing for the body than the head, or a different one for the head than the mouth. Arms and hands help in phrasing dialog: much can be said with the eyes.

Phrasing and timing can also be thought of as texture. We are used to thinking of texture as the surface quality of cloth or of other materials. Some have an overall design or texture, like the warp and woof of woven cloth, or like a tapestry or Persian rug. Others may have small groupings of texture on a field of plainness. Likewise a scene may have an overall linear pattern (texture), a scene of great and sustained activity taking place, like a hall full of dancing people, or a bleacher full of home team fans during a grand slam home run, or it may have almost no texture, like a lazy summer afternoon scene in the country — the hillbillies from the Martins and Coys are lounging on the hillside. Certainly, the timing of each of these last two scenes would be different. The fans in the bleacher scene would require several violent extreme poses and the idea could be put over in a couple of feet. The hillbilly scene could probably be done with only one tranquil pose and might require several feet to present the idea that nothing is happening.

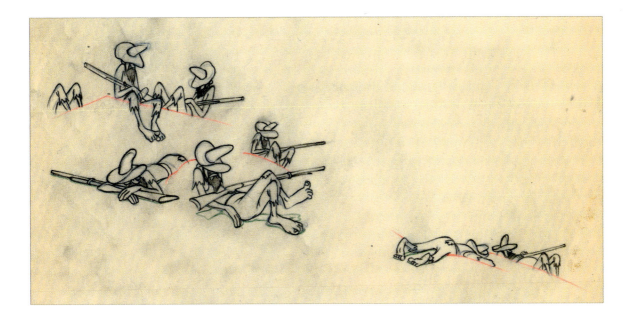

42 Symbols for Poses

SYMBOLS FOR POSES

HERE ARE A SET OF SYMBOLS WHICH SUGGEST MOOD, STATES, BEHAVIOR OR CONDITIONS. THEY SEEM TO BE INHERENT IN THE NATURE OF THINGS, OR AT LEAST IN OUR INTERPRETATION OF THEM. IF THIS IS SO, THEN THESE SYMBOLS CAN WORK AS A SORT OF EMOTIONAL SHORTHAND, AND WHEN USED IN A DRAWING OR AN ACTION, CAN SUBCONSCIOUSLY AROUSE IN THE OBSERVER THE EMOTION WITH WHICH THEY ARE ASSOCIATED.

DRAWINGS ARE BUT SYMBOLS. THEY ARE AN ARRANGEMENT OF LINES AND SHAPES WHICH MERELY REPRESENT REAL THINGS. TO THE EXTENT THAT THESE SYMBOLS CAN BE INCORPORATED IN A SCENE (BOTH LAYOUT AND ANIMATION DRAWINGS) TO THAT EXTENT WILL THE EMOTION BE COMMUNICATED TO, AND HOPEFULLY BE AROUSED IN THE VIEWER.

USING THESE SYMBOLS CAN NOT ONLY ENHANCE THE SCENE BUT ACTUALLY WORK AS A SHORT CUT TO ILLUSTRATING YOUR IDEAS.

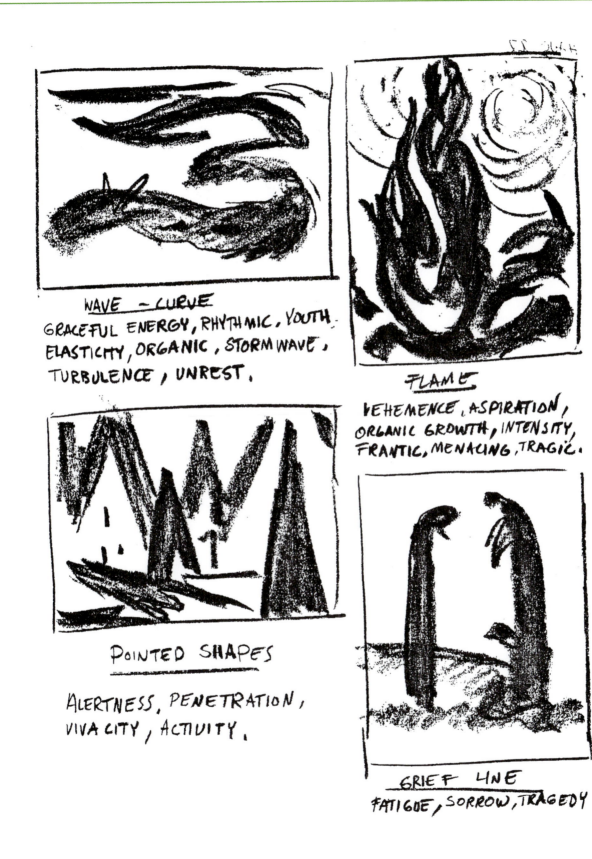

WAVE – CURVE
GRACEFUL ENERGY, RHYTHMIC, YOUTH.
ELASTICITY, ORGANIC, STORM WAVE,
TURBULENCE, UNREST.

FLAME
VEHEMENCE, ASPIRATION,
ORGANIC GROWTH, INTENSITY,
FRANTIC, MENACING, TRAGIC.

POINTED SHAPES

ALERTNESS, PENETRATION,
VIVACITY, ACTIVITY.

GRIEF LINE
FATIGUE, SORROW, TRAGEDY

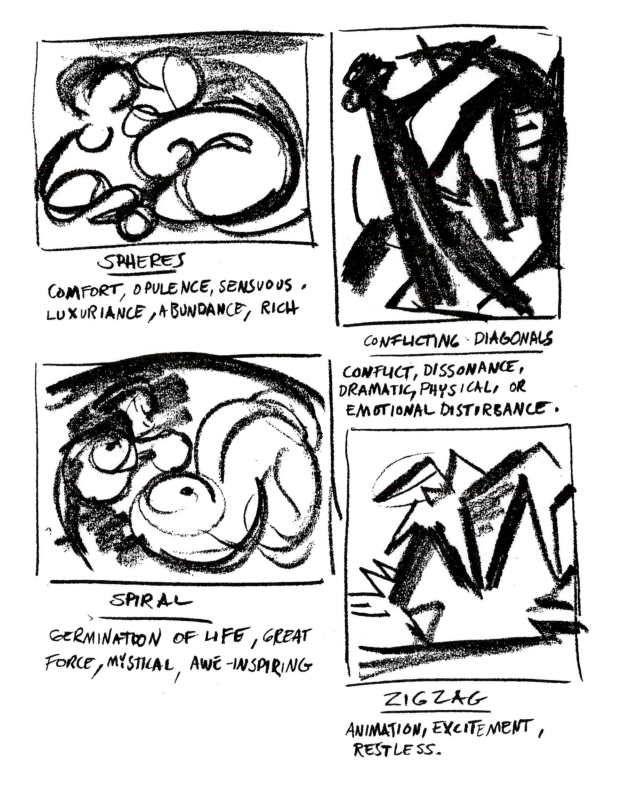

SPHERES
COMFORT, OPULENCE, SENSUOUS, LUXURIANCE, ABUNDANCE, RICH

CONFLICTING DIAGONALS
CONFLICT, DISSONANCE, DRAMATIC, PHYSICAL, OR EMOTIONAL DISTURBANCE.

SPIRAL
GERMINATION OF LIFE, GREAT FORCE, MYSTICAL, AWE-INSPIRING

ZIGZAG
ANIMATION, EXCITEMENT, RESTLESS.

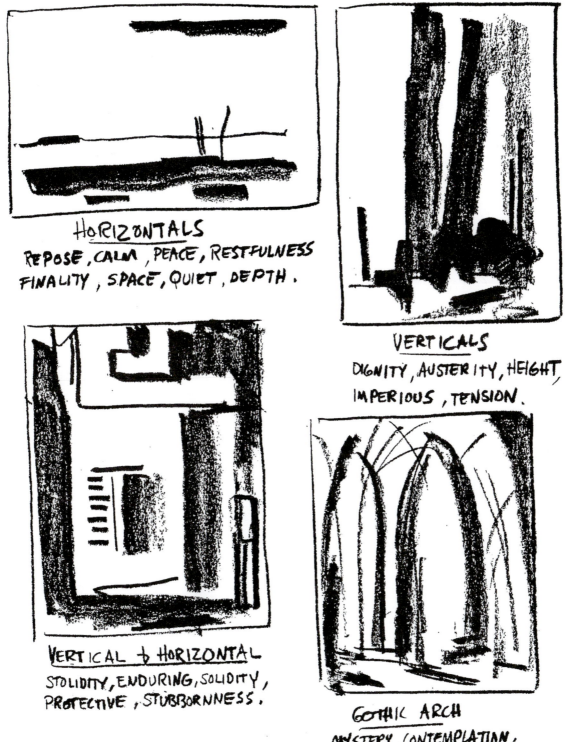

HORIZONTALS
REPOSE, CALM, PEACE, RESTFULNESS
FINALITY, SPACE, QUIET, DEPTH.

VERTICALS
DIGNITY, AUSTERITY, HEIGHT,
IMPERIOUS, TENSION.

VERTICAL & HORIZONTAL
STOLIDITY, ENDURING, SOLIDITY,
PROTECTIVE, STUBBORNNESS.

GOTHIC ARCH
MYSTERY, CONTEMPLATION,
ASPIRATION, SPIRITUAL, AWE.

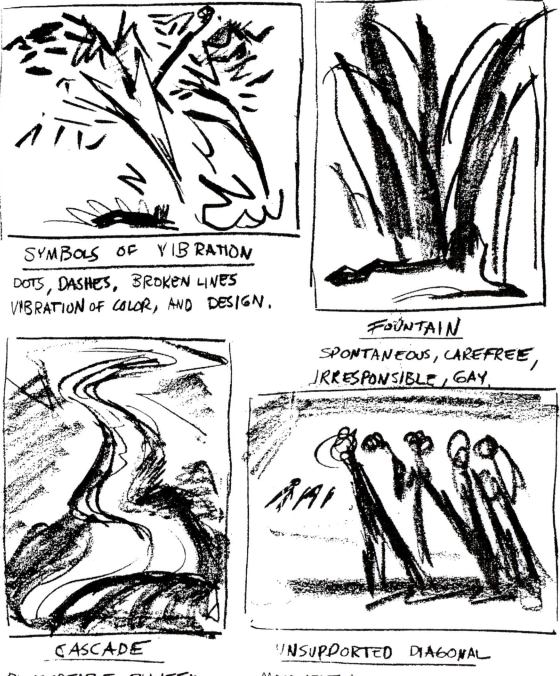

SYMBOLS OF VIBRATION

DOTS, DASHES, BROKEN LINES
VIBRATION OF COLOR, AND DESIGN.

FOUNTAIN

SPONTANEOUS, CAREFREE,
IRRESPONSIBLE, GAY.

CASCADE

PLEASUREABLE, PLAYFFUL
SWIFT, POWERFUL, RHYTHMIC

UNSUPPORTED DIAGONAL

MOVEMENT ACROSS OR IN AND OUT
OF SPACE.

43 Positive and Negative

Positive and negative shapes can be used to great advantage in both layout and in animation.

For instance, a background can help set the mood for a scene through proper staging, utilizing the positive/negative. This allows the animator to capitalize on the mood suggestion and carry it even further in his animation.

A story is naturally packed with a variety of moods. The gambit runs from happiness to sadness, gaiety to seriousness, and defeat (or the possibility of defeat) to victory (or the anticipation of victory).

A series of scenes where a character feels threatened could be enhanced by using dominant negative shapes, placing the potential victim in ominous compositions.

On the other hand, if the character is "on top" of his situation, he can be the dominant positive filling the screen with his victorious stances or with his boasting attitude.

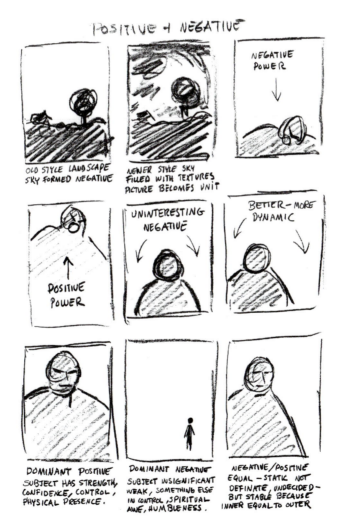

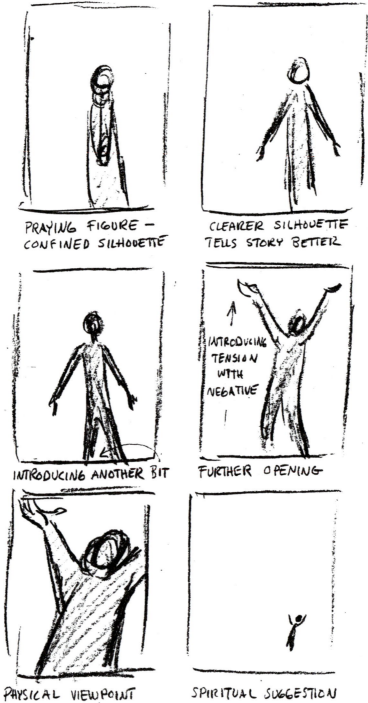

PRAYING FIGURE —
CONFINED SILHOUETTE

CLEARER SILHOUETTE
TELLS STORY BETTER

INTRODUCING ANOTHER BIT

INTRODUCING TENSION WITH NEGATIVE

FURTHER OPENING

PHYSICAL VIEWPOINT

SPIRITUAL SUGGESTION

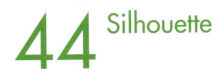 Silhouette

Here are some more examples of excellent silhouette patterns. Note that even without the help of the eyes and mouths or other detail, the moods of the characters are instantly evident: pleading, caution, delight, rejection, contemplation, sadness, playfulness, etc.

Lines define all the moods, yes, but the essence of each pose lies in the general shapes in alliance with specific shapes, in the positive shapes versus the negative shapes.

All this must be discovered by the animator and rediscovered by the cleanup person.

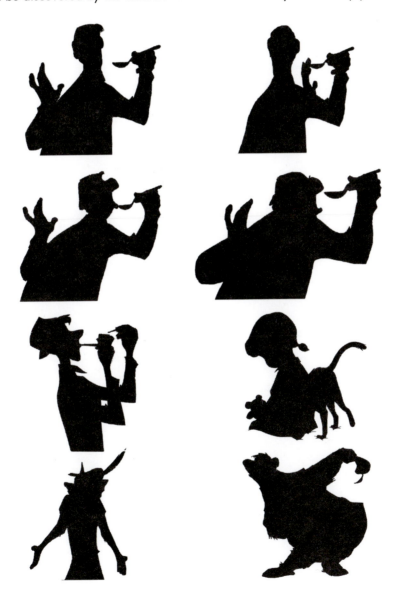

45 P.S. The Metaphysical Side

Certain "new thought" religions have a positive theme running through their teachings; they feature life, peace, happiness, health, and success. One way to get in tune with all this goodness is to start the day with a positive affirmation. One might say something like this: "Today brings out the best in me, if I bring out the best in today."

For artists (animators), drawing takes up a large portion of the day, so perhaps a positive statement for making successful drawings would be in line. For instance, say "today's drawings bring out the best in me — if I bring out the best in today's drawings." It becomes an expectancy factor and attitude factor, and those two things are a great energy source. Athletes usually do better at home games because their home fans cheer them on. It helps the team's expectancy/attitude factor.

You as artists don't have bands playing, banners flying, cheerleaders, or a friendly crowd of admirers to bring you up to creative heights. But you can have a quiet, affirmative, efficacious word with yourself daily, to make sure all your wheels are on the track.

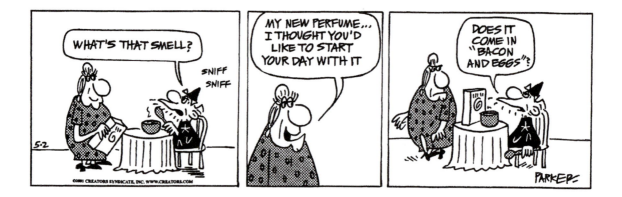

46 Draw Verbs Not Nouns

A sure way to keep from making static, lifeless drawings is to think of drawing verbs instead of nouns. Basically, a noun names a person, place, or thing; a verb *asserts*, or *expresses* action, a state of being, or an occurrence.

I speak often of shifting mental gears and here is another place to do it. The tendency to copy what is before us without taking time (or effort) to ferret out what is happening action-wise is almost overwhelming.

Let's say, for example, the model (and this also goes for making a drawing without a model) is leaning over with her elbows extended. If you approach the pose from the standpoint of drawing nouns, you will name and draw the parts (humerus, radius, ulna, scapula, biceps, triceps, deltoid, etc.) and place them as best you can in the positions suggested by the model. With good hand/eye coordination, or a good memory, or either a model or a good anatomy book handy, you can produce a fairly handsome drawing of nouns. If you approach the pose from the standpoint of drawing verbs, you will simply be using those nouns to produce a drawing that portrays a woman *bending* over, *stretching* her arms, *pulling* her hair, or about to *push* the towel over her hair to *dry* it. You feel the hair below her left hand *hanging*, you feel the right arm cocked and ready to *push forward*. You feel the back *stretching* and the left side *squashing*, and you feel the downward motion set up by the angles of her forearms. The body is also *balancing*, *twisting*, and *angling*. You feel she is thinking about what she is doing — not just frozen into a still life.

Now there is a list of verbs that should develop into a drawing that has the breath of life in it. The pose could be described by nouns: "woman after bath," but verbs would charge it with the life-giving qualities of bodily movement, rhythm, motion, and action allowing the viewer to participate vicariously.

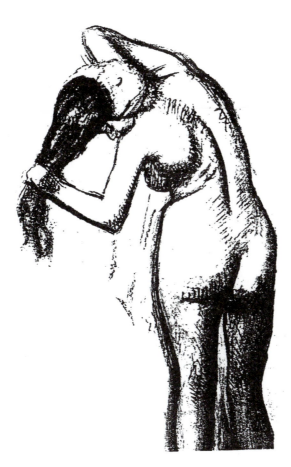

47 Osmosis

Glen Keane was pinning up some inspirational drawings in his room one day as I happened by. He explained that he hoped that some of the artist's genius would enter him through osmosis. Glen laughed, but he was serious. And serious he has a right to be for osmosis works.

The conscious mind must be selective of the things that vie for one's attention because it can only process one thing at a time. You could liken it to a telephone line where the voice travels over a single concentrated vehicle. The conscious mind "listens in" to whatever it desires to pay attention. The subconscious mind, however, receives an unbroken deluge of information, not through a single line but more like radio waves that travel in all directions. The subconscious mind receives constantly from all directions; all the information picked up by the five senses (and psychically) in the form of subliminal "osmosis."

Most everyone is acquainted with the classic example that took place in a theater some years ago. A subliminal advertisement for coke and popcorn was flashed on periodically during the film. The flashes were so fast the conscious mind couldn't pick it up, but not so the subconscious. It picked up the message and acted on its own — the coke and popcorn sales rose by something like 20 or 30%.

Later, some fellow capitalized on this method by recording several tapes of a positive thinking and self-help nature, but with only the sound of waves breaking at the seashore audible. The problems the tapes deal with are common everyday problems such as procrastination, self-image, eating problems, and the like. The person seeking help listens for an hour a day (or something like that) and while the conscious mind is soothed by the wave sounds, the subconscious deals with the subliminal suggestions in its mysterious but inevitable fashion. The premise is that a lot of negative influence has gotten by the "guard" at the mind's door and has polluted the whole thinking process, and consequently, the mind and the body — one's whole life in many cases. Testimonies from those who used the method are quite fantastic (and a heartening sense, that is).

So, be convinced that osmosis (subliminal input) is a very serious business, and a potent vehicle to guide your mind in the direction you want it to go (or change some undesirable direction it has inadvertently taken).

By all means, as artists aspiring to excel in animation, avail yourselves of this excellent form of self-help. If there are those who don't aspire, then you need to work on that missing link.

In a previous handout I said positive thinking comes in many forms. The subliminal form is one of the more potent and effective. Besides, it can make life rather pleasant — surrounding yourself with the best drawings you can lay your hands on and perhaps a few "quotable quotes" of a positive thinking nature. Your subconscious loves to take all this information and find some way to express it. It has nothing else to do for 24 hours every day but manipulate and match bits of information, trying to piece something usable out of them for you to use. It's quite impersonal, so it can also build an evil and destructive think tank — without you being aware of it. Remember it is *sub*conscious and aimless unless you consciously control it.

In the book, *The Power In You*, by Wally "Famous" Amos (the chocolate cookie man), there are interspersed throughout, encased in "boxes" to set them off, some choice bits of wisdom. They are designed to sum up the surrounding text, but are gems in themselves. Here is a sample.

"Each of us has free will and we have chosen the results in our lives, either passively or actively."

"That goes hand in hand with the "guard at the door" bit — you can either choose what you want to feed your mind (life-improving nourishment) or you can be passive and allow just about anything to get in there and take root."

"Success is the result of an attitude that can find the positive, worthwhile aspects of everything it comes into contact with and denies anything that may be negative or hindering."

So if the guard at your mind's door has been letting you down by letting a lot of negative stuff in, maybe it's time for a "changing of the guard." Some exciting things could be directed into that cauldron of creativity you're carrying around up there.

In the space left, I have crammed in a potpourri of visual delights to feast your hungry subconscious. Incidentally, you don't have to look far for good drawings — these were all done by fellow Disney artists.

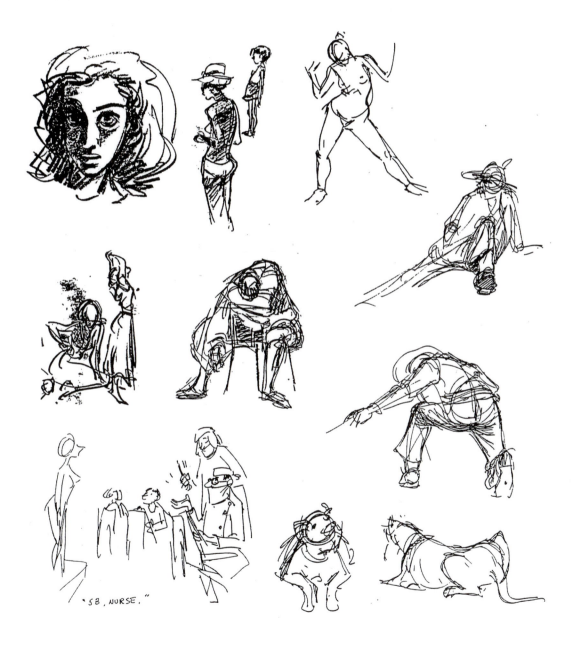

48 Drawing and Caricature

We have talked about taking advantage of the model's build, that is, if he is tall or paunchy or lithe and trying to capture those distinguishing features in your drawing (there is a tendency to draw the ideal figure, the one that frequents the anatomy books and the ones we clip or Xerox and pin up above our desks). The same applies to heads. The model may have a pinched nose, a double chin, baggy jowls, a long upper lip, beady eyes, or a low forehead. These are the things that help determine and emphasize the gesture. Even as the structure of the body determines the possibilities and the uniqueness of a gesture so does the construction of the head and the features of the face, especially if those features can be recognized and caricatured. -

Don Graham said, "It isn't how well we draw the joints or the different parts of the anatomy, but how well you know where they are, how they relate and how they work. That's the important thing." And as Woolie Reitherman said, "Get the spirit of the thing. That's the most important and then after that you can add to it." Ward Kimball said if he could take something apart and put it back together again, he could draw it. Perhaps we could approach drawing the head in that way. If we could analyze the construction of the head, the types of features, and the meaning of the gesture we could draw it.

In animation, the ideal model sheet is one that clearly describes the head shape and the features. The proportions and types of features are all defined and clearly recorded. It will even suggest, somewhat, the extremes one might go to in animating that character. Even then it is not easy. And it is less easy with a live model. Here it is up to us to discover the idiosyncrasies of that person and use them to reveal and enhance the gesture. A reproduction of an anatomy book illustration will not do — no more than it does for the model of one of our characters in a cartoon feature. The basic structure will certainly be useful, but as for an individual character — each person is unique, and the gesture that comes from that uniqueness is what we are striving for.

For the animation artist the ideal lies somewhere in that vast area between realistic/anatomical and cartoon/caricature. Walt's definition of caricature was "The true interpretation of caricature is the exaggeration of an illusion of the actual, or the sensation of the actual put into action." Eric Larson said "Caricature comes from the old word, 'caricatura' which meant to overload, so we do just that: overload. Caricature implies laughable exaggeration of the characteristic features of a subject, human, animal, building, prop, etc. But caricature needn't be thought of only as humorous or ludicrous exaggeration — it can be and is simply, "distortion by exaggeration of parts or characteristics" (as per Webster's Dictionary).

The spirit of the thing as Woolie termed it can more easily be portrayed by exaggeration. It need not be comical. Many very touching drawings of serious and poignant subjects are subtle caricatures of reality. I don't suggest we remain as subtle as Norman Rockwell or as far out as Gary Larson (*Far Out*), but don't forget, we are essentially cartoonists who are in the entertainment field, so with that in mind our model studies should perhaps lean in that direction.

On the following pages I have made some drawings that might be literal sketches of a model, then beside them I have placed some exaggerations of their features to show the possibilities of augmenting both the character and the gesture.

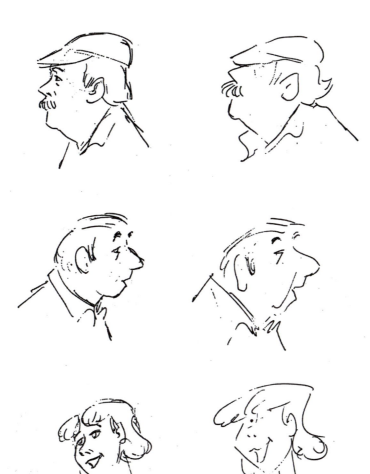

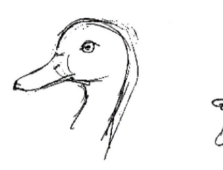

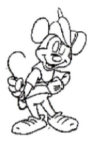

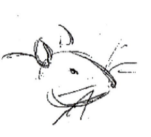

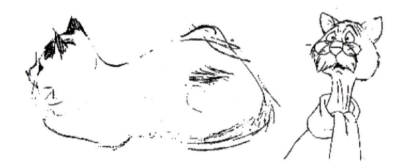

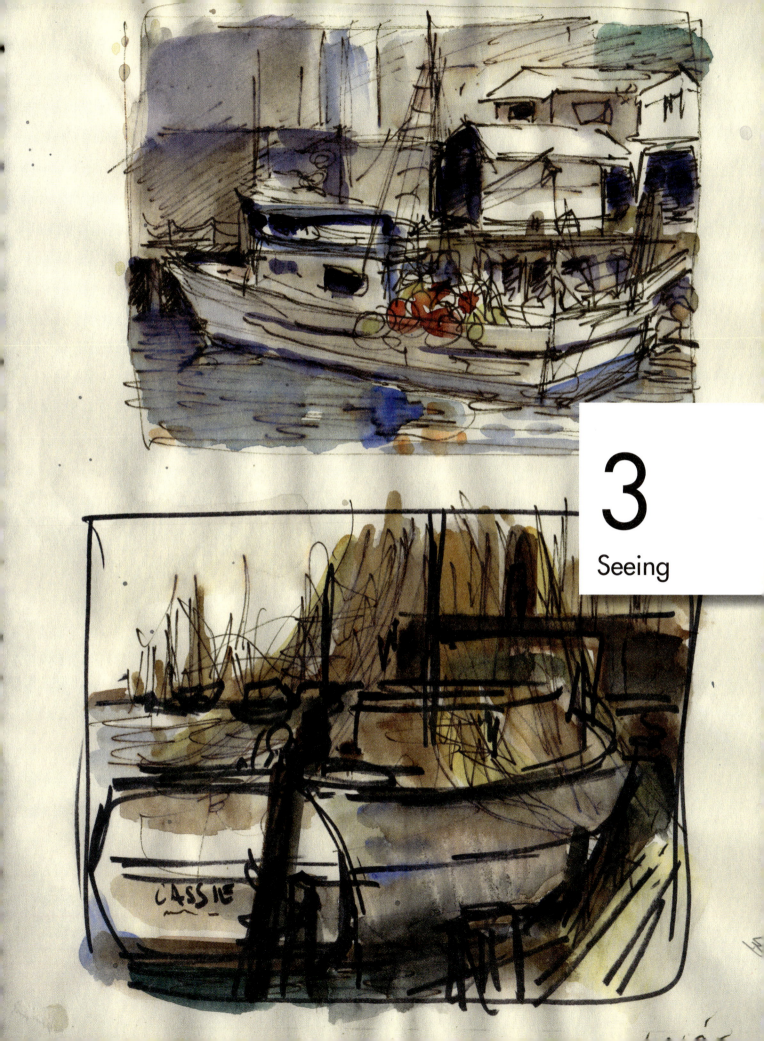

3

Seeing

CASSIE

49 What Not to See

One of the things you have to look for when sketching from a model is what not to see. Random bumps and bulges often occur, demanding interpretation. Clothing sometimes acts contrary-wise to all common sense. An excess of cloth will often defy the main action and seemingly do something on its own. When you see this happen you have to take the matter into your own hands and make sense where there is none. I think the best way to handle this problem is to constantly refer back to your first impression of what the person is doing, as opposed to what the cloth is doing, assuming of course, that you have "named the pose." Naming the pose is a natural outcome of studying the pose for a first impression. You could think of each pose as a one drawing drama, or you might think of it as just 1/16th of a foot of animation.

A GOOD BIT OF BUSINESS

One thing that helps an animator is a "good bit of business." If the story point is clear and definite, that gives him something solid to work with. I have often heard the admonition, "If you can't make it work — it's probably because your concept is wrong." Many an animator has struggled with a drawing, taking it off the pegs and shifting it around, tracing it with minor differences, then putting it aside in favor of a radically different approach. The concept was wrong — or at least difficult to put over.

WHEN YOU ARE WALKING, YOU ARE WALKING...

A still drawing of a model, if there is not a solid concept of what one is drawing (gesture-wise or story-wise), can turn out to be a jumble of muscles and bone and bulges of cloth. On the other hand, if you as artist/director/story man, can establish a clear-cut concept of what your actor is doing, you can then make a good clear statement. There is a Zen saying: "When you are walking, you are walking; when you are eating, you are eating...." Should not your drawings be as definite and simple as that?

DINNER FIRST, THEN DESSERT

Other things not to see, especially in the initial stages of a drawing, is anything that complicates or dilutes your first impression. The first impression should be as simple and direct as you can possibly make it. Constant vigilance has to be exercised to keep temptation at bay. My mother used to say "Eat your dinner and then you can have some dessert."

BEADS WITH NECK OR NECK WITH BEADS

I have seen some sketches start with details, which is like hanging a necklace in mid-air before the neck is drawn. Sounds silly but we all do it to a certain extent. Decide at the beginning what is the main course — saving the dessert for later. You are not drawing a necklace with a person attached to it; you are drawing a person doing something. That something is either suggested by the model, or conjured up in your mind for the purpose of making the drawing a one-drawing drama, thereby giving it a reason for being. The person might just have a necklace on at the time.

SHIFTING GEARS

When you see a play or movie, you allow yourself to look past the actor and see the acted. A shifting of mental gears takes place. A similar shifting takes place when drawing. You look past the model to that illusive but capturable gesture. You don't draw a costume with a person somewhere underneath (there only to hold the costume up), you draw a person, dressed in a costume, influencing that costume in the unique way that only that person can.

A GESTURE LIGHT

It would be grand if we had a light that would illuminate just the gesture of the model. It's light would filter out all the superfluous stuff. Well there is such a light — it's within us. Illumination means "to throw light on a subject in order to see it better."

WHAT WILL THE VIEWER SEE?

An author pictures something in his mind and he writes it down. Each time the passage is read the picture reappears in the mind of the reader.

An artist pictures something in his mind, he draws it and each time the drawing is viewed, the artist's impression reappears in the mind of the viewer. If the artist lets his strong first impression (the essence of the gesture) slip away, the drawing will surely turn out to be just a copy of the multitude of details before him, bumps and bulges and all, and that's what will be re-emerge whenever the drawing is viewed.

SEEING INTO THE POSE

We have been fortunate lately to have some models that stimulate us to go beyond the parts and details so we don't just see the pose, but we see into the pose. You know when that happens — the illumination light comes on. I don't profess to be a great cartoonist, I just do it for relaxation, but I do know that feeling of illumination while doing it. I plant a theme or subject in my mind and something in the mind takes it and runs it through my mental computer and in seconds there is a gag with the characters, the composition and the gag line complete. It's like picking fruit from an in visible tree. Somehow the gestures that come match the gag line as if the subconscious has a director in there that stages everything and prompts the actors.

DON'T BLOW IT WITH DETAILS

Drawing from the model (or developing action for a scene of animation) works that way too. You send the problem quickly through your mental system and if you can keep the parts and details from "blowing it," the computer mulls it around and sends it back to you in an illuminated form, the composition, the character, and the essence of the gesture.

FIND THE LIGHT SWITCH

All of you get that feeling when your drawing "goes right," but when things go wrong you wonder what happened to that feeling — where did it go — why did it leave me right when I need it most? Whenever that feeling comes to you, just don't sit there and enjoy it, analyze it and see if you can call it up at will. And if you see someone walking around with a dazed, euphoric look on their face, you can be sure they found that light switch.

Here are a few drawings from a scene by Milt Kahl. Study the costume. Notice how, even in a complex action, it is kept simple — no meaningless bulges or bumps. In the last drawing it settles into the epitome of simplicity. The garment, bulky as it is, echoes the gesture of the body underneath.

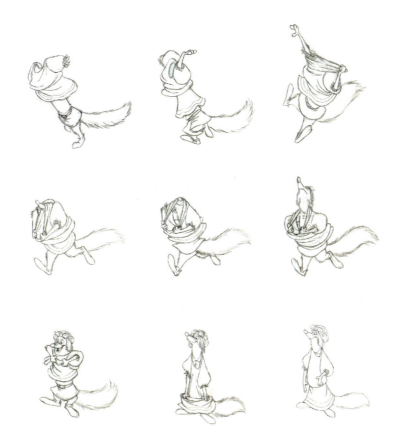

50 A Bit of Introspection

We are all beautiful people but also strange in some ways. We all have psychological quirks that whisk us through life, along many paths that often are not really of our own choosing. Why did we choose art for a career — certainly not because we were good at it. If we were good at it we wouldn't have to struggle so hard to make a go of it. But we plug along, each at our own pace, some eager and industrious in improving ourselves — some of us sit back and wait for the "light" to come on. Some of us are driven by some invisible urge to create. Others need some project imposed on us from outside to stir us into action.

Animation has a unique requirement in that its rewards are vaguely rewarding and at the same time frustrating. We are performers but our audience is hidden from us. We are actors but there is no applause. We are artists but our works are not framed and hung on walls for friends to see. We are sensitive people whose sensibility is judged across the world in dingy theaters by a sometimes popcorn eating audience. Yet we are called upon day by day to delve deep into our psyche and come up with fresh creative bits of entertaining fare. That requires a special kind of discipline and devotion, and enthusiasm. Our inner dialog must be amply peppered with encouraging argument. We sometimes have to invent or create an audience in our minds to draw for. Our fellow artists only partially serve us in that respect. We go to them for criticism not for praise. The directors are necessarily merciless. We at times almost connive rather than create to get a scene by them. I used to sing in operettas, concerts, etc., so I know what real applause is. It is heavenly. A living audience draws something extra out of the performer. A stage director once said to the cast of a play on the opening night:

> You've had good equipment to work with, a theater with everything it takes to put on a show but you have been handicapped — one essential thing has been denied you. Tonight there is an audience out there, now you have everything you need.

Well, we do have an audience out there. We'll be denied the applause but at least there is a potential audience to perform for; one to keep in mind constantly as we shape up day by day our year dress rehearsal. Even as we struggle with the myriad difficulties of finalizing a picture — what is the phrase, "getting it in the can" — we can perform each act for that invisible or mystical audience. We can't see our audience, but it is real and it is something to work for.

So, all you beautiful people, if you are the kind that needs a little mental manipulation to keep your creative juices flowing, perhaps this has been of some benefit; if not, well, so be it.

51 It Ain't Easy

Drawing may be compared to driving a car. While driving there are a number of things that need to filter through the consciousness and be constantly monitored: destination; steering; judging distances and speeds of other cars; working the gas pedal, the brakes, or the clutch; driving in the right lane at the right time; checking the panel for gas, temperature, oil, seat belt, sun visor, etc.

In drawing one must continually run through the list of prerequisites for making a successful drawing. There is the brief study to grasp a first impression, then the start of the sketching — the size, the pose, the perspective (including overlap, diminishing size, surface lines, foreshortening), anatomy, squash and stretch, angles, tension — then back through the list again, perhaps in a different order, depending on the needs of the drawing at that particular stage. But one must always go back to the first impression lest the drawing be allowed to drift off into "just a drawing." So, in driving, one has constantly in mind the destination lest one ends up just driving around.

One must visualize the ideal drawing (gesture) and then monitor the progress and state of the drawing to keep steering it in that direction. Hopefully, the analysis of the pose to acquire the first impression was a good one.

Talking oneself through the drawing is one technique. You might say, as your pen or pencil busies itself with your orders and desires: "Let's see, do I have enough straights, enough curves; should I strengthen these angles; what can I do about this tangent? My first impression was thus and so — am I sticking with it? I will stress this tension, accent the lift or the stretch. How can I make this clearer?"

This may sound like an overly involved process just to get a gesture drawing down on a piece of blank paper, but you see this is not just any old gesture drawing — this is the one you are working on now, at this moment of your life, you don't want to toss it off casually as if it were less important than another. Until all, and I mean *all*, of these prerequisites for a good drawing become second nature, some method has to be used to make sure each of these things is attended to. Just as you wouldn't think of driving a car without checking the fuel, planning your route, and for sure, tuning the radio to your favorite station.

"It ain't easy,", as Ollie Johnston said. It requires a lot of thought and loving attention. Bill Berg said "I love to draw." Did he not speak for all of us? So in animation there is not just one pose to "lovingly" attend to, but hundreds and eventually thousands of such poses. So added to the above list of prerequisites are endurance, "stick-to-itness," and a sustained enthusiasm — things which in themselves require a special nurturing.

It might seem that all this mental manipulation might impede the so-called creative side of drawing, because all these rules and the overseeing are a left-brain activity. But left to its own, the right brain may take off into some Picasso-like freedom and we end up with some "creative" but inappropriate drawing. We must be creative within the bounds of our media, so it is legitimate to call upon the left brain to help out in that respect.

Most important to the success of a drawing is that first impression. If it is perceived wrongly, the preliminary sketch will be off and all the work put in it from then on will be a waste. You may think I'm being overly hard-headed about this. After all, if you finish the drawing and it looks nice, what the heck…. The point is, you want to sharpen your skill and sensitivity to the point where you can express any gesture you are called upon to draw. It is thrilling to see a well-done anatomical drawing, but it is deeply thrilling to see a drawing that expresses some gesture, mood, feeling, or meaningful action.

Following are a set of drawings that do just that. The artist's knowledge of anatomy has been transformed to conform to the character he was drawing. His adaptation of the anatomy of the human body was only a tool to attain his intent. His sensibility to the personality of the character and the resultant appropriate gestures are quite phenomenal.

(I would like to interject a word of praise and respect for the cleanup people, including inbetweeners, for many is the time when the sensitivity of the animation drawings came to full fruition in the cleanup department.)

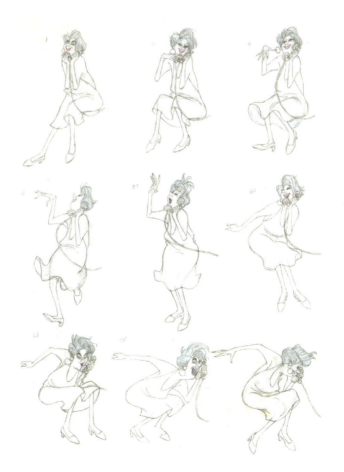

52 A Good First Impression

Try this experiment: look at your surroundings — a panorama of scenery is ideal for this — and direct your mind to slip in and out of some selected modes. First concentrate on color. You should be able to eliminate all the other elements and see just areas of color. Then switch to dark and light, then to masses, then to the third dimensional qualities of things near and far. Now, try to see all of those things at once. Your mind may have to do a little jig, skipping back and forth between them, for it's rather hard to concentrate on more than one thing at a time. But if you keep at it, it will all come together and the *totality* of the scene will hit you like a bomb. That's the first impression I speak about. It is sometimes referred to as a moment of inspiration; a moment of utter clarity; that instant of pure seeing that Betty Edwards (*Drawing On The Artist Within*) calls the "Ah-Ha!" moment. Actually it is just an extremely vivid summation of all the important elements before you. It hits you so hard and clear it is relatively easy to recall when you need a fresh look at it.

The practical application of the ability to isolate the elements of a scene, or in your case, a posing figure, is to quickly analyze the components of the pose and to put them all back together again into a good, strong first impression, any part of which you can call to mind for reference as your drawing proceeds.

Depending on the purpose, meaning, or story behind the gesture you will search the figure for (not necessarily in this order) overall structural personality or character (tall, thin, graceful, soft, doll-like, comical, etc.), then phase in on the essence of the gesture (the one-pose story, how this particular figure enacts this particular pose, the feeling it evokes; you may want to refer back many times to that feeling because it is important), then you will want to phase in on each of the rules of perspective (see my rules of perspective), mentally superimposing them on the figure to locate them there, then file the findings in your short-term memory for handy reference. Especially mode in on the all-important angles and any squash and stretch. This may all sound very complex, but it all happens in a split second.

Once these things are established in the mind, you can go back to the whole figure and start drawing. If you bog down in some area, don't fight it — simply switch modes and call up that first impression for just long enough to revitalize your original intentions. This kind of drawing, in a sense, is finished before you start, so there is less struggling during the crucial periods of drawing and it frees you of laborious deliberations, vacillations, backtracking, and getting sidetracked. This is not to say any new information coming to light should not be considered, but only as far as it is relevant and will help plus your first impression.

In animation you usually have *one thing to say at a time*, so everything on your drawing should relate to that one thing. Forming a good first impression will establish that *one thing* and keeping it in the forefront of your mind will keep you on the right path. Simplicity will prove to be one of your best allies, both in your concept of the gesture and in the process of drawing it.

The first impression is the right brain's summation of all that lies before it. Often as the drawing proceeds, the left brain will want to step in and have you start drawing all the details — the buttons, the stitching, the pockets, or some piece of clothing that for no particular reason has formed a little bump. You don't have to waste any energy fighting such temptations. Just press the "CLEAR" button and your first impression will flash back on the screen again with all the consequential information, the strong angles, the simple shapes, the squashes and stretches, etc. You don't have to "put the left brain down." Relegate to it a job like switching back to the first impression every minute or two — it is eager to help (it thinks it can draw better than the right brain). But if you allow the left brain to dominate it will copy what is before it, insignificant details and all. Both sides of the brain are eager to help but you have to let them know what you want.

While watching the finals of a tennis tournament between Agassi and Paul Anacone, I sketched a little. This is quick sketching at a fairly fast pace. I tried for two things in these drawings: (1) to capture the action itself and (2) to draw the player's identity — the action (that is, so they could be identified as those two players). I can only guess at the time involved — perhaps one hundredth of a second to analyze the gesture and from between 15 and 45 seconds to draw it. This is good practice for it forces you to lock in on a good solid first impression because in one second the pose has changed and you're stuck with how much information you have gathered in that Ah-Ha! moment. In a classroom situation where there is a model to copy from, you often have to remind yourself that it is the gesture you are after.

53 Stick to the Theme

An orchestra conductor, in a discussion on conducting Mahler's 1st symphony, said he had to be careful not to have too many climaxes in the performance. It is a relatively long symphony, fifty-five minutes in length, and is full of delightful passages that could be featured each in their own right. But there needs be control over such a temptation so that the overall theme of each of the three movements shall prevail.

Drawing is like that. We are the conductors who are tempted to feature the many interesting passages on the model. Some passages — a wrinkle, a belt buckle, a hairdo — are sensuous to the point where we want to render them into little masterpieces of nonessential detail. Usually, a drawing has but one theme and that theme must be featured or the drawing disintegrates into a montage of unrelated climaxes.

There is a story to be told in drawing whether it is one drawing of a model, or many drawings in a scene of animation. True, in both cases there are secondary actions and costuming that must be dealt with, but the story (theme) is all important, while all else must be kept in a subordinate role. Subordinate doesn't mean unimportant. *Everything* on the drawing is there to help stress the story. Every line drawn should help direct the eye to the theme.

An obvious example, but to the point. (pun meant).

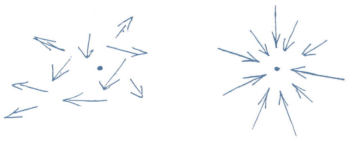

Every scene of animation and every single drawing has a theme upon which the viewers attention should be directed. Every line in the drawing must help. It is much more difficult in music and literature. To keep a central motif going in music for fifty-five minutes takes some advanced know how and discipline. An author has a similar problem. Whether writing a love story or a psychic thriller; the words chosen are like the lines we use in drawing. They help reveal and build the substance of the theme. A wrong choice of words or phrases will spoil the mood. Things that are not basic to the story (plot, mood, or gesture) have to be left out.

Below are two sketches from the drawing class that illustrate the "centering down," the "gathering of the forces," and the aggregation of certain elements crucial to telling the story. (I like that word aggregate — it means a mass of distinct things gathered together — a total).

The first sketch if carried further would have been a good drawing in the sense the artist would have finished it with a certain amount of expertise.

The second drawing immediately centers your attention on the story. A sailor has tossed a line to some destination. You feel the force of the toss. The secondary action of the held end of the rope indicates that it has not reached its destination yet, which is commensurate with the throwing arm still at its extreme position. His body is bent forward and down front the forward thrust of the toss, which caused another secondary action, the belly-hanging-over-the-belt-bit. The straight of the right leg plus the force exerted by the left leg, along with the open "channel" set up by the two arms and the splayed out rope, and even the unseen face, open a "passage" (one of Don Graham's favorite words) for the attention of the viewer to dwell on, or pass through. That is where the story is told, and every line in the drawing is contributing to it.

So drawing is not just recording a leg here, an arm there, a head and hands, etc. A drawing is like a parable, which is a story told to convey a lesson. If the story reveals the meaning of the lesson it is a success, but if it is just a cute story, it falls short of its reason for being.

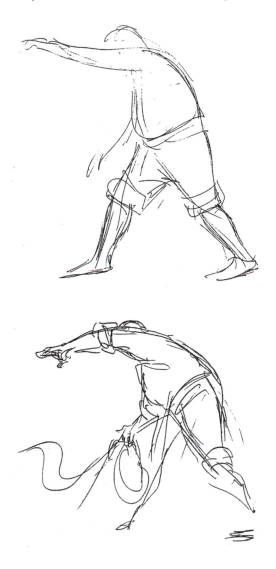

54 Sometimes I Wonder Why I Spend the Lonely Hours…

In a sense, drawing is learned by accumulating a visual vocabulary, just as speaking requires a verbal vocabulary. And as a certain amount of sentence structure, syntax, and voice inflection must be learned to communicate verbally, so must there be some rules of drawing that need to be learned and used to communicate the meanings of your drawings. We think of communication as "normal," but in the distant past there were no words, and at that point man had limited ways to communicate his thoughts — simple as they probably were. Our present way of communication has evolved … and is still evolving. In our class we're attempting to make another leap in drawing communication by seeing the gesture at once and putting it down in all its freshness and lucidity.

It is not an easy thing to do. You have studied anatomy and have spent many hours admiring your favorite artists until a foregone conclusion as to how to draw something sets in. Now you are bombarded with new gestures and new concepts. You are called upon to see the essence of the gesture and get it down before it slides back into a watered-down pose or before your foregone conclusions alter your newfound vision.

Before I get into specifics, let me congratulate you for your recent accomplishments. Your drawings in the last class were superb.

One thing most of you have to work on is angles. You still have that subconscious desire to straighten things up.

Try this experiment: hum a couple of your favorite tunes. Notice the angles the melody takes. If you took out or straightened out those angles where would the melody be? You would end up with a kind of monotone. The same thing can happen to your drawings if all the angles are straightened out.

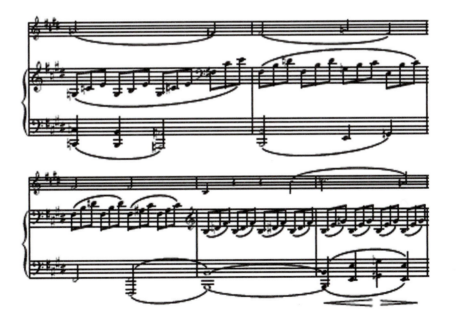

Music is a linear or two-dimensional thing, it moves along in one direction-while drawing, illusion-wise, is three dimensional, adding to the problem. But through a creative use of the principles of drawing, the most difficult and subtlest gestures are within your grasp. Not stiff drawings, as if done by formulae, but loose and fluid and meaningful.

Here are two corrections I saved from the class. They have to do with angles, which unlike melody, which is two-dimensional, are three-dimensional and come at us from all directions. Two of the simple rules of perspective, overlap, and surface lines are applicable here.

Notice how the male figure stooping over needed more angle to bring him forward at 3/4 view. The head mass placed over the chest mass illustrates the overlap rule.

The tilt of his head illustrates the surface line rule.

In the woman's head the same problem is present and the same rules are the solution — the forehead overlapping the cheeks, the cheeks overlapping the chin and the ear, placed on a surface line, overlapping the jaw.

These so-called principles of drawing are a lot of fun after you get them to work for you. They actually help you to see the construction of the figure in relationship to the gesture it is assuming. They are like a friend that points out the good things in life that you might somehow by negligence or misdirection have missed.

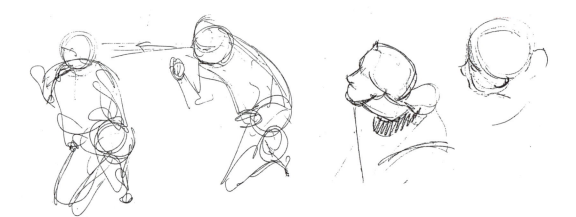

55 Cleanup — General

Study model sheet and/or examples of character to date. Discuss character with knowledgeable person. Acquire key drawing.

Get acquainted with scene; know what it is portraying and how it is portrayed. If there are any doubts, talk to the animator, director, key man, or study ruff reel.

Flip scene several times, then roll the drawings five at a time or from extreme to extreme. Pay special attention to breakdowns and inbetweens, making sure arcs and overlaps are used and followed. Make rough corrections or suggestions on drawings that need adjusting.

Also check dialog and/or pan movements, if any.

Remove inbetween drawings and lay aside.

As you proceed to clean up the scene, try to go through the process of animating the scene mentally to capture the animator's original creative intentions.

Note the "high" points in the scene, so that the greatest emphasis may be placed there. Note the poses that require the most "punch."

Compare several key extremes to make sure sizes are consistent throughout the scene. If there is a variance, the proper size will have to be decided upon and the corrections made on separate sheets of paper before starting to clean up the scene.

In some cases it may be best to clean up several key extremes and treat the balance of them as breakdown extremes. However, in most cases you may begin with the first extreme and work more or less straight ahead.

Where a character increases or diminishes in size throughout the scene, it is best to clean up the first and last drawings so the change in size will be consistent.

Ideally it is best to rub down the animator's drawing slightly and clean up directly on the original, careful not to erase so much that the essence of the drawing is lost. Very often there may be a special or subtle action that could be lost forever by rubbing down too far, especially if the drawings have to be altered to bring them closer to the model. If you see that this may be a possibility, be safe and work the problem out on separate sheets of paper. At times like this you must respect the animator's efforts, making sure you retain what he has attained.

The animator may have spent many laborious hours on a small and/or subtle action, which could conceivably be lost in cleanup in 30 seconds. Actually it is not the cleanup person's job to merely save what the animator has done, but to try to better it.

When the ideal is not present; that is, when the animation drawings are quite rough or they are off model, it will be necessary to make new drawings. This is where special care must be taken to transfer the essence of the animation to the new drawings. Do not destroy the original drawings; there may be a need to refer back to them at a later date, especially if some effects suggestions must go with scene to the Effects Department.

The cleanup person's *goal* is to make good drawings, and it is his *responsibility* to enhance the animation. As a matter of fact, sometimes it is up to the cleanup person to put into the scene even what the animator has failed to put there.

Check field size. A small field will necessitate more careful work. Also there may be a lot of drawing outside the field that need not be worked on. If it is a close-up or a slow movement, more care must be taken. If it is a long shot or fast moving scene, it may be handled more loosely with more attention given to the broad lines of action rather than to details. Time is always a factor to consider so, in effect, times may be "banked" on the fast scenes.

If possible, keep the first drawing on the pegs or at least readily available for constant checking for size, detail, and character throughout the cleanup process.

Any doubts about the approach to be used, problems, or questions should be settled before getting too far into the scene. It could save a great deal of time and effort.

Ideally the first few cleanup drawings should be brought to another person who is acquainted with the character and have him analyze them. You should be less reluctant to show your drawings to the person whose job it is to help you, than to let it go and then have a hostile and critical audience see them.

Stick-ons are a must. Your drawing will be handled by several other people and not always gently.

Occasionally the backs of your drawings will become messy from picking up lines from other drawings, especially if soft lead was used. Since Test Camera uses a bottom light, this mess may show up in a cleanup test. If this seems likely, erase the backs. Then too, the "messy" backs of the drawings worked on will work as a carbon paper and transpose random marks over the face of the new drawings already completed.

One of the cardinal sins in animation is working on a drawing without flipping it with the extreme drawing preceding it. In some cases, two or three extremes before and even extremes following might be needed to capture the essence of the action.

Remember, you are moving shapes in space, so to see that shape and to draw it accordingly you must know where it came from and where it is going. The only way you can do justice to a stretch drawing is to work it out of a normal squash drawing or vice versa.

An anticipation, for instance, is sometimes broad, sometimes subtle, but always directly related to the "normal" drawing before it and to the action that follows. Refer to Eric Larson's notes on anticipation in "Drawings that Live" in your workbook.

If anticipation is that important, it deserves the full attention and efforts of animator and cleanup person. The only way this can be done is by constantly flipping as the drawing progresses. Flip to make sure this shape moves properly; flip, still, to determine if this squash or stretch could or should be stronger; flip to make sure angles, volumes, and perspectives are natural and honest.

Flipping and rolling is like seeing in slow motion what later will appear on the screen as a continuous motion. In speech you can cough, hesitate, stop in the middle of a sentence and start again with a whole new thought and still communicate an idea, but in animation there has to be a continuous marriage of one drawing to the next throughout the entire length of the film. This can only be done by constant flipping and/or rolling the drawings.

56 Cleanup

Historically, perhaps cleanup (CU) was done with greater emphasis on simplicity than it is in the present time of Xerox printing. Formerly, the drawings had to be drawn with enough clarity to allow the inkers to do their task with the least problem. Now, Xerox clearly prints whatever we draw, or don't draw, and then it's up to the painters to fill areas which may not define the painted cell with the kind of shapes we would like to see. Examples of these shapes are facial areas that do not clutter up the face but leave the expression defined and readable, straight lines working against curves, small "busy" areas against large unadorned spaces, etc.

WHEN STARTING A SCENE FOR CU

First, know your scene. Study the scene thoroughly. Do not merely do the first drawing and work your way through it chronologically, hoping that somehow it will all work out for the best. Spin, or flip, your scene from time to time as you're working on it. Stay acquainted with it.

Before you begin, study the scene to learn and feel the essence of the action! Try to spot the two or three key moments in the scene. At this time, do the three or four key drawings in the scene. Study them — are they "in drawings" doing what they were meant to be doing? If the extreme ruff had good "drive," a dominant "force" through it, does you drawing retain it, or make it stronger? Or does your drawing look weak and mush by comparison?

DEVELOP GOOD WORK HABITS

To some, this has become a trite cliché, but do learn to roll and flip the drawings without reducing them to limp, demolished pieces of "paper towel." No need for excessive gripping and wrinkling of paper. If done, it makes follow-up work, checking, etc., more difficult. Practice thoroughness. Be neat and definite.

When drawing, especially in cleanup, it is often a good idea to talk the scene over with the animator. During the cleanup phase, keep three or four preceding drawings on the pegs so you know where you are "coming from." It is often a good idea to have two or three ruffs under the drawing worked on; these would be in reverse numbering so you would be rolling these drawings backward into the one on which you are working. This process gives the cleanup person complete knowledge and, hopefully, control of what has been animated. The result will be a scene that should have no "mechanical" spots in it, and one in which the drawings work fully and three-dimensionally.

DEVELOP ACCURACY

One way is to learn the "dot" method. With the bottom light off, place a dot on the bottom paper. Drop the two top papers down and place a second dot precisely over the first one. With concentration and periodic practice, you will be able to quite accurately do inbetween drawings with accuracy and dispatch. Also, for the person doing the cleanup, it is helpful to know the preceding and following scenes, just as it is for the animator.

To do final check or finished "final" drawings, always reverse the drawings on the pegs. This has the drawings working in the opposite direction of what has become too familiar, and will help you spot mistakes, which your tired eye was unable to spot previously. As the drawings are checked, watch for "traveling lines," i.e., lines whose endings do not all follow a precise arc or path.

KEEP THE PAINTER IN MIND

Do not draw in such a way that you leave tiny enclosed areas, causing the painter to misunderstand them or have difficult painting them in. This is costly, and it diminishes the viability of the drawing. It may also cause honest misjudgments on the part of the painter, causing him to paint in wrong color areas and creating "glitches" and flickers on the screen. If a small area of the background shows through on the character somewhere, be sure you indicate it. Otherwise it may be painted on varying cells as part of the character.

57 Inbetweening

Inbetweening is not merely putting line in between line but actually moving shapes and volumes to conform to some predetermined action. True, when inbetweening a slow movement where the volumes are very close together, one sees only line going between line

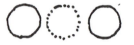

but when inbetweening a broader movement the lines will be further apart and the volume itself must be considered or

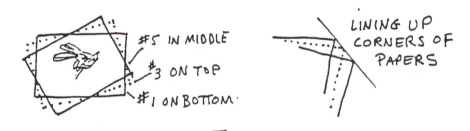

in the first case, inbetweening is usually pretty mechanical, i.e., put one line in between two others and that's it. In the broader movement the lines may be so far apart as to forgo any attempt to merely inbetween lines. However, there is a short cut to doing such drawings, which is called superimposing or place and trace. This is simply putting the two extremes on the pegs, say #1 and #5 plus a blank sheet for #3. After sketching in roughly the character's inbetween position plus an accurate drawing of all lines close enough to inbetween, extreme #1 is left on the pegs while extreme #5 is placed over it in a superimposed position and taped to the desk leaving the part to be flipped free. Then superimpose the sketch and tape down also. You may double-check the position of #3 by "eyeing" the corners of the paper to see if they line up. (This will only work if all the papers were punched alike.)

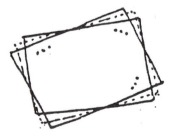

In extremely critical and/or exacting work the dot system may be employed. This entails placing three dots near the corners of all three drawings (#1, #3, and #5) traced accurately one over the other.

Then in the same manner as in the above method, line up the dots as if "inbetweening" them, tape all papers to the desk and proceed with inbetween. Make sure the dots are out of the field lest they show up on the Xerox cel. Another aid when inbetweening a particular shape is to be conscious of these things: note the angle, length, width, and overall shape of the extremes and keep these things in mind while drawing. For instance, if you have a shape like this

to inbetween, first of all establish the angle of the extremes and indicate an inbetween angle lightly on your paper.

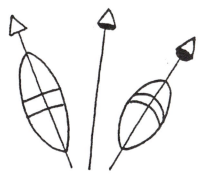

Then establish the length of the extremes and indicate the inbetween length on your paper with a couple of dots.

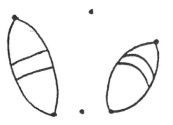

Then, starting at one of the dots, proceed to draw the inbetween with its width and overall shape, plus any subtleties constantly in mind, drawing your way to the other dot.

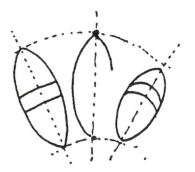

Then add the details. This may seem mind-boggling but is really quite simple. Once the procedure is learned and becomes second nature, it is much faster and much more accurate than floundering amidst a maze of confusing lines — with a hesitant approach with stops and starts, a little drawing here, a little drawing there technique with its enervating and time-consuming meandering. And soon all of this can be handled with a minimum of consternation — even on a Monday!

Another technique may be especially helpful when working on the "microscopic" drawings that are so small that flipping hardly differentiates the lines. This technique forgets trying inbetween lines but rather concentrates on the shape and its details; for instance, a leg. Note first the angle of the upper leg, the lower leg, and the foot.

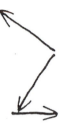

Note that there is a hip, a knee, and an ankle, for all cartoons are constructed roughly on human anatomy, unless it's an animal's hind foot that also has a hip, a knee, and an ankle only in a slightly different arrangement.

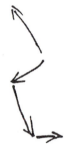

You have started with the basic structure, flipping often to make sure your drawing is falling in place (inbetween), then add details until the drawing is complete, having had all this time, running constantly through your mind, all those elements of drawing that are contained in the extremes.

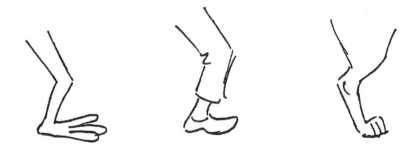

Very often, if not most of the time, an action does not move in a straight line but in an arc. Sometimes the animator will indicate the arcs lightly with a blue pencil. But whether there is an indication or not, one should place several drawings on the pegs and check. Let's say if drawings #17 and #21 look like this.

it might be tempting to make the inbetween look like this.

But if drawings #13, #17, #21, and #25 are placed on the pegs, they may look like this.

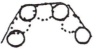

This calls for an arc to assure a smooth flow from one drawing to another.

Meaning the inbetweens #15, #19, and #23 should follow the arc.

If they were merely inbetweened the action would be jerky.

Try to swing your arm or move your head like that and you will see how important establishing the arcs are before attempting a drawing.

Another consideration is timing. Again, whether there is a chart on the extreme or not, one should check to be sure. Actions are full of slow-outs
and slow-ins

and if they are not heeded the action will lose its snap. Rolling several extremes on the pegs will reveal any need for slow-in or slow-out consideration. It takes just a moment to check for arcs and slow-ins, but in the long run may save either later rework or avoid a possible not too crisp movement. If there is any question about whether or not to do this on your own, discuss it with the animator — he will be pleased that you have shown an interest. Slow-outs occur when a character or a part of a character, having been still, begins to move. It will not take off like a bullet out of a gun, it has to start slowly and gain speed. At the other end of the action it will slow-in, meaning it cannot just stop abruptly but must ease into the pose.

Any "follow through" on clothing (sleeves, coat tails, dress hems, ties), long hair, tails, ears, etc., will involve slow-outs and slow-ins. For instance, when a character with a long tail comes to a halt after a move, the body may go into trace backs (or a held cel when permissible) while the tail eases into its final position, perhaps many frames later.

58 Problems with Drawing in Line

One of the problems in using line alone to draw with is that there are very few lines in nature. Even the outline of an object is not truly a line, because if the object were turned one-quarter on its axis toward us, what was the edge would now be the center.

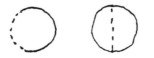

If we think of that circle as a head and put a round nose on the profile, when it is turned toward us it will still be a round nose.

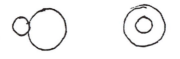

But if we have a real human head with a real human nose on it, the complex shape of the nose changes drastically as we look at it straight on. What was a line on the profile becomes a non-line on the front view. The principles of perspective help to overcome this dilemma. For, instance the rule of overlap

tells us what is in front and what is behind, and helps us differentiate between the two and to draw them that way. The human face (head) is a very complicated set of planes with very few areas that can be described by line alone. But if the areas that are in front (closest to us) are seen and drawn as such, then at least it presents something to work with.

A face straight on in reality is a conglomerate of planes molded on top of each other — very few lines. So for a line drawing we invent some symbols to indicate which shape or plane is closest to us and its general shape. For instance, a nose in rendering might be drawn this way.

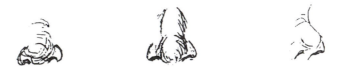

While in line alone it might have to be done so.

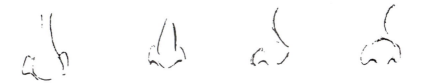

Depending of course, on the type of character drawn.

In animation the symbols we use for noses are kept simple. The fewer lines there are the less chance of jitters, and when lines have no anchor point it is hard to keep them from "drifting."

I didn't mean for this to be a "how to draw noses" paper, it is really about drawing layers of things in line alone, using the simple rule of perspective and overlap.

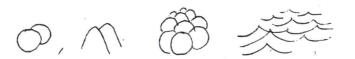

There are many ways of stating it and infinite ways it can be used, for it happens on *all parts* of *every drawing* you will ever make. Knowing the problems you are dealing with and better yet, how to deal with them is what we are really getting at.

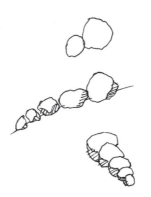

What I am suggesting is *everything* in a third dimensional environment is one thing overlapping another in space, whether they are connected like the parts of a leg (or a nose) or are separate. Even then, nothing is really separate, for all things are connected by the matrix of space that they occupy. In painting we can use atmospheric perspective to show where the objects are in space if they don't overlap. In drawing with line we can use another of the principles of perspective: diminishing size or surface plus diminishing size.

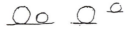

59 Superficial Appearance vs. Creative Portrayal

In the course of animating on a picture, you will be called upon to draw many different actions, each one calling for a distinct set of gestures. Your character night have to display a variety of expressions like happiness, anger, confusion, determination, and so on, with actions that match each of those emotions. The character will no doubt have to walk, turn, stoop, stretch, extend arms, etc. There will be a number of characters in the film and each one of them will have different personalities that will require appropriate gestures, none of which will be repeated — at least not in exactly the same way.

In a classroom situation where you are studying a live model, it is nearly impossible to anticipate those action requirements, so you have to concentrate on the ability to capture those gestures the model performs for you. This, in effect, hones your sensitivity for seeing bodily actions, so that you are better able to apply your skills to future needs. It is nearly impossible also to find models that are "look-a-likes" to match the characters in the various stories. This may be a blessing in that if you could find them you would surely be tempted to copy the superficial appearance of the model, rather than using the time and opportunity to further your skills in gesture drawing. After all, gesture drawing to the animator is what acting is to the stage or movie actor. *What the actor portrays on the stage or before the camera is what the animator draws on paper.*

So a perceptive and keen observation in regard to gesture (acting) is essential to the animator.

Completion (of a drawing) does not depend on material representation. The work is done when that special thing has been said.

Robert Henri

The purpose of working with a live model is to sharpen your awareness of the possibilities of the human figure to tell a "story" with body language. In my estimation, anyone (all of you) who has made it past the "board" with your drawing portfolios, has enough knowledge of basic anatomy. You know where the knees are, how they work, and their general functions — likewise all other parts of the body. At this point, to merely copy what is before you would be just to solidify your position on a plateau, short of your potential. Now is the time to transcend that ability to make a carbon copy likeness of the model, and to discover, reveal, and disclose the rich assortments and subtleties of body language.

Then you will be better equipped to formulate the future needed variations and apply them to whatever character you happen to be working on.

> The wise man brings forward what he can use most effectively to present his case. His case is his special interest — his special vision. He does not repeat nature.
>
> Robert Henri

All of the above try to convince you to stop tiring your eyes by glancing back and forth from model to paper in an attempt to make a pretty copy but rather to "shift mental gears," looking past the flesh to the spirit of the pose and to draw that. Think caricature, think essence of gesture, think going beyond to a better than average drawing, one that blows up in your "emotional face." There will be rejoicing in the village if you can *draw not the facts, but draw the truth*.

My apologies if I sound preachy, such is not the intent. I consider myself more a kind of coach than a teacher. You have all had teachers. They have "taught" you to draw — I'm just trying to help you *see* more clearly so you can put that drawing ability to a more fulfilling use.

Reproduced on the following pages are some drawings that came from one of animator Art Babbit's lectures. They show how he thinks in terms of caricaturing live action for use in cartoon action.

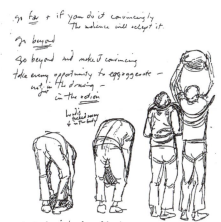

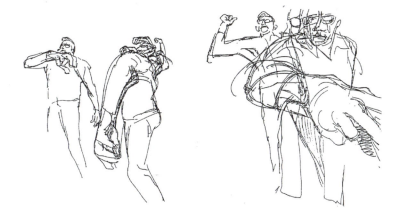

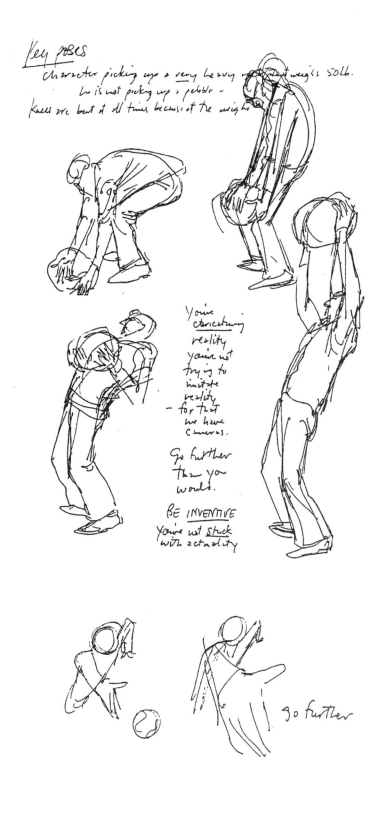

Key poses
character picking up a very heavy object that weighs 50lb.
He is not picking up a pebble –
Knees are bent at all times because of the weight

You're caricaturing reality you're not trying to imitate reality – for that we have cameras.

Go further than you would.

BE INVENTIVE
You're not stuck with actuality

go further

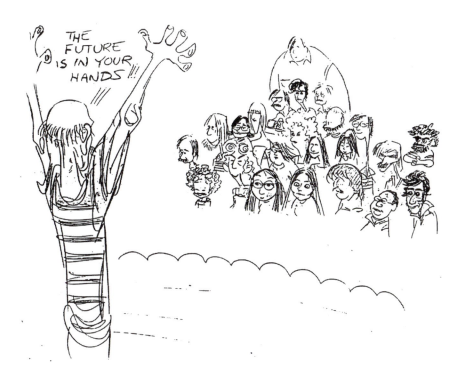

Here is a bonus page with a caricature by Dan Haskett. He captured the spirit of my "teaching" many years ago at the Disney School of Animation. It is quite a prophetic drawing too, for the audience are two of your current directors — Clements and Musker. Spot any others? Maybe Jerry Rees? Ed Gombert? Bluth, Pomeroy, and Goldman? Even the artist himself is there.

There are different faces out there now, but the sentiments are the same.

60 Creative Energy

I've always been one of those ordinary guys, you know, just a plugger — nothing outstanding. I have a short memory so if I've done something great I can't brag about it because I can't remember it. Maybe that's why I am prone to look forward rather than back. What is happening today and tomorrow are the important things. And for a person that has that forward-looking trait, I think it's especially important for him to have a good solid philosophical and psychological undergirding. The word gird is very apropos here because it means to prepare (oneself) for action. The action, in our case, is drawing; that impassioned desire to express oneself, that urge to create that ingrained need to interpret one's surroundings. It is the need to make or create a tiny bit of order, it is the need to *express* some of the myriad of *impressions* we have gathered in all our hours of looking and seeing and observing, it is the pleasure that comes from corralling form and content and assembling them into a new thing — preferably something that no one else has done before — at least not quite in the same way.

All of this takes energy. Energy of a special kind. For an artist, energy is in constant use and demand. A gardener cuts his lawns, trims his bushes, and his work is done — he can go home, open a beer, and watch TV. A cartoonist or an artist draws all day then goes to a drawing class at night or studies a book on anatomy, heads, composition, perspective, caricature, acting, or some related subject. If he watches TV he is either sketching the actors or studying the action or the way the dialog is delivered, thinking how he would have improved this or that scene if he were the director. In all his waking hours (sometimes in sleep) he is mentally transposing his environment into compositions, delineating certain lines, stressing certain shapes — working one against another. He talks to someone, missing whole sentences while concentrating on *how* the lines are delivered rather than what is said.

Clearly and simply, man, and the artist in particular, is a creative being. If you take that away from him (or if he relinquishes it himself), he is less than his potential. So who needs potentials? I'll tell you who needs them — you do, I do. This world was created by some creative energy (you name it as you see fit) and that creative energy that founded it and now runs it, is working in and through you now. Do you not feel that surge of energy and awareness tingling at your fingertips and it's motor humming away in you solar plexus. Is your mind not spinning with thoughts and ideas — is it not always searching, searching, searching. The awareness of it will be strongest in the springtime when the earth around you begins to hum with the renewal of life. But here's the wonderful thing — man's renewal is not dependent on springtime. A mere re-dedication to creativity is all man needs to start the creative juices flowing and then suddenly there is energy to "pull it off," energy that seems to feed upon itself, so that each moment becomes a fresh start, each experience a new event, and the vision is forward-looking with anticipation and wonder — not backward looking, full of regrets for neglected opportunities of the past, or negative influences that creep in and block our vision.

Yes, the action is drawing and the preparation is aligning us with that creative energy, becoming a channel through which it can find expression. Think of the universe as full of energy (it is, you know) and that energy is swirling around us waiting to take on some form. All we have to do is open up our consciousness and allow it to enter — and in a way that no one else in the world can, we express it.

61 More Meanderings

From time to time it is good to go back and take a fresh look at basics, for as they say in tennis "The first rule you learn is the first rule you forget." So starting from pose number one (so to speak) take the normal upright position. It is not what you ordinarily think of as an action but actually to stand is an action. Stand is a verb. Just think what you have to go through to remain standing. There is constant muscular adjustments and according to our individual physical structure, our attitude and the conditions around us causes everyone's "stand" to be slightly different. It is utterly impossible for a person to do *nothing*. So in effect *every* position a person gets into is a pose. There's a challenge for you whenever you are drawing — though the figure *seems* to be doing nothing, this isn't the case. You must sometimes seek out very subtle nuances to capture the pose or gesture. When you begin to radiate out in all directions from that upright pose into the millions of variations of poses and gestures the human figure can assume it *seems* to get easier. It *seems* like instead of shooting an arrow at a tiny target, it is more like shooting it at the "broad side of a barn." But it just *seems* that way. There are as many if not more subtleties in a broad pose as there is in a subdued one.

It may not take as much concentration to draw an action pose as a subtle standing pose, for you can get away with more. With a little extra effort in seeking out the subtleties of a broad pose as you *must* do for a lesser active one — you would end up with a really nice drawing — not merely a recognizable action.

So don't settle for merely recognition — go for the subtleties. If you are animating and leaving those subtleties for the cleanup person to find, you are expecting quite a bit. A cleanup person *should* be skilled enough to "cover" you, but it is usually enough for the cleanup people to hang on to whatever the animator has drawn.

If you are a cleanup person, it behooves you to train yourself in those subtleties, so when they are needed in a scene of animation you are ready and willing. Cleaning up may not have the most glamorous aura about it, but it is an integral part of animation. After all, ours are the actual drawings that are seen on the screen. It is my contention that it is easier to animate a loosely drawn character in a scene that it is to clean it up. On the other hand, if the animator has worked clean and has all the subtleties carefully drawn, then the cleanup person's job is a cinch.

So, whoever you are or whatever you are doing — take all these things personal. Make them personal. It's not the other guy I'm talking about; it's you. And then you will be proud...very proud. Pride is not a bad thing to have. Among you are the future "nine old men of animation," which is not a bad thing to be.

62 Those Who Cannot Begin Do Not Finish

"Those who cannot begin do not finish."
Robert Henri, from his book: *The Art Spirit*

In searching the model's pose for a good first impression that says — "this is what the model is doing, or thinking" — don't look for the elements that make up the figure (anatomical parts), but rather look for the elements that make up the pose. They will vary with the gesture, but usually will feature something like

1. **Weight distribution**. How the figure balances itself because of what it is doing.
2. **Thrust**. Body language usually requires a hip to be thrust out, a shoulder up, knees apart, or an arm out (as in throwing something or pointing), etc.
3. **Angles**. Straight up and down figures are generally stiff and static. Angles will add life and a feeling of movement.
4. **Tension**. Whenever one member of the body moves there is tension set up between it and its counterpart. You can capture an effective pose by working one elbow against the other elbow; one knee

against the other; likewise the feet, hands, and the shoulders. Never draw one appendage without planning a counter move with its opposite. .Never.

5. **Straight against curve**. All work and no play makes a long and dreary day — or something like that. All curves and no straights make a dreary drawing. Straights and curves tie in perfectly with one of animation's key tools — "squash and stretch". Straights and curves used indiscriminately are but trickery, but when used logically they can emphasize and clarify the gesture.

6. **Extremes of the pose**. Extremes in animation usually mean the farthermost extension of some pose or the drawing just prior to a change of direction. A single drawing also has extremes, which, in a "flash," explains what is happening in the pose. Those extremes are vital to such an explanation. To the degree they are missing or diluted, the drawing will deteriorate from "expressive" to "bland" to "confusing" to downright "boring." Silhouette almost explains "extreme," but not if it is thought of as a tracing of the outside of the figure. Forces are at play in a gesture and it is force and thrust and tension that generate an extreme.

A perceptive *overall distribution* of all these elements concentrates the viewer's attention on the vital aspects of the gesture. To gloss over them in a muddled and nebulous way is to cheat the viewer out of a clear look at what you are trying to "say." Here is another quote from *The Art Spirit* (I replaced the words portrait and painting with the word drawing).

An interest in the subject; something you want to say definitely about the subject; this is the first condition of a drawing. The processes of drawing spring from this interest, this definite thing to be said. Completion does not depend on material representation. The work is done when that special thing has been said. The artist starts with an opinion (first impression), he organizes the materials (the elements I spoke of above) from which and with which he draws, to the expression of the opinion (first impression). The things have no longer their dead meaning but have become living parts of a coordination. To start with a deep impression, the best, the most interesting, the deepest you can have of the model; to preserve this vision throughout the work; to see nothing else; to admit of no digression from it...every element in the picture will be constructive, constructive of an idea, expressive of an emotion. Every factor in the drawing will have beauty because in its place in the organization, it is doing its living part. It is only through a sense of the right relation of things that freedom can be obtained.

An actor may have a pleasant voice, perfect diction, proper emphasis, all the qualities necessary to make a good performer, but if his accompanying body language is unclear, the audience is left in a "no man's land" and up goes the sign, TILT. The audience is left with some undecipherable bits of information. Likewise the artist. This may be an appealing technique, but if the message is garbled, the purpose of the drawing is lost.

The accompanying drawings all contain corrections that illustrate the above-mentioned, all-important elements. The corrections (suggestions) were not done to teach anyone "how to draw,", but rather how to *see* those elements and to make them the basis for all drawings. They are easy to spot if you look for them when making your first impression. If you start your drawing without locating the elements, you may find yourself drawing without a purpose or your purpose may evolve into a desperate search to find out what went wrong with your drawing.

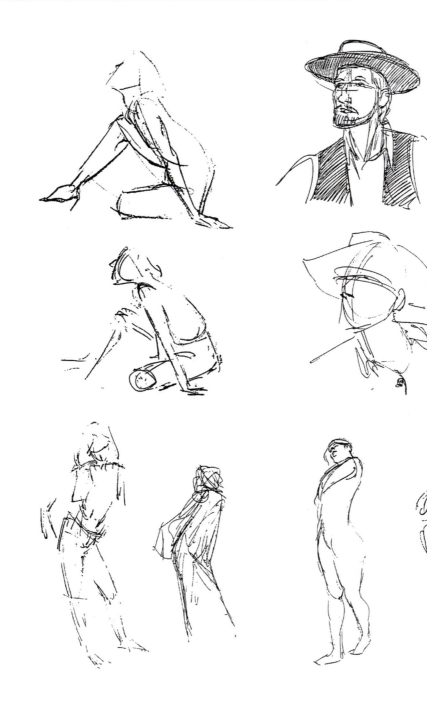

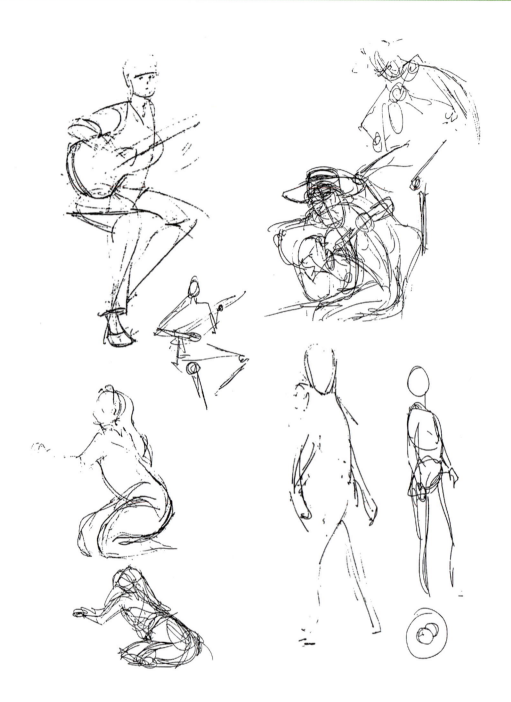

63 Body Language

Body language is vital to animation. The uses of body language in visual communication ranges from subtle eye movements to great sweeping bodily gesticulations. Each of these movements has meaning and has been developed to a high degree of spontaneous understanding between people of like cultures.

There are some non-verbal messages that are "universal." These are basic human emotions such as joy, sorrow, anger, tenderness, submission, domination, fear, surprise, distress, disgust, contempt, and shame. It seems these emotions are tied in with the physiological structure of humans. Some scientists (who study kinetics) believe that the brains of all humans are programmed to react bodily in a similar fashion to these emotions.

Other forms of body language are either learned by copying, or by strict codes or rules devised by individual cultures. Often these gestures are the exact opposite from those of other cultures. For instance, nodding the head is our Western culture's non-verbal way of saying yes. There are societies in India, however, where a nod of the head means no.

Messages of the body are used to establish one's "space," of which there are many kinds — personal, social, public, territorial, etc. Body language is used to reveal one's social position, one's attitude, and one's needs; also there are gestures of love, friendship, and hatred. Gestures are used to create an "image" of self as honest (watch the candidates on TV), sexy, or physical or caring, etc. The kinds of gestures and their uses are practically limitless. Every gesture we make or contrive is used to explain our thoughts or actions and the degree to which we display the movements establishes our character as extrovert or introvert, aggressive or passive, thoughtful or insensitive, comical or tragic.

In animation, of course, the story and its characters dictate the types of gestures needed. In most cases whatever the character, caricaturing the action is necessary to "punch" the business. Caricature is the animators means of making sure there is no doubt in the viewer's mind what is being portrayed. John Lounsbery animated what he thought was a cute Italian gesture for Tony, the waiter, in *Lady and The Tramp*. The director, Geronimi, knowledgeable in Italian matters, suggested he change it because it happened to be an obscene gesture.

Poetry can, for instance, be nebulous and suggestive in order to evoke personal images in the mind of the reader, but a cartoon has to "read" in an instant with no need for retrogression. In a film, everything unfolds at 24 frames a second and all must be "spelled out" so everyone arrives at the ending at the same time and with the same conclusion. Gestures that "ring true" are needed to attain that goal. Practice, observation, constant sketching, "osmosis," and even emulation of the Disney masters past and present should be among your daily pursuits. Drawing gestures is like using body language — it requires the context of an entire situation (story) to be thoroughly meaningful.

We learn drawing by studying parts; we *practice* drawing by assembling those parts into a meaningful whole.

Here are some drawings from Joe Ranft's sketchbook, done recently on a trip to Australia. They are what I call "unselfconscious" gesture drawings. As you study them you will see that there was no attempt to impose upon them any more than that they record some activity (body language) in its most direct and simplest form. In every drawing he seems to fuse the gesture into the context of the situation he has chosen to draw.

(Incidentally, this "handout" was triggered by reading the book, *Body Language* by Julius Fast.)

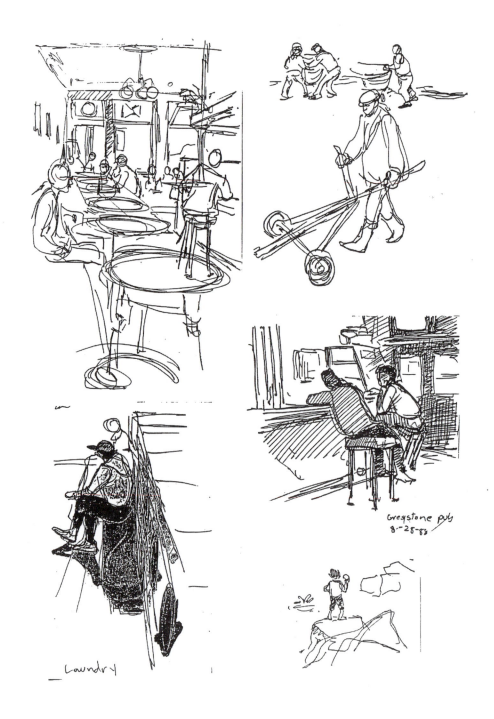

Greystone pub
8-28-83

Laundry

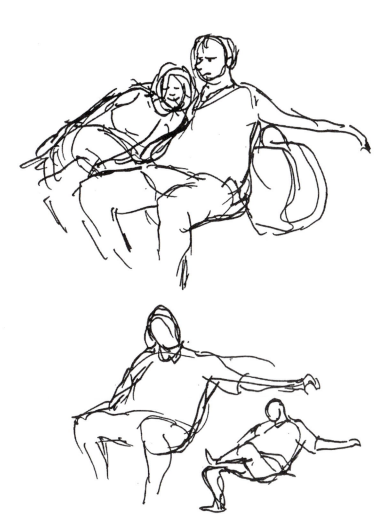

64 Note Taking and Sketching

If you haven't been a note taker — become one. Hundreds of potentially fertile ideas have drifted through your consciousness and have spun out into oblivion to be lost forever. You often hear or see things that, like a potent horseradish sauce clearing the sinuses, sparks a clear vision of some illusive point, perhaps some clearer way to draw a wrinkle or some better way to draw hands or knees. It seems so clear at the time there seems to be no reason to make a note of it. Many, perhaps dozens of ideas have bombarded your sensitive receptors during the day (and night), the overload adjusting itself in favor of a few of the most impressive messages, not always the most useful. So write them down, or sketch them, they may prove very valuable at a later date. A seasoned note taker will often hear a seemingly dull bit of information and, either on the spot or later, translate it into a meaningful bit of wisdom. Once down in writing or in drawing form it can be like a seed planted in fertile soil, burgeoning into growth when given the proper inducement.

Taking notes, like sketching, sharpens the mind, hones it into a more sensitive and receptive instrument, more ready when needed than one that is allowed to "flow with the tide." It can be the difference between being a reactor or an actor. The reactor drifts along awaiting opportunities from others before making a move. The actor checks his notes and comes up with a positive move of his own. Most, if not all, artists, composers, authors, scientists, etc., have been and are avid note takers and sketchers.

A three-ring, loose-leaf notebook with unlined paper is ideal for writing, sketching, and storing notes in. It may be too large to carry with you everywhere, so augment it with a small note pad that will fit into a pocket or purse. The notes taken in the small pad can be removed and taped or glued into the larger book. Record the source, or initial and date those of your own origin. It will be a great focus of learning and a pleasurable hobby, and will help keep your mind alert for new ideas and to new vistas of creative thinking.

Here's how Robert Kaupelis puts it in his book, Experimental Drawing:

I suggest that you wed yourself so thoroughly to your sketch book that it almost becomes a physical extension of yourself. And now what you must do is draw and draw and draw and look at drawings and draw and draw and draw and look at drawings and draw...

In *Cartooning Fundamentals* by Al Ross, he says:

Finally, I cannot stress too strongly the value of carrying a sketch book at all times. In it you can record notes and ideas and, above all, a continuous record of your development as an artist or cartoonist.

Your note/sketch book can and should contain both writing and sketching. Memories are often useful in creative work. Present day experiences are worthy of recording, saved, and savored. Jot down only the pertinent details. Sketch scenes and expressions making comments beneath the sketches. Describe people you know and meet. Don't correct your impressions later; it's better to write or draw new ones. Develop your senses by becoming aware of them. Record them in a straightforward manner and/or caricature them to some humorous extreme. What you will be doing is sharpening your sensibilities, increasing your susceptibility to impressions, and refining your ability to perceive and to transpose them into graphic form. Soon you will find yourself exploring your world for impressions and the recording of them will buoy you up mentally, physically, and spiritually. Remember my formula for this: impression – expression – depression. So become a note taker, start collecting things — not through one ear or eye and out the other, but graphically, through your fingers with which you have chosen to express yourself. Copy words, phrases, bits of articles, drawings, paintings, anything that awakens a spark in you.

That great teacher Robert Henri (*The Art Spirit*) said:

He (the artist) moves through life as he finds it, not passing negligently the things he loves, but stopping to know them, and to note them down in the shorthand of his sketch book...He is looking for what he loves, he tries to capture it. It's found anywhere, everywhere. Those who are not hunters do not see these things. The hunter is learning to see and to understand — to enjoy.

One more quote and then we'll take a break with some examples of sketchbooks.

From the book, *Cartooning For Everybody*, by Lawrence Lariar, comes this excerpt:

Sketching is sketching. It involves a model, usually, whether the model is a buxom nude or an old tomato can. It is copying, after a fashion. The cartoonist, when he sketches, is going through a process of study. He concentrates upon the model, plumbs its movement, bulk, and outline. Then he sets it down, remembering that he wants only the spirit — the guts of the thing he's after. He puts into his drawing all his experiments. He isn't concerned with anatomy, chiaroscuro, or the symmetry of "flowing line." There's nothing highbrow about his approach to the sketchpad. He is drawing because he likes to draw! All types of sketching benefit the artist. Never stop sketching! Sketch at home, in the subway, on picnics, in art school or in bed. But SKETCH!

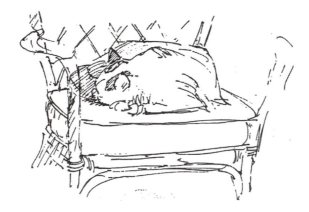

While sketching a boxing match on TV I cat-ch (pun intended) a disinterested non-viewer. Quite a switch from the violence on the television screen.

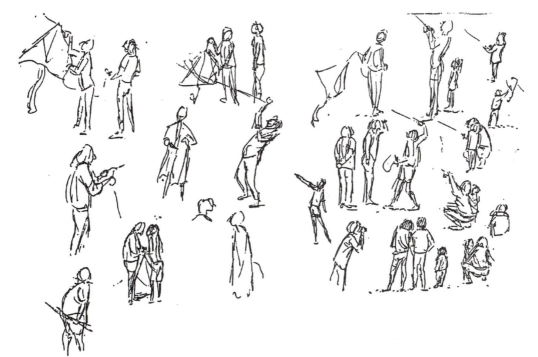

Arming yourself with a sketchbook will put you at the ready when opportunities present themselves. One day while searching for driftwood and shells (for my driftwood mobiles) and seaweed (for my wife's basket making), I ran into this group of kite flyers at the beach.

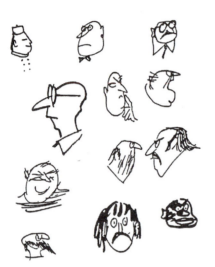

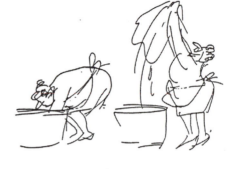

.. FROM THE SKETCH BOOK OF AL ROSS, CARTOONIST

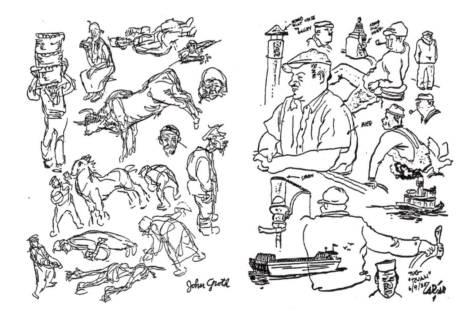

A page from the artists, Lariar and Groth. Styles and subject matter differ, but the benefits and rewards are the same. For the artist or cartoonist there is more realism here than if photographs had been taken.

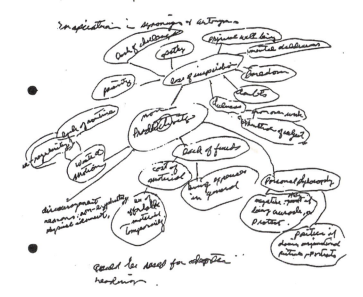

A good way to take notes or to gather your thoughts on any subject is to state the problem or subject at the center and circle it. Then as related thoughts come or as you gather research, attach them to the center by a line and into groups that are more closely related. It is a wonderful means of focusing the mind.

I was working on an inspirational book for artists who find themselves in the doldrums. These suggestions for a title could have been jotted down in a restaurant or while driving.

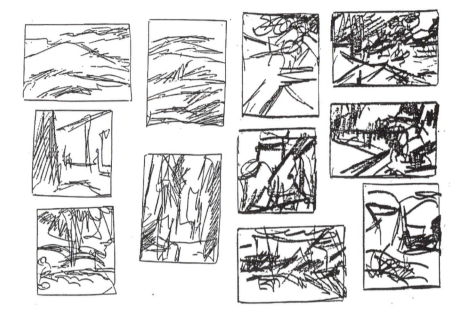

They were done inside a cardboard template with the eyes closed. The borders were added later. Good exercise!

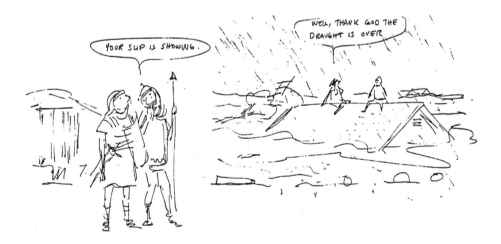

These were done with the eyes open.

65 Using the Rules of Perspective

As artists we see through eyes that constantly search for shape, gesture, color, contrast, etc. When we draw from the model (or from life in general) we have a tendency to feature shape. A thing is either round, oblong, or rectangular or some combination of each. These in turn create the two-dimensional negative space that forms a relationship between one or more objects or parts of one object. It requires an extra nudge of observation to see things as third dimensional an two extra nudges to translate that third dimension onto a two-dimensional surface. The rules of perspective such as

(diminishing size)

(overlap) and

(surface texture) are invaluable for this purpose.

Also, since we do see things as basic shapes, we must think of the shapes as being third dimensional. For instance, a rectangle

is as flat as the paper it is drawn on. But add the rule of diminishing size and we get a somewhat third dimensional shape.

Add some bulk to that shape and the third dimensional feeling (or illusion) is augmented.

Add a slight angle or give it a twist and the illusion is even more apparent.

It is more difficult to achieve three dimensions with an orb or spherical shape, but it can be done with the aid of the rules of perspective. For instance when drawing a head, the nose, forehead, cheeks, ears, and chin may be thought of as shapes that overlap other shapes.

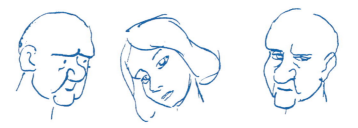

If the model strikes a pose that forms a rectangle viewed straight on

that rectangle from a three-quarter angle would look like this.

The degree of diminishing size (perspective wise) would depend on how close to the model (or object) we are and at what angle we are seeing it.

If our eye is one foot from a rectangle measuring 17 × 20"

at a 7/8° angle

the far side will appear to be about 7 inches high. Meaning that within 20 inches the upright line has diminished by more than one half. At 6 feet it is only 4inches shorter, and at 12 feet it is only 2 inches shorter. So the ratio of diminishing perspective lessens as the distance increases.

So the factors that concern us are how far from the object we're and what the angle of perspective is; that is

One-quarter, or

three-quarters. We have gotten a little technical here but it is only to stress the importance of thinking and seeing things in third dimensional space. If we carried the premise of the diminishing rectangles further we could divide all space into cubes. Lay-out and background artists are more apt to think in these terms because they deal with scenery that involves space and objects in that space.

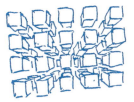

For the artist drawing or animating a figure, whether human or cartoon, we are dealing with only one cube of that space at a time, a variable cube that encompasses the perimeters of the figure and its gestures.

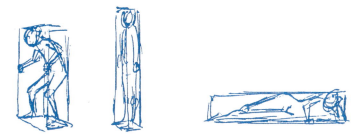

The imaginary cube reveals the third dimensional negative space so important in capturing a third dimensional drawing on a two-dimensional surface. If all the rules of perspective aren't considered while making a drawing or animating a scene, the character would end up looking as though it were confined between two panes of glass, forcing it to do its thing on a two-dimensional stage. Extending that plane into the third dimension gives the character depth as well as lateral space to move in.

Third dimensional negative space can also be helpful in creating tension in a pose or action.

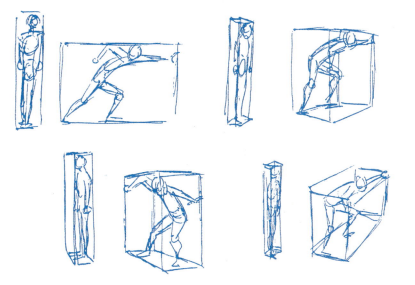

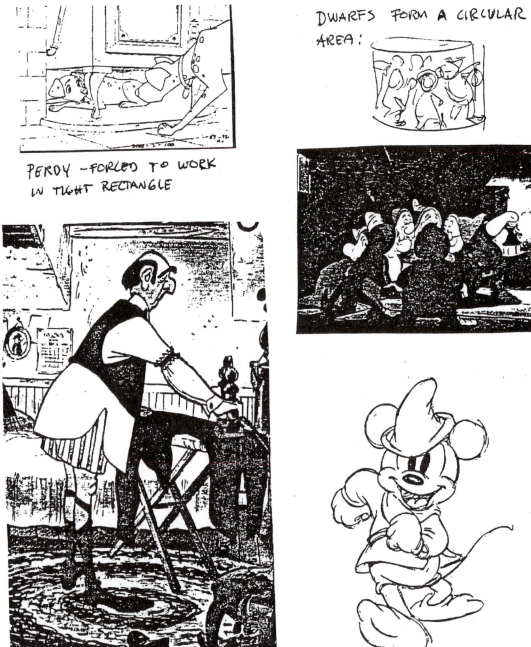

PERDY — FORCED TO WORK
IN TIGHT RECTANGLE

PROPS SUCH AS THIS IRONING
BOARD AID IN CREATING DEPTH

DWARFS FORM A CIRCULAR
AREA:

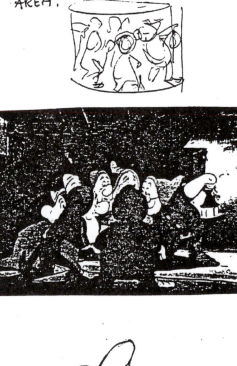

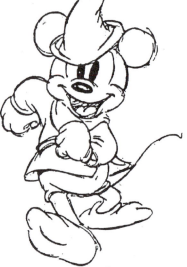

EXCELLENT THREE —
DIMENSIONAL DRAWING
OF MICKEY.

66 Applying the Rules of Perspective

Whenever I think of drawing, my thoughts go back to those principles of perspective I mentioned a while back. The more I think about them, the more I come to believe they ought to be called the "All encompassing principles of drawing." I never make a drawing without being conscious of them, and when I am having trouble with a drawing, I delve into those rules and they are a sure help. For those of you who were not privy to those simple but very valuable rules (which I "borrowed" from Bruce McIntyre), here they are.

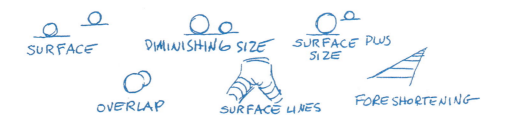

Take the one about diminishing size. That has to do with establishing a vanishing point on the horizon and having all things diminish in size from an established height in the foreground to that vanishing point. In animation we work with a layout that has that kind of perspective built in, so we have to draw our characters with a somewhat matching perspective. Let's consider how these rules may be used to accomplish a desired third dimensional effect. This may seem like an unlikely approach, but let's take five dimes (minus the detail). Knowing they are all the same size, if we drew them all the same size, they would all appear to be the same distance from us.

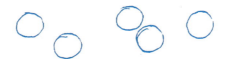

If we varied the sizes they would appear to be at different distances from us (rule: "diminishing size").

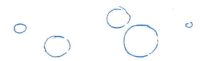

If we put two of them side by side, we create and are aware of the space between them (two-dimensional space).

Now if we place one behind the other (rule overlap) plus making one of them diminished in size (one of the rules of perspective). we create a third dimensional negative space.

If we take just one portion of our dime drawing, we would have what I once saw in a book on drawing, the "T" principle.

There will be numerous occasions where we can use the whole dime thing, for instance, in foreshortening the figure at some acute angle, the head (one dime) in front of the chest (second dime), the chest in front of the hips, (third dime) etc.

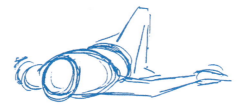

Those areas are easy to relate to a circle (whole dime), but when we are faced with longer and straighter shapes — an arm or leg or fingers foreshortened — is when we can use just a small portion of the dime, or the "T" section.

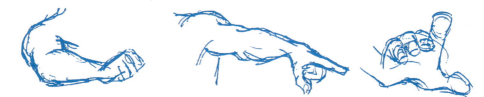

Using the dime bit or the "T" section principle creates depth (one thing in front of another) whereas if it were absent, all those lines would run together and depth would be destroyed by what is called a tangent. A tangent is when two or more lines meet or merge into one another so there is no differentiation between the parts that they describe.

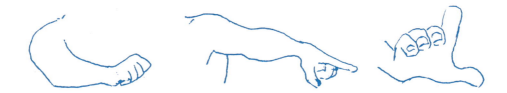

Here is a good illustration of a tangent problem and its solution.

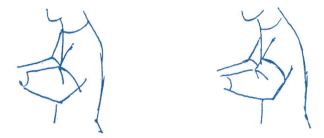

Along these lines (slight pun intended) we might introduce the "L" rule. In cases where one thing meets another but is neither in front of nor behind it, (changes direction but does not overlap) but where differentiation is needed or desirable, use the "L" rule.

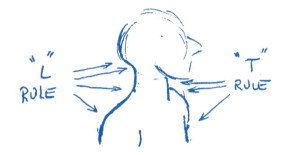

Actually the "T" principle also coincides with the surface direction rule. To show surface direction on a foreshortened object we just think of the stem of the T as the vertical angle and the cross as the horizontal angle. Thus

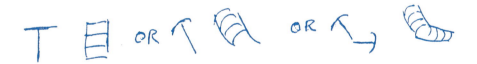

We may be tempted to think of surface lines as belonging only to striped blouses or trousers, but actually everything has surface lines, though not always visible. Take the mouth for instance. It is situated on the head (a modified sphere) and changes its surface line as the head is tilted up or down; likewise the eyes and the ears.

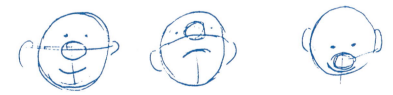

Even the line of the nostrils does the same thing

and likewise the brows, cheeks, etc. Anything on a curved surface will do it. Surface lines on a flat surface work differently. When they are tilted they simply get closer together:

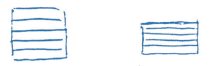

But back to the problem of making a third dimensional drawing with the limiting, restrictive, two-dimensional lines we are forced to use — those ever helpful elements of perspective are present in *every* area of *every drawing* we will ever make. Being conscious of them will be a great help, plus a great comfort in our quest for good draftsmanship. Not that draftsmanship is the ultimate goal, but it does take draftsmanship to express oneself in animation. Knowing and using these principles when needed is like having a good road map when traveling in unfamiliar places.

67 Copy the Model...Who Me?

When working from a model you must keep in mind the fact that you are not copying what is before you, but that you are searching for a gesture — one that will be applicable to any character that you might be called upon to draw (animate); for instance, the mermaid, one of the sailors, or the prince in the *The Little Mermaid*, Mickey, or Goofy. Again I use the term "shift gears" (mental gears) to picture the release from the shackles of any false burden, responsibility, or obligation to copy the model.

The poses in our class are purposely kept short so that a quick first impression can be summoned, worked on, and developed. Short pose sketching also excites you to a higher pitch of awareness so the creative juices flow more freely, and *seeing* becomes more acute. Quick sketching promulgates a feeling of spontaneity in the drawings. Short poses thwart any attempts to get you involved in unnecessary details. Most important, the short pose condenses the whole process of drawing so the wholeness of the gesture predominates and the gestural qualities of the pose permeate the entire process of drawing.

Any of you who have worked on photostats or have used live action in animation know the devastating effects of copying and tracing. What is acceptable for live action becomes bland, vapid, and uninteresting when braced into line. There has to be an appropriate interpretation and restatement into a cartoon style. The term "caricature" pretty well explains the transformation. So in a classroom situation that same transformation has to take place. You should strive for a release from the "live-action-ness" of the model and extract from it, not what it is, but what it is doing — the same as you would while sitting at an animation desk working on a scene.

   Here is a photograph of a chap picking up a box. The drawing next to it is a tracing, while the rest of the sketches were done (albeit, crudely), to demonstrate how slightly caricaturing the action can bring out different nuances of the pose without drastically changing the original pose. A Mickey and a Goofy were added also to show a possible application of such a pose in a scene of animation.

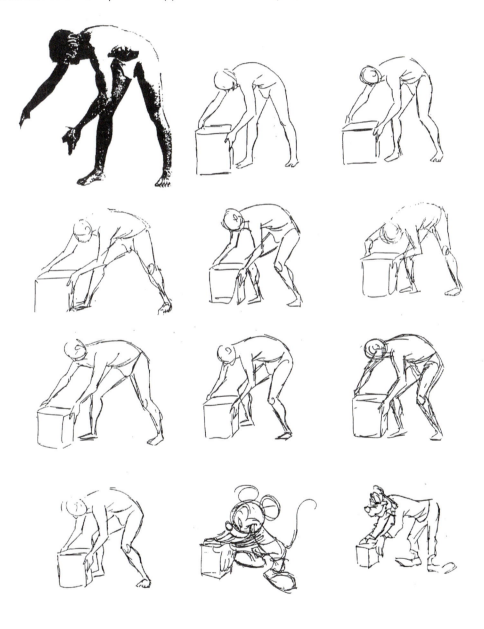

68 *Talk* to Your Audience — Through Drawing

I have been trying to find a way of saying "drawing is mental." I mentioned "positive thinking" a couple of times but received no feedback, so I figured that sounded a little too much like I was trying to sell a religious denomination or something. It is religion but only in the sense that it is a system of belief. Positive thinking comes in many forms.

Some years ago I took a modern painting class at Valley College. The instructor, Danielli, told the class on the first night: "Anyone who wants to paint dewdrops on roses, don't bother to come back." I accepted that as a challenge, painted a rose with a dewdrop on it, and brought it to the next session. He said, "That's nice — very tasteful, but I don't want any 'taste' in this class." I said, "What? I've spent 40 years trying to acquire taste and now you tell me 'no taste.'" He said, "You've been trying to turn people 'on.' now I want you to try to turn them 'off.'"

That may sound very anti-social, but taken in its proper sense, he was telling me to relax — quit trying to force my paintings into some preconceived mold. We're going to try to be "creative" in this class. We're not going to "copy" the old dewdrops on roses thing. We're going to abstract the essences of color and shape and mood and design from nature and release ourselves from the old conventional ways of painting a picture.

The effect on me was phenomenal. I felt a great weight fall from my back. I am still, 29 years later, impressed by that lesson.

You may recall a "handout" a while back, wherein I told of a similar thing with a singing teacher. He told me to quit "singing" to the audience. He said, "You are telling a story — so just talk to them (on the tones of the melody, of course.)" Again, a "shifting of mental gears" took place. What an eye opener! Singing suddenly took on a whole new meaning. I was able to put aside the concern with voice (anatomy) and began concentrating on telling the message and meaning of the music.

So, what does all this have to do with drawing? You're telling a story in drawing, and you want to tell it in the most enjoyable and creative way you can. You don't want to burden your viewers with how much you know or don't know about anatomy or how well you draw belts and dress seams. Just tell the story with simple, easy-to-read gesture drawings.

Recently the people in the drawing class were starting off very stiffly, bearing down on tightly gripped pencils, trying to trace the model's anatomical physique. I pleaded with them to stop trying to "draw" the model. They were drawing the muscles, the head, the arms, etc. I had them grasp the pencil farther up the shank, releasing themselves of all the responsibilities of drawing the model. "Let the pencil do the drawing," I said. "Allow it to search out the gesture...allow it to tell the story."

What followed was a joy to see. I have reproduced one of the artist's works here to show how quickly and thoroughly he got the idea. This was not a slow transition — it happened on the very next drawing, and continued for the rest of the session. The first two drawings are representative of his first sketches. They are rather stiff and frozen and seem to be an attempt to tell the viewer how the model was built. The ones following are expressive, loose, graceful, and tell the viewer, in an interesting way, what the model was doing.

It's tough having to come up with some nice drawings after having become tired and tight from drawing exacting line drawings all day. But here is where the mental part of it enters in. To continue in the same vein will further tire you. What is needed is some form of release that will be exhilarating and liberating. Again, one of my favorite phrases, a "shifting of the mental gears" into a different mode will be rewarding both as a study period and for some wholesome relaxation. Try to forget "singing" (drawing) to the audience — just *tell* the story.

If you were called upon to translate these drawings into Ariel, or any other character for that matter, the latter ones would certainly be by far the easiest, for they express a gesture, but without the inhibiting, overpowering influence of the anatomy. In the first type of drawing a gesture is used to show off the figure; in the latter drawings the figure is used to show off the gesture.

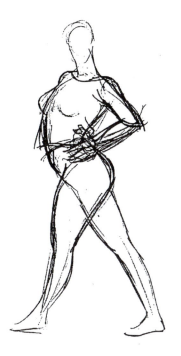
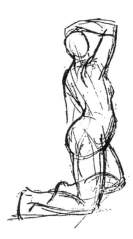
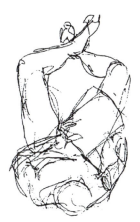
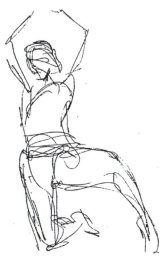

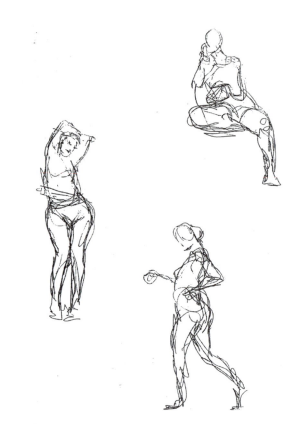

69 Getting at the Root of the Problem

You can have a nicely shaped fruit tree by pruning and trimming it, but if you want that tree to bear fruit abundantly you have to get at the roots — feed them and water them.

This is also the case in drawing. By cleverness and superficial arrangement of line and flurries of "action lines," one can very often come up with a nice looking drawing. But to continually draw meaningful drawings that portray a desired effect (tell a story), you have to develop the roots of draftsmanship; that is, the principles of good drawing, fertilized and watered by a good feel for acting, storytelling, and some plain old fashioned insight. If you try to make a nice looking drawing without including all the above, you are batting against pretty high odds. In tennis we call it a low percentage shot. Any line or shape you put down on the paper should mean something to the pose, if it doesn't the odds get higher. If it helps to reveal the pose or the gesture, good, that helps you to proceed because you have something down for all the rest of the lines and shapes to relate to. For surely, every line and shape you put down should relate to every other line and shape and to the overall gesture itself: Every line and every shape!

In full animation an arm move will cause a reaction in concentric rings of diminishing influence throughout the whole body. Real live people do not move in "limited animation": hold the body–move the arms, hold the head–move the mouth. When a woman winks, she winks with her whole body. When a man points, he points with his whole body. To try to draw a pose by concentrating on the local trimmings alone would miss the essence of the pose for sure. The roots of the body — the structure and the farthermost parts of the body like the hands and feet — must be considered as parts of the gesture and related to it in whatever proportion they deserve.

When you taste a well-cooked dish, you get a certain sensation, a oneness of taste, though many ingredients have gone into its creation. This is also the case with a gesture drawing. Many parts have gone into its creation (head, neck, arms, legs, etc.), but it takes that oneness of sensation, a blending or marriage of all the parts to make a well-drawn gesture. There is a shifting of mental gears wherein you shift from low gear (the parts) into overdrive (the oneness of the overall).

I used to sing in operettas, concerts, weddings, and churches. There was a similar problem to overcome — to stop singing notes, words, and tones and to concentrate on telling the story. One of my singing teachers kept on me to stop "singing"…just "talk" the song on the proper pitch…tell the story. He taught me to study the "parts" well while learning, but while performing forget the notes, the dynamics, the key, the beat — all the parts — and just tell the story.

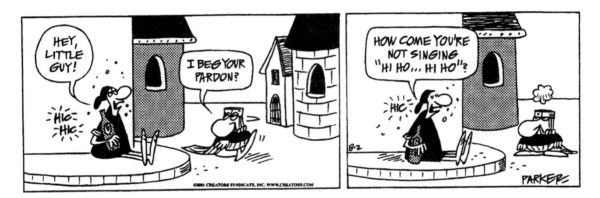

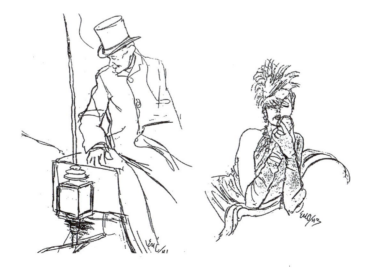

In the two beautiful drawings by Carl Erickson at the bottom of page 151, there's a lot of "overlap," "diminishing size," "surface lines," and "foreshortening." Observe how every line and shape and detail seem to direct your eye right to the center of interest, with the center of interest being a look. Every line on the woman carries your eye to that space between her eye and the mirror. The man's hat brim and shoulder form a path for his look to travel on. The book I got this from has this to say about Erickson and his drawings:

They give the impression of having sprung to life without suffering the usual labor pains. But his performance looks too easy; its nonchalance is deceptive. It is not accomplished without a struggle. Erickson, indeed is a hard-working man, a very serious artist who is usually practicing when not actually performing. In spare moments he is usually drawing from the model and his sketchbook goes with him to the restaurant and to the theatre.

70 Doodling vs. Drawing

To doodle according to the dictionary means to scribble aimlessly. A drawing, on the other hand, has an aim; it has a reason for being. It may be an illustration, a depiction, a caricature, a recording of some incident, a person, or a decoration. When making a drawing for animation or for animation study it must be saying something; that is, depicting an action or a mood, otherwise it becomes a mere doodle.

To further investigate the use and importance of gestures to portray an action or a mood, I have taken a couple of simple but expressive drawings that were made in our action analysis session and altered them to fit other possible meanings. The two drawings have what you might call a basic stance, one standing and one kneeling. Notice how, by changing some of the extremities, the whole attitude is changed. That is because these postures and gestures are a part of the universal language of gesture. Posture, pose, carriage, manners, bearing, and movement all tell what kind of person it is and what that person is doing or thinking. When certain gestures are drawn we "read" the pose quickly because we are educated as to their meaning. This makes it possible to communicate in a visual way. A good pantomime can tell all manners of stories by gesture alone. This is part of the animator's "vocabulary" too, for in telling a story in cartoons he must use visual means. He cannot relax into the luxury of doodling, for his drawings have to "say" something, they must communicate something.

So...whenever studying drawing to better yourself for animation, don't doodle (draw aimlessly), draw with a purpose — go for the gesture. Save your doodling for telephone calls.

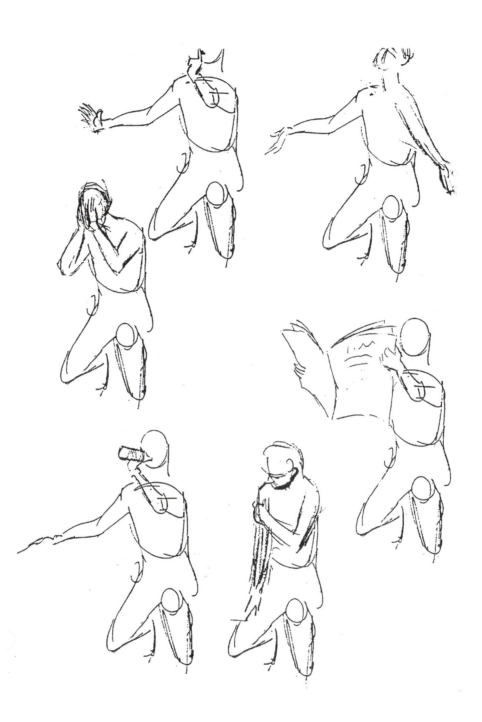

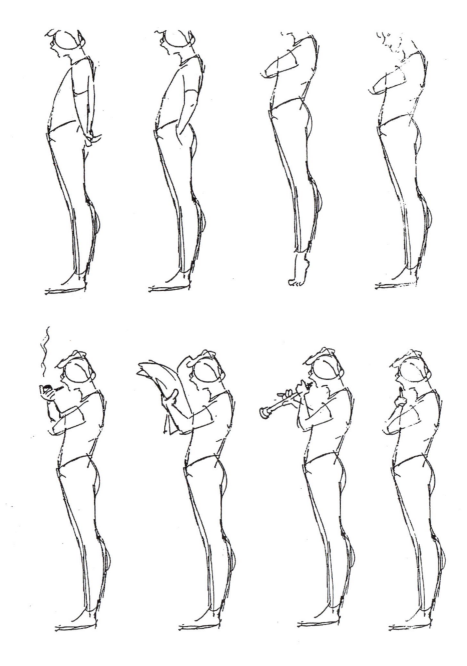

71   Purpose in Drawing

The study we are involved in is *gesture* and is designed to help us when the need arises (which is on practically every drawing) in animation. It seems that old seducing habits prevail when new goals are not clearly stated, re-stated, and kept constantly in mind. Some of those old habits or tendencies that are likely to creep into one's drawings are

1. Thick and thin lines. They are hard to perform with a ballpoint pen, which is one reason why we are using them. I think a heavy line is done to emphasize a tension, thrust, or a pull if it serves to delineate the gesture, but not for the purpose of creating a shadow or to balance a lopsided drawing, or for texture.
2. Shading. Shading may enhance a gesture in a painting or a rendered drawing, but the animator does not enjoy the luxury of such devices — best to reserve shading for portrait study.
3. Putting more details in one area than others. Sometimes one becomes fascinated by some detail, or the mind wanders or is marking time somewhere on the drawing. Or perhaps it is an attempt to raise the whole drawing up into the minor masterpiece level. It's sufficient for it to be a simple gesture drawing.
4. Adding texture under the pretext of locating key points in the drawing, such as the positions of outstretched hands or feet, or dots that profess to locate balance or other alignments. This becomes obvious when there are a lot or marks where there are no key points. Sometimes a stipple effect is charming in illustrations for children's books and other stylized drawings. Spattering with a pen is a much-used technique in ink drawings. Watercolorists often throw spatterings and drippings of paint by flicking their brushes at their paintings. It adds a kind of loose and exciting texture and also suggests the artist was so inspired and exuberant in getting down his creative impulses that he was lost in a flurry of involvement: heedless of his surroundings, the time, the heat, the mosquitoes, and neatness was far from his mind. This is not to suggest that animators should not become exuberant and totally involved, but for our study purposes we need to direct our attention to our *particular* goal.
5. One of the most offensive habits is putting down lines simply to get lines down; for instance, tossing in a couple of lines with no thought of which leg is supporting most of the weight of the body. It takes no longer to draw the lines in the right attitude — it just takes a little prior observation and thought.
6. The same goes for a multitude of lines where one line would have done the trick, which could have been avoided with a little more searching out the gesture before the pen or pencil was applied.
7. This one is not a devious way to achieve a nice looking drawing but it is a sure way to miss the gesture: drawing down one side of the body or working on isolated areas with no thought of their correlative opposite. One should never draw one elbow, hand, knee, or foot without considering the relationship to its opposite. I should say to its "companion part" for all joints and parts work in conjunction with their counterpart. They are either complimenting, balancing, opposing, or in someway relating to one another.
8. One of the most common techniques used to accomplish what "seems" to be gesture drawing is copying the model. An artist who has drawn a lot and has a good hand/eye coordination, can simply by multitudinous looks at the model and back to his drawing, reproduce fairly accurately what is before him without ever noticing or feeling the gesture. This is almost like photography. Later, of course, when one is called upon to draw Mickey or Donald or a mermaid in some particular gesture, there will be nothing to copy or "photograph." One may be required to conjure up a multitude of gestures, heaven forbid, from one's imagination.

So there in eight nutshells (an incomplete list, to be sure) are some tricks we need not concern ourselves with in the study of gesture. We are not striving for drawings that say, "Look at me, aren't I an attractive drawing." But that will say, "I have life, and feeling, and purpose," and the drawing will reveal that purpose.

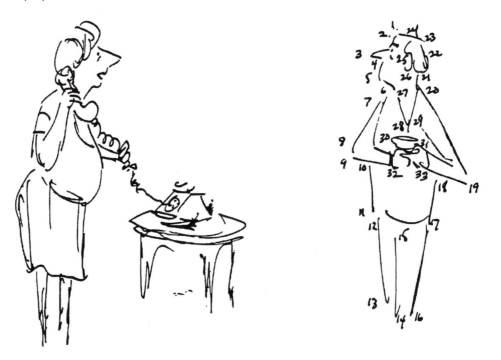

"It's a Mr. Stanchfield from the Disney Studios — wants to know if you'll pose for a drawing class."

72   When Acting (Drawing) is an Art

We have been using pen and ink exclusively in the gesture sketching class. The reasons for this was and is to try to transfer the function of drawing to the mind and away from the hand — to eliminate a tendency to render and to train the eye to see the gesture at a glance rather than feel it out on the paper with a multitude of searching and superfluous lines. Ultimately, the searching method may be the style you will use in animation, for there will be no model before you to lean on. I have contended that in a model drawing situation the pose is already there so searching is not necessary. Using a pen forces one to distill the essence of the pose in the mind's eye and in turn draw it the way one sees it. On the other hand, using a multitude of lines borders on doodling, which I am not putting down, can become a habit and one may come to rely on it; for it sometimes accidentally locates things in its meandering lines from which all one has to do is pick out the best ones. Of course, when there is no model and when a needed gesture is not clear in the mind, by all means start searching. On the other hand, using our kinetic sense of motion we stressed in the gesture drawing session (the feeling the pose in our own bodies — the "living" the pose) and being at one with the gesture and "knowing" it, will in every sense be a short cut to capturing it on paper. Both methods of drawing are invaluable. But I think it is important to know the difference and be able to use either of them at will.

Stanislavski, in his book, *An Actor Prepares*, said "...the organic basis on which our art is founded will protect you in the future from going down the wrong path." The "organic basis" he spoke about is that emotional empathy and those natural body gestures that we are striving to see and know — know in our own bodies and minds so we can transfer them to paper. For as Stanislavski says: "...if we are not living our art, imagination evaporates and is replaced by theatrical claptrap." On another page he writes "...in our art you must live the part every moment that you are playing it, and every time." And on still another page, "...you must be very careful in the use of a mirror. It teaches an actor to watch the outside rather than the inside." In our classroom situation we are not using a mirror, we are using a model, which is no different than a mirror if we merely copy it. Stanislavski cautioned "...never allow yourself externally to portray anything that you have not inwardly experienced and is not interesting to you."

Translating all that to drawing from the model: copying or drawing by formula, that is, with anatomical diagrams, symbols of shapes and parts, or copying photographically will simply be drawing by the numbers. There is indeed a kind of universal "body language," but it differs with each person's (or character's) use of it. Charlie Chaplin's reaction to some particular stimulus such as grief or joy might be the same, emotionally, as John Wayne's, but would differ greatly gesture-wise. If you attempted to mimic those actors, it would come from your mental image of their gestures, with an adjustment of your own bodily movements to reproduce theirs. This is the very thing we do when drawing a model's gestures, except we do not mimic them with our bodies — we use a pen or pencil.

All the above just to say see it in the mind, and feel it in the body before trying to draw it on the paper.

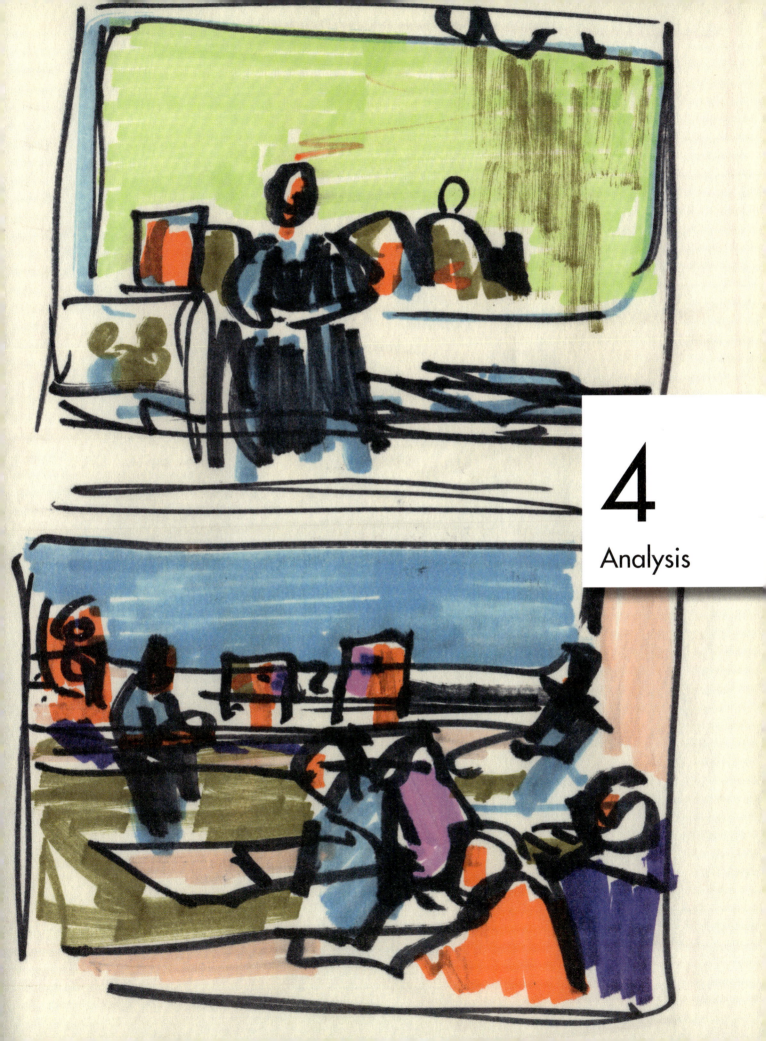

4

Analysis

73 Action Analysis Class I

The action is the thing here. There is absolutely no sense in trying to get a likeness, that is, a cosmetic likeness or a personality likeness — the essence of femininity, yes, the essence of a coy or seductive pose, yes.

Don't be shackled by the model. If the model is short and you want to draw a tall girl then draw a tall girl. If the model's hair is short and you want long hair then draw long hair. If the model strikes a pose you think you could improve by altering a little here or there then do it on your drawing.

Take a moment before you start to *see* the pose. Feel yourself and experience the pose subconsciously. Actually feel the tension of a reach, the folding up sensation of a squash; feel the pressure on the leg that the body is standing on, the weight of the body on that foot; feel the relaxation of the other leg. Show it relaxed to emphasize the *tension and weight on the other leg*. If the model's head is turned to the right, turn your own head to the right Feel the wrinkling of the skin as the chin squashes against the right shoulder. Feel the left side of the neck *stretch*. That is what you want to draw — that squash and stretch.

Drawing for animation is not just copying a model onto paper — you could do that better with a camera. Drawing for animation is translating an action (in this case a pose) into drawing form so an audience can retranslate those drawings back into an experience of that action. You don't just want to show the audience an action for them to *look at it*; you want to visualize an action for them to see; that is, to experience. That way you have them in your grasp, your power, and then the story can go on and the audience goes on with it, because they are involved. You have allowed them to experience it.

I have Xeroxed some sketches I made at the airport, the underground, and a museum to show the possibilities of a direct approach to capturing a pose with a minimum of line. Notice the emphasis of putting the weight on one leg in the standing poses; the emphasis on relaxation in the sitting poses. There was no penciling in first — they were done directly in ink!

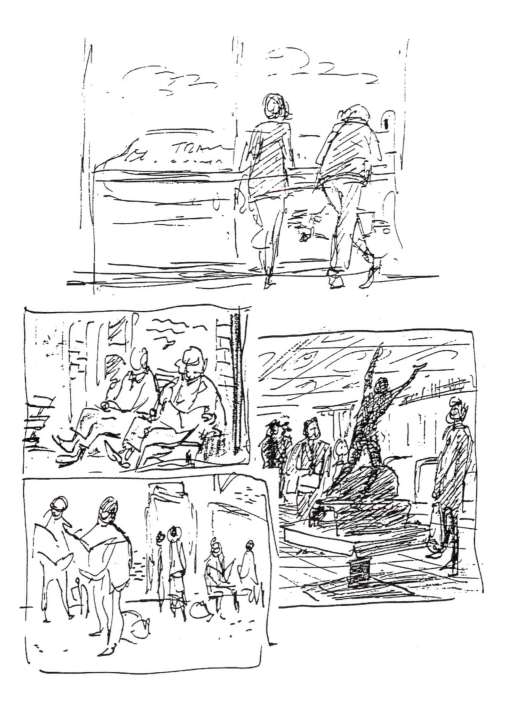

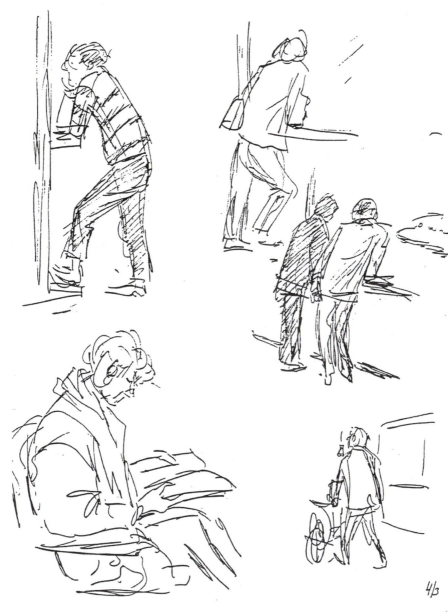

4/3

1-169

74 Action Analysis Class II

Here is a sheet of figures drawn by Glenn Vilppu, life drawing instructor and layout man. This is an excellent simplistic approach to sketching the figure for animation purposes. I suggest you study them and for the purpose of the action analysis class tonight (and next week) try to emulate them. The model will be clothed but I am suggesting that you think of the structure and attitude of the body rather than the clothing. After capturing the pose begin to consider what affect that pose has on the costume. The idea is that you don't animate clothing running around doing its thing — you animate a character which is a body that just happens to have some clothes on it.

If you want to experiment and use a cartoon character in place of the human figure that is fine. In any event try to caricaturize the pose, which means to go a little farther with the pose than the model has done (or even could do — not being a cartoon character).

If you've taken life drawing classes you are probably used to copying poses or attempting to locate the muscles and bones and depicting them as realistically as possible. But for the action study's sake forget the muscles, forget the realism, and go for the action. I say action rather than pose because although we use poses in animation, every pose is in reality an action. No one ever just does *nothing*, especially in animation. If there is a pose it is either because something has just happened or is about to happen. If something funny has just happened give the audience an additional thrill by ending up with a funny pose. If something is about to happen, give the audience that superior feeling that they have figured out that something is about to happen. In true life the wheels of the mind turn undetected by observers, in cartoons that thinking process has to be caricatured. The story line takes care of a lot of that but the bulk of it is done visually. That is why we have such broad anticipations, "takes," squashes and stretches, arcs, slow-ins and slow-outs, follow-throughs and overlaps, and long moving holds where you want to build up to some situation or let down from one — some pose you want to "milk" for all its worth.

So for the purposes of studying life drawing for animation, one pose does not tell enough, because seldom will the animator be faced with just a one-pose scene. So ideally there should be at least three poses to study and portray each action:

1. The Preparation: Telling the audience something is going to happen
2. The Anticipation: Gathering the forces to carry through with the action
3. The Action: Carrying out of the intended action. Plus, of course, all the follow-through, overlap, and resulting residuals such as dust, smoke; wind, destroyed property, chaos … whatever.

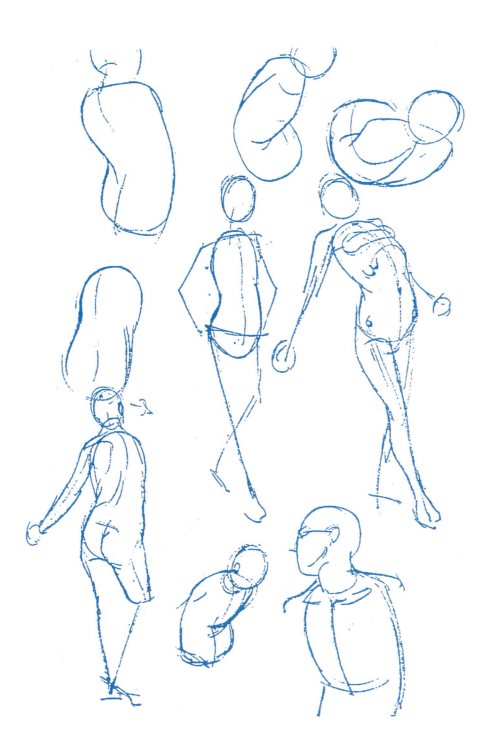

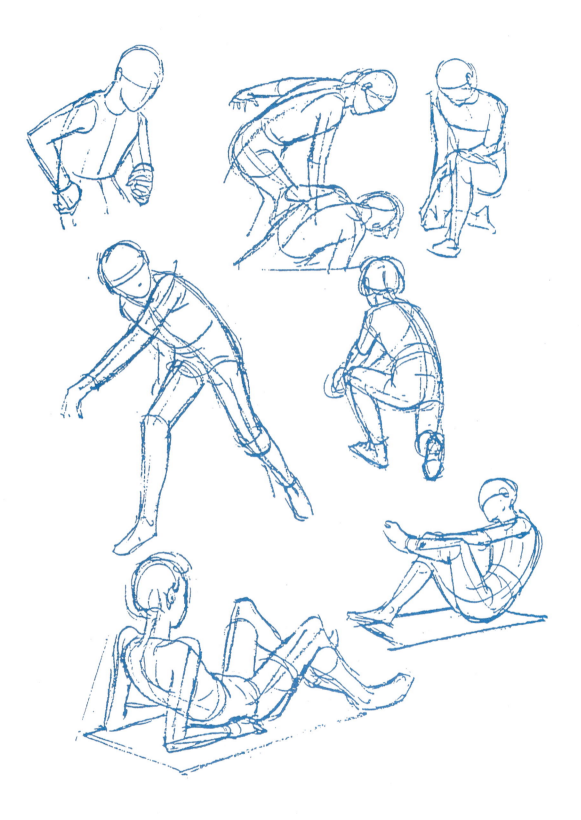

75 Using Cylinders

I was preparing a paper on using cylinders for the parts of the body, when I came across a book, *How to Draw the Human Figure,* from the Famous Artists School. Lo and behold, they recommend the very same method as a means of studying the figure. They also stress the importance of *seeing* to learn to draw well, and to first feel the gesture before attempting to draw it. They also strongly advise assuming a new mood with each change of pose, bringing a freshness and spontaneity to each and every sketch. To carry the idea further, it would help to quickly assume the pose yourself, to feel it, and to experience it, in order to jettison yourself into the proper frame of mind. Further into the book I find other points that were brought up in our classes such as gesture drawing is more than just copying the action of the figure. It has, especially for us, to do with capturing the inner meaning, the essence of the pose — what is happening at that moment. With and through that first impression sketch, a good final drawing is assured.

In the case of the cylinders for drawing, they can be used to establish the basic shapes and their angles, directions, and relationships — then it is an easy matter to add the details. Again, the details only *after* the basics are well established. Don't be impatient — the foundation first. To avoid "doodling" while practicing this form of study confine yourself to these shapes:

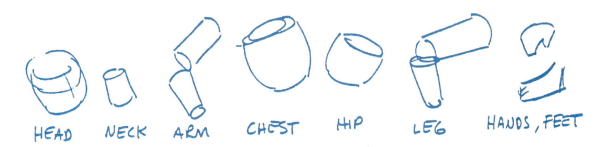

HEAD   NECK   ARM   CHEST   HIP   LEG   HANDS, FEET

There are only four lines per cylinder and if it takes you twenty lines to make one — you need help!

See the cylinder in space. Perhaps envisioning an arrow inside each one will help capture its direction and angle.

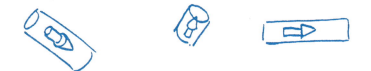

This will help you establish the shape in space rather than on a two-dimensional surface, and in the simplest of terms. Also, the bulk of the figure is automatically built up and available for further delineation. If you have a difficult time seeing these shapes in space and relating them to the overall pose, sketch in just enough rhythmic gesture lines to suggest the pose. Then before getting too involved with them, "throw" on the cylinders with gusto and bravado and watch the figure take shape. Remember, of course to embellish them with some suitably angled hands and feet.

This basic drawing with its essence of pose can then be humanized or cartoonized according to the needs. If it is a nude you are working on, add flesh, joints, wrinkles, etc. If you're working on a clothed figure, add clothes, costume, features, wrinkles, and other detail. If you're working on a cartoon, caricature it accordingly, add costume, etc.,...and win yourself an Oscar.

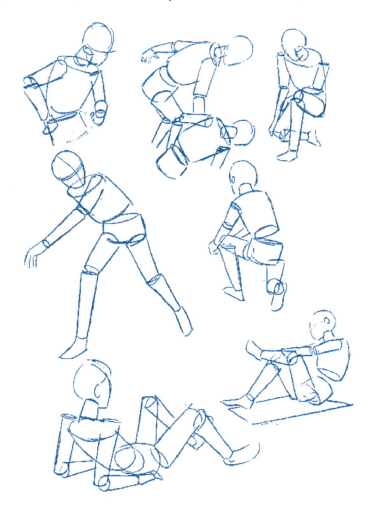

76 Action Analysis — Hands and Feet

In life drawing classes there is a tendency to start somewhere around the head and end up somewhere around the knees. Perhaps the students are influenced by the thousands of sculptured torsos and portrait paintings that fill the museums, galleries, and art books. However, for the animator, such a restricted area of study is for all practical purposes useless.

Pantomime plays an important part in animation, especially in scenes that contain no dialog. Even those scenes with dialog are greatly enhanced and, of even more importance, caricatured by pantomime. If the animator were to study the mime, he would find that the hands and feet are one of the most important parts of the body in the representation of an action or of a character, a mood, or a gesture.

To emphasize the importance of the above premise I have selected some illustrations, which are presented in two different forms — one showing the head and torso, one showing the lower legs and feet plus the lower arms and hands. I submit that the latter drawings explain the poses much better than the ones with the head and torso only. I am not suggesting that you begin an extensive study of hands and feet, but only that when studying the figure you put the emphasis on the parts that explain *what* you are drawing. Otherwise your study becomes a mere repetition of torso after torso, after torso, after torso, etc.

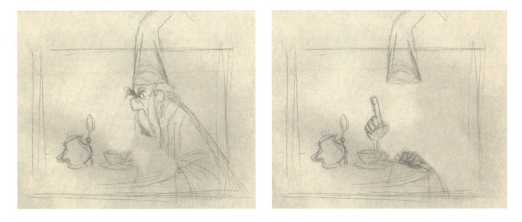

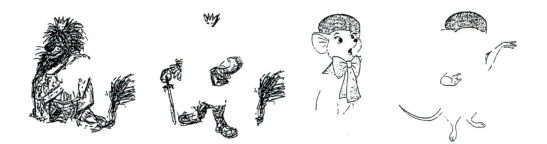

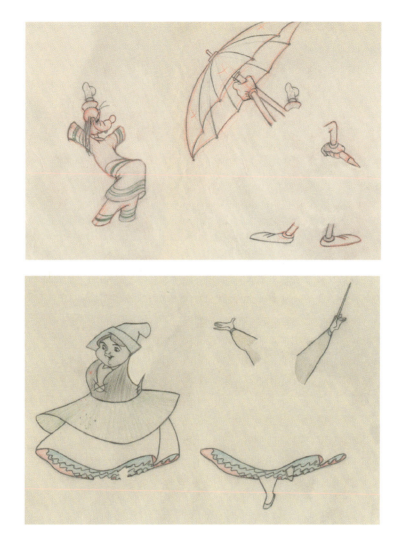

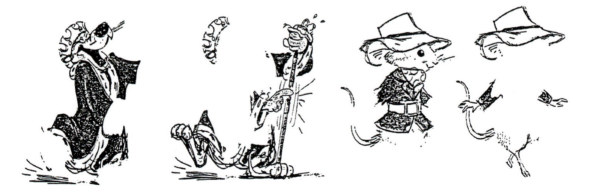

77 Angles, Angles, Angles

I often speak of angles in drawing. Sometimes I get a blank look. I finally decided to look the word up in the dictionary to hopefully find a definition that would apply to drawing. I didn't get much help, for it stated that an angle is the shape made by two straight lines meeting in a point, or by two plane surfaces meeting at a point. That meaning might apply to an arm bending at the elbow, but in drawing there are numerous angles that do not meet at a point; for instance, a person's legs while sitting or running.

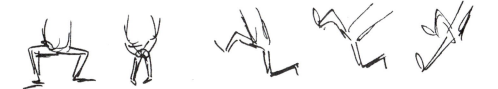

In mathematics the acuteness of an angle is measured in degrees with 45 degrees as a pretty well-known angle. Almost anyone can describe a 45 degree angle without a protractor. An artist's perception of an angle is not measured in degrees, but just whatever angle best serves his purposes in describing a gesture. The intensity of the angle usually depends on the intensity of the emotion or mood behind the pose, or the need to use a convincing angle to make the gesture seem physically logical.

Here is one artist's drawing of the model leaning back in a chair in a somewhat relaxed manner. To make it more logical I increased the angle of her body and angled her shoulders — after all her right arm is lifted over the chair back and the other arm is reaching down to her knees (pulling the left shoulder down with it). The more acute angle of the body puts some weight into the lean, and gives a reason for the neck stretching forward. Remember that if a model, or anyone for that matter, looks natural in a pose, it's because their body just naturally does these things. We all have learned enough body language to express things bodily. In drawing it is different — there is a thought process that has to be consulted and activated. In effect your pencil has to be directed to do what your body does unprompted. (see the drawing below).

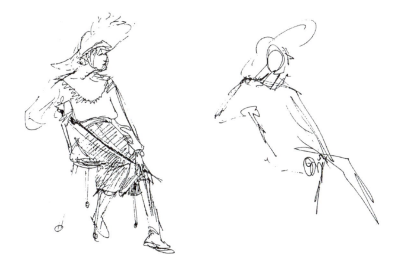

Here is another drawing that is quite nice. All the elements are well drawn, but the angle of the magazine disturbed me. I felt the look was glancing off the magazine page and carrying our attention off to the right. I suggested lifting the left side of the magazine so the audience's attention would be corralled, so to speak, in that all-important area between the eyes and the magazine — the area I call the "stage" of the drawing. That is where the drama is taking place. Also I angled the shoulders differently to accelerate the look in the direction of the magazine.

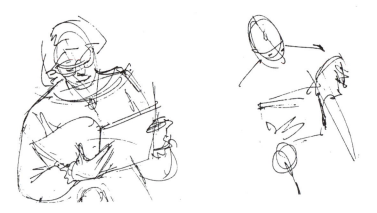

Angles refer not just to lines but to surfaces or planes as well. Notice on the previous figure that the whole surface, though it is curved, angles toward her eyes — not just the lines but the whole plane of the page. Likewise not just the angle of the head and eyes, but the plane of her face points toward the page. In just drawing a magazine one might spend a lot of time drawing the details but neglect to select a contributive angle — one that helps the gesture or the story point. There must be purpose behind everything you draw, and in animation, story is that purpose or the raison d'être.

Here is another drawing, same pose, different view. Nice drawing, but this time it's the head angle that's off. That is, unless according to the story she was reading and watching TV at the same time.

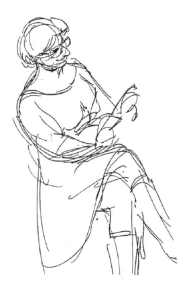

Last week we had a wonderful model named Bobby Ruth Mann. She was no "spring chicken" but she was full of fun, and a good actor. Lureline Weatherly seems to have charmed this beautiful drawing into being. The suggested story was a gypsy woman adjusting a rose in her hair. It's a very forceful and expressive juxtaposition of angles.

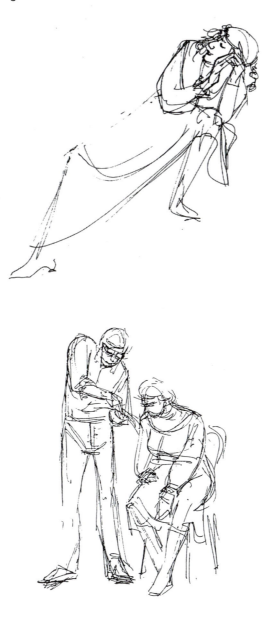

We had some male students join in the act to set up a relationship to draw. Here are three artist's drawings of the same pose. Roger Chiasson's on the left, Dave Woodman's below that, and I apologize for being unable to identify the other artist (I tried). In all these drawings there is an intense concentration of interest in what the gentleman is pointing at. The problem was to establish a relationship between the two. Notice how that relationship was realized by the use of angles — angles of lines, planes, and negative spaces. One word summary:

THRILLING.

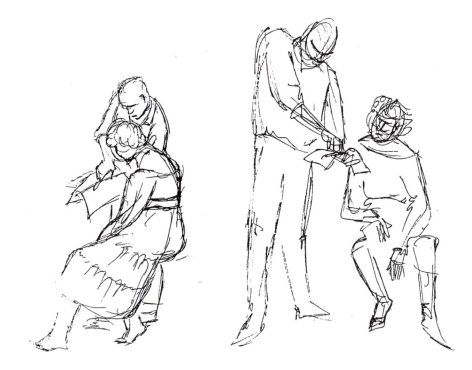

78 Using Angles

I can't resist pushing the idea of using angles in your drawings. At first it may seem that you might end up with a very abstract or stiff drawing, but that doesn't have to be the case. Perhaps there is a subtle difference in saying "a drawing is angular" as opposed to saying "angles have been used in drawing."

    Certainly these drawings of Medusa can be considered angular, and so they are for she is an "angular" character.

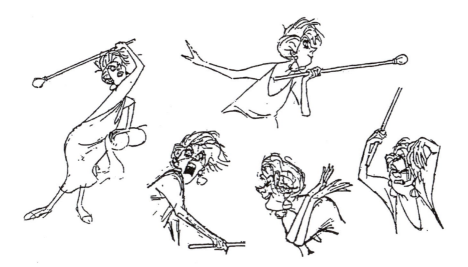

On the other hand, these drawings of Snow White, Cinderella, and Freddy Moore's drawings are quite angular but at the same time soft and feminine.

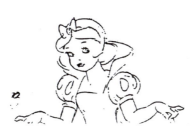

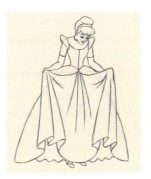

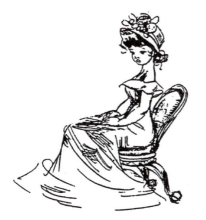

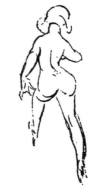

In the more cartoony characters, angles are indispensable. Notice how expressive these actions are and how angles play such an important part in capturing those actions.

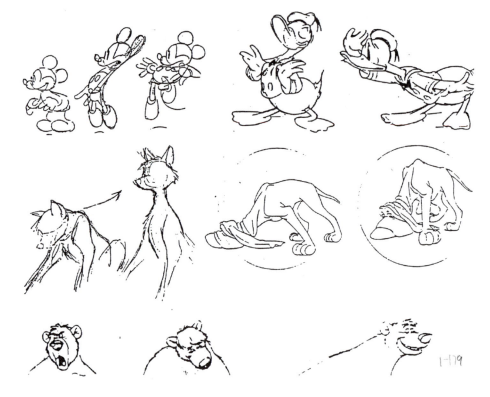

79 Angles and Tension

Angles and tension are important elements in drawing. Little has been said about them in books on drawing and in drawing classes. They can be the difference between a do-nothing drawing and an active, dynamic drawing. Tension is brought about by the appropriate use of angles in a drawing.

It is easy to imagine how a running figure can create tension by the angle of his body. Any time you pull a figure off its perpendicular norm you create tension. The figure is pulling away from one border and pushing toward the other. There is also a tension set up between the figure and the ground surface — for it would fall if something weren't done to stabilize it. There are tensions set up within the body, also, such as between the outstretched arm and the opposite outstretched leg. That tension is eased as the body prepares to change from one leg to the other. Then the tension is set up again on the opposite side.

Of utmost importance is any deviation from the perpendicular axis. We humans are very sensitive to it. We can't stand pictures hanging askew on a wall; Venetian blinds that are lower on one end than the other, neckties that hang askew; if the tree we planted has started to lean, we drive a stake beside it and tie it up straight.

You've all seen and probably have a copy of Muybridge's, *The Human Figure in Motion*. Muybridge knew the value of using vertical and horizontal lines behind all of his photographs so any deviation of angle could easily be seen. I submit that without those lines the untrained eye would miss a great many of the vital angles that were and are necessary to enact those actions and poses.

As I have pointed out many times in the drawing class, there is a compulsive urge to straighten up the model's pose. The whole purpose of a gesture class is to nurture the ability to capture those subtle angles and tensions that make the pose enjoyable, picturesque, charming, and unique or whimsical and humorous or even sad or wretched.

It's been tough! We have had models with costumes for the past month or so. There dangling and sparkling before us have been those hundreds of eye-catching do-dads that cried out to be a featured part of the drawing. It took resistance and discipline to put them in their proper place. As Ollie Johnston often said: "It ain't easy."

Try this. Whenever you make a sketch, keep a mental vertical line going through the figure somewhere. Realize that even this is an angle — it is a 90-degree right angle to the horizontal plane. Any deviation from this (in mathematical terms) would be an obtuse or an acute angle. In drawing, this deviance would set up a tension. Or to put it in less formal terms, it is what we humans use in our body language, and body language simply put is our every day form of acting, and as animators, acting is our business.

The author E. B. White wrote "When you say something, make sure you have said it. The chances of your having said it are only fair." He could have been talking about drawing.

Here are a few corrections I made on drawings in class. All the problems were the same — a tendency to straighten up the pose and in effect iron out the gesture.

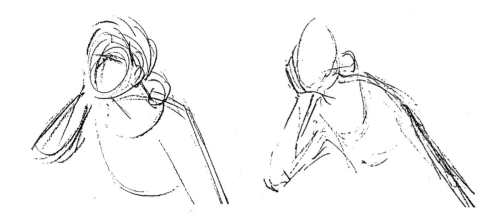

In this drawing the gesture was turning out to be of an "Oh my tooth hurts" nature, rather than one of reflection or deep thought. Strengthening the angles also helped to show the weight of the head on the hand, allowing for a more definite angle of the wrist.

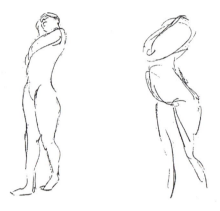

This is another case of overlooking the life-giving qualities of angles. Even a still drawing should look like it has action in it (even repose is an action), and a skillful, bold, adventurous use of angles will contribute to its presence.

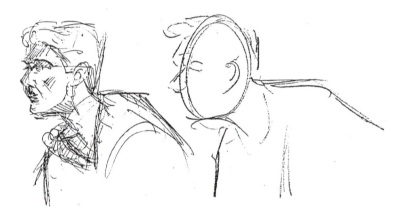

In this drawing it looks as though the artist tried to straighten the body up and even make a front view of it, interpreting the angles to suit those intentions. One doesn't have to invent angles to interpret a gesture — the body with its solid–flexible construction will dictate them for us.

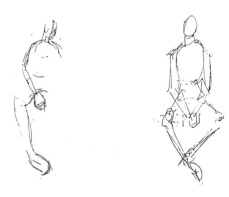

I always advocate, urge, and even plead for the termination of the practice of drawing one elbow without the other elbow to relate it to or one knee without the other, or a hand or a foot or shoulder, etc. Observe people at play, at work, or at rest. There is a constant relationship between the joints and appendages. They are complimenting, opposing, or balancing each other. It is this relationship that creates the angles and tensions that are the tools of expressive gesture drawing.

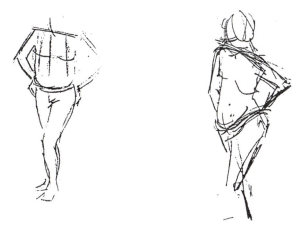

This is a case of straightening up the angles and losing the gesture. Even a subtle gesture should be unmistakable. A judicious sprinkling of angles will go a long way in ensuring its readability.

80 Applying Angles and Tension in Our Drawings

One day as my wife, Dee, and I were coming home from the tennis courts, we stopped along the country road so she could clip some reed-like plants for use in her basket making. While stopped, I, as usual, took up pen and pad and rather unthinkingly sketched what was before me — a multitude of things that were not a good setup composition-wise. I simply went through the motions of sketching. I got a lot of it down but it was a hodgepodge. Suddenly, I realized that if one of my students had done that, I would have reminded them of the rules of perspective and certainly because it was so fresh in my mind, having worked up a handout paper on angles and tension that week. So I corrected my sketch — several times — attempting to simplify and clarify things, aware that I was now drawing, not copying. The possibilities became infinite. I was no longer confused or intimidated by the array of bits and pieces — by the parts. I began to see the scene as a whole, with all the parts fitting together into what I thought of as landscape gestures.

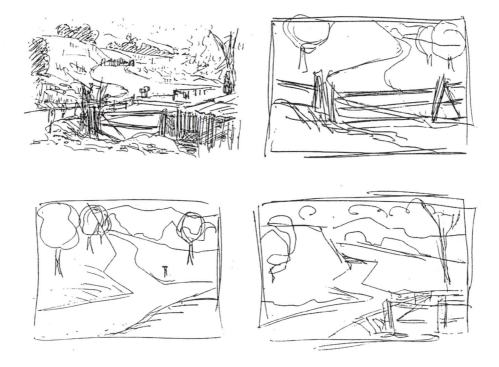

The subject was a landscape but the process of sketching it was the same as if it had been a live model. I make no special claims for the drawings as they are crude and quickly drawn. Their only purpose is to demonstrate a shifting from copying to creating. Betty Edwards (*Drawing on the Right Side of the Brain*) would have said "Shifting from the left side to the right side of the brain."

How can we apply all this to figure drawing? On the following page I have reproduced a class drawing, and for the short time in which it was done, it is quite anatomically solid. But it reminds me of my first sketch of the hills —we were involved in copying, getting lots of this

and not enough of this.

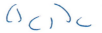

In animation squash and stretch is one of our greatest tools. Drawing a stretch with these will in no way put the idea across. We have to learn to shift our mental gears so that when drawing a stretch, we lean less on our knowledge and infatuation of anatomy and simply draw a stretch.

Here is the drawing along with three sketches I made to suggest a simple and more direct approach to the problem of capturing the pose. I changed the angles of the arms, torso, and legs slightly to illustrate what I mean when I speak about using angles to clarify a pose or to bring out some desirable nuance of gesture. In one of the sketches I straightened out one whole side of the figure to show that an almost straight line can be used for a stretch and still retain some semblance of anatomy. Notice in one of the sketches I copied the angles of the lower legs, while in the other two sketches I varied them. Also notice how some sharp angled lines were used on the figure's left foot to make it read clearly as it works against the right leg. The student's drawing is a little nebulous in that area. As for tension in the drawings — imagine a large rubber band connected from hand to hand, foot to foot, knee to knee; hand to knee, head to foot etc. Tension is simply the stretching, pulling, elastic force, pressure, or exertion that takes place in a pose or an action. So in effect, to capture the essence of this pose, we would not merely be drawing the left hand and the left knee, but more important, the tension between them.

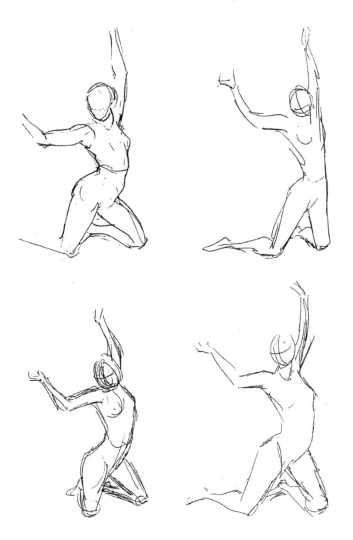

81   Tennis, Angles, and Essences

One thing is for sure, to acquire a certain degree of skill or expertise in any undertaking the basics must be studied and conquered. Drawing, animation specifically, is no exception. Once the basic rules and principles are thoroughly ingrained, they can be applied to all the variations of problems that will confront us — and confront us they will.

The game of tennis has a few basics that when once learned are applicable throughout the game. For instance, once you learn what a "forehand drive" is, you soon realize that that shot doesn't cover just one tiny area of the total. It covers any ball that comes to your right side (if you're right handed), anywhere from the ankles up to around head height, providing it bounces once on the court before it gets to you. Beginners who are not yet aware of this as a category of shot will be confused, because it comes at them anywhere from the center of the body to way beyond their reach, and as I mentioned, from the ankle to head height. It's like being "splayed" by a machine gun of tennis balls. You may find a waist shot at arms length fairly easy to handle, but these things are coming at you like swallows entering their nesting place at sundown.

So you study and learn this one stroke, the forehand drive, which requires, more or less, one particular "principle" of stroking. Just knowing that much makes it easier to adjust to the variety of heights and distances and speeds of balls, so you can adapt your body movements, weight distribution, speed of racket, footwork, etc. Anything over the head merges into the area of an "overhead" shot, which requires a technique of its own. Anything that bounces just before you hit it is a "half volley" shot that has its own rules for handling. The forehand drive is just one of many shots a tennis player should have in his arsenal of shots.

I didn't mean to bore you, but I thought it might illustrate the fact that *knowing* a particular problem so you can deal with it on its own terms makes sense. It takes all the mystery and confusion out of it. It allows one to isolate a problem and to work on it alone and by repetitive practice, "groove" it to perfection, and to learn it so well that it becomes second nature. Not that you won't have to think anymore, but that thinking about it will not cause you to lose your main trend of thought, which of course in animation is acting out your characters' parts on paper.

The use of those rules of perspective I mention so often may be likened to shots is tennis. To avoid belaboring those rules too much, let's use angles as an illustration of a "stroke" in our arsenal of shots. Every gesture or pose is loaded with angles, but if they are not recognized as potential point winners, we might just gloss over them. I don't want you to gloss over that word gloss either. It means superficial quality or show — a deceptive outward appearance; to make an error, etc., seem right or trivial. If we gloss over enough of those kinds of drawing "strokes," we will end up with a "love game," in other words a nothing drawing.

Back to angles. If you want to make a strong statement, and even subtle poses and actions can be strong statements, pay special attention to angles; especially if you work roughly, then "clean" your drawings up later. (after the initial spurt of enthusiasm and clarity of vision has left you). Then later a cleanup person will work on it, who never had your enthusiasm or clarity of vision, and perhaps soften the angles just a little more. Your accolades will be soft too, for it is the strong statements that get the oohs and ahs. Don't confuse angles with angularity. Some of the most graceful people are put together with 45-degree angles. Watch them — they seem to have studied how to play one angle off another to create those tantalizing poses. Sometimes the changes of angles of cheek against neck, or hand against cheek are so subtle they are felt rather than seen. If you are just looking they are seductive, but if you are drawing, they suddenly become almost invisible — difficult to see and capture. That's why sometimes you have to draw not what you see but what you know is there or what you feel is there.

Last week while making suggestions on some of the class drawings I concentrated on angles. Sometimes the angles were just barely discernible on the model and needed special attention to find. Once found they needed accenting to make sure they would still be subtle, but at the same time a strong statement.

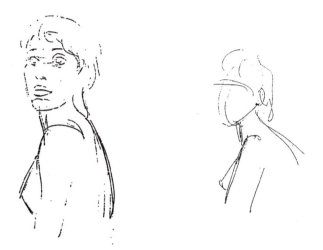

This was beginning to be a nice drawing, but was also becoming a straight up and down thing. The pose had some subtle angles that I tried to point out.

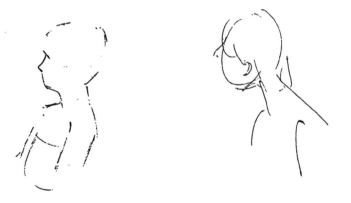

If I had not interrupted this sketch it might have turned out to be a very sensitive drawing. But the whole gesture was overlooked. Note the acute angles the gesture needed to get its story told — not just the neck angle but the face angle against the neck, the front neck angle against the back, the neck angle against the shoulders. One should never work one angle by itself. Angles must work against other angles to contribute to the overall maximum statement.

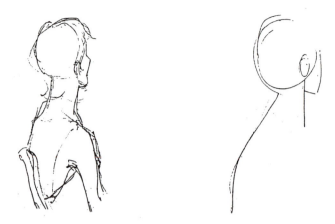

This is not a bad drawing, but I felt it missed a very subtle thing going on in the pose, which a few lines and some definite angles captured.

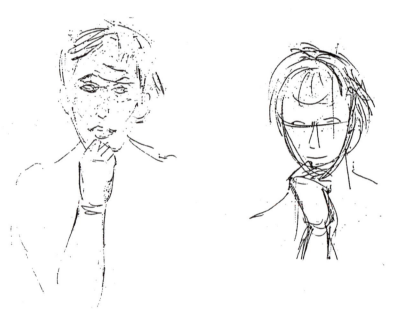

In this pose I didn't feel the head was leaning on the hand. Through the use of a "surface line" I lowered the face so it angled into the fingers to show the weight of the head. The hand and arm became a tangent so I bent the wrist to introduce an angle (which helped to show the weight of the head also). The trapezius muscles and shoulders became too symmetrical so I offset them with more interesting angles and introduced a neck with its third dimensional "overlap."

82 More on the Same

I have been stressing "essence" drawing and may be running the word into the ground, but I feel strongly about the word. Anatomy and mechanics are always present, too, but in the end the essence of each pose must prevail if we want to win the award for best-animated scene ('scuse me — scenes). Things to think about include proportion, anatomy, line, structure, weight, negative space, angles, squash and stretch, perspective and more, but you can be off in lots of those areas *if you have the* essence of the pose. The word essence to me is almost philosophical in meaning — "that in being which underlies all outward manifestations...." Applied to drawing it is the motive, mood, or emotion as displayed through the gestures of the physical body.

Ideally, of course, there will soon suddenly, then hopefully, constantly appear in your drawings all of these elements in a satisfying blend. A little study *each day* spent on one or another of them will net wondrous results. You will be pleased and much prospered when they all start to fit together and the exhausting battle with each separate one is over. We are all at different stages of development so must search out our own weak areas and concentrate on those. I'm not a master in any sense of the word, but would relish the opportunity to discuss your class efforts or your studio work in a one-on-one attempt to analyze your weak and/or strong areas. If I bomb out — so what! If I can hit home with some effective and fruitful suggestion then let's hear it for the spirit of search and discovery. Any time is a time to be adventurous if it spurs you on to some worthy goal.

The essence thing appears in all the arts — not just sketching. In literature it is when the writing goes beyond just words, beyond just reporting. In music it is when it goes beyond just notes and lyrics, when there emerges an essence that touches the heart. There are only 26 letters in our alphabet — only a couple honored words we use in daily communication — but the artful way those are juxtaposed set them apart as memorable and meaningful. In drawing you have 360 degrees in which to vary your lines and the choice and variance determines whether or not your drawing will be worthy of the effort you've spent on it.

There used to be the belief that certain muses attended to the inspirational needs of the artist, today we speak of using the right side of the brain. Certain metaphysical teachings speak of expanded consciousness or awareness. In Psalm One it says the man whose delight is in the law of the lord...whatever he does prospers. Regardless, it is a shifting of the mental gears from the ordinary to the inspired area of creativity.

Here are a few bars of Mozart. How can anything so beautiful be put down so simply? When a good pianist plays it, it sounds like an ethereal orchestra playing God's own symphony.

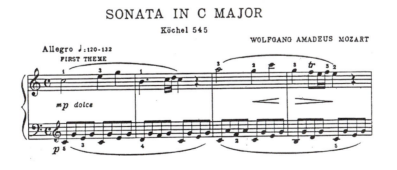

SONATA IN C MAJOR

Köchel 545

WOLFGANG AMADEUS MOZART

"Popular" music has its essence passages too. Here's one that came from our own studio.

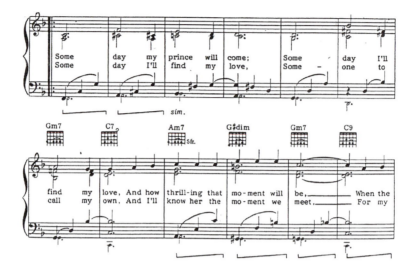

Guys like Robert Frost, the poet, spent their whole lives on the razor-thin edge between the ordinary and the inspirational. How thought provoking, his poem *The Road Not Taken*.

THE ROAD NOT TAKEN

Two roads diverged in a yellow wood,
And sorry I could not travel both
And be one traveler, long I stood
And looked down one as far as I could
To where it bent in the undergrowth;

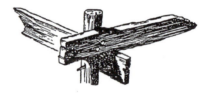

The poem goes on for three more stanzas but ends with these three exquisite lines:

Two roads diverged in a wood, and I—
I took the one less traveled by,
And that has made all the difference.

How pithy the first line of his *Mending Wall*, it has the essence of all our feelings about being fenced in.

MENDING WALL

Something there is that doesn't love a wall,
That sends the frozen-ground-swell under it,
And spills the upper boulders in the sun;
And makes gaps even two can pass abreast.
The work of hunters is another thing:

As for drawings and sketches that "tell all" they are all around us and we recognize them immediately. They imprint their vivid essences on our mental retinas. Fancy talk, eh, well this is fancy stuff. You can't just pass over this stuff with a "Hey, Man," you've got to worship it and make it your religion.

This is getting out of hand, but I feel compelled to…well…overkill.

It all starts with preparation, which is the "open sesame" of all genius. Even the geniuses admit is 99% hard work and 1% genius.

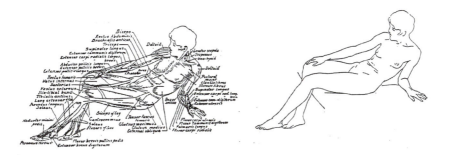

Here are two drawings by Forain — a master of simplicity and gesture.

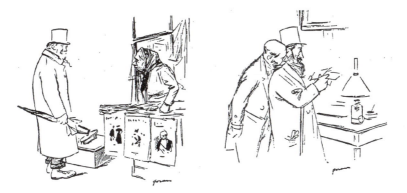

A playful caricature by Ward Kimball.

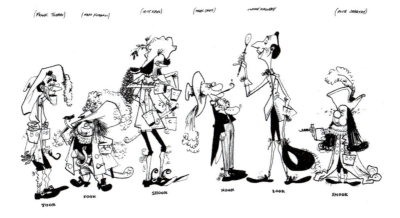

The cartoonist too has to get at the essence of his subject

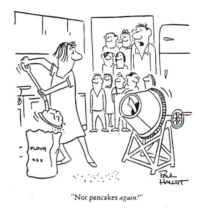

"Not pancakes *again!*"

and in the business so dear to our own hearts — animation. Cliff Nordberg was a genius at simple, direct action. This is the latter part of a weightlifting demonstration.

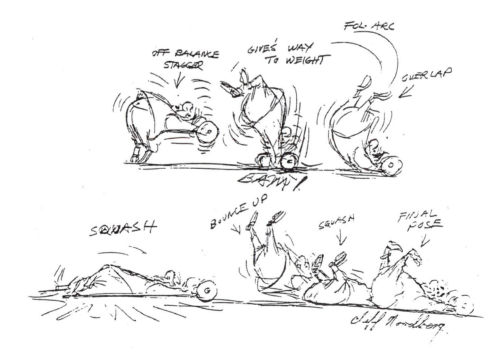

Ollie Johnston has done some of the most sensitive animation and drawings this studio has seen. I give him the title of "Mr. Essence Man."

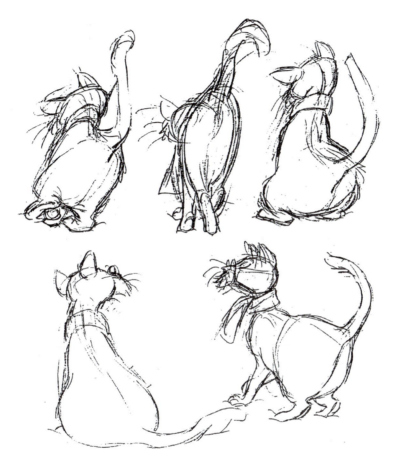

83 More on "Essence" Drawing

You might think of drawing as composed of two elements of life — mental and physical. The physical is the knowledge of anatomy and the mechanics of how that anatomy works. The other part is the mental, which involves the whole gamut of moods and emotions. Our job as artists is to somehow tie those two elements together into a readable expression of whatever it is we want to illustrate. In our sessions we have been emphasizing the mood and emotional part of the gestures. Needless to say both areas are necessary for a maximum of expression. But whereas the mechanical part of anatomy is traditionally taught in anatomy classes, the mental and emotional side has been left for the artist to develop according to the artist's needs or preference. Ultimately, in animation one must face up to the emotional gesture when called upon by the director to inject it into his scenes.

As an example of the marriage of the physical and mental take the breaking of a vase. The physical act of breaking a vase can be accomplished by simply dropping the vase on a hard surface. But to show the emotional reason for breaking the vase would require the artist to imagine himself in such an angry state that would cause him to break it, and get that feeling into the drawings. Each artist would have his own subtle manner of doing it but basically there is a sort of universal body language that says "anger."

There is no doubt that there is a physical universe but we deal with it in a mental and emotional way. A physical being without emotions would make a lousy roommate. A scene of one of our characters, perfectly drawn but without some mental motivation be of much help to the picture. A roughly drawn scene, off model but containing the essence of the story line would be much more desirable. Then let the one who draws so well clean the scene up, but retain all that emotional gesture so vital to the making of a good Disney film.

Hours and hours should be spent with anatomy books, old Disney films, and scenes of the old masters like Milt Kahl and Ollie Johnston. Also much time must be spent flexing one's emotional muscles with "essence" sketching, reading a great variety of authors — novels, biographies, psychology, metaphysics, and of course, humor. Don't be like a friend who used to say he was waiting for the "light to come on." Well, he was a real charming guy but he retired before the light came on. Moral: Don't wait. Immerse yourself in the search now.

I have Xeroxed some drawings that Frederick E. Banbery did for the book, *The Posthumous Papers of the Pickwick Club* by Dickens. I think they're an excellent example of "essence" drawings. There is a minimum of line and rendering, but a maximum of gesture and feeling. And they radiate the type of humor the story calls for.

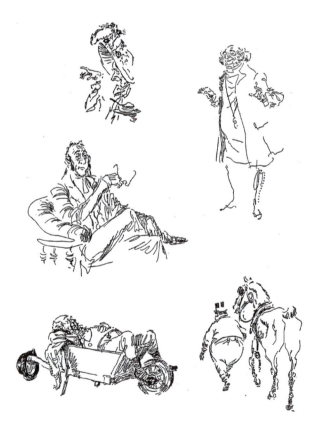

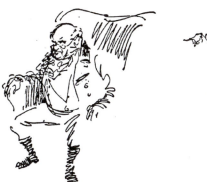

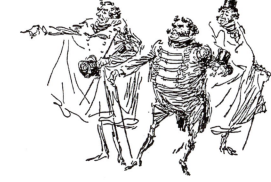

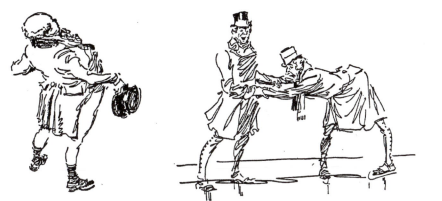

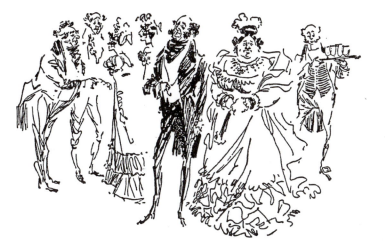

84 Driving Force Behind the Action

In the evening drawing sessions I try to direct your thoughts to the gesture rather than to the physical presence of the models and their sartorial trappings. It seems the less the model wears, the more the thinking is directed to anatomy, while the more the model wears, the more the thinking goes into drawing the costume. It's a deadlock that you can only break by shifting mental gears (there's that phrase again) from the "secondary" (details) to the "primary" (motive or driving force behind the pose). Remember, the drawing you are doing in class should be thought of as a refining process for your animation drawing skills.

I found something in Eric Larson's lecture notes on entertainment that may be of help to you. Please bare with the length of the quote, it is put so well I couldn't edit it without losing some of the meaning. As you read it keep your mind on gesture drawing.

…As we begin the 'ruffing out' of our scene, we become concerned with the believability of the character and the action we've planned and we give some thought to the observation of Constantin Stanislavsky. 'In every physical action,' he wrote, 'there is always something psychological and vice versa. There is no inner experience without external physical expression.' In other words, what is our character thinking to make it act, behave, and move as it does? As the animator, we have to feel within ourselves every move and mood we want our drawings to exhibit. They are the image of our thoughts.

In striving for entertainment, our imagination must have neither limits nor bounds. It has always been a basic need in creative efforts. 'Imagination,' wrote Stanislavsky, 'must be cultivated and developed; it must be alert, rich, and active. An actor (animator) must learn to think on *any* theme. He must observe people (and animals) and their behavior — try to understand their mentality.'

To one degree or another, people in our audience are aware of human and animal behavior. They may have seen, experienced, or read about it.

Because they have, their knowledge, though limited, acts as a common denominator, and as we add to and enlarge upon said traits and behavior and bring them to the screen, caricatured and alive, there blossoms a responsive relationship of the audience to the screen character — and that spells 'entertainment.'

How well we search out every little peculiarity and mannerism of our character and how well and with what 'life' we move and draw it, will determine the sincerity of it and its entertainment value, we want the audience to view our character on the screen and say: 'I know that guy!' (or in the case of gesture drawing: 'I know what that person is doing, what he or she is thinking.') Leonardo da Vinci wrote: 'Build a figure in such a way that its pose tells what is in the soul of it. A gesture is a movement not of a body but of a soul.' Walt (Disney) reminded us of this when he spoke of the driving force behind the action: 'In other words, in most instances, the driving force behind the action is the mood, the personality, the attitude of the character — or all three.'

Let's think of ourselves as pantomimists because animation is really a pantomime art. A good pantomimist, having a thorough knowledge of human behavior, will, in a very simple action, give a positive and entertaining performance. There will be exaggeration in his anticipations, attitudes, expressions, and movements to make it all very visual.

The pantomimist working within human physical limitations, will do his best to caricature his action and emotions, keep the action in good silhouette, do one thing at a time and so present his act in a positive and simple manner for maximum visual strength. But we, as animators, interpreting life in linear drawings, have the opportunity to be much stronger in our caricature of mood and movement, always keeping in mind, as the pantomimist the value and power of simplicity.

Below are some excellent examples of what Walt must have meant by, "...the driving force behind the action is the mood, the personality, the attitude of the character...." They are sketches Mark Henn did while at a recording session for the Great Mouse Detective.

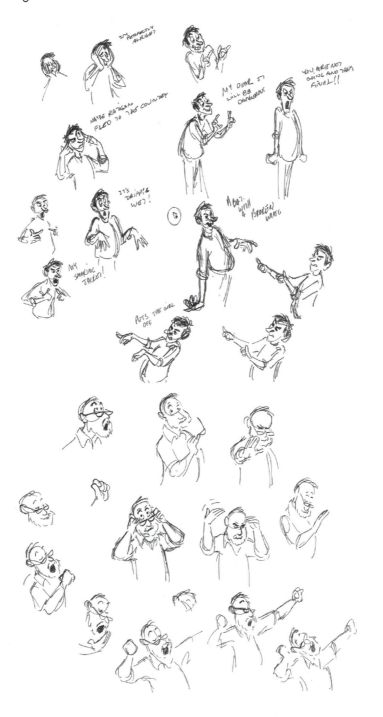

Actually we create nothing of ourselves, we merely use the creative force that activates us. And when we draw we are not using the left brain to record facts — we have shifted gears and are now using the right brain to create a little one-picture story with, of course, the facts that the left brain collected and named and itemized in former study periods. This is not a study period; this is a show-and-tell period (any time we are not studying).

We are not the car parts in the design room or where they mold the parts or on the assembly line. We are the car full of gas, traveling along the Pacific Coast Highway, heading for a nice seafood restaurant in Carmel.

Do you feel that you are too limited in knowledge? Robert Henri, that great teacher of art, said that anyone could paint a masterpiece with what limited knowledge they have. It would be a matter of using that limited knowledge in the right (creative) way. Have you ever seen the "knowledge" or drawing ability of that great painter Albert Ryder? Probably not. But when you look at his nebulous paintings of ships at sea or skeletons riding around with nothing on, you sense the drama and have a feeling a story is being told. If its facts you want, pick up a Sears' mail-order catalog.

I'm not advocating abandoning the study of the figure. Anatomy is a vital tool in drawing, but do not mesmerize yourself into thinking that knowing the figure is going to make an artist of you.

What is going to make an artist out of you is a combination of a few basic facts about the body, a few basic principles of drawing and an extensive, obsessive desire and urge to express your feelings and impressions.

The violinist Yehudi Menuhin started out at the "top" of his profession. He played in concerts at a very young age and in his late teens was world famous. Suddenly (if late teens is sudden) he realized he'd never taken a lesson — he didn't know how he was playing the violin (the right brain had not been discovered then).

He worried that if that inspired way of playing ever left him he would not be able to play. So he took lessons and learned music (finally getting the left brain into the art).

It didn't alter his playing ability but it bought him some insurance.

I'm suggesting that somehow he had early on tapped the creative force and bypassed the ponderous study period, like all geniuses seem to do. I have a Mozart piano piece that he wrote when he was around nine years old. I've been working on it for years and still can't play it. Who does he think he is anyway?

I've been studying piano for umpteen years and I still don't know the key signatures. The left side of the brain is absolutely numb. But when I sit down to play the piano sometimes that creative force takes my hands and extracts a hint of emotional sound out of the music. That's all I really care about. My sketching is the same way. I don't know a scapula from a sternum but when I venture out into the world with my sketchbook, I am able to distill my impressions into a one-frame story that totally tells my version of what I saw. When my wife Dee and I go on a vacation, she takes the photos and I sketch. She records the facts — I record the truth.

Shift gears! With the few facts you have go for the truth!

85 A Drawing Style Appropriate for Animation

Have you ever said, "Oh, if I could just draw well"? Ah, yes, you could express yourself to the nth degree. You could animate or clean up scenes that would evoke oohs and aahs. Work wouldn't be so much like work. You could get it all down on paper and leave at 5 o'clock feeling good.

Most of you draw well. A lot of you draw better than I do. And in all the years I've been in the business, I've never seen a more industrious and devoted staff of artists. It makes my job of trying to help you better yourselves a pleasure.

I got a late start in life. The first five or six years in the business were a "walk through." I was a dilettante, toying with poetry, painting, singing, and socializing. Then 10 years as John Lounsbery's assistant, and 10 years as Ollie Johnston's assistant helped me to "center" myself. Those guys worked hard and were completely devoted to their jobs, which taught me to work hard (and study hard to catch up). The next 20 years were not easy but were very satisfying.

Sometimes I wish I had a magic wand that I could wave over you and say, "You are now learned artists — go and draw to your heart's content." But maybe it's better that you do it yourself and become your own self-starter. The learning process should be fun. One thing that it does is it tears down a lot of false pride. To seek help is a kind of humbling experience, a very necessary one in as much as animation should be thought of and practiced as a group effort. I consider a person who is not ashamed to seek help to be a wise person.

In the *Illusion Of Life* Ollie or Frank had written a paragraph on cleanup people which lists some of the functions of a cleanup person that coincide with some of the things I keep stressing in the drawing class — a crisp line against a soft shape (using angles), designing shapes that work with the action rather than copying, emphasizing squash and stretch, and drawing detail only as it furthers the action and the drawing and especially, "telling the story" whether it's a scene of animation or a still drawing.

The quote, reprinted here in full, refers to cleanup people but it could as well refer to animators and inbetweeners. All of the above classifications make drawings that go into a scene and so the same training is necessary for all.

"They studied line drawing, training on Holbein, Degas, Daumier, da Vinci; they watched drapery in movement, noting the difference between filmy scarves, woolen skirts, flowing capes, and even baggy pants; they learned the value of a sharp, crisp line against a large, soft shape; they knew how to keep a design in the free-flowing changing shapes of animation rather than make a rigid copy. They always extended the arcs of the movement, squashed the characters more, stretched him more — refining while emphasizing both the action and the drawings. They understood the business of the scene, what it was supposed to achieve, worked closely with the animator in deciding which parts were developing well and which parts needed a little help, and they could see the characters start to live as they "rolled" the drawings on the pegs. This required a special kind of talent as well as study — not every artist could master it."

So you see, there is something special about the thinking that goes into animation drawing. Don't ease up on your search — success is just around the proverbial corner. I am reprinting some ruff animation drawings to remind you of the style of drawing that seems to serve the purposes of the animators best. I am constantly apologizing for maybe interfering with your style of drawing, but if you are serious about making animation your life's work, it behooves you to take as many tips from the pros as you can. Try to use this kind of an approach when drawing from the model, then you won't have to make an unnatural switch in styles when working on animation.

Draw ideas, not things; action, not poses; gestures, not anatomical structures.

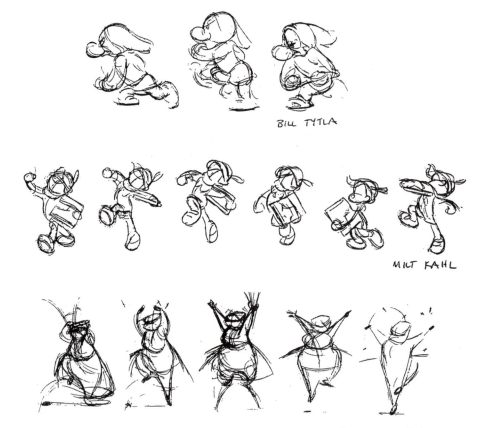

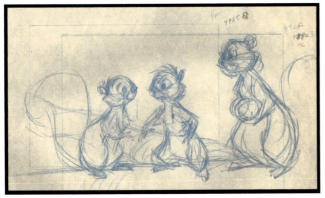

Frank Thomas

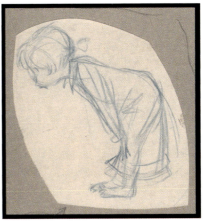

Ollie Johnson

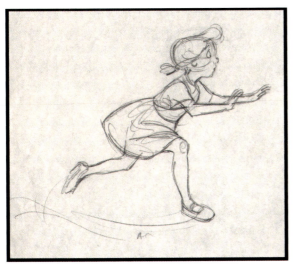

Milt Kahl

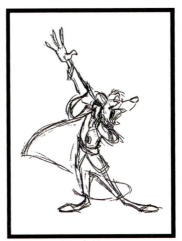

Mark Henn

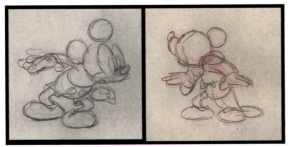

Fred Moore

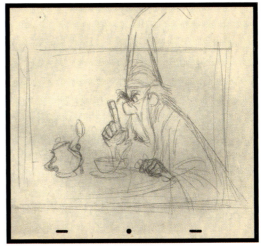

Milt KahlL

86 A Drawing Style for Animation, Part II

Last week I reprinted some roughs as examples of a style of drawing. appropriate for animation, which I knew at the time were not fully explaining my point. They showed some beautifully drawn roughs that were loose and expressive, but didn't explain or even given a hint at how they were arrived at.

Let's take one of the drawings from last week's "handout" and analyze it. The animator, Mark Henn, was not interested in

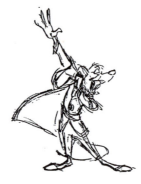

telling the part of the story that occurred on that particular frame of film. If he were interested in parts and the audience were too, this kind of thing would have satisfied both:

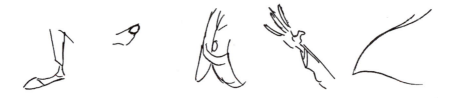

Animators are not just recorders of facts; they are storytellers, using their drawing vocabulary instead of words to spin a tale. They have at their disposal many exciting and dramatic ways to make expressive drawings, some of which are squash and stretch, twisting, contrast, angles, tension, perspective, and thrust. These are not physical things but they are what give *life* to physical things. (I emphasize "life" because without those things in a drawing it would be stiff, dull, and as I often point out in the drawing class, "too straight up and down").

You can be sure this drawing wasn't started with a detail of the head, or some other part of the body (as some of you are still tempted to do when drawing from the model).

It was started with a simple sketch of the whole action, then (and only then) were the details and finishing touches added.

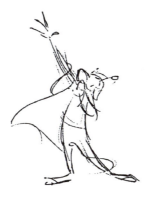

At some point after the initial gesture is established, certain tensions and forces important to the gesture should be chosen, including all parts involved, and worked on as units of action. Every drawing will have a weight distribution or a stress or a thrust or a twist — a squash and stretch, a pull, a push, a drag — some action or actions that you will want to emphasize.

Choose those themes, story points, gesture topics, or whatever you want to call them and with all your awareness concentrate on them and accentuating them, "pressing home" their importance in what you are trying to say —in a word, caricaturing them.

For instance, in Mark's drawing Basil is yakking about something as he goes through a flurry of putting on his coat. At this point in the action he has thrust his tight arm through the armhole, causing a stretch, and is pulling it over his shoulder with his left hand. That is one unit of action — the two hands pulling away from each other. There are others: the lower jaw pulling away from the nose area, the left foot pulling away from the right foot, and the corner or the cloak swinging away from his body. They are all part of the action, but they directly relate to one another.

So, to get the most out of these areas of action, you work one of the related parts against the other — never draw one part of the unit alone — but concomitantly the whole unit. For instance, you would not draw two unrelated parts such as his left arm and his left leg.

Rather you would work his left arm against his right arm.

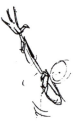

Then (but not necessarily in that order) you would draw the two feet that work as a unit, pulling away from each other.

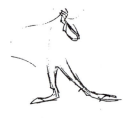

Then you would concentrate on the action of the corner of the cape as it stretches out away from his torso.

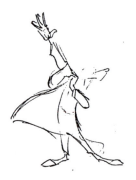

Then the head thrust, which is set up by the sum total of all the other parts. Notice how the nose direction is a continuation or rather a culmination of the whole body action. It's clear from the left toe but also the belt line, the cape line, and the straight lines of the arms is almost like a "sounding board" for the yakking that is going on.

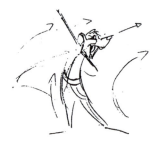

Some of the subtle poses that our models assume may be less extreme or dramatic but all the more reason for us to be cognizant of the importance of those vital elements in gesture drawing. It is so easy for a subtle pose to become another one of those "straight up and down," self-conscious postures. On the other hand, it is "goose bump" time when those eloquent, meaningful, storytelling gestures come through in your drawings.

May the forces and stretches and angles and all other drawing helps be with you.

87 Learn to Cheat

No, I am not trying to lead you astray. "Cheating" in drawing is a term used when some part of the figure is adjusted to help make the pose read more clearly. One of the most obvious places to introduce a cheat is in establishing a good silhouette. First, let's look at a drawing with a fairly good silhouette.

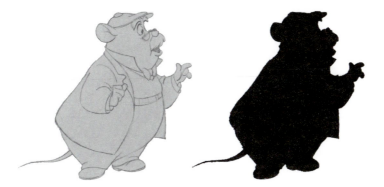

This drawing of Dawson clearly defines his hat, nose, mustache, mouth, hand, coattail, legs, etc. The stance, mood, and personality are unmistakable. Incidentally, the third dimensional elements in the drawing work equally well in making it a readable drawing.

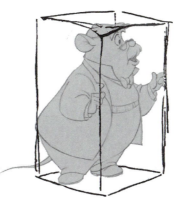

If the drawing had not been so successful, "cheating" a little here and there would have helped. For instance, the coattails, the fingers, or the hat could have been lengthened or in some way made more obvious. Let's take a less clear silhouette and see if it could be improved without substantially changing the pose. In the first attempt Dawson's left elbow was extended to avoid the tangent it was forming with the back side. His right elbow was shortened to expose more cheek, and the tip of the hat was more clearly defined. In the second attempt the left arm was shortened and the backside extended (the opposite from the first) with a little of his shirttail extended, which helps to divide and define the upper body from the lower.

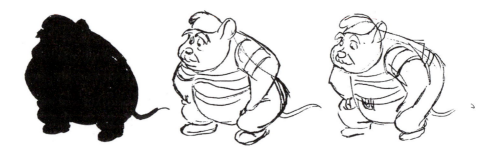

The fear of straying from what is before you while drawing from the live model can sometimes "tie your hands" (your drawing hands). An innocent little cheat may do such wonders for your drawing that any deviation from the "facts" will go unnoticed. A good place to practice cheating is while drawing from the human figure. Very often in a classroom situation you will be stuck with a difficult angle where things that explain or complete the gesture are hidden from you. The challenge of adjusting the pose to better tell your story can be invigorating. The important thing is you are not bound to copy what is before you, but on the contrary, you are bound to tell the story of the gesture, even if you have to cheat to do it.

Caricature, one of the animator's most valuable tools, is a total cheat. An effective caricature can be so exaggerated that not one line of realism remains. Even so, a good caricature can be more "real" than a photographic copy. Tracing photostats for a scene of animation is sufficient proof of that.

So start now. Discover that creative freedom that releases you from the conventional copycat type of seeing, thinking, and drawing — become a good cheater.

I saved two drawings from the evening class that may help to illustrate the point. In the first one, the model had assumed a rather haughty, officious air. It was subtle and the drapery was no help at all. One artist got trapped in the multitude of curves in the clothes and figure, and in attempting to copy what was there, missed the aloofness of the gesture. In my suggestion, I "cheated." I took out all the curves (I have a tendency to go to extremes when pointing out things like this), thrust the shoulder up, straightened out the hanging shirttail (thus accenting the shoulder lift), stretched the neck, and added a better angle to the folded arms, and *voila* — instant arrogance.

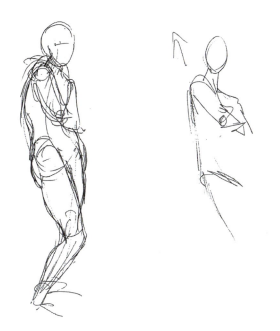

The other drawing was again from a deceptive pose, in that the clothes contained a lot of soft curves. In cases like this, one has to cheat a little and introduce what they know is happening rather than what they *see*. For instance, in this pose the girl's right shoulder had to lower in *shape* as well as position, the front of the neck had to *stretch* to reach from the raised chin to the lowered pit of the neck, and the coat had to hang with some straights to contrast with the bunched up cloth at the elbows.

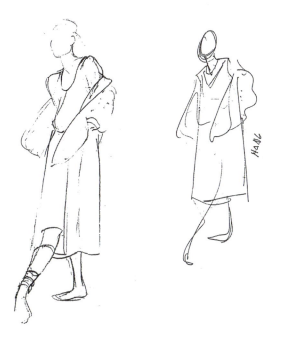

88 One Picture Worth A Thousand Words?

Some friends gave me a book for my 69th birthday called *Medical Makeover* (gosh, do I look that bad?). My birthday was in July, and tonight, November 27, I opened the book for the first time to peruse it. Peruse means I don't have time to read it now, but at least I can spot some things for future investigation. I always begin a book by starting at the very first page and then reading every word, clear through to the back cover, usually ending up with tons of notes sparked by the text. Anyway, on the seventh page of this book there is a dedication that struck me as a more than an ordinary book dedication. It goes "To my parents who have helped me realize that medicine is more than a profession." Wow! Isn't that a beautiful thought? I don't mean "Hurrah for the parents," or "How thoughtfully thankful the son"; I'm thinking, we as artists should realize that drawing is more than a profession. We are privy to a form of communication that many aspire to but few attain.

Man alone in the animal world has developed a language. It is our way of communicating what goes on in our complex minds. Animals have been taught words, but they are not able to use those words to transfer thought. I must qualify that by relating the story of a lonely chimp who was taught some English sign language and who, after a period of isolation from friends, when meeting a friend, said with that sign language: "Please — help — out."

Right-brained people have developed a language of drawing. Their language is not like the sign language that animals can learn such as nouns and other left-brained things, but is an emotional language of emotions, moods, gestures, and story-weaving. Right-brained activities especially include the ability to gather things together and to summarize, and describe the findings in some "artistic" way, visually or graphically, for instance. It is a wonderful area of human activity. An old Chinese adage expresses it very well: "One picture is worth a thousand words." But again, a qualification has to be made — only a descriptive, expressive picture is worth a thousand words.

Yours is a unique role in our civilization. With your drawings you reach many thousands upon thousands of viewers who look to you for escape or thoughtful viewing pleasure or maybe some form of impersonal communication.

A friend of ours took their two children, three and six years old, to see *Oliver and Company*. The kids were so absorbed in the picture they forgot to eat their popcorn. These kids know nothing about following a model sheet, animation timing, dialog sync, or any of the other fine points of animation. They are just right-brained little folk who are able to tune into a medium that speaks their "language."

In speech, a lot of words, no matter how perfectly spelled or legible, do not make a sentence. The words have to be arranged into syntax, which helps to clarify the image. So in drawing such as a lot of parts, arms, legs, ears, etc., do not make a drawing. Visual syntax (gesture) has to be employed, whether in a still drawing or an animated scene.

I have had many opportunities in my forty some odd years in animation to not only observe, but to experiment with animation and cleanup drawing. One thing stands out in my mind as an absolute ingredient in making a drawing or a scene of animation "work." Certainly, many factors go into the making of a drawing or the animation of a scene such as faithfulness to the character (model), logical anatomical structure, and all the principles of drawing and animation — perspective, squash and stretch, timing, etc. Those are all somewhat mechanical things, things that can be measured with a ruler or a stopwatch. You could make charts and diagrams, and use reference material to accomplish that area of animation.

But the primal thing that sets a drawing or a scene above the "basics" level is sincerity of gesture (acting). If your drawings or your animation is bringing forth the true guts of what you want to say, you can get away with murder regarding much of the other requirements. You could have the most perfect model drawings in the world in a scene, but if the integrity of acting was lacking, the reaction would likely range from detachment to disgust. However, if the opposite were true, the audience's eyes would be much more forgiving than their emotions. A strange thing about the eyes, they fill in for missing parts, they adjust differences and contradictions. They are very chameleon-like. But the emotions are very demanding. They have standards that have taken years to develop and do not, I repeat, do not like to be fooled around with, toyed with, or in any way taxed, coerced, or deceived.

So learn all the mechanics of drawing and animation that you can. Surround yourself with reference material. But also *study gesture — both humorous and dramatic*. There is no way in the world that you could collect enough poses and gesture reproductions to cover all your needs. You just must sensitize your ability to see those actions in your mind and with the help of the mechanics of drawing and animation, get them down on paper.

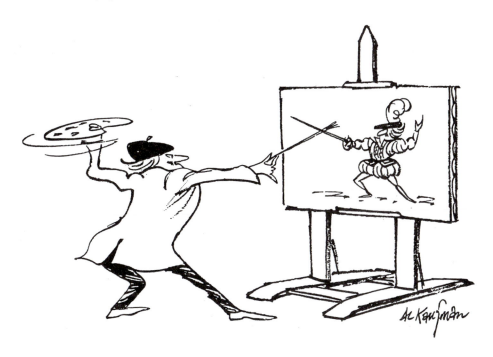

89 Double Vision

We are going to try an experiment in the Tuesday and Wednesday evening classes. There will be a model in a costume that is only close to the production model that we are going to transfer him into. This will give you an opportunity to break away altogether from copying the details of the live model. The production model's costume is so simple it won't require any special attention. Try to capture the pose the live model is offering you, but just "throw in" the shapes and costume of the production model. The poses will still be relatively short, so you won't have time to get involved in detail or "cleanup." At first you may think this is a waste of a perfectly good live model, but as you get with it, I think you'll find it to be a revelation. It might even become addictive.

There will be a model drawing and a large paper clip supplied that will hold the copy erect on top of the drawing board where it will be visible at all times. This can be a real fun session — and a learning one. Do not attempt to copy anything on the live model except the gesture and do not try to copy anything specific off the model sheet. Just sketch in the most general terms. Think of it like this: rather than throwing a tiny dart at a small target, throw a handful of pebbles. If you get even one pebble on the target then you are a winner.

Occasionally a bit of live action film is used as source material for animation. Since it is impossible to find actors who are constructed like the cartoon characters, the animator has to extract the essence of the action from the film or photostat and transfer that to the drawings. It takes a kind of "double vision" — you are looking at the live action but you are seeing the cartoon character. You may be looking at a person seven heads tall but drawing a cartoon character three or four heads tall. It requires a special knack, but it is a learnable knack.

In the early 1930s when the use of live action was first tried, it was a period of discovery, a period of great excitement. *That* discovery is history and now artists have to discover for themselves the merits and even the necessity of using live action, whether in the form of live models, film clips, or photostats. After all, all cartoon characters, no matter how cartoony, are built on human traits or attributes.

Learning to see in this "double vision" can be fun. In their book *The Illusion of Life* Ollie and Frank state: "And the spirit of fun and discovery was probably the most important element of that period." Don't let the statement "that period" squelch *your spirit* of discovery, pursuit, and involvement.

Again I quote from the *Illusion Of Life*,

"But whenever we stayed too close to the photostats or directly copied even a tiny piece of human action, the results looked very strange. The moves appeared real enough, but the figure lost the illusion of life… Not until we realized that photographs must be redrawn in animatable shapes (our proven tools of communication) were we able to transfer this knowledge to cartoon animation. It was not the photographed action of an actor's swelling cheek that mattered, it was the animated cheek in our drawings that had to communicate. Our job was to make the cartoon figure go through the same movements as the live actor, with the same timing and the same staging, but, because animatable shapes called for a difference in proportions, the figure and its model could not do things in exactly the same way. The actor's movements had to be reinterpreted in the world of our designs and shapes and forms."

So come to the class and do some discovery of your own. It will be a cartoony character we will be working with, which means you can sort of, as the saying goes, hang loose. And to show you how loose you may be I have taken some class drawings of Craig, our model, in other costumes and turned him into Louis the chef. I even used a female dancer and a little girl to demonstrate that it is not so much the model as it is your ability to adapt the human figure to the cartoon figure. These are my first tries at the character, so to the trained eye may be disgustingly off model, but for our purposes anything faintly resembling the character will do.

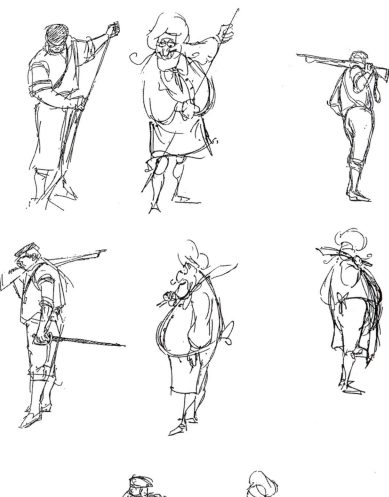

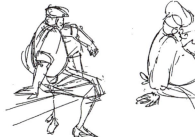

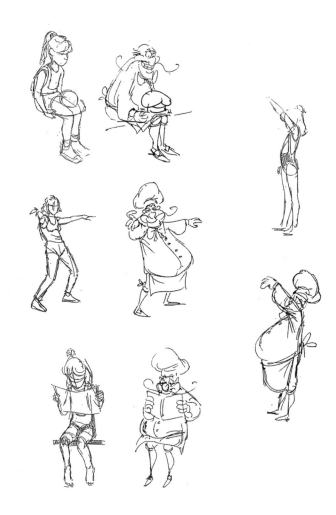

90 Lazy Lines

While talking to Dan Jeup one day, he mentioned "lazy lines." He was referring to lines that didn't describe anything like shape, texture, softness, or hardness. It's like what you get when you trace something, an overall sameness of line. Granted, when you are using a mechanical pencil as we are on "Mermaid," that in itself cuts down on possible variations of line. However, the problem of lazy lines goes deeper than just the surface patina, it has to do with the lack of basic drawing.

For instance, the same pencil makes a line for a bird's beak as for its feathers. If the artist does not *feel* the difference and try to inject that feeling into the drawing, then both lines will look alike — these are lazy lines. And incidentally, they look like a tracing.

Many factors go into the drawing of any part of a bird, and the mind must be focused on each thing separately yet simultaneously. A Zen saying may help to clarify what I am trying to say: "When I am walking, I am walking; when I am eating, I am eating." It simply means that when you are walking, enjoy the fact, instead of planning what you are going to do about the rent payment or what you should have said during yesterday's discussion on politics. Now is the only moment you have — *live in it.* Someone said "Thank God we only live one moment at a time — we couldn't handle any more than that."

Back to walking. When I am walking, I am (just) walking. I feel the cool breeze or the soothing warmth of the sun, I hear whatever sounds pass into my consciousness. I feel my heels strike the ground as they make contact. I enjoy the sway of my body as it negotiates for balance and forward motion. I watch the scenery go by and am aware of the third dimensional quality unfolding around me. These factors are all happening simultaneously yet can be enjoyed separately. The same goes for every activity of your daily living. It is possible to go through life (or sometimes just big chunks of it) in a sort of dream state wherein you don't really experience the things you do. And so it is possible to make a drawing (many drawings) without being wholly conscious of what you are drawing.

To apply that philosophy to drawing you simply have to realize, when you are drawing a beak, you are drawing a beak; when you are drawing a feathered head, you are drawing a feathered head. And that goes for any of the hundreds, or will it be thousands, of separate parts you will be called upon to draw. This may seem contrary to my usual preaching about not drawing details in the gesture class. It is a matter of sequence — first the rough gesture drawing, then the detail. The line used to lay in the pose or action (acting) can be all one kind of line, as long as it is flowing, expressive, flexible, searching, and basic. The line to "finalize" the drawing must describe the shape, texture, and malleability of each part. So when drawing a bird's beak, you should aspire to make the drawing say "beak." When you get to the feathered part of the bird, you shift gears or press the "When I am drawing feathers, I am drawing feathers" button.

I fully realize the pressure levied on you by the production schedules, but it really takes but a split second to alter your thinking as you move from one texture or shape to another. Just being aware of what you are drawing will help to elevate your line from "lazy" to "expressive."

The bird beak and feather thing is pretty obvious, so for a demonstration I'll use a character with a metal crown, some areas of hard and soft flesh, and some hair and cloth:

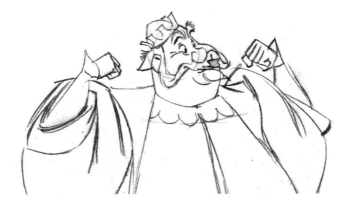

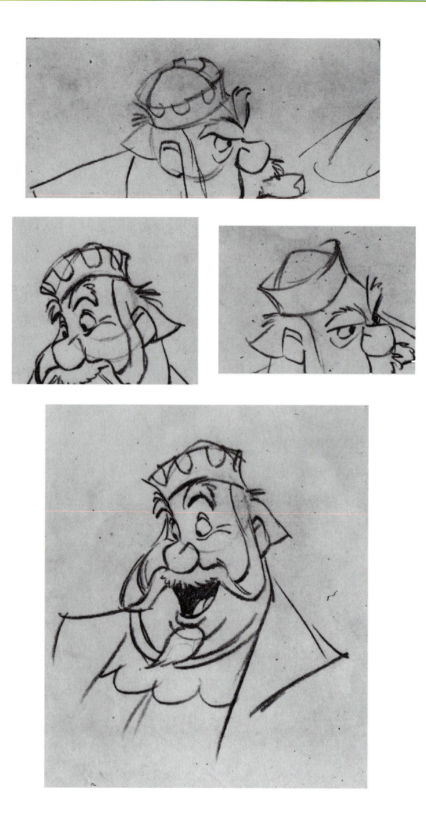

Let's start with the crown. In reality it is a very inflexible, rigid, and lifeless object. It must be drawn so it looks like metal, though in animation liberties may be taken with its shape. For instance, to enhance a raised eyebrow or a frown, it can be contorted to accommodate the expression. Its shape may be altered to help other actions too; for instance, here the crown of the crown still fits snugly onto his head but the brim leans forward helping the direction of the look. Also notice that since the head is tilted to our left it sets up a squash on that side and a stretch on the other side, and the contorted crown shape contributes to that very important animation gimmick, squash and stretch. Even so, it remains rigid and must be drawn so as the surrounding hair and flesh work against it with their softness and of course, more extreme flexibility; that is soft and flexible non-lazy lines.

Take the hair. Its basic shape is this.

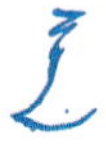

In movement it never loses that basic appearance but may squash and stretch and overlap to enhance the head moves.

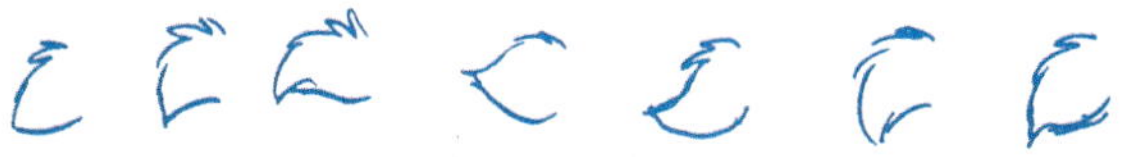

So, as you "Zen" your way through the drawing, you come to the face. You say, now I am drawing the bridge of the nose,

now the top of the nose,

now the front of the nose,

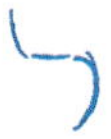

now the part under the nostril,

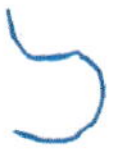

now the back of the nostril

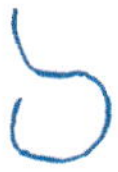

And now the top of the nostril.

Those are all separate parts of the face and must be kept in mind *as* you are drawing them. If you think of all that as just one big shape it will end up as a lazy-line drawing.

When drawing a cheek it is not just a line you are putting down, it is a shape made of very flexible flesh over a fairly rigid bone structure. So when the chin is pulled down, the cheeks stretch and usually there is a bag under the eye. At this stage it is a bag you are drawing. When the mouth smiles, it pushes all that flesh up and pretty soon you are no longer drawing a bag under the eye — you are drawing the top of the cheek. The highest part of the cheek is found at a point where the mouth would have touched it had the mouth line continued up that far. So then you say, I am drawing the bottom of the cheek as it hangs over the corner of the mouth, which in this case is covered by the mustache, not a lazy-line mustache, but one that is drawn in a way that suggests a smiling mouth. Now I am drawing the flesh that is slightly more rigid, which is trying to stay where it belongs. It is connected to the other line but is a different thing and requires thought to depict it as a separate thing. Now I am drawing the front of the cheek as it bulges forward over the backside of the nostril wing. Suddenly it is not the back of the nose you are drawing — it is the cheek.

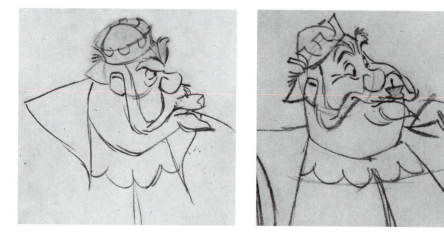

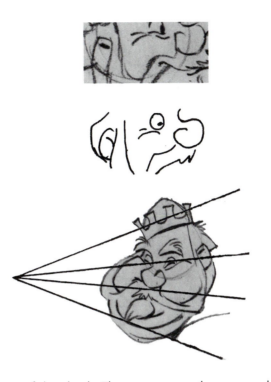

Now I am drawing the top of the cheek. The part nearest the nose and the ear try to stay put, so you get a bulge of loose flesh between two ends that trail off to where they are attached more firmly.

Lazy lines would not spell out all that action. They would simply be there, not describing what is actually happening in a realistic manner.

And as if all that wasn't enough, to keep you thoroughly occupied, you have to fit all those parts into the perspective of the layout. So you have to constantly remind yourself of where the vanishing point is and see that each of parts are loyal to the layout.

If you are a "lazy line" person all this will seem like an unbearable burden, but if you love to draw and can incorporate the "When I am drawing this, I am drawing this" bit, your job of drawing will become very meaningful and sparks of enthusiasm will put a twinkle in your eyes and a sparkle in your drawings.

91 Spot It for Yourself

You have all no doubt experienced the exasperation or perhaps the mortification of having someone else, with seeming ease, spot a problem in a drawing of yours and sketch a solution for you. "Why couldn't I have spotted that?" you say. Well, you can spot it, though it's not so easy after you've drawn it, for your eyes have a tendency to cover up for your shortcomings by finding some false logic to convince you it's okay.

For instance, if this was correct

your eye would find a way to convince you that this was okay

and perhaps it would be okay for some other occasion.

Yes, you can spot it for yourself, but usually it has to happen before you put it down on paper. It happens in the mind — in the planning stage. There are exceptions to the rule, of course. Frank Thomas and Dale Oliver were experts at improving their drawings once they were down on paper. They could work a drawing over until the paper was tissue thin and come up with a gem. Some of us, though, work over a drawing and all we do is intensify the error.

Drawing is like other activities, in that it has to have a purpose behind it, otherwise it is like being set adrift on the Sargasso Sea.

In sports for instance, whether tennis, football, baseball, or basketball, you pick a spot for the ball to go to. Once that goal is chosen, the rest is mostly "mechanics" or "pick and shovel." You use what you learned during those long periods of training you've undergone to help you accomplish the goal. In drawing, you have a goal, too, that is, you have a story to tell, and all your training is put to use in attaining that goal.

Say you are a quarterback and someone is out for a pass. A lot of two hundred and fifty pounders are rushing at you to scrunch you. Your goal is to get the ball to the receiver — not to watch to see which linesman is going to clobber you. If you spend all your time and energy running around dodging these guys the pass is not so likely to get thrown.

In drawing, the goal is not just to get a drawing down on paper, the goal is to tell a story. That is your goal, and if you are dodging around drawing arms and legs and hair instead of getting at the story, very likely you'll be "clobbered" by some 250-pound muddle that has crept in.

I am reproducing a few drawings from the class accompanied by my suggestions. These aren't drawing corrections, such as anatomy or proportions, etc., but suggestions for a kind of thinking that leads to the goal of storytelling.

In the first one the model was bending over, leaning on the back of a chair. He was a rather portly gentleman. On my correction/suggestion, I reasoned that the guy was *bending* forward with his head *resting* on his hands; his knees were *spread* apart because his ample stomach had in a comical or caricatured way, displaced them. If there is a "story" already there, capitalize on it; if no story, try to make one up. It is better to fabricate a goal (story) than to try to make a good drawing out of a nothing situation. To further analyze my thinking, I used a bent line on his back to show that he was bent over. Then I tucked his head lower into the chest area to accent that "bent-overness." I brought his shoulders forward because that was the kinetic feeling I got when imaging myself in that position. I pulled the feet a little closer together (unseen) which accents the knees being pushed out by the stomach. So you can see, it's not so important *what the model is doing*, as it is *your interpretation of what the model is doing*.

In the second drawing I reasoned that the model was looking up. That to me was the "story." So I simply stretched her neck, which is what happens when someone looks up. Then since the front of her neck is a stretch line, the back of her neck could be a squash line and I used her hair to suggest that. And since too many curvy lines have a tendency to cancel out any strong action line, I straightened out the back of the hair, reasoning that since the head was slightly tilted back, it would disengage the hair from the shoulders and back, and allow it to hang down freely. Seems simple doesn't it? Being logical has a tendency to simplify.

Making one drawing is no different than producing a whole animated feature, in that the story always comes first.

In the third drawing I noticed the model was inspecting the sharpness of his knife as if he were farsighted. This required that he back away from what he was looking at. To logically do this, his back had to be arched, which in turn gave an opportunity to play up his belly again. Also, as happened in the first drawing, only in reverse, it allowed the belly to project outward and upward, to displace the elbows. Also, and this may be most important of all, *it got his eyes out into the open, clearing an uncluttered path for his look*. After all, looking down the blade edge is the story here.

In the fourth drawing, the model was stretching for something with his left arm. That was the story. There was nothing else to tell! That was it! So I shoved his left shoulder forward, stretched his arm (all the way from his left foot), setting up an interesting twist in his body. This made what I call an "active still drawing."

In *That's Not What I Meant*, a book on conversational style, the author tells of a man who was stopped by the customs authorities. He had a briefcase filled with sheets of paper covered with odd symbols and sentences that were unable to be interpreted. The customs agents asked a lot of questions that he answered with truthful but not informational answers. The whole thing looked very suspicious. Actually, he was a visiting college professor, and the marks on the papers were not spy codes, but linguistic symbols that were to serve as illustrations for a speech he was to deliver at a university lecture. Local university representatives were waiting outside with his hotel reservation, etc. Just giving the authorities the information they had asked for was not enough to clarify his reason for being there.

In drawing it is not enough to supply your viewers with factual information, like how many arms a human has or how many heads tall he is. The viewers want to know why you are presenting this image. The viewers know what a human being looks like — they've seen thousands of them. No big deal! And they have, no doubt, seen some pretty interesting action and poses, too. So the viewers want to know: "What is this drawing portraying that is supposed to interest me? And you, my friends, have to come up with the answer.

Robert Henri, that great teacher of art, said "A public which likes to hear something worthwhile when you talk, would like to understand something worthwhile when it sees pictures. If they find little more than technical performance, they wander out into the streets where there are faces and gestures which bear evidence of the life we are living…."

And also from his teachings, compiled in the book, *The Art Spirit*, he said, "The artist is no mere entertainer come with cap and bells to amuse and perform graces before a paying public. The true artist regards his work as a means of talking with men, of saying his say (telling his story) to himself and to others."

And: "Gesture, the most ancient form of expression — of communication between living creatures."

And: "To recapture gesture as a means of expression would mean not only added powers of communication but would mean also a greater health and strength."

Finally, and I include this excerpt not so much pertaining to this particular "lesson," but more as an encouragement for you to keep on keeping on: "It takes a tremendous amount of courage to be young, to continue growing — not to settle and accept."

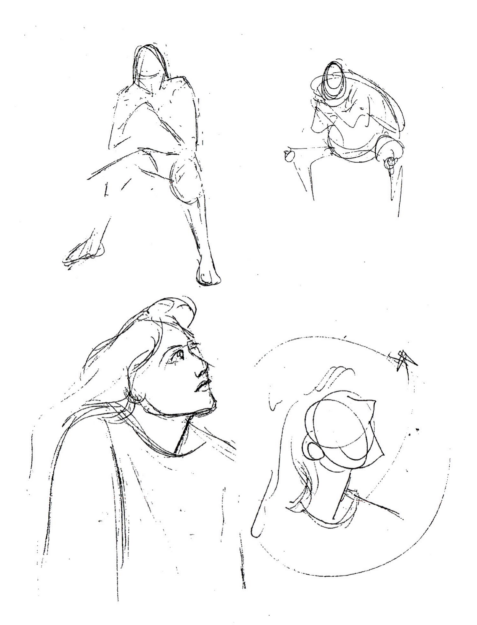

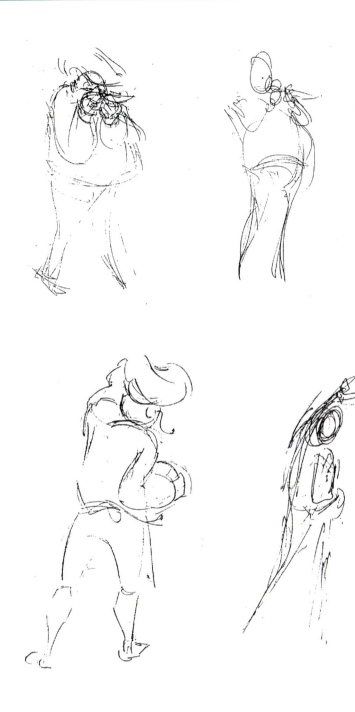

92   Do You Promise to Draw the Action, The Whole Action, and Nothing But the Action?

When you perform a movement of some kind, your body, without you having to think too much about it, does it for you. All you have to do is tell it to pick up a cup, or open the newspaper to page three, or pull the starter cord to start your mower motor. Each of these actions takes a different set of muscles, in various combinations of bends, stretches, twists, and balances. It is truly amazing how dexterous you can be with little or no practice. You might even appear graceful, forceful, serious, or comical, depending on the nature of the move, also how you desire to appear.

When you do these moves, you don't get involved with what muscles are used or what bones those muscles are attached to. And you certainly don't have to be concerned with how many heads tall you are. If you're short you don't have so far to reach for something on the floor, but farther to reach for something over your head. But whatever, your body takes care of all the necessary adjustments. What goes through your mind is simply "Reach for this, bend for that, lean into this, twist for that," etc.

How does all this apply to drawing? In drawing, you suddenly have to become conscious of the action that is required; you have to draw a bend, or a stretch, or a twist, not just do it as in real life, without having to analyze the component parts of the move. Up until the time you decided to draw, you lived without having to give all this subtle body manipulation a second thought. So now you have to investigate, examine, study, dissect, and think through what you do when you move.

One of the great violinists who played in concerts at a very early age, realized, in his teens, that he didn't really know *how* he played the violin. If suddenly this ability left him, he wouldn't be able to perform. So in his late teens he took violin lessons.

You are in a somewhat similar position, because all your life you have performed an infinite combination of bodily movements that required only the desire or need to do them. Then when you have to draw those movements you tend to forget or fail to "call up" the feel of those moves. Consequently, there is a tendency to straighten every thing up, take the twists out, and equalize the angles — all the things that make a pose or action exciting.

Most artists are rather reserved and (self) reflective, rather than demonstrative. Dancers, athletes, and actors are usually bombastic and physical in their expression. Artists, in deep thought while drawing, become still and withdrawn. Unfortunately, some of them even have a tendency to project that stillness into their drawings. This tendency has to be guarded against for it is contrary to their "calling." Don't, for heaven's sake, allow your posture to influence your drawing, unless of course, you are consciously assuming the desired pose. I often tell the students to feel within your bodies the action you are drawing. If your character is stretching or straining, get up and stretch or strain, so you can feel what is going on — what you have to "put over" in your drawing. The fact that you are relaxed in your soft, padded chair, listening to your favorite music, all cozied up in your corner, surrounded by your favorite paintings and drawings can work against you as well as for you.

The thing is when you perform an act, your body adjusts to the complexity or the difficulty of the task, say, an extra need for balance here, more bend there, etc. So when you draw a similar action you have to conjure up those physical needs and inject them into the drawing.

I saved a few drawings from a recent class to illustrate this problem. *In each case the artist, if he (or she) were performing these acts in real life, would not do them in the bland, not total, partway manner they have drawn them.*

In the first drawing, the model was leaning forward looking at a paper. The primary action, of course, is looking at the paper. The secondary action is the head supported by the left forearm. If the back isn't bent forward enough there would be no weight for the left arm to support.

In the second drawing there is a similar action. The right arm is supporting the head as the model assumes a kind of reflective pose. Again, if the body isn't leaning, there will be no need for support. I placed the hand lower on the head which affected a pushing aside of the chin, increasing the angle of the head which accents the "reflective" attitude.

In the last drawing, angles played a big part. Again, the model was bending forward leaning on his left arm. I intensified the bend, which clarified his sitting posture, plus the function the left arm plays in retaining his balance. I angled the right leg more toward us to clarify the leg positions. The angles on the student's drawing of the legs cause a tangent (the deadly destroyer of third dimension).

In closing, I quote myself from earlier in this handout: "In each case, the artist, if he (or she) was performing these acts in real life, would not do them in the bland, not total, partway manner they have drawn them."

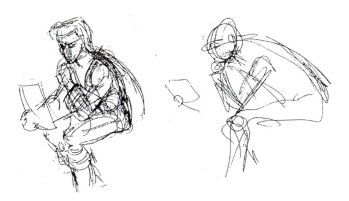

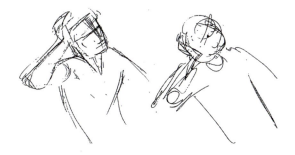

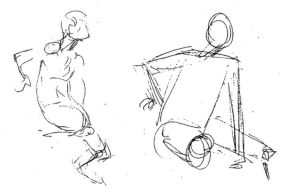

93 The Pose — A One-Drawing Story

The body is always in motion — always squashing or stretching. Even while at rest it is doing something. You might say that a body is incapable of *doing nothing*, for even doing nothing is *doing something*.

People *do* things and everything they do is important and interesting. It is their little bit part in the exciting drama of life. Only the blasé cannot see it so. When an artist draws, it is from this drama of life that he gleans inspiration and subject matter. Resting, reading, running, playing, contemplating, talking, laughing, crying, on and on; these activities unveil the "dance of life" and call up images with which to portray it.

We see a lot of still photos in newspapers, magazines, etc. We must be careful not to let these influence us, for nothing in real life is still. When we make a drawing it is not a *still* drawing; it is a piece of some action, one drawing of a pose which is one pose in thousands upon thousands of poses which comprise the model's full complement of daily poses. It is one extreme, minus the inbetweens.

Don Graham — that great teacher of drawing, painting and animation — said of the extreme: "Instead of being just a turning point, or a rest point in the action, it (the extreme) now became a drawing of great and special picture interest, a story-telling drawing" (the underlining belongs to Don Graham).

Most of the poses in class are rather subdued. The girls look in their purses or drink from teacups; the men try to look masculine by doing something physical to make their muscles flex. I usually shove a prop at them to assimilate some contact with reality. They talk on the phone or read from a paper. Those are vital activities. Much or our own lives are spent doing them. And yet I often have to remind the students that "Hey, she can't be reading with her eyes looking off in another direction." Or "Hey, how can he be reading from a paper, you don't even have a paper in the drawing."

You must *enter into* the drama — I call it a one-drawing story — or your drawing will be like an astronaut floating off into space without a tether line.

If all you had on your drawing were two eyes and the paper the story would be communicated. What you draw around that can be anything from a beautiful girl to a character like Triton or from an Adonis to a character like Goofy. They become the actors, but the story is two eyes looking at the paper:

I keep searching for ways to persuade you to draw ideas (story), rather than to draw drawings (things). Last week the model was bending forward looking interestedly at something offstage. The student, whose drawing I have Xeroxed here, was starting to make a drawing of a head, never mind the back bend or the support the arms were providing or most important of all, the *look*.

"Telling" a story stimulates you to use things in your drawing that reinforce your concept of the pose. In my correction sketch, I accented the bend, which helped to thrust the look forward. It allowed me to pull the left shoulder back farther, clearing the space into which the look had to travel. The lines of the back and chest act as directional helps for the look. I got a little extra movement by utilizing one of animation's most valuable principles: squash and stretch — the front of the neck stretching, and the back of the neck squashing. Bending forward also allowed me to have the front of the shirt collar opening hang down, creating an ellipse that also helps to project the look forward by forming a sort of springboard for it. All these things work in tandem in putting over the one-drawing story concept.

You've seen the commercial "Don't leave home without it" (credit card). Here's one for drawing: "Don't make a drawing without it" (story).

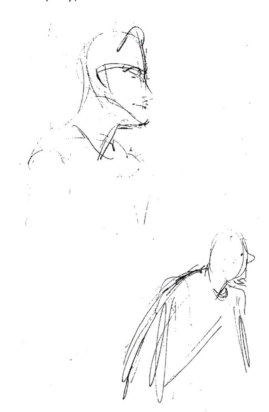

94 My Eye Is in Love

It's strange and mysterious and truly wonderful how some important things repeatedly pop into one's mind. It's as if their importance needs to mull around in the subconscious until their meanings can reach all the places where they might reveal their special significance. Like last year Bill Berg said, "I love to draw." That thought has haunted me ever since. Not that I wished I loved to draw, because *I* already do, but possibly because I desired to some day use the statement to inspire others to unabashedly embrace the same thought.

Last week one of the young artists in the intern program asked me: "What artists are best to study for ones preparation for animation?" My immediate reply was "All accomplished draftsmen would be good to study. Each one may have something different to offer." One thing to consider in ones study is the fact that future Disney productions will require a very broad area of expertise. They will require, on the one hand, drawing extremely cartoony characters like Roger Rabbit, and on the other hand, somewhat realistic (even classical) figures as in *Beauty and the Beast*. So perhaps right next to your volumes of ancient and modern "masters," you should have a selection of MAD magazines, some Disney classics, a set of Rien Poortvliet's masterfully illustrated books on men and animals, etc. If you weren't born a genius you're going to have to work hard to become one. Studying to become a genius can be a lot of fun, but becoming one is something I'll never be able to comment on.

Another statement that reverberates in my memory happened recently when I explained how to accomplish a certain gesture. The artist said "I wish I could think like that." It would be an oversimplification to say, "It's just a matter of being logical." Behind the logic of directing and acting, which is what you do when you make a drawing, goes a great deal of observation, study, sensitivity, and awareness.

I think being logical about telling a story in drawing is a lot like reading a road map. First one must have a destination, and then one must pick the streets that lead to that destination. When making a drawing, the goal (destination) for making the drawing must first be established (the story). Certainly making a drawing of a petite lady drinking a cup of tea would differ greatly in all ways from drawing a husky boxer preparing to knock out his opponent. The requirements for depicting either of these are quite obvious. Those requirements will hopefully be found in one's background and training, and must be activated as the drawing is being made.

Last week I analyzed some drawings in class wherein the model was looking at something. All looks, of course, are not the same, but one thing is for sure, the eyes if they are looking at something must be pointing toward the object being looked at. Not the zigzag course one would have to take following a street map, but an "as the crow flies" course. That is basic. To strengthen that look, the rest of the body must be drawn (no matter what the pose) in a way that helps to augment that look, and also to explain the meaning of the look.

I will spend more time on that subject in future handouts, but for now, I would like to end with a quote from a book called *My Eye is in Love* by Frederick Franck. It is a very inspiring bit of writing and it contains some thoughts that are apropos to the plights of all of us. Also it carries Bill's thought about loving to draw a bit further, perhaps a bit too dramatically, but so what! I rather enjoy people getting dramatic about the things they love.

> My eye is in love with this world. My eye is in love with its own perception of life. It affirms and rejoices. It is alive.
>
> Through my eye I relate to the world around me. The images on its retina are so poignant that I have to draw. For where the eye in love perceives, the hand involuntarily follows the forms as if to encompass them. Here is the beginning of drawing.
>
> To me then, drawing is a way of living a way toward life's fullness. It is not just a technique and certainly not mere skill. It is a total response. When I see a thing my first desire is not to possess what I see, or to eat it, to buy it, to name, to classify, or to change it. My first desire is to draw it.
>
> Political man, economic man, historical man, may well have contempt for this apparently senseless response to life. To me drawing, like singing or dancing, is an activity that temporarily delivers me from history. Maybe it transcends it.
>
> Drawing, while born from awareness, leads to an even greater awareness which involves me totally, yet impartially with all that passes before my eye: with mountains and human faces, city streets and humblest weeds, nude bodies, and the pebbles and shells of the seashore.
>
> What started as a book about drawing became a book about seeing and hence about being humanly aware and alive.

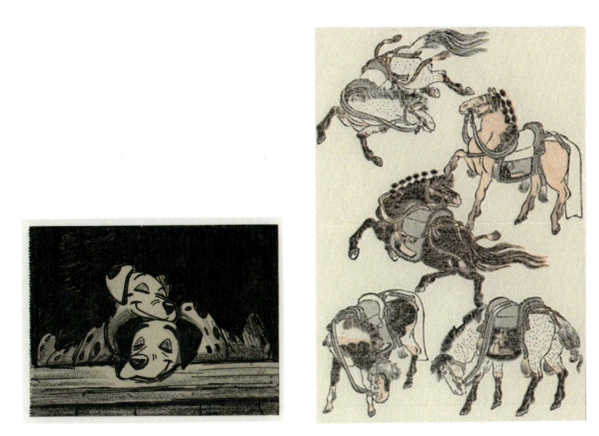

95 Become the Director

It helps to look for the abstract qualities of a pose. In a real sense that is what you do when you caricature something. To abstract means to "take out"; that is, "separate or isolate." When drawing a gesture, whatever it happens to portray, you have to, right from the beginning, decide what it is that you are going to say about it (in your drawing). When drawing from a model, for instance, you must "isolate" the important thing you need from the pose, subjugating all else to the role of support team. Ask yourself, — better yet, *tell yourself* — what is going on there, what is the story behind the pose? You have to separate or isolate just the vital thing that needs to be told. Isolate it so you can better portray it to your audience.

"It, it, it. What is this *it* you keep talking about?" you ask.

"It" is simply what you would *say* if you were describing the action or pose to someone in words. "He is bending over looking at something." "He is leaning on something." "He is sitting, leaning back on his right arm," etc.

I sang in a light opera group for ten years, having the privilege of singing several lead tenor roles. It was an eye opener watching the director work with a group of amateurs. He had to be very precise in his direction for there wasn't time to teach everyone how to act. His approach was much the same as an animator's approach to a scene of animation. That is, keep it simple, put over one idea at a time, and play it so the audience can see it clearly. I wish all of you could attend some stage play rehearsals to watch the director work, see how he molds all the elements of a play to move along unencumbered by distracting trivia.

Literally you, the artist, are the director of each drawing you make. A stage director does not tell the actor how to act. He encourages the actor to use gestures and movements that carry the story forward in a sincere, convincing, clear, and properly motivated manner.

If you would adopt the role of director as you draw, you might be less inclined to settle for (copy) what the model has presented to you. You would say to yourself, speaking to your drawing, because your drawing is the actor that is going to perform for the audience, "This is what you are trying to put over, so use whatever resourcefulness you can conjure up, to do it. If you need weight, here, I will give you weight. Do you need more stretch? Here, by golly, is some stretch. Do you need some squash because of what you are doing, okay, you got it."

Squash and stretch and weight are things that you don't find in anatomy books, but are abstract qualities that bring drawings to life. If the artist doesn't move in and take over the role of director, the drawings may deliver their performances in an amateur-like manner.

I saved a few of my correction drawings (again) to help put these ideas over. Sometimes the "story" as the model presents it is not too clear, and must undergo the director's touch. This was the case in these drawings. I think Craig is a great model, nevertheless, his poses are as with all models, only the embryo of a storytelling drawing. We the director/artist have to take the stage and re-mold the pose to make sure it has all the necessary elements to put across the "story."

I apologize for the lengthy explanations. It takes many words to explain all this, but as you who have watched me make these corrective sketches know, they take a matter of seconds (except when I keep on doodling long after I've illustrated the point). They will take *you* a matter of seconds also when you take over the directorship of your drawings.

Let's delve right into the first drawing (story: man leaning on lance). He won't look like he is leaning on something if he is standing straight up and down. One way to accomplish a lean is to thrust the hips back so the upper body is in a sense hanging in space with little or no body support, thus the rod suddenly takes on the function of support. Angling the legs into a triangular shape sends the eye upward, causing the hips to move backward and upward. Tilting the head to the left, away from the rod, forms a triangle like an arrow point, which helps to force the upper body downward. Lowering the shoulders causes the elbows to pull downward, which makes the hands become the support for all that weight and downward thrust.

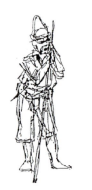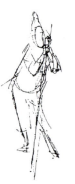

In the second drawing, (story: man sitting, leaning on his right hand), to get more weight on that hand, he must lean back farther. A good clear angle at the fanny and a straight line at his bottom helps to put more weight on his fanny. A roundish line can be too balloon-like. Keeping the lower half of his body where it is, and stretching the top part back to the left, allows the belly to be "played up." Angling the right leg toward us a little eliminates a feeling that everything is drawn in profile, and introduces a feeling of third dimension. Altering the angles of the legs sets up a nice tension — you can almost feel the left leg move inward.

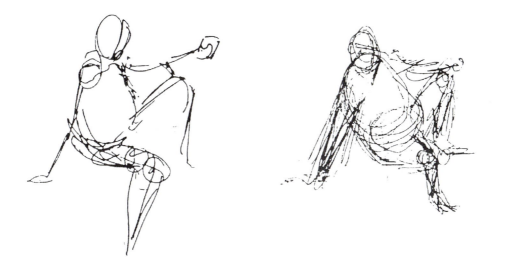

I made a couple of extra sketches to explain the leg angle thing, and to show the difference if the angles had gone the other way. If there are two parallel lines

||

they are static. But if one of the lines is angled

/|

it sets up a movement — to the left in this instance. When I angled the lower legs as I did, it set up a movement in the direction of the lean of the body, amplifying it (supporting role).

The next sketch angles this way,

|\

which causes a move to the right. That's what the model would do if he were going to straighten up.

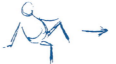

Another pose was an intent look at something being held in the hands. A good director would never allow the "story" to be hidden from the audience. He would tell the actor to re-stage it so everyone would know what was taking place. So I got his right shoulder out of the way, to clear a path for his look to travel in. I bent him over, intensifying his interest in what he was looking at. I pulled his fanny back to the left allowing the left leg to stretch out, causing the spectator's eye to sweep right up to the center of interest.

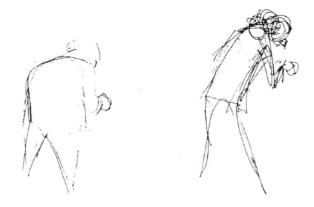

In the last drawing there is a solution to a problem a lot of you faced when turning the model into one of the fatter characters in the "Mermaid." This pose was one of many where a *look* was the story. Creating a massive body covered up the look in the student's drawing. Actually, the abstract of the pose was something like this — with look in the clear:

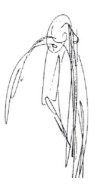

At any rate, one solution to the problem is to simply get the shoulder out of the way and project the head forward a little more. I attained the necessary bulk by humping up his back and featuring the belly a little more. The eye is not the farthest thing at the edge of the form, but at least it is in the clear. Note how the angle of the gun and the humped back help to project the look forward.

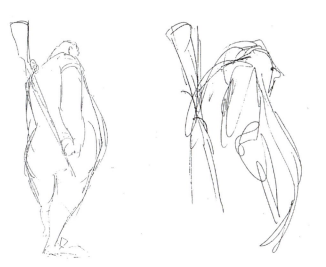

Different directors may find different ways of putting over a story point. There is no one "right" way — only logical, plausible and convincing ways. Any pose can be drawn a hundred ways and all of them be right. Right, that is, if it leads the viewer to the right conclusion, the story point.

One director working with several actors doing the same role would have to vary his directions and adapt them to each individual personality. But in each case his goal would be to sway the audience in the direction of the story. Likewise in drawing. Fifteen artists may be drawing the same pose, so there would likely be fifteen versions of the pose. However, each version must contain that one much needed common factor — communication — the communication of the story idea.

So as you draw, assume the role of director. Your drawings are the actors who are professionals and who are receptive, willing, responsive, adaptable, and even submissive to your expertise as a director. You are the one who reveals the true meaning of each action or pose. Without your presence and your special skill, the drawing could very easily end up just another drawing, just another, albeit well drawn, "map" of a figure.

Arouse your sense of the dramatic and resolve to weave a tale with each line you make. Let your drawings take new direction.

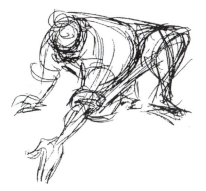

Here's a drawing that needs no criticism.

96 Hone Up or Bone Up

A little honest self-examination goes a long way. And since some of us have a long way to go (boy, am I nasty), it wouldn't hurt anything to just sit back for a moment to see where we are in relation to where we want to be. It's no secret that our shortcomings are the main bugaboos in our quest for advancement, both in our personal life and in our work skills. When we talk of skill, we're talking good old-fashioned study, observation, and application. There is no other way. Anyone who wants to learn and develop a skill must first pinpoint the basic essentials, shore up adequately in those, and from there one may fine-tune acquired skills to whatever degree they are so inclined.

How does one properly and effectively self-examine ones own place on the scale of excellence? Even those who are 8 on a scale of 10 should still feel the urge to improve. Perhaps a checklist will be revealing. If I were to propose one for animation cartoonists, it might look something like this:

1. A fair knowledge of anatomy and the ability to apply it.
2. A feel for depicting action and the ability to apply it.
3. An understanding of the rules of perspective (overlap, diminishing size, etc.) and the ability to apply them.
4. An understanding of squash and stretch and the ability to apply it.
5. A feel for how to adjust a pose to bring out the story point and the ability to apply it.
6. A sense of timing and the ability to apply it.
7. A sensibility for staging and the ability to apply it.

This list is by no means complete, but for starters, read it again checking off the categories you might need a little help with. Bear in mind that each point in question ends with "… and the ability to apply it." I have known some who talked a good drawing or animation, but when it came to practical application, theory outran applicability. So be honest. This is self-examination. Others may care about you and want to help, but cannot invade your privacy. That's your domain.

I think you'll feel good if you actually check off some of the items on the list, and especially if you make the check become a resolve to hone up on the ones that are "iffy," and to bone up on the ones that are absent.

Resolve to start (or continue one already in progress) some program of self-betterment, one that is streamlined so it does not become a great burden time-wise or any-other-wise. It's surprising how much progress you can make if your problems are isolated so you can concentrate on them. This also allows you to measure your progress, and each small goal reached helps to build confidence and helps to clarify your overall goal.

So hone up or bone up! Or both. You'll feel good about yourself, and with good reason.

One further word. We have a tendency to blame our shortcomings on our parents, our acquaintances, our memory, our lack of time, etc. But let's acknowledge the fact that we have all the opportunities (or can create them) that any other person has ever had. Some of the greatest achievements were accomplished by people who had mental, physical, or emotional problems to overcome. A real heavy-duty inner strength emerges from overcoming the things that seem to stand in your way. One way to gain muscle is to lift weights. So in the skill area grapple with the roadblocks and your creative muscles will grow.

Here is an interesting formula I once saw in a book on writing:

$$T + S = J, \text{ Talent} + \text{Skill} = \text{Joy.}$$ May *your* life be filled with Joy.

97 The Illustrated Handout

Last week I nearly got lynched because of a handout with no illustrations, so in self-defense, if nothing else, I submit to the insatiable appetite of artists for illustrated texts.

Herein are some more drawings from the evening class with my suggestions. Please understand these are not "how-to-draw" corrections, they are suggestions designed to encourage the artist to analyze the pose rather than simply attempt to copy it. If the model is bending over, for instance, the thought "bending over" must register in the artist's mind. This allows her or you to say, okay, the model is bending over, what can I do in my drawing to put over that idea. By imagining the feel or sensation of bending over or by actually getting up and mimicking the pose you can personally experience the tensions on certain muscles, the distribution of weight, and whatever else it takes to carry out that particular task.

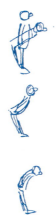

The "whatever else" depends on what the story is behind the bend. For instance, a simple bend might require just the hips (tail end) to protrude as a counterbalance.

If the back is arched, the head will automatically raise, for the neck has a tendency to continue the action of the backbone.

If the back is bent the other way the head will be forced to lower itself because the spine is bent over and the neck is part of the spine.

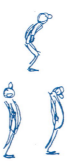

If the knees are bent, the hips do not need to protrude so far in back, because when the knees bend forward there is less need for counterbalance. Besides, the hips have to follow wherever the knees go.

When the back is arched the other way there is more flexibility in the neck area so the head can tilt straight up or almost straight down.

These things may all seem boringly obvious to you but you can see how important it is when interpreting a gesture with a bend in it — to say nothing of all the modifications and combinations involving arms, legs, knees, hips, shoulders, etc. Mind you, I have just touched the surface of the bend. There are limitless poses that require the same careful analysis to make sure they are appropriate anatomically and gesturally. Physiognomy is a good word to contemplate in this regard. It means, in part, "The art of discovering temperament and character from outward appearance… hence inner character as revealed outwardly."

Sometimes when drawing a model in a bending pose, the action is not all that apparent, so to get some dynamics into the drawing, you have to either know what is taking place intellectually, or feel it kinesthetically. Here is a fairly nice drawing of a possible Ariel (done by the way, from a male model with a sailor outfit on) in a bend that is slightly passive. I suggested two alternate bends that might have conveyed the impression that the character was a little more excited about what she was looking at.

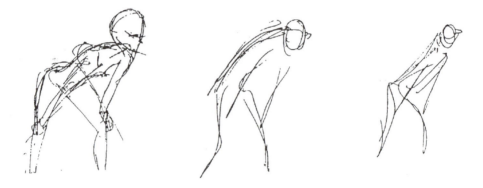

If you try to pick out lines on the model to copy, you will often be thwarted, for the lines needed to put over the action may not be there. In such a case you would have to "feel" the action and create lines that would communicate it. In this next pose the left side of the model was a nebulous jumble forming an almost straight vertical line. All it yielded by way of expression was a tangent — clear from the shoulder to the ankle. It needed a clarified line to depict what was happening.

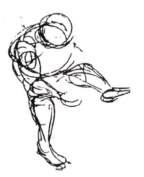 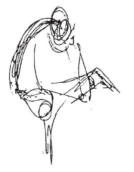

The next drawing is a very interesting one. It is an expressive drawing, but the model happened to be bending into the point of interest quite a bit more, hence my suggestion.

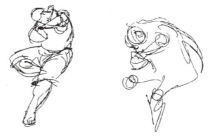

The next pose was a very subtle one where the model was slightly bent over, staring blankly into air as if contemplating something. I suggested a little more bend with the face (and eyes) protruding as if looking into a mental image-balloon a few feet in front of him.

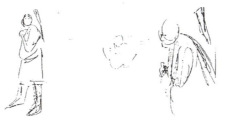

The next pose is one where the model was reaching for something below the edge of the model stand. To strengthen the pose I merely planted the right hand, right knee, and left foot, then stretched (and bent) him *forward into the stretch*. This brought his right shoulder forward causing a forward tilt- ing angle on the right arm. It also thrust his chest and head forward so there is more weight on the right hand. Plus it got his eyes out in the open, creating an uncluttered path for the look. These things can be spotlighted if the pose or gesture is analyzed from the standpoint of the "story" behind the pose.

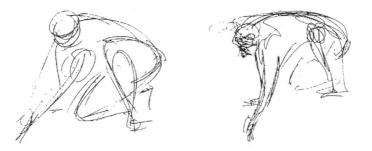

In the next drawing, I stopped the artist before he had a chance to work out his problem. The man is tired from carrying this heavy box. He is slumped over, perhaps looking back to see if anyone is fol- lowing him. Is there something valuable in the box; perhaps his entire belongings? Or has he stolen something and is edgy about being apprehended? Any such story points will inspire you to select the essential elements for putting them over.

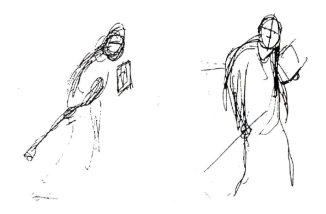

One of the interns asked me, what about days when you just can't seem to draw anything? I suggested he create a project like drawing a bend or a stretch or some action like that, which requires getting involved on a "story" level, where he can forget "drawing." Working out ways of putting over a story will suggest ways of drawing it. When you say, "squash or stretch," "joy," "fright," or "take," there suddenly appear ways of depicting these actions or emotions. You don't sit down and start drawing muscles or clothes or legs or arms. What you draw is a squash or stretch or joy or a "take," etc. If one of the lines you put down seems to suggest what you have chosen to illustrate that line will inspire others that will "chip in" and help. On the other hand, if you are too involved in "drawing," per se, you might forget what you started out to do.

Drawing is not easy. It requires a lot of thought. So keep your mind agile. Flex it constantly so that it doesn't atrophy. Give it the reins and let it soar at times. Other times subdue it and utilize its fantastic range of possibilities.

Here is one more drawing in this series. It's not a bend problem, but a tangent problem. The right leg seems to go right back to the left hip. A simple adjustment remedies the illusion.

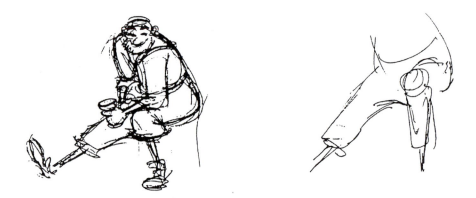

The last page of this handout is a bonus selection, devoted to some excellent drawings that are translations of the live model into a character from the "Mermaid." These are "cold" translations by artists who have not drawn the character before. It is heartening to see such resourceful and skillful powers of adaptation.

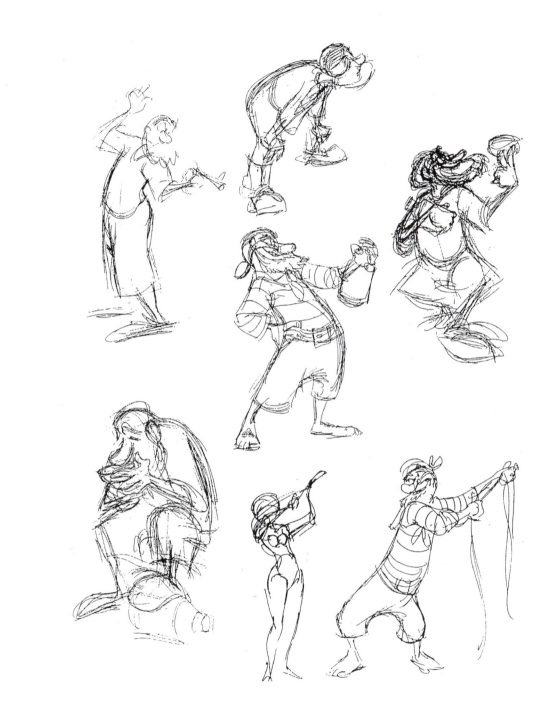

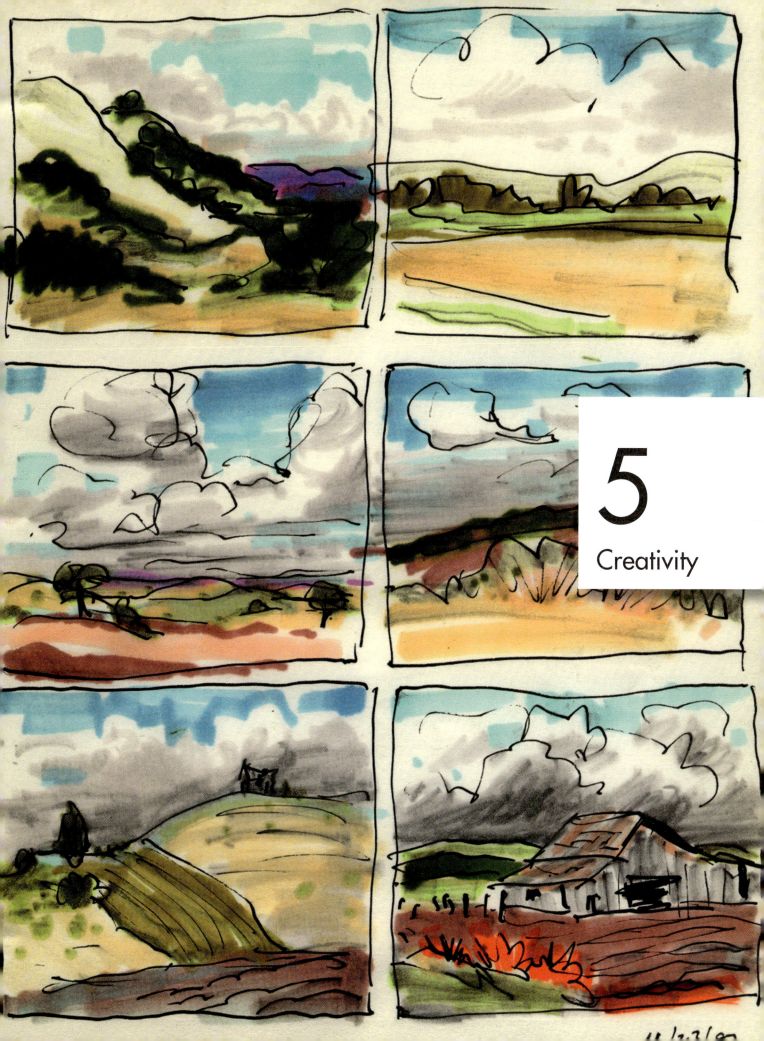

98 Drawing on the Artist Within

It's sometimes beneficial to assume the role of investigator, explorer, or researcher. That prompts you to ask questions such as "how does this affect me?," "where has it gotten me?," or "have I been given enough information to benefit from it or to draw any kind of personal conclusion?" There's nothing wrong with this kind of attitude — it isn't negative in any sense of the word. Especially in a pursuit like yours where drawing is your business, and you have to ferret out all the usable information you can from all possible sources.

One case in question was the lecture on the book *Drawing on the Artist Within* written by Betty Edwards. The necessarily limited time given it forced me to go back to the book to renew the impression I had gotten from it. I think the idea of having lectures, films, and a research library are a praiseworthy contribution the studio has offered the employees for their growth and progress. But I also feel that it is up to each person to glean from the material what they feel is needed for their personal improvement. I thought you might benefit from my reaction to the lecture. Much of the lecture had to do with using a kind of "automatic" drawing for problem solving. Since I'm not pre-occupied with solving my problems, I reread the book for what I am interested in, seeing and thinking more clearly in regard to drawing. The book is a "gold mine" for such things.

Inspiration loomed up on the title page that made me want to read on and to open doors of awareness: "An inspirational and practical guide to increase your creative powers." Then, the very first sentence of the preface is a mood and attitude setter: "Writing this book has been a process of discovery." I haven't really gotten into the book yet and my mind is spinning with anticipation. It's not that I am so interested in Betty Edwards having experienced a process of discovery; I want to experience the process of discovery myself. She goes on to say that, "direct perception," a different kind of "seeing," is an integral part of thinking and hence the creative process. The purpose of the book, she says, is: "The role the visual language plays in the creative process." Also, learning to draw is not the end. "For in learning to draw, I believe you will learn how to see differently. And that, in turn, will enhance your powers of creative thought."

Pretty heavy stuff!

One of the many visual conceptions of creativity that Betty Edwards found was this one by a French mathematician Henri Poincare.

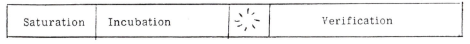

Saturation	Incubation		Verification

Illumination

It's a graphic depiction of a very nebulous mental process called creativity. This creative process does not belong to artists alone. It applies to people in all walks of life — business people, mechanics, inventors, writers, musicians — you name it. For the purpose of drawing, there is an attempt to pin it down to make it more available. In the drawing class I try to get the students to look at the model for a few seconds of intense "seeing" to form a first impression of the essence of the pose, then strive to put that first impression down on paper. If the drawing starts to slip away (and this is important) go back to the first impression. Better still, hang on tenaciously to that first impression as you draw. Graphically it might look like this (after Poincare).

First Impression		Draw it

Illumination

Here is a more flowing version of it, wherein the left section shows a search for, and forming of a first impression (saturation and incubation), the middle section is the formed impression (illumination), and the final section shows the illumination stage sustained throughout the drawing process (verification).

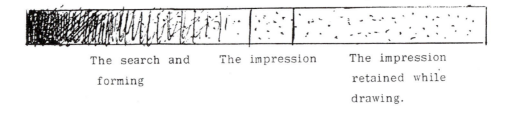

The search and   The impression   The impression

forming   retained while

                                              drawing.

The research and discovery of the two major modes of the human brain by Roger Spery in the 1950s, which earned him a Nobel Prize for medicine, has led to a better understanding of the creative process. Betty Edwards bases most of her teaching on the activities of the right and left sides of the brain.

I was once tested on a feedback machine (electroencephalograph) to measure my alpha wave capabilities. When the alpha wave was attained the machine's normal squawking sound (beta wave indication) soared into a high and pleasant bird-like tweet. I reached that desired state in seconds. The tester engaged me in conversation to see if that would cut the connection, but the tweet continued. He then had me count from 100 downward by 2s, but the tweet continued. He said that was quite amazing, and what did I think or feel was the reason or process that allowed me to think on an intellectual plane and still retain the relaxed state of alpha. I said it was as if I had two sides to the brain (this was before we had heard of Betty Edwards) with one side of the brain I could think and talk while with the other side I could remain in a meditative state.

Since then I have experimented with a sort of dialing in and out of the left and right modes to different degrees of intensity. In knowing for instance, a certain amount of L mode activity, that is, intellectual maneuvering and use of detail is needed in drawing, along side an interpretive, storytelling, and emotional R mode involvement, it is up to me to generate a compatible blend of the two. It's not magic. It's just that once you have summed up all the information into a first impression (R mode); you have to enlist the help of the L mode to manipulate the pencil in the physical process of drawing (making communicable marks on a piece of paper). If the L mode starts to isolate parts or details and tries to take over to verify its knowledge of "things," you simply have to dial it down a bit and dial up the R mode, which is patiently holding on to that first impression and is eager to communicate it through the drawing process. If, on the other hand, the drawing becomes a mess of scribbled lines, though expressive (R mode loves this), then the L mode has to be dialed up to reestablish a touch of realism.

"Mode dialing" can also work for you when you are tired and need a pick up. Turn up the R mode to full capacity for just a few seconds and the alpha state will have the effect of a battery charge. I don't think Betty Edwards gets into this use of the brain waves, but a little additional research may prove interesting and/or helpful for you.

Well, all that, and I haven't gotten beyond the first chapter of *Drawing on the Artist Within*. Maybe I'll get on to the next chapter some time in the future — if you're interested.

I'd like to close with a little anecdote. When someone in the class is making a very expressive drawing, I like to grab it from them at its peak stage (before it gets bogged down with detail) and show it to the rest of the class. It opens up possibilities, stirs up the "juices," and charges the air with a sense of creativity — a "something is happening here" thing.

A couple of weeks ago I grabbed a drawing from James Fujii and a visiting artist next to him said, "He doesn't even let the guy finish his drawing." I said to him, "The point is not to finish the drawing, the point is to get the *idea*." And James had gotten the idea.

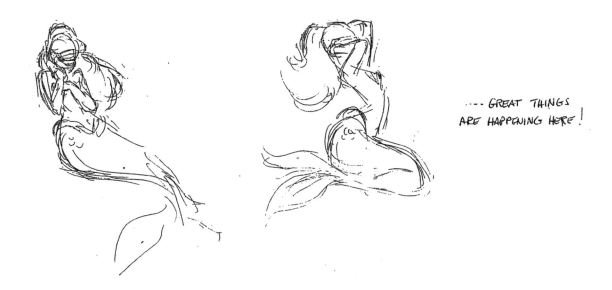

---

99 Fine Tuning the Gesture

Every artist must know the basic structure of the human body (animals, too) and how the parts work in action. These bodily movements are what all mankind uses for gestural expression. You shrug your shoulder to indicate doubt, not knowing, or resignation. And to complete the gesture you raise your eyebrows, the corners of your mouth curl up, and your cheeks puff up causing your eyes to squint. You duck your head to accent the uplifted shoulders. The structure of your torso, shoulders, and face are the parts you use for the action. You twist around, squint, and cup one hand over an ear in a listening attitude. Again, you must know how the body parts work; their capabilities, and their limitations to convincingly draw that action. Even so, every person (character) having a different personality; a slightly different body structure, or enacting the move for a different purpose or in a different attitude, all require a sensitive use of an otherwise mechanical action. You are naturally interested in the mechanics of anatomy, for that is an important tool used in drawing and animation. But you are also interested in storytelling, so it is important to sensitize yourself to the established forms of body communication.

Knowledge of basic anatomy is necessary to adequately portray the gestures. After all, in the overall development of mankind, the physical body came first and the gestures only after our brains developed to where they had to invent a means of dramatizing our thoughts. There ensued an almost universal language of body gesture. Everyone uses body language according to their physiological makeup and their personality. The artist (you) has to be able to capture any number of gestures and actions depending on the needs of the story and character,

In the Tuesday and Wednesday evening classes we attempt to carry drawing a step beyond just copying the pose. We try to fuse the anatomical model with a gestural "story," wherein the various parts of the body supply the fine-tuning for the overall gesture. In other words, what does the body have to do to accomplish this or that gesture? The study serves two purposes. First, the study perfects our facility in drawing, and secondly it is in a sense studying acting, so that when we are faced with an acting problem (for animation) we can skillfully merge the two purposes together into a first rate drawing or scene, one that is well-drawn and well-acted.

I saved some drawings from a recent class that might help to illustrate the kind of reasoning that one might undergo (and nurture) to accomplish that goal. In the first drawing the model was carrying a coat over his right shoulder. I reasoned that to keep the coat from slipping off, he would lift that shoulder higher. In thinking through such actions, if there are any doubts in your mind, be the pragmatist and assume the action yourself to get the feel of it. You certainly want to be authentic in any gesture you use. When the right shoulder is raised, the body adjusts by raising the left hip. Not only does it establish the pose as genuine but it also adds more dynamism to the drawing.

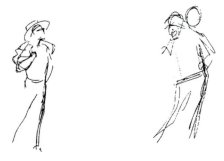

The second example is the same problem only by a different artist. This neglect to "enter into the spirit" of the gesture seems to be universal.

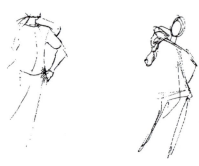

In the third drawing the problem is similar. Again, the body does certain things to produce certain body language. Every drawing you make should go through your action analysis computer to make sure whatever you put down will be convincing to the viewer. In this drawing I reasoned that he could have his thumb tucked in his belt and could be pushing down (typical western pose) while the shoulders and hips do their usual thing. In doing so I eliminated the duplication of angles in the two arms. And, when your shoulders tilt to the left, your head tends to tilt to the right.

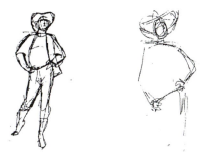

In the fourth drawing the problem was increased by having to draw the angle of the shoulders from the side. Telling yourself that the right shoulder is lower than the left is one clue to the solution.

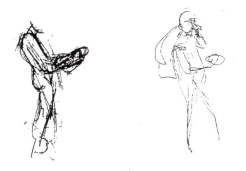

In the fifth drawing the problem was similar. Again I used the angles of the shoulder and hips to do away with the duplication of angles on both arms, and to tilt the head in opposition to the shoulder angle. Another common error is to tilt the hips but still have the upper leg connections level.

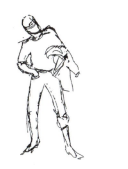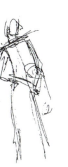

These corrections are not meant to infer that there is just one right way to draw something. The point is that all actions should be done in a logical way, both physically and gesturally to get the maximum impact or impression out of the drawing. Naturally, great liberties can be taken to accomplish a desired effect. It can be an impossibility as far as real life authenticity is concerned, but it has to seem logical. The more cartoony or caricatured the character is, the more wild the action can be and the more liberties may be taken to affect it.

I couldn't resist adding a page of drawings that needed no correction. These are delightfully expressive. Lots of nice angles, no parallels, no tangents. Outstanding analysis of the poses. In a word — extraordinary.

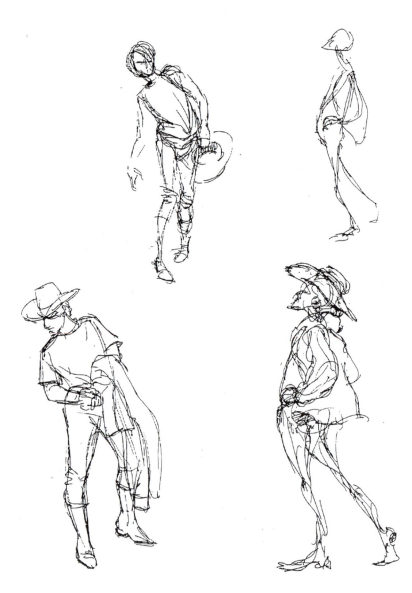

100 For a Better Gesture, Adverbs

In an earlier handout I suggested the concept of drawing verbs instead of nouns. The idea was that a verb is active (run, bend, twist, gesticulate, etc.) while a noun is a motionless object (man, woman, arm, leg, clothes, etc.). Thinking of your drawing as a verb will add life and movement to even the subtlest action.

You can carry the thought a little further by adding an adverb. This will add character, personality, and acting style to your drawings or animation, because it tells *how, where, when,* or *why.* For instance, he runs *gracefully, up a hill, in the morning, because he is in a race.* And, he bent his body *sharply at the waist, just before* tossing the ball, *to get snap into* his attempt at a basket. I stretched those sentences to include how, where, when. and why. Just the *how* is indispensable in forming a good first impression for a gesture drawing and a great help executing it. For instance, instead of drawing a character just bending over, he could bend over gracefully, awkwardly, or using his knees because he was going to pick up something heavy, or obsequiously, as if bowing to a superior. All of those adverbs or adverbial phrases describe how he bent over. The when, where, and why have more to do with staging, story, and reasons, but are never completely absent, especially in animation where they are integral parts of the story.

Imagine yourself acting a part in a stage play. You have the first entrance to make. How, where, when, and why are all factors that would have to be worked but. What kind of play is it — comedy, drama, low-key, or melodrama? What kind of a part do you play? Do you stumble onto the stage, saunter on, swagger on, sneak on? The verb is *walk* and the adverb is how, when, where, and why? They are important. The mood of the whole play might hinge on your entrance.

I once did such an entrance in an operetta. I was a smartly dressed lieutenant, a lead tenor part. I made the appropriate how, where, and when but the why escaped me — I forgot my lines. I was fully aware of the need to keep in character (or in this case, establish it) so I ad-libbed some lines in an appropriate way to some ladies already on stage. I was careful to stay near the back of the stage, though, so I could hear the cue person prompt me. In a classroom situation where we are doing gesture drawings from a live model, the *how* should suffice to bring off an expression befitting the character and the pose.

How does he look? Glare, squint, surprised, leaning forward, tilting head, "down the nose," head turned slightly aside, one eye cocked, passively, disgustedly, happily, elatedly, sleepily? All those looks are different and have different meanings, and if you want your drawing to have meaning, you'll have to pick the appropriate attitude and build your drawing around it. If you are a person who gesticulates a lot while talking, you enjoy body language and would not pass up an opportunity to "punctuate" your dialog with a well-chosen gesture. You do it to emphasize your meaning, and in some cases your personality. You've seen some people who wave their arms around like a lame windmill, the emphasis is five frames off and inappropriate to begin with. Actor/animators can't afford to do that while drawing — they have to pick the proper verb to illustrate the gesture and emphasize it with the proper adverb (and time it just right, to boot).

How a character carries off a gesture depends on his individuality, and the reason for the gesture. The two added together will pretty much decide how it is to be done. Mickey could twist aside apologetically, smile sheepishly, and say, "Ah, gee whiz." But can you picture Roger Rabbit doing that. Roger would be bouncing off the walls, yelling "holy mackerel" or "may day, may day."

Even the most professional of professionals sometimes sweat over seemingly simple gestural problems. Last week director Burny Mattinson showed me some sketches he had drawn for a Pluto reaction in the *Prince and the Pauper* storyboard. I have no idea how many were thrown away but I retrieved

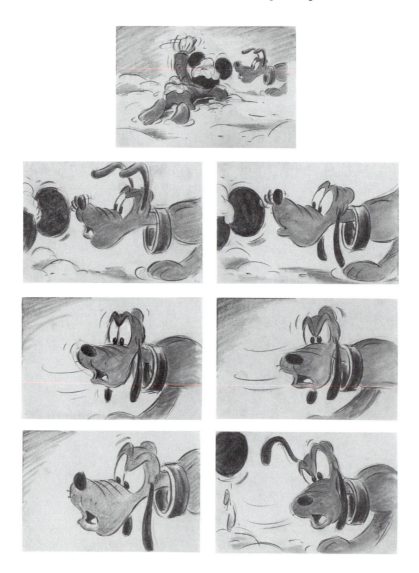

several of them to illustrate his concern in getting the proper gesture; Pluto's reaction is a verb, but how he does it is an adverb. Here is a partial list of verbs that might describe his reaction: muse, contemplate, reflect, study, deliberate, ponder, wonder, conjecture, guess, or speculate. Adverbs that might tell *how* those verbs were acted upon might be intently, confusedly, searchingly, comically, seriously, or deeply. At any rate, this is all just to suggest that even a "cartoon" sometimes needs some serious analysis. And the solution, most of the time, can be found in choosing the right verb and adverb.

I was going to end right there but I didn't want you to think that you would have to go through that kind of a thinking process every time you make a drawing. Actually your brain computes such things in a matter of seconds, with just a little guidance on your part. But of course the more you read, study good movies and plays (both drama and comic), and observe; the more reference material your brain will have to work with.

Now, as long as there is some space left over on this page, perhaps a drawing from last week's session would be nice. As you might have guessed from its sketchiness, it was put down in short order. And naturally since you're seeing it in this stage of completion it means I snatched it from the artist before he had a chance to go any further. It is a charming drawing. But since I'm being paid to find fault, how much more charming it would have been if the upper arms didn't form a strong "V" shape for that, along with the inverted "V" of the legs, sets up an hour glass image.

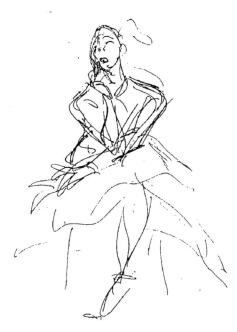

101 *Omni — on Creativity*

In the April *Omni Magazine* there is a good article on creativity. I highly recommend it. But I can't resist writing about it also. To begin with, a very reassuring statement appears at the head of the article, "No correlation between measured IQ and creativity exists. Intuition, more than rational thought, appears to be vital to the creative thinking process." I don't know what my IQ is — it's probably so low that I purposely forgot it. Hopefully yours is high, but if not — take heart. According to Candice Pert of the National Institute of Mental Health, creativity comes from the spiritual realm, the collective consciousness. And the mind is in a different realm than the molecules of the brain. The brain is a receiver, not a source. Pretty heady stuff, eh?

Colin Martindale, University of Maine psychologist, thinks the creative state of mind has a broad, unfocused sort of attention. But in focusing your attention, you essentially defeat creative efforts. This is interesting because in animation the mind has to be focused on a great many things. That is why

I think the concept of a left and right mode of the brain is helpful. (Though this article points out it may more likely be the front and back modes.) If while creating, in terms of drawing and animation, one can be aware of the possibility of calling on one or the other mode, or a percentage blend of the two, both needs can be fulfilled. For instance, in our classroom situation, we try to deal with the need to call upon our knowledge of anatomy and other necessary details (left brain activity), while at the same time attempting to resolve the elements before us into a coherent whole, a meaningful gesture (right brain activity). The article points out that *one of the attributes of the creative person is Mental Mobility.* This allows us to observe the model, while at the same time adjusting what we see to better tell the story we have attributed to it. *Another trait is the willingness to take risks.* It requires a certain amount of risk taking to part from the model to better caricature the gesture. To just sit and copy the model is playing it safe — not taking risks. The article says *creative people are not so responsive to stimuli as other personality types.* So it should be easier for the creative person not to be held down by the stimuli of the model's presence, but use the information in an innovative way, and take risks. "Along with risk taking, comes the acceptance of failure as part of the creative quest, and the ability to learn from such failure." No one knows better than we ourselves how many bad drawings we've made, but they just make us more determined to succeed — we use them as stepping stones in our "creative quest." Perkins of Harvard says "Contrary to popular image, the creative person is not a self-absorbed loner." He can put aside his ego and seek advice from trusted colleagues. Important, though, to the whole kit and caboodle, is the fact that "... the driving force behind creative effort is inner motivation."

Lest you are harboring the idea that creativity can only be associated with such things as hit songs, award-winning novels, painting masterpieces, and mind-boggling inventions, let me suggest that any activity you undertake each moment of your life can be creative. Every drawing you make has whatever portion of creativity you choose to instill in it. Every time you resist copying the model and instead draw or caricature the "story," you have distilled from the pose, you are creating. You are strengthening your ability to create.

I have only skimmed the surface of the article, so if you have an opportunity, read it. You will probably find things in it that will mean more to you than those I have picked out. Here's one last "mind blower." We may sometimes feel like such a small part of the whole picture, but this suggestion of University of California's Frank Barron may help put it into perspective: "Creativity is a unique force in the universe." So in light of this, may the force be with you.

You've probably heard the saying, "there's nothing new under the sun." Well, that may or may not be true, depending on your philosophical bend, but according to Webster (I think it's Webster — my dictionary has lost its cover long ago), the act of creating (creativity) is the "presentation of a new conception in an artistic embodiment." That is what you do when you draw your conception of a subject, be it from a model or from your imagination. It would be pretty hard for you to invent a new gesture, but there are infinite ways you might bring into being an exciting, spine-tingling version of the ones you do draw. Remember the quote from the *Omni Magazine* article: "The driving force behind creative effort is inner motivation." Well, whatever dictionary I have says that motive means "that within the individual, rather than without ..."

So motivation is your own unique, inner thing that prompts you to draw something the way you do (or want to). I say, want to, because a lot of times you see a gesture in your mind but it doesn't come out that way on paper. That's the hang-up we're working on — how to short-circuit that impulse to copy the model. How to form a "story" in our minds and draw that story the way we see it.

Here is a drawing from last week's class. The student's drawing has some nice touches in it, but it just doesn't say "guy leaning back, with hands clasped at knees." The motivation for making the drawing should have been to describe that action in the artist's own unique way, but certainly in a creatively convincing way. In my sketch I tried to let the viewer feel the lean back, the pull of the arms and the ensuing sensation of balance.

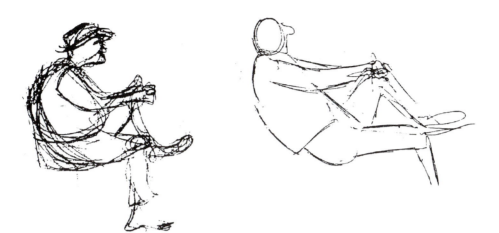

102 Metamorphosis

On April 4 and 5 we had Ken Martin, mime, posing for us in the evening class. I watched him closely as he changed from one pose to another. Coming out of a pose was like deflating a balloon that had been blown up with some magical life giving gas. Then there was a pause as the human mime shifted his human body into what the human mind had contrived. You could see the mental wheels turning; you could sense a process of metamorphose like when a butterfly emerges from the pupa stage, or when mixing red and blue paint together and they become purple. Suddenly out of nowhere there was this pose. It was like being transported into a small portion of some fanciful world — just the mime's portion of it — isolated there on the model's stand. And he would hold that intense, fanciful preoccupation for ten or fifteen minutes. His concentration on that pose seemed constantly fed by some power source within him, so that, even as electricity flows continually into a light bulb to sustain the light, the mime's intention flowed into the pose, keeping it alive. And each time you looked at it, it was as if seeing it for the first time.

You, the artist, are in a sense, a mime too. *They* do it with their body — *you* do it with pen or pencil. Read that paragraph again substituting yourself in place of Ken. *You* are performing for the viewer. *You* are the one who has to bring that fanciful world to life, to a kind of reality. *You* are the one who has to shift into that fanciful world. *You* are the one who has to sustain that intensity of interest until the job is completed. *You* are the one who has to summon up constant renewal from within, as with electricity which sustains the lamp's light. It is *you* who has to get a good, exciting, imaginative gesture down on paper. And no matter how difficult the job (or how tired you happen to be), it has to look as fresh as when you first saw it or conceived it: just as exciting, shocking, or awesome; just as new or deep-felt.

Ken will be with us this week again. In these sessions he will tell us about his methods, his inner motivation, and how he translates that into its physical counterpart. It should be very exciting.

We were fortunate to have the San Francisco Mime Troupe give a demonstration and workshop. We learned that their approach to theater is to satirize people and ideas, provide music and entertainment, and to give a "shot of hope." They shun subtle revelation of character, intense psychological truth, and deep probing of personal relationships. They practice two forms of theater: commedia, designed to make you laugh; and melodrama, designed to make you cry.

To bypass having to develop their characters as the play progresses, they have developed (or distilled) eight types of characters for commedia and eight types for melodrama. As soon as one of these types walks on stage, their character is instantly recognizable, so the audience is not waiting to find out who they are, but what they will do, and what will be done to them." The actors merely learn the physical attributes of each stereotype, and play that to the hilt. Some of the animation characters are, for instance, Donald, Goofy, and Bugs Bunny. The way they enter a scene tells you that something of a stereotypic nature will inevitably happen. Most of our feature characters have some of the attributes of the 16 mime stereotypes but usually their character is developed as the story progresses.

Animators can benefit from a general knowledge of the stereotyped characters, but their acting requirements extend far beyond merely pigeonholed characterizations. Cartoon features are more complicated than melodramas, so they require more versatility than the mime has. There is need for a wider scope of acting ability. The animator must be thoroughly grounded in drawing and acting techniques. Drawing alone is broken down into a knowledge of anatomy, perspective, foreshortening, squash and stretch, silhouette, overlap and follow through, caricature, and much more. The animator's range of acting abilities must cover human, animal, birds, fish, mechanical props, and special effects, such as water, smoke, etc.

There is a similarity to both the mime's and the animator's techniques. Neither should rely on their knowledge of the stereotyped characters or stereotyped action. True, there is a sort of universal body language, but its application should be always fresh, imaginative, and creative.

I saved some drawings from the class that suggest possible solutions to some of the problems that plague us. In the first one, a view of a pose which seems to hide what is really happening, I advocated "cheating!" I merely turned the subject enough to clarify his stance. There is nothing meritorious about reproducing a straight-on pose, unless you have accepted it as a challenge, but you do owe the viewer a clear picture of what is happening to your subject (your actor). Remember, a drawing that does not tell a story can never be good, and one that does tell a story can never be wholly bad.

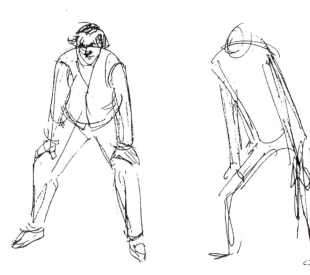

In the second drawing it was the same problem — a straight-on view. Just because you get stuck with a bad view of the model doesn't mean you can't re-stage it slightly. As a matter of fact, sometimes it best that you do.

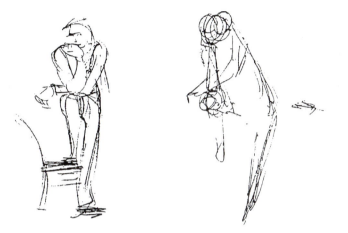

In the next drawing I tried to create a deeper interest in whatever the model was pleading to. If it was some kind of supplication, perhaps it could be a little more emphatic, passionate, or deeply felt. Everything in the drawing should point to the object of his plight.

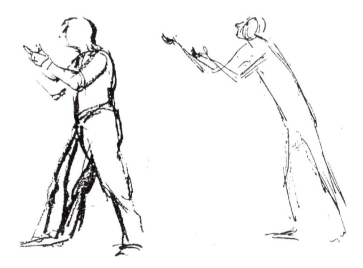

This was a similar pose. When interested in something, you have a tendency to move in for a closer look. Extending the right arm helped to project the look. Opening a passage by separating the arms and staging the hands so they form a kind of tunnel or channel that point toward the object of his pleading, frees that area for the look and attention to travel unimpeded. In the student's drawing — the elbows touching, the thumbs pointing back, the whole body leaning backward — all tend to focus the attention on the model's apparent dilemma, perhaps fear, anxiety, or cowardice.

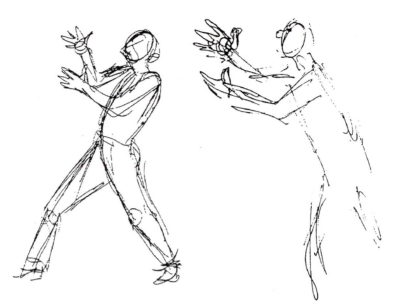

In the next pose, angles and spaces are important in focusing interest on whatever he is looking at. I opened up more space around the left palm to more freely receive the look. I angled the fingers of the right hand to help project the look down to the palm. In the student's drawing the right hand angles upward toward the face, directing attention to that area, as if making a sounding board for his voice. I made use of angles to propel the interest to the palm. The angles of the student's face and hands sends the attention in an outward direction.

It also encloses an area between the neck and the arm, which traps you into a circular motion. You are soon exhausted trying to find a way out. The principle behind the angles is that two lines like this

are static. By angling one of them, a motion is set up.

Three or more such lines accelerates the movement.

Anyway, here is the drawing and suggestion.

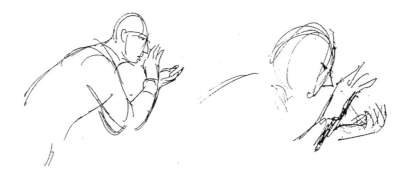

Later I made another sketch angling the right hand even farther.

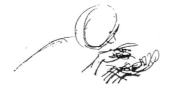

Then I decided to get the right hand out of the way altogether, clearing a direct channel from the eye to the palm of the left hand. Compare it with the original.

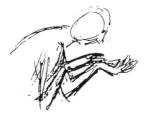

Now everything on the drawing converges on that point. Notice how the angles of the upper arms help

the lower arms, too.

Even the angle of the hands help.

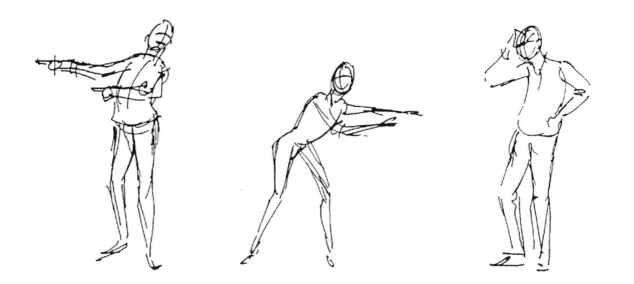

103   Mime

We had mime, Ken Martin, as our model for a second time. In this session he lectured and posed at the same time, illustrating his talk with appropriate gestures. I taped his voice, but the buzzing of the overhead lights interfered badly. I will try to get it transcribed and made available through the research library. I transcribed a bit of it and have woven it into a handout.

Pantomime, the art of silence. Possibly it was the first language. Before the word was the gesture; before the gesture was the need. Everything starts with a need. All art begins with feeling. This need or urge or feeling as it evolves in the body becomes a gesture. Gestures define ideas. Ideas generate energy. This energy travels through the body and emerges from the body in a particular way depending on the idea, and the way you choose to express it much like music. The musician uses notes, tones. His ideas form themselves in his mind as tunes and melodies, which he puts down on paper to be eventually played by himself or by an orchestra. Other people's needs emerge from their bodies in terms of painting or sculpture. The painter uses line, form, color, space … his ideas come out that way. The dancer uses his body in space. His feelings, needs, and urges come out in terms of rhythmic, physical movement. The writer expresses himself with words, putting his ideas into words — written so other people can read them. The mime uses only his body in space.

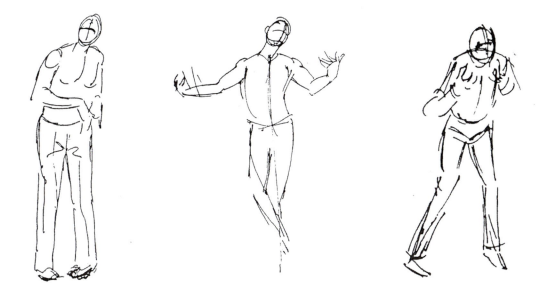

Ken said the mime's job is to create a kind of outline, minus props and sets, and the audience fills in with their imagination. In contrast, the animator uses props, plus third dimensional backgrounds, plus dialog to convince the audience, leaving nothing to chance. But the artist should employ the mime's techniques of body language and gesture. A good drawing or a good scene of animation should be easily "read" even without the props, background, and dialog.

The mime uses gestures, he uses attitudes of the body, and he uses illusion. Attitudes of the body suggest what the character is feeling. The mime has to show more than one thing: what the character is like, how he is involved, his traits, his environment, and what is motivating him. For instance, the attitude of his body should display what is going on in his mind by basic, universal gestural suggestions. The audience sympathizes with the actor because they recognize and understand (clearly) the gesture. The mime "magnifies" the truth — he doesn't just exaggerate. This is an interesting concept, for we animators think of exaggeration when we caricature a character or an action. "Magnify" seems to be less mechanical, less surface adjustment. Character and feeling and ideas are from deep within, they are the truth of the character and therefore to magnify their truth seems more completely expressive.

In the olden days they used tableaus instead of acting out the scenes. Everything had to be "right on" to express what was going on (the story). There is a similar requirement for making a still drawing. It has to be "right on" or the meaning is lost. What worse fate can you think of than to have no meaning.

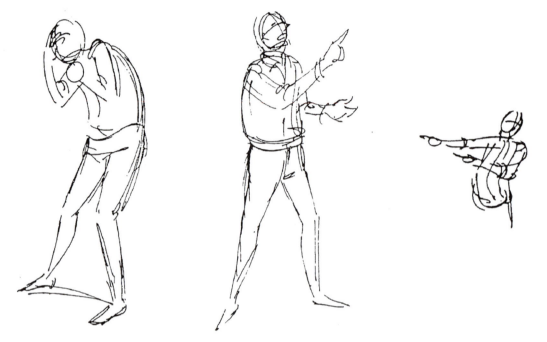

Ken acted out a character that comes on stage and is startled by something. He described with the body and facial expression that he was scared. Part of him wants to leave, post haste, and part of him is curious and wants to stay and see what it is. This is called an opposition.

There are three great orders of movement the body is capable of doing.

1. There are oppositions where two parts of the body are trying to go in different directions at the same time. No sign of stress or stretch can be shown without them.
2. Then there are parallel moves (parallelisms), two parts go in the same direction, not necessarily a strong movement, but (sometimes) decorative.
3. Then there are successive movements where one part follows another. In animation this would be called overlapping action.

He said the strongest thing a mime can show on the stage is a straight line. Take a straight line and bend it — all kinds of things begin to happen — feelings and ideas are suggested.

The mime has to show two kinds of energy, inner and outside. These are forces that are manufactured inside the body, and forces that control his body from the outside. The mime has to understand where the source of energy is coming from to be truthful to it.

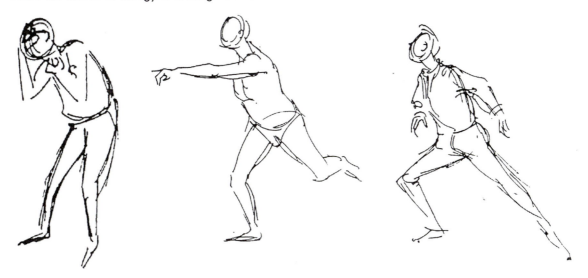

Francis Delsarte (The Delsarte Method) said the body is divided into three basic centers. First the *intellect*, (the head) where all the intellectual energy goes to and comes from. (By gestures we can tell when someone is thinking.) The torso is the *emotional center* containing aesthetics, feelings, falling in love, etc. Energy flows out from that area. The *physical center* is in the hips and pelvis area and from there down. Gut feelings, sexual feelings, and anger are expressed with that area.

Even random parts of the body seem to express certain emotions. For instance, the insides of the arms are the emotional parts of the arms. Those are what you expose when praying or when you embrace a loved one. The elbows and shoulders are the more aggressive parts. Delsarte said the shoulders and the elbows are the thermometer of the will. The eyes are the emotional part of the head; the mouth and lower jaw are the physical parts.

Delsarte categorizes not only the gestures of the body, but also the space around the body. We as artists are also concerned with the space around the body — not just the silhouette, but the third dimensional space that in a real sense becomes the boundaries within which our characters act. We, like the mime, use body language and gesture to illustrate our stories, but we have to *create* the illusion of depth — something the mime is blessed with by merely being on the stage.

Drawings courtesy of Ed Gutierrez.

104   True Gesture Drawing

While I was at the Florida animation studio, we had several drawing sessions using live models. One of the best models was Max Howard's beautiful baby daughter, still in diapers, and a born "ham." She presented us with an infinite number of gestures and poses. It kept everyone on their toes because most of the poses were held for perhaps three or four seconds or less.

It was an opportunity for me to suggest the idea of registering the pose in the memory (as if taking a Polaroid photo), the "first impression" thing I keep stressing. I pointed out how if too much time were spent "drawing" the head then by the time they got to the body, it would have changed. Then while drawing the body, the arms would have changed. So by the time they began to draw the arms their attitude would have nothing to do with the body or head gesture. Then, of course, the legs would be added to a drawing that already is a mixture of three or four gestures. It brings to mind the creations of Dr. Moreau, H. G. Wells' mad doctor, who created strange animals by using parts of different animals.

It was a perfect opportunity to drive home the idea that the gesture was the important thing — not the shape of the baby's arms or legs. After all, Baby Herman was the object of the study. I urged them to stop "drawing" and start "capturing the gesture." There was a great step forward made as each artist attempted to "go for the gesture."

Jeff Dutton, whose drawings I managed to confiscate (to share with you) typify the effects of trying to "capture" the gesture rather than trying to "draw" a baby ala Rembrandt. The drawings he made before these were factual as far as shape, proportion, and detail are concerned, but suddenly, he began to record the gestures, which I believe is the foundation of draftsmanship. It is tempting to suggest that there is a rule to cover all rules: "Stop trying to draw, and just get the gesture down." The drawing will take care of itself.

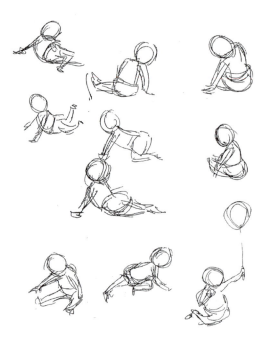

105 A Second Chance to Make a First Impression

For a drawing session in the Florida animation studio we had one of the actors from the studio lot pose for us. The poses weren't inordinately long, but long enough for Garrett Ho, a former intern from Glendale, to investigate ways to better his interpretations of the poses. This, to me, is a truly creative use of the model. Such a practice of probing for other possibilities is fundamental to animation, for if the first sketch does not fully tell the story, the option to search out a better gesture is ever present, and is in fact a necessity. Garrett's vividly expressive drawings speak persuasively in favor of "going for the gesture."

In some TV commercial I heard the line "You never get a second chance to make a first impression." In drawing, that is only partly true, for if your first impression doesn't work, you can always conjure up another first impression. One of the hazards of putting too much work into a drawing that isn't right, gesture-wise, is that you are likely to fall in love with it (you worked so hard on the details) and hate the thought of changing it, even though you know it needs improvement.

Garrett's spirit of search is commendable. An actor should never crystallize his performances. If he does so, his acting will appear commonplace or hackneyed. Sure, there is a universal body language that we use to express ourselves, but it must remain forever flexible, always seem spontaneous- like gestural reactions in real life.

Maybe it would help to hold the thought that there is no ideal way to draw a gesture — only one of many that seems most appropriate to put over the particular one you are dealing with at the time and one that suits the character you are working with. Say, for instance, a certain gesture is called for as a reaction to something. The gesture may be a universally recognizable one, but would certainly have to be adapted to the character, be it Mickey, Goofy, Roger Rabbit, or Ariel.

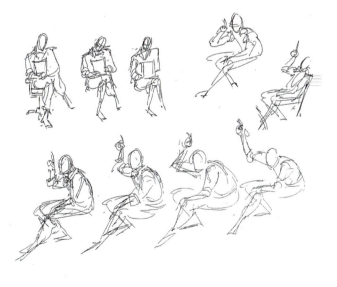

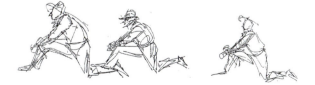

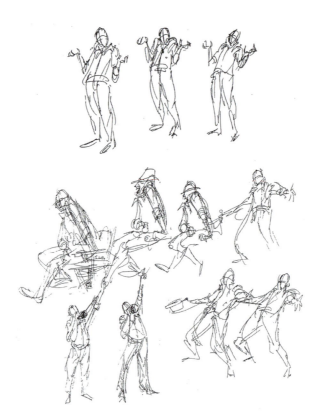

106 A Good Sketch Is Like a Good Joke

I still love to draw. After sixty years of drawing (I probably started around 10 years old) the subject matters have not depleted nor has my desire to "tell it on paper" been exhausted. Whenever Dee and I go anywhere, we don't call it a vacation, we call it a "sketching trip." She loves to drive and I love to sit on the passenger's side and sketch.

Having been in animation for so many years has influenced my drawing. I try to get movement (life) into my sketches. I think drawings, though still, ought to have a feeling of liveliness, animation, energy, and must describe or dramatize an action. A drawing should be "charged" with persuasion. You know how a baby will smile when you smile at it, or cry, or act frightened — that is how I would like the viewers of my drawings to react. If I draw someone sitting down, I don't want the viewers to register anything but that. I want them to feel the "sitting downess" of the sketch. Like the baby that involuntarily reacts to emotional suggestions, I want the viewer to react to my drawings. I want them to take part in the drama I have tried to portray. Granted, the drama is usually pretty subtle, unless the subject is a football game or a boxing match, but subtle things are part of our everyday living experience and have a place in art.

A good sketch is like a good joke. The teller builds the groundwork as succinctly as he can, then, when he has you "hanging on the cliff," delivers the punch line. It hits you in a climax of emotion and suddenly it is so crystal clear that you explode with laughter and delight. Part of the pleasure comes from the fact that although the teller spun the tale, you were the one that put it all together in your mind and figured out the climax or punch line. Likewise the artist builds a groundwork in the sketch, one that has a one-drawing story as its base and also weaves the "punch line" into the drawing in the form of the gesture. One look at it should tell the viewer how to react. The idea or feeling of looking, resting, walking or carrying something should burst upon the viewer, like the climax of a good story or the punch line of a good joke. If the joke has to be explained it is a bad joke — the same goes for a drawing. If a drawing doesn't "say" what it means at first glance, it is a failure as a drawing.

"Great art," said Tolstoy, "is when a great man who has the highest life-conception of his time tells what he feels. Then infection is universal. Everybody understands it and at once." Also, "Infection (sharing something with or influencing your audience) is only received (accomplished) when an author (artist) has, in a manner true to himself, experienced the feeling which he transmits and not when he passes on another man's feeling, previously transmitted to him." In other words, for you to infect your audience with your story/drawing, you have to be infected by it yourself. You have to feel the pose as if you were experiencing it yourself. Then your rendition of it will be sincere and infectious, and the punch line won't have to be explained.

Better a real, living, expressive scribble than a superficial, stiff, death mask-like copy.

Well, having tried to say all that eloquently and persuasively, I now put my integrity on the line by reproducing some sketches I made at the airport on a recent trip to Florida. You will notice that I spent little time on chairs or benches that people were sitting on. For one thing, people are so fidgety you have to move right along on your sketch or they will change positions on you. Also, it is sometimes a challenge to sketch someone sitting, and do it so deftly that the chair can be imagined. It is like the mime that does his act minus props but causes you to imagine they are there. If a chair were drawn, it should be done in the same spirit as the sitter, that is, a person *is sitting in the chair*, and conversely, the chair *is being sat in*. They are both part of one action and the chair's action should be part of the "punch line."

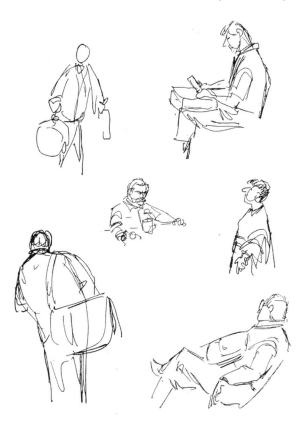

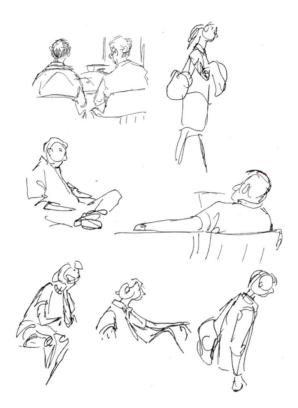

107 Opposition

We were most fortunate and privileged to have Judith Harding, mime and storyteller, for our model recently. It was very stimulating to see how she was able to do in her posing, things that animators are constantly called upon to do. "With a flick of the wrist," as the old saying goes, but actually with all parts of her mind and body, she displayed truly classical ballet poses, traditional and abstract mime poses, and demonstrated her new art form — telling stories, using body gestures. She could also switch to a bashful, comical, almost "cutsey" character. It gave us a chance to study all of those styles in one evening.

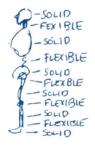

Judith is well acquainted with the solid/flexible make-up of the body. She would turn her chest area to the right, her head to the left, lean her body one way, and tilt her head the other way, while her feet seemed to be walking away from it all. For that, she used the term, "opposition" — things working against each other causing a feeling of movement, life, and conflict. But hear! Conflict does not mean, necessarily, strife or warfare. Even a pose in the attitude of prayer can contain opposition. The face and eyes pointed hopefully to heaven, while the hands push downward at the end of straight, tense arms, seeming to signify a rejection of earth and all it stands for. Opposition in a pose tells us that the person is living, thinking, and deciding — wrestling with a problem, real or fictitious. There has to be options or there can be no life.

In animation, a classic example of opposing forces is "anticipation." When a character wants to rush off stage to the right, he first leans to the left to gather his forces, holds it until the audience gets the picture, then he zips off in the opposite direction. That's opposition in a linear sense. It accents the move. A still drawing can have movement too, if it contains some opposition.

For example, when a hip is protruding, it's because it is being thrust out in opposition to the centerline of the body. Feel that thrust as you draw it. Don't think of it as a hip just sticking out — think of it as a hip *thrust* out there by the character in the drawing. There must be some indication that it took some conscious, physical effort to get that hip out there. Make the hip look so much like it is being thrust out, that your viewers will inadvertently shift their hip — like when you yawn and someone sees you they yawn, too. Here are some suggestions I made in class in regards to thrusting the hips out. The rule applies to every part of the body like the neck, shoulders, elbows, knees, feet, even the eyes, nose, ears, etc.

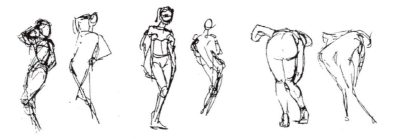

When people see a good actor doing his thing, they may be unskilled in the art of gesture, but will know what is being portrayed and will be able to empathize with the actor. To a degree, they experience the gestures vicariously, feeling it is actually happening to them. In drawing you have to convince the audience they are experiencing the meaning of that pose, so they will say, "Oh, that's great," because through your skill you have persuaded them to enter into it as a personal experience. It allows everyone to get involved.

Georgia O'Keefe felt "invaded" because her works were misunderstood. "Critics wrote their own fixations or autobiographies into hers" (quoted from her current exhibit catalog). And because of that she did make an attempt to be a little more objective in her paintings. Abstract art is subject to personal interpretation and that is one of the charming things about it. In animation there is little room for the abstract. The audience must get the artwork pretty well interpreted for them by the artist or it will be hard for them to follow the story. Even the gestures that we recognize as "universal" vary from culture to culture, so a thorough study and knowledge of body language is indispensable for animation artists. I think that is one of the fun things about drawing — capturing a clear depiction of a gesture. When I paint abstracts or write certain kinds of poetry, I try to leave much room for multiple interpretations, but when sketching or drawing, I try to "go for the throat."

I confiscated a few sketches of Judith from Roger Chiasson and James Fujii, which are reproduced here in that order. Their techniques are different but each artist captured the poses well. A good model helps in that respect, inspiring artists to bring out the best in themselves. The ability is there, a good model just helps you prove it.

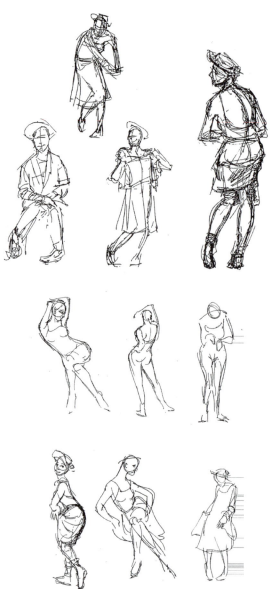

P.S. At the expense of being accused of "overkill," allow me to explain the verb thrust, not in an "English" sense, but in a "drawing" sense. It means "to push with sudden force," or "continuous pressure" (Webster). There is an overtone of movement suggested. A drawing should have that overtone in it. Go back to the drawings made by Roger and James and study them for opposition and thrust. Notice how the hips are thrust out, even when they are hidden behind clothing. Notice how some heads have been thrust out, up, or down. Go through them again and check the elbows for thrust — notice how the elbows work against each other (opposition). Check out the knees. In many instances they are forced together. When that happens, there is a tendency for the heel to be ('scuse me — here it is again) thrust out. When the legs are spread apart, the toe has a tendency to thrust itself out farther. Notice how when the left knee is pushed to the right the face looks in the opposite direction. These are excellent poses and they are excellent drawings.

108 Elastic Band Tension

Whether you are drawing from a model or from the imagination (as in animation), you should always be aware that you are not drawing bones, muscles, and cloth, or a model sheet drawing — you are drawing an action. Think of the figure as having gone from a "normal" relaxed pose to the gesture you are drawing. Attach, in your imagination, a rubber band at all joints at that normal position. Any part of the figure that moves will have to be moved under the strain of stretching the rubber band. Try to draw the effort it takes to stretch into the change of pose. Feel that if the figure relaxed it would snap back to normal. That is called "tension." Being aware of whether it is an extensor (a muscle that pushes out or extends) or a flexor (one that pulls in or contracts) may help, as long as you keep in mind that it is not the muscle you are interested in but rather the idea or motivation behind it all. Look for the tension between foot and foot, elbow and elbow, or any part that pulls away from or pushes toward another part, or twists or any kind. Try this, but don't think of it as an experiment, think of it as one of the main weapons in your arsenal of drawing helps.

Here are some examples from an earlier class. My correction drawings are necessarily simple, sometimes overly exaggerated and often crude. Anyway, most of you know by now that I think more highly of a crude sketch that tells a story than an immaculately rendered drawing that looks like a freeze-dried corpse. The first correction was an attempt to get the artist to loosen up. Holding the pen tightly right down near the nib plus trying to "draw" all the parts of the figure as parts of the figure has a stiffening and stifling effect on drawing. I suggested holding the pen farther up the shank and start drawing the action, i.e., the stretches, tilts, twists, and tensions. Feel the tension (the rubber band-stretch) between the upraised right shoulder and the outstretched right knee and foot, the tension between the two knees, and the twist caused by the arm having to stretch over to the left knee. You can even feel some tension in the neck as it strains to hold the head upright. Feel the whole figure pulling away from what would be a normal sitting pose.

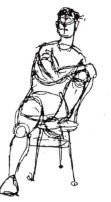
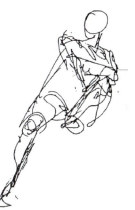

The next pose was a difficult one. Ordinarily you would think of the shoulder as lifting higher if it is leaned on. In this case the other arm was stretched straight as she pushed on her leg, forcing that shoulder higher. It meant having to show some of her upper back to suggest that it went up beyond the neck (here is a front view of what is going on) where it could logically meet the pushed up shoulder of the straightened arm. If you are looking for lines on the model to divulge something to copy, they may not always be there. You have to look for the "story" in the tensions, twist, stretches, and squashes that will reveal that story.

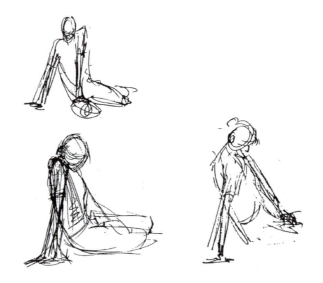

Here is one where I perhaps went a little overboard, but you can spot the crux of the problem quickly. You can feel the "elastic bands" pull from all points to all other points. This kind of tenseness is not rigidity or stiffness, it is the stretchable, flexible, resilient, supple kind. It allows your figures full play (and beyond) in performing their body language. There is a study in contrasts here also, where the knees are forced dramatically apart while the hands are pressed together with the pelvic area establishing a solid base for the rest of the body, which has suddenly taken an interest in something off stage right.

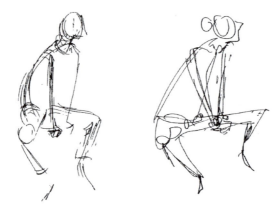

Just as some drawings are only an illusive nuance away from being breathtakingly expressive, so are some drawing techniques one untried idea away from becoming successful, forceful, and dynamic. So strive for a drawing technique that is flexible in helping you to communicate the story you are trying to tell. Communication is what makes an artist a great artist.

109 Get Out of the Way

In last week's handout, there was a reproduction of a drawing by Brad Kuha. Next to it was a sketch I did to suggest a way for him to draw a little more loosely. Here again is his drawing and my suggestion.

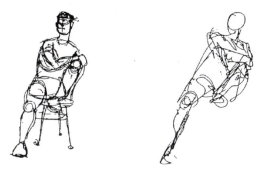

When I do this, I encourage the artist to hold the pen looser and farther away from the nib and *let the pen do the drawing.* If the drawing turns out good, take the credit for it, if it turns out bad, blame it on the pen. But don't "draw" — let the pen do it. It gets you out of the frame of mind of "What is this part I am drawing and how do I draw it?" into the frame of mind of "Ah, these lines are going down so easily, I feel I can push the top part of the figure over a little farther, and stretch the arm a little more, and etc. Wow, this helps me to forget the anatomy charts and to go for the gesture." Here are a few more of those somewhat stiff, structural drawings. Anatomically and proportionate-wise they are good, but they have a slightly mechanical look.

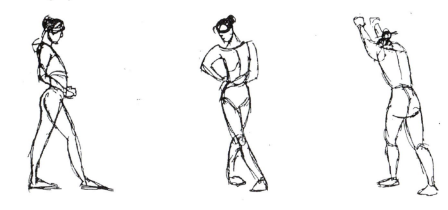

Now let me show you some of the beautiful, loose, life-filled sketches Brad made after that one drawing suggestion. These, if you'll excuse the expression, are damned nice drawings.

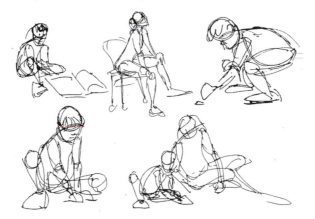

And while we're on the subject of damned nice drawings, Mike Swofford, who studies drawing seriously, did some too. Mike takes the drawings he makes in the class and reworks them later to perfect them (and himself). These don't need any working over.

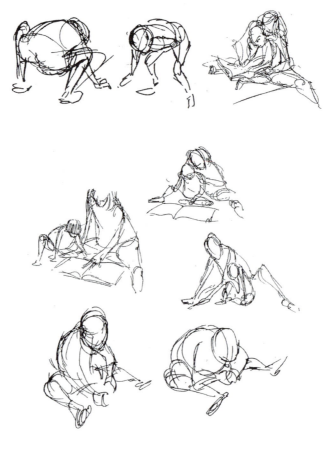

A newcomer in our midst is Ash Brannon. He attended the class on the night of four-year-old Kyle Brown's explosive modeling performance, got caught up in the excitement, and "drew up a storm" of his own. Here are some of his sketches.

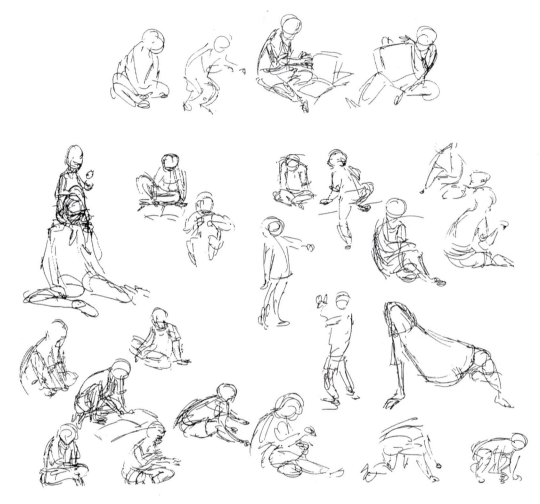

Realize, I am not trying to sell these artists to anyone, I am trying to sell sketching — the quick and intensive kind where there is no time to atrophy either in the mind or on the paper. When you slave over a drawing for hours it should still have the appearance of spontaneity, as do these quick sketches. Having to rev up the engine, to floor the adrenaline pedal while sketching a moving subject, makes one fall back on one's sixth sense where reactions are instinctive rather than intellectual.

In a book called *Inner Tennis* the author says your body knows what to do — just get out of the way and let your body take care of the strokes. Sometimes we try to force the drawing into being. We intellectualize. We name parts and attempt to draw them, when all we need to do is "get out of the way" and sketch (tell) the story which is unfolding before us. If we were verbalizing something we wouldn't proceed by analyzing our sentence structure, syntax, and spelling. We'd be tongue-tied in a minute. In drawing something, all we're really doing is verbalizing with marker and paper. So, "get out of the way" and let it be told the way it really is.

110 Play-Acting

Storytelling, which is what animation is all about, is 95% play-acting and 5% genius. All of you pass the 5% genius prerequisite but as for play-acting, some of you have "grown up" and have gotten "serious" about drawing. People who grow up become sober, somber, sedate, and solemn and risk losing what it takes to become a performer, especially an illustrator of fantasy. Moviegoers want to be entertained. They don't give a hoot about how well you can draw a model or copy a model sheet drawing. They want their amusement to whisk them out of their already too serious life. Most of them have forgotten how to play-act. Growing up takes its toll. But they seek to acquire it vicariously. So along comes the Disney cartoons, designed to whisk them into an hour or so of pure fantasy. Escape from the "normal" everyday sane world of serious living. And that's where you come in — adding the visual stimuli to some very ingenious and amusing story material.

So what happens? You have to train for the job. What can be more serious than training, especially for something so illusive as drawing? Take studying to become a typist as a contrast. You learn the typewriter keyboard in two months. A couple of months of extensive training and you're up to 45 or 50 words a minute. Two more months and you can put an ad in the paper, "Excellent typing done at home." But after 6 months of art school, what kind of credentials can you come up with? Even after 4 or 5 years we still can't capture a damned gesture. It's enough to make you slightly solemn if not downright downcast. And being downcast is apt to filter down into your drawings, and another vicious circle is begun. But be of heart, the solution is not far. Attitude is a reversible coat. One side is seriousness and the other is play-acting. Wear the side out that gives pleasure, both to you and to your audience. Bring play-acting back into your life, at least into your drawing. You can be as sedate as your lifestyle calls for, but when it comes to cartooning you should be as flexible as a politician and as good at play-acting as a child (at least with pen and pencil).

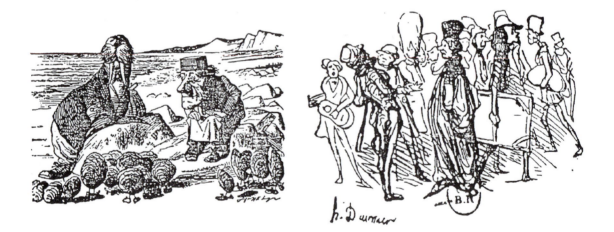

Study this drawing by John Tenniel for excellent drawing and rendering and at the same time, play-acting He was a cartoonist for the magazine Punch, but as you can see was a very fine artist to boot. He was even knighted for his high esteem.

Honore Daumier is an outstanding example of a fine artist who caricatured life, especially political life.

He had an eye for the grotesque. He saw through the protecting solemnity of the magistrate's billowy black robes and found many of them to be mere windbags of the law. He concentrated the attention of the public upon their vapid expressions, upon their hideous Adam's apples and their coarsened features.

Howard Simon — *500 Years of Art in Illustration*

Gustave Dore was one of the finest and most prolific of artists, ever. There was not a mood or emotion he could not evoke. His humor stood out like a precious gem. Check out this illustration of a pompous woman and her (perhaps sycophantic) attendant. The gesture tells all. Even the horses prance along as if they were accompanied by some Leonard Bernstein music.

Energy and life flow from every line, shape, and form. Is it serious acting or is it play-acting?

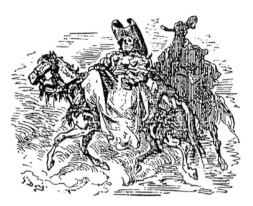

And of course who was more adept at play-acting than the great Japanese artist Hokusai, a fine artist in the Japanese tradition, but also a master of grotesqueries and caricature. His facile brush probed all aspects of Japanese life and landscape.

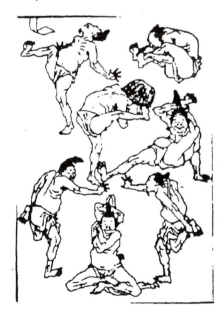

The great Disney artist/animators of the past were well acquainted with these masters of drawing. Their works were inspirational not just for draftsmanship but also for acting — play-acting to be specific. Here are some drawings of the typical "Disney" style. They all have the same quality of play-acting that all great illustrators possessed.

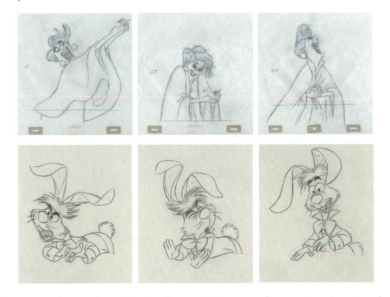

Few know play-acting better than Ken Anderson. Ken went from animation into layout many years ago (now retired) and developed the function of visual presentation to a very high degree. He made numerous studies to inspire the directors, story men, layout men, and animators to squeeze out the maximum possibilities from each character and situation. Here is a page of his foxes. At the top is a rather serious realistic drawing of a fox by Ken Hultgren (*The Art of Animal Drawing*), as a contrast to Ken Anderson's approach.

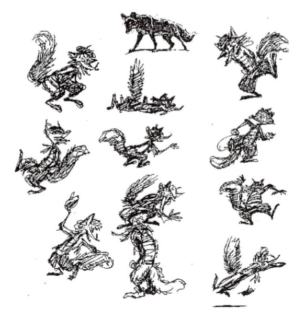

Is play-acting any different front just plain acting? Yes. Acting is where an actor acts out a part so the audience will believe it is the character he is portraying, and not himself. Play-acting is where a child, for instance, imagines he is someone else or somewhere else or in some otherworld situation and play-acts that he is actually experiencing it. Kids are fun to watch when they are doing this. They often become absolutely oblivious to their surroundings and are released of all ties with reality. They assume another personality and emote in ways completely foreign to their own. And there are no inhibitions — they go all out. It allows them to act out roles and make gestures that they might feel too self-conscious to do under normal circumstances. Play-acting is a magical emancipator in that respect.

I think that is why mimes make such good models. They are able to cross that line between everyday reality and some invented reality. Our mime models, Ken Martin and Judith Harding, do it. Craig Howell does it. He comes dressed as a carpenter, and with a tape, measures things on the walls and pretends to saw pieces of wood and to plane them. Kind of strange to see a grown man doing these things but a great opportunity for cartoonists to sketch someone at play-acting. Lalla Lezli is another great model who creates little vignettes of characters for us. She pouts, grimaces, leers, and sells plastic flowers shawled and bent over like an old lady. She will be modeling for us this week. So you who come to draw her, take advantage of her play-acting and allow a little of it to "rub off."

111 A Storytelling Drawing

Don Graham, that great teacher of drawing and painting, who was so instrumental in getting the Disney style of animation off and running, said an animation drawing is a "storytelling drawing." That thought should be uppermost in our minds whenever we are drawing from a model or animating. For the sake of clarifying that thought and to drive the point home (make it your own), let me quote further from Don Graham's book, *The Art of Animation*:

The extreme, the important drawing of every action, represents the outside limit of an action or a gesture. It indicates at what point the direction of an action changes. If an arm swings backward, at some point it must swing forward. The extreme also represents a momentary pause, or rest, in the action. A bouncing ball, at the point of contact, or at the height of the bounce, seems to be stationary.

At about the time of the *Three Pigs* this pause in the action suggested a new use of the extreme. Instead of being just a turning point, or a rest point in the action, it now became a drawing of great and special picture interest, a storytelling drawing. By making this drawing more expressive and by having it suggest what was about to happen or what had already happened, the intervening action could be suggested, rather than delineated, to an unbelievable degree.

Watching straight-ahead animation is like watching a buzzard or a hawk wheeling and gliding in the sky. The action is continuous but monotonous because we see a series of poses of equal interest. Watching animation is like watching a hummingbird darting from flower to flower. The action is continuous but exciting because we are able to see separate poses which are made possible by definite rest periods in the action.

That is by no means a complete formula for animation, it was only quoted to stimulate you into thinking that *whenever* you are drawing you are drawing a storytelling drawing. The mere thought should help to focus your attention on the purpose at hand — at that very crucial moment when all the elements of your drawing converge. This is when the right side of the brain assembles all the left brain's research and creates a "storytelling drawing." Supposedly the left brain has done its work. You have studied anatomy, cartooning, perspective, composition, acting, and pantomime. Now it is all brought together in one electrifying moment of unification — when a storytelling drawing is brought to life. I see it happening every night in our drawing class. Here are some examples of bringing all that hard earned knowledge and sensitivity together. These are Joe Ranft's drawings of mime, dancer, storyteller Judith Harding and Alex Topete's drawings of former dancer, actress Lalla Lezli. If I were to try to tell you how nice these drawings are, and how close they come to describing the storytelling genius of these two models — you would be turned off by my "gushiness." I'll let the drawings speak for themselves.

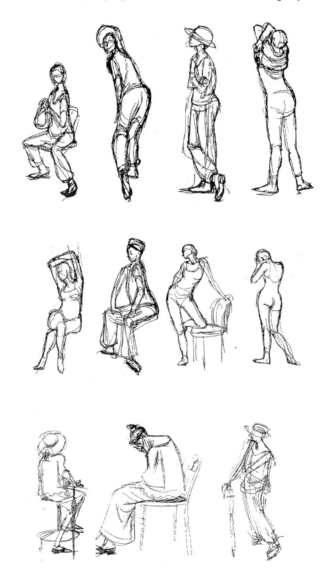

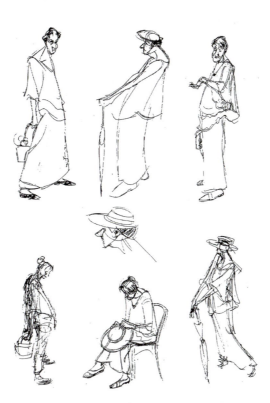

Of course sometimes work takes its toll, or we can't gather our thoughts together, or our biorhythms are nose-diving, so I have to intervene with the "magic formula." Here are a few examples. Oh, incidentally, and this is important, if some of these drawings look bad, it's not because the artist is bad — it's because the concept of the gesture was not fully comprehended or energized. When the concept is clear it suggests and inspires ways of drawing it well.

Here is a drawing that you can see the artist lost all interest in. If he had gotten a better concept of it I'm sure he'd have pulled it off.

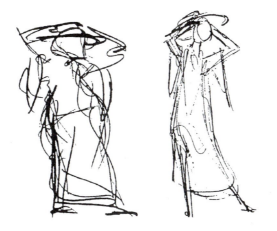

Here is a similar problem, and as you can see I interrupted the artist at an early stage, and suggested he introduce some opposition, which is what the model was doing anyway — the head angled in one direction the torso in another, and the legs in still another. It's not an invention of mine. It's a very natural gesture. Stand up and try it.

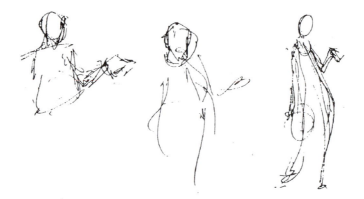

Here is a case where an important storytelling aspect got overlooked. If the artist had rehearsed the story in his mind — *she is leaning on her elbows, cogitating* — he'd have no doubt made her "lean." Bending her forward puts some weight on the elbows and says, "lean."

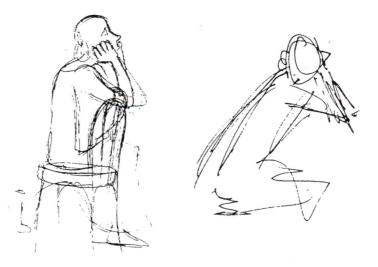

In this last one Lalla was selling flowers. In the artist's version, she doesn't seem to be making any appeal to a possible buyer. To get someone's attention and make an appeal, universal body language requires that you lean toward the person. This intensifies the eye contact, in the hope of making a more sure contact, arousing interest, or even pity.

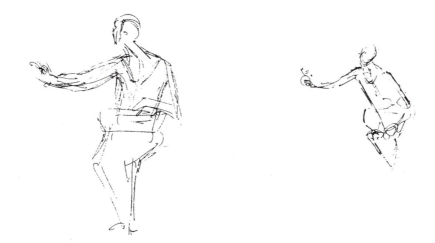

112 Drawing Techniques

Drawing techniques vary from person to person, which is as it should be. One should feel comfortable and as free as possible while drawing. This is one case where the means is justifiable if the *end* is achieved. And as we all agree (I insist on it) the *end* is a good "storytelling drawing." It could be though that if you're not achieving the "end," your means may be faulty. And if this is the case, some adjustments are in order. Most of us tend to unthinkingly fall into habit patterns (good or bad) that as soon as they take hold, seem normal. So it's sometimes difficult to spot our own— how shall I say — shortcomings.

Technique seems to imply a surface attribute. But according to Webster's Collegiate Dictionary the word actually means *"the method* or *the details of procedure* essential to expertness of execution in any art, science, etc.,"* and so has to do with any function that goes into the drawing, including the mental. The mental part is the desire, inspiration, concentration, and sustained interest.

Many times I have (as I "stalk" behind the artists in our evening class) watched someone start a drawing and sensing it was not coming up right, abandon it and start again — only to do the very same thing. I have seen as many as five or six starts that looked like Xerox copies. Here is a six-starter and below that a three-starter with my suggestions following. The first one didn't feel good to the artist because the figure wasn't leaning over far enough to put some weight on the elbows. I think habit drove him to repeat the "shortcoming." To chip away at those habits one has to keep the mind flexible at all times. Don't let some behavior pattern control your act of drawing. A good formula for overcoming those devitalizing habits is to talk to yourself as you draw. Say, "The guy is bending over and is leaning with all the weight of his head shoulders, and upper back on his elbows. I know what a straight line looks like — it looks like this:

and I know what a bent line looks like — it looks like this:

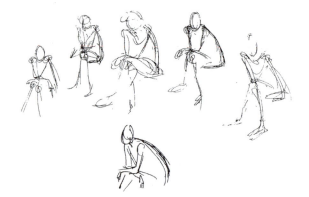

so I will use a bent line for the guy's back so I can get some weight on his elbows."

In this second group the artist was trying get the stoop-shoulder look, plus a belly protrusion. What he might have said as he talked his drawing into being was, "Okay, the belly is protruding. That's a verb. So to make it protrude, I'll thrust it out, putting some tension between the elbow and the belly, let the shirt hang over to accent the protrusion. I'll even look up into the sleeve, as if it were coming at me, because he's as wide as he is potbellied, causing the arm to fan out toward me."

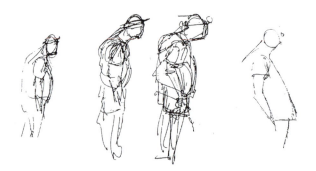

It may seem cumbersome as you read my suggestion but while drawing this all happens in an instant. Logic has a way of cutting through any ponderous cogitation. My sketches are much more simple and direct which has nothing to do with technique — it has to do with thinking and seeing. I simply distill the essence of the gesture and leave everything else out.

In animation, technique has been a relatively controllable variable. All animators draw a little differently, but thanks to an excellent cleanup crew, the drawings are all brought "on model," and the result is it appears like one person did the whole picture.

Here are two techniques that are very different, on the surface, that is. The first is Kent Culotta's technique. His drawings are carefully built up from the inside out with layer upon layer of graphite. The searching for the gesture is really done in the mind first — not on the paper. The searching lines on the paper are more to find the final statement.

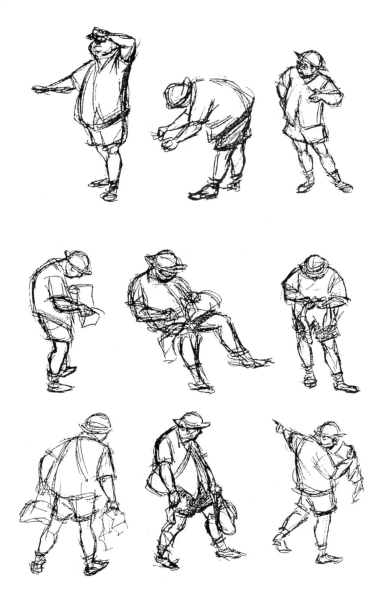

The second group of drawings is these nice, crisp pen sketches that appear, at casual glance, to be more spontaneous. Yet if a cleanup person was called upon to bring both sets "on model," the same spark and flair and basic gesture would be present in both groups, regardless of the artist's techniques. Model Craig Howell's personality, mannerisms, and his play-acting as a "tourist," would be there, too, as they so unmistakably are in these drawings.

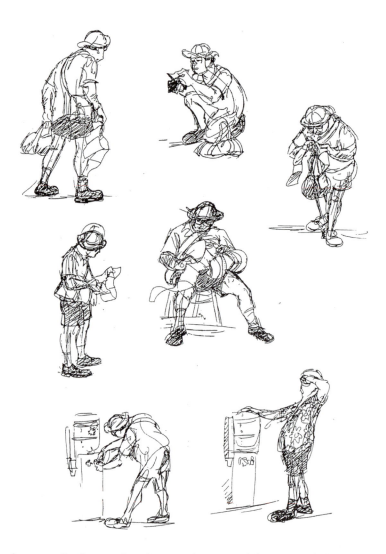

So as you employ your "technique," make sure that your definition includes the basics of drawing — not just the superficial appearance of the drawing. Robert Henri, in his book, *Art Spirit*, advised his students (and us) to

...start with a deep impression; the best, the most interesting, the deepest you can have of the model; to preserve this vision throughout the work; to see nothing else; to admit of no digression from it; choosing only from the model the signs of it; will lead to an organic work. Every element in the picture will be constructive of an idea, expressive of an emotion. Every factor in the painting (drawing) will have beauty because in its place in the organization it is doing its living part. Because of its adjustment, it is given its greatest power of expansion. It is only through a sense of the right relation of things that freedom can be obtained.

Which brings to mind the second sentence in this "handout," and I quote myself: "One should feel comfortable and as free as possible while drawing."

113   Step Into It

In *Unlimited Power* by Anthony Robbins, a book on personal achievement, the author uses "acting like" as a tool to do what you want to do and to become who you want to become. Part of his premise is that physiognomy has a great deal to do with the way you feel and how you achieve. Physiognomy means the art of discovering temperament and character from outward appearance.... External aspect; hence, inner character as revealed outwardly. He teaches that even the attitude or stance one takes, signals the brain and the whole nervous system of the body, enabling it to carry out its "acting like" or pretended intentions. Even Charlie Brown understands this:.

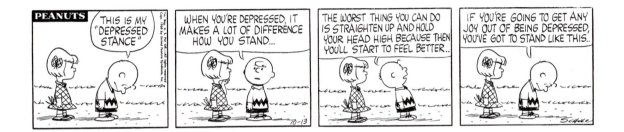

I see this as an important tool in drawing, too. Most of the drawings that come short of the mark are the ones where the artist didn't "act like" (mentally or physiognomically) the gesture of the model or something drawn from the imagination. To illustrate this, let me ask you to imagine yourself having to pound a big spike into a thick piece of hard wood. Your mental picture will certainly not be like the actions you would take to place a cup of hot tea into someone's hands. No, you would picture yourself lifting the hammer high enough to get some power and speed behind the swing. You'd lean back, putting what you might consider the maximum distance that you could accurately swing the hammer and still hit the nail head. You'd turn your shoulder for extra power; you'd tighten the muscles of your stomach for additional support, and you might even squint your eyes and grit your teeth. Then you'd unleash all that gathered power in one great manly whack at the nail.

When you are drawing, such a mental picture would be transposed into graphite or ink onto paper. And it has to be a conscious, active, and assertive involvement. It's not too complicated. We're talking simple (but energized) things like a stretch or a squash, or a bend, or a twist; or a couple of angles working against each other. We're talking perspective — things that are close appearing larger, things far away, smaller. We're talking things coming at you or going away from you in space. We're talking weight distribution and balance and tension, push and pull — all the things you would do naturally with your body if you were to carry out some action or gesture, things that you would have to rehearse mentally before you could do them, or draw them.

Drawing is total involvement. You can't "stand off" and watch it being done — you have to "step into it" and do it yourself. I recently read a book called *Lost in Translation* by Eva Hoffman. That title suggests an explanation for many aborted attempts to draw a gesture. We may see the pose perhaps in a shallow sense (maybe we look but don't really see it). Then when we try to draw it, the kinesthetic feeling having not reached the true sense of it, or the picture being weak in our minds, allows it to get lost in translation.

I have a few drawings here that I hope will graphically illustrate the point. In the first drawing the artist has the body at ease as she peers down into her blouse opening, and as they say of some animation, "it moves but it doesn't animate." In my suggestion sketch I have her straighten up slightly, forcing her neck back, making it

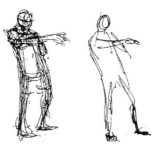

easier to look down, and I thrust the left elbow out for a cleaner pull on the collar. Looking from one drawing to the other you can see it become a stronger look.

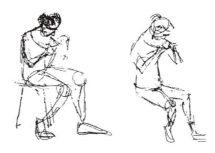

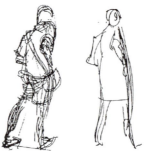

In the next pose, the model was bending at the waist. The long, curved, sweeping line from heel to shoulder cancels out any hope for a clean bend at the waist. Also with the definite angle of the upper torso, it gives the right arm a better stretch. This is an example of opposition — one part going in one direction and one part going in another. It adds power and spark to a gesture.

In this next drawing the artist has a lot of curved lines, which when used in such profusion, have a tendency to cancel out anything of a definite nature. The model was standing alertly looking at something. In this attitude one thrusts out the chest and stomach, stretching the whole body. It makes a clean "springboard" for the look to travel to the object of its interest, unheeded by a lot of unnecessary clutter. Curved lines can be used at the rear of the figure to help identify the shapes.

Here is a similar problem where the *stretch side of the body was drawn with mostly angles and curves.* The solution was to introduce a more definite "stretch," which in turn intensified the pose.

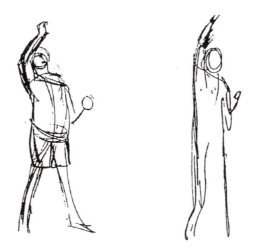

In this last illustration the model was bending back at the waist drinking a glass of water, his right hand resting on the water dispenser. The act of drinking water (or whatever action) should be imagined and felt in your body before starting to draw. The thrusts and stretches and bodily tensions will then be apparent, and easier to transpose onto paper.

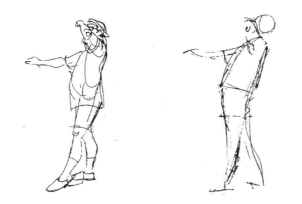

114   It Could Be That....

Sometimes I come on pretty heavy with a subtle or even questionable suggestion in our evening class on how to capture a pose or the meaning of a gesture. Occasionally I can't pull it off myself, and I'm embarrassed and the student is frustrated. Sometimes I explain before I start that "I may not be able to draw this, but it could be that...this is what is happening," and then I make a sketch. My hope is that the "it could be that...." will stick in the mind and not the success or failure of my sketch. "Could be" leaves the path open for unlimited possibilities.

If we are relatively consistent in achieving an acceptable result, we may become complacent and stop growing. "Could be" leaves an open-endedness that may lead to great drawing, rather than merely good drawing. Look at some of the great Disney feature cartoons. You'll spot the greats, as opposed to the goods, and especially as opposed to the get-by-ers. Some of the get-by-ers may eventually stretch their talents and become goods or perhaps greats — some of them will be satisfied to stay on the get-by plateau. So if you sometimes can't see the extra possibilities in the model or in your mind, don't stop searching. You want to be a better actor (storyteller) than a model. Maybe the model is just a "good" model and you want to expand your drawing ability to "great." The extra "punch" (could be that...) will have to come from within you. Complacency, fear of failure, or self-satisfaction will keep you from even trying. I love to pick on the good artists because they are so close to breaking through to greatness. Maybe just a little "could be" here and a little "could be" there will do the trick.

Let's consider some of the "could bes" that might transport a good drawing into a great drawing. We'll have to do it without the model here. But with or without a model, "could bes" are a legitimate and worthwhile pursuit.

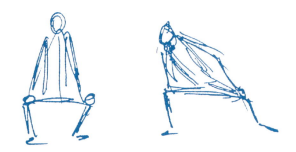

In this first example the artist seems to have gotten the gist of the pose. But when (and if) you consider where the figure started from and the extent to which it has gone (see illustration at right), it could be that his head and right hand have gone past the right elbow. If the figure is looking at something it certainly gets the look out into the clear. It could be that he has leaned over far enough to straighten out his left arm a little more, making it look like it pushes everything into the look. It could be that since the right lower leg is more vertical; that knee will be higher than the other one. If you're into negative shapes, and you should be, the opening enclosed by the left arm being elongated will help the lean. Negative shapes also squash and stretch. And it could be that if the left hand were wrapped over the leg in a pushing attitude it would compliment the whole action.

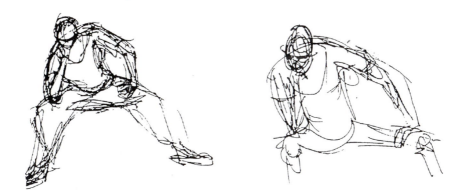

In the next sketch the model was clutching a box that had just come from her boyfriend. She was in the process of opening it. The artist seems to have chosen a "could be" that she was clutching the box eagerly as if it contained something precious (a good concept). In searching for another "could be," I pictured her wrestling with a huge box that she could hardly get her right arm around (later to open it finding only a small gift). Actually my box is smaller than the artist's, but it seems larger because of the way it's held.

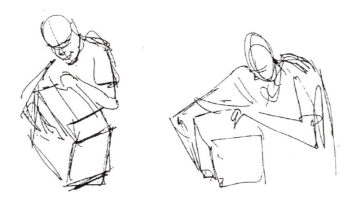

Notice the angles of the forearms in the artist's drawing are almost parallel, which is rather static. I have a theory about angles that I will explain briefly. Simply put, two parallel lines are static.

Angle one of the lines and it sets up a movement.

It can produce domino effect

or a kicking effect,

depending on how it is used in a drawing. In the artist's drawing, the static effect is the result of the right arm clutching the box and the left arm (hand) pulling up on the box lid, causing them both to do the same thing (no opposition). In my sketch I have the two arms working against each other, setting up a little tug-of-war action. The angles, instead of

which are static, have two sets of kicking-up angles — the upper arms

and the lower arms.

Of course it could be that she had gotten her left elbow up into a pulling position, while pushing down with the other hand, see 1. Or she could have positioned her right thumb on top of the box to oppose the pull of her left arm, as in 2. Or it could be that she was so eager to get into the box, she just sort of tries to crawl into it, as in 3.

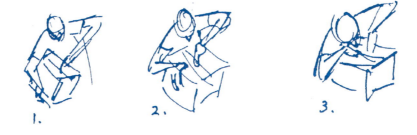

In this last example, the model was engrossed with her shoe lacing. The artist's conception was not a fully congruent depiction of a figure interested in what it was doing. The flow of attention somehow gets interrupted. In my sketch I angled the back in a way that would feature her stretched neck. I angled, even slightly distorted the head into a more intense look at what she was interested in, and stretched the shoulder and arms more to direct the attention downward.

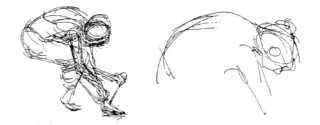

The point being that all characters should be really interested in what they are doing, inspiring the viewers or audience to be interested too. Perhaps thinking "it could be that..." will help you to search out the best way to put over the story point and to get all the elements in focus. And incidentally, don't shy away from this kind of investigation, thinking that the picture deadlines force you to put quality on the back burner. That's one of the reasons for your continued study: to be able to arrive at a more desirable drawing in less time. Knowing where to put a line should take a lot less time than not knowing where to put it. So if you figure it's going to take sixty or a hundred hours of intensive (but enjoyable — if you like drawing) study to get to that comfortable position — start counting.

I apologize for the ponderous text, but I don't know of another way to show the thought process in arriving at these things.

115 A First Impression — Your Intended Goal

Last week I touched briefly on my theory of the use of angles for getting movement in still drawings. I also have a theory about establishing the pose solidly in your mind before starting to draw. It's called "first impression." It allows you (actually forces you) to first of all decide what the pose represents to you story-wise. In doing so you get the juices flowing. Energy is gathered to carry off your goal. If you don't have anything to "tell" in your drawing then your energy is not aroused or is dissipated on a non-goal.

In *Unlimited Power* by Anthony Robbins, he puts it this way, "When the mind has a defined target, it can focus and direct and refocus and redirect until it reaches its intended goal. If it doesn't have a defined target, its energy is squandered."

Establishing the goal of a drawing puts you in a position where you are committed to success, thus helping you to be more resourceful — it emboldens you to achieve and calls forth and inspires the means to pull it off. Whatever the opposite of a vicious circle is, is what happens to you. "An important point worth adding is that there's an incredible dynamism inherent in this process. The more resources you develop, the more power you have; the more strength you feel, the more you can tap into even greater resources and ever more powerful states." That rousing quote from *Unlimited Power* was meant to be applied to anyone wishing to achieve some goal — well, drawing is a goal, and it takes energy to draw. So if it seems enticing, why not try its refreshing and energizing promise. Don't squander your energy on a poorly conceived first impression. Get the ball rolling with a pre-programmed story-telling drawing (backed by all the above promises).

You may be thinking of figure drawing as a still life — the model takes a pose and you struggle to capture it as it is. But for the purposes of studying for animation, think of each pose as one that has just come from another pose and will soon move into a new one. The model is an active person and has merely slowed down long enough for you to sketch just one tiny part of his or her daily actions. But it is not a still life. It is one action isolated from a whole series of actions.

Don't study the model for the pose — study yourself, as if it were your body posing. When you have to make an animation drawing, you're not going to have a model handy. You'll have to do it in your head, and with your sense of kinetics. So if the model is pointing or stretching then do that yourself.

Feel the muscles that pull, feel where the weight has to be to do that action. Notice where the stretches are and the squashes. Actually get up from time to time and assume the pose yourself. Then when you look back to the model for reference to make your sketch you will know what you are drawing — you will know it personally. And when you have to draw a similar pose sometime when there is no model handy, you can concoct all those feelings of a pose physically and mentally — and go right to it. It's not out there on the model, it's right there in yourself.

Of course you are mainly interested in three phases of an action listed variously as preparation, anticipation, and action; or preparation, action, and follow through. It is a good practice when sketching to consider the pose as being one of those phases. Ask yourself, would this make a good anticipation drawing or would it serve as a main action? Imagine an anticipation drawing in front of it and a follow-through drawing after it. If it seems like it might be a good main action drawing yet is not quite extreme enough. Take it upon yourself to push it to the extreme you desire. Go beyond what the model is offering you.

As you study the model for a first impression be careful not to think of it as a still life. Think of it as an action that might occur in a scene of animation. The model doesn't know your problems. You have a special problem. And your problem can be solved, not by copying the model, but by observing how the figure arrives at certain gestures so you can apply that process to whatever character you happen to be working on, whether it be a human character like Eric or Ariel; or a cartoon character like Roger Rabbit or Mickey.

116   Gallery of Class Drawings

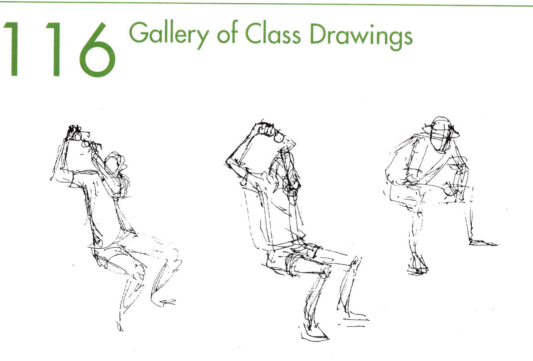

Ash Brannon did this nice loose, expressive sketch. Right next to it is Pete Docter's version using different tensions in the body. And another simple but solid sketch by Pete.

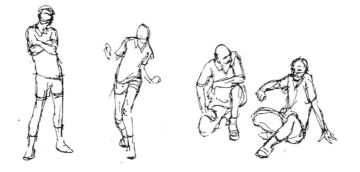

James Fujii's drawings are slightly more finished but nonetheless loose and expressive.

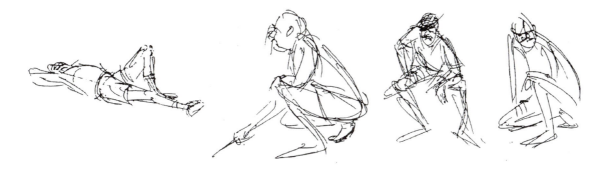

Dan Boulos whips in his drawings with gusto, so they are usually crisp and simple.

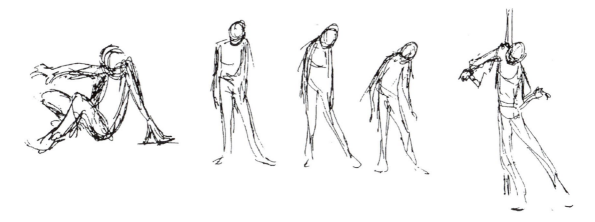

Brenda Chapman-Lima likes to experiment with the poses as shown here. The chap upper right is scratching his back, not being hung.

ADDENDUM: Thought you might like to know I practice what I preach. On Saturday, August 19, I took part in the 3rd annual "Quick Draw" along with eleven other artists, each of whom show their work in one of many art galleries in Los Olivos, California. The artists are given 45 minutes to sketch, draw, or paint a model (this year a sexy gal in a sexy barmaid outfit.)

I completed two 11/14" pen drawings into which I worked some watercolor. I had just written some stuff on the first impression thing and it was fresh in my mind. The scene was tense. I sat there on my tiny portable camp stool (this is in a park in Los Olivos) solidifying my first impression, because, of course, with pen and ink you can't back up or erase. There was a crowd of people gazing over our shoulders, anxiously waiting to see the artwork take form. Country western music reverberated throughout the little town with its quaint, late 1800s and early 1900s architecture.

Mentally I checked the proportions, angles, perspective, and general feeling of the set up. The impression jelled. I could hear the crowd release their long held breath as I began to dash out the drawing with vigor, flair, and confidence. After the 45 minutes were up, the works were auctioned off to the spectators with half of the money going to the artists and the other half to the town to buy some old fashioned streetlights. My drawings sold for $150.00 apiece.

117 Think First....

Last week I attended an animator's meeting held at the Hart building. It was a most inspiring session and everyone present seemed to be enthusiastic about it. I hope such meetings can be an ongoing happening. James Baxter showed a British Television comedy and handed out some material that Richard Williams has been collecting — possibly for future publication.

As I glanced through the writings and quotes of the contributors, one thing that stood out in each animators approach was: *think first, then draw*. Let me just quote some of them briefly. And bear in mind these are not just "aids" for drawing — these are basic to their way of working,

9 out of 10 times before I animate I *know exactly* what I'm going to do. The worst thing you can do is to get into anything before you *know* what you're doing.

Milt Kahl

Think about your work before you sit down to do it. You must think and plan — you can't wing it.

Art Babbitt

Planning it so that you know exactly where you're going...

Grim Natwick

I think it's in the planning. If you can plan the stuff out so you really know exactly what you're gonna do ... if you know exactly what you're going to do — and have it visualized — why you can do it pretty fast.

Ollie Johnston

"The only advice I know is to think it all out in your mind and then draw it the best you can....
                                                                              Ken Harris

In a class such as we have on Tuesday and Wednesday evenings, it is very difficult to get into specifics of animation. One thing that is missing when making a single drawing is the advantage of watching the change take place in the poses as you flip one drawing over another. For instance, having an anticipation drawing on your pegs makes it *easier* to draw a stretch drawing coming out of it. I emphasized easier because I'd like to suggest that just because it's easier, does not mean it is the *only* way of drawing a stretch drawing. I have always said that drawing is a mental activity, especially when drawing for animation, which is inextricably tied in with the story. The whole purpose of drawing is to put over a story point, and that story point has to be firmly established *first in the mind* before starting a drawing.

So in a classroom situation, the artists should realize that every pose is the study of a gesture. If the drawing happens to involve a stretch, then in the absence of another drawing to flip from, a good approach would be to imagine where the figure had come from (anticipatory pose). This is tantamount to saying that every drawing you make should be an action analysis exercise. In other words, ask yourself "What is the story here and how would this gesture fit into a bit of animation action?" That is the mental side of drawing.

Let's consider how one might "think through" a pose. Take, for instance, a woman sitting down, brushing her hair. First of all there should be a feeling of squash where her body is plunked down on the chair. No real need for another drawing to flip from — a squash is a squash. It doesn't need to be spread all over the chair seat but it should look as though it is supporting the weight of her upper body. She pulls at her hair with her brush. Naturally she would lean into the pull to free her hair from her neck and shoulders causing a stretch in the direction of the pull. To help that action you might use the opposite leg to help push the body into the action. You might tilt the head in the direction of the pull of the brush to emphasize that activity. You might show some of the hair being pulled away from the head in a good clean silhouette and angle the arms to help in the outward pull of the brushing. You don't need another drawing to figure all this out. You just need to *know what is happening* and then incorporate the principles of drawing and physics to illustrate that.

It just so happens that there was such a pose in one of our recent drawing sessions. One of the drawings was coming off in a rather stilted manner. There seems to be a kind of intellectual attempt to incorporate angles, anatomy, negative shapes, and clarity in the drawing. But one thing seems to be missing — a total involvement on the part of the woman in brushing her hair. My accompanying sketch is an attempt to make brushing her hair the story point and to direct all attention to that one thing. I agree that a great variety of poses will be employed as a woman brushes her hair. The artist's may well be one of them. Or perhaps the story point could have called for the woman to hear something disturbing, like a burglar trying to pry open the bedroom window, and she freezes in this position as she listens.

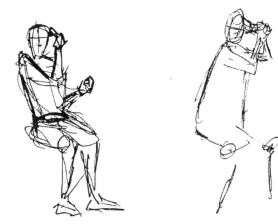

A gesture is a body doing something. Certain things have to happen to facilitate the body in doing it. Those certain things are the things we are interested in, whether it is in an animation drawing or in a simple still drawing. Better yet, it is the mental manipulation that helps us find those things that we are interested in, for if we can picture the gesture in our minds, then we can draw it.

118   Piles of Nuts

No one would dream of starting out to create a car by assembling piles of nuts, bolts, and miscellaneous parts. Nor should you dream of starting a drawing by assembling a bunch of bones, muscles, and miscellaneous parts. My observations in the Tuesday and Wednesday classes (and as animator/key cleanup for many years) has led me to believe this is the most self-evident roadblock standing in your way — starting with the parts. Somehow you will have to look beyond that beguiling surface appearance with its hypnotizing bulges of clothing and lines that so often misrepresent what goes on underneath. The model in class or the model sheet at the animation desks are merely there to identify the character used to perform the story you are telling.

There is an overwhelming tendency to draw the outline of the figure rather than the energy and thought within the body that is behind the move or the pose. A varying degree of mental and physical effort is put forth in executing an action. That effort involves *muscular tensions, weight distribution, balance and counterbalance.* Those are the things you must concentrate on — the outline of the body doesn't always reveal them. The outline is only the edge of the figure from where you are observing it. Move around the figure and the edge changes. The tension, weight distribution, balance, and counterbalance doesn't change. They are, you might say, the guts of the pose. If you make *one* line that doesn't further reveal those things then it is like chaff and should be blown away by the wind. For all parts and lines of the body synchronize to form the pose. There are many parts with but one thing to say.

Picture a wave breaking on the beach. There is an energy behind its move — the wind and the moon's pull. And the shape it takes on the shore is the shape of the beach. There are subtle hills and valleys of sand, and the water creeps as far as it can up into the valleys. All along the wave's path are foamy patterns that are stretched out, visually defining the path and direction of the move. The circular forms of foam elongate in the direction of the flow. All the parts of the wave help to define the move. That is what happens when a figure makes a move. Or if the figure strikes a pose — that is like the wave at some chosen point in its journey. The forces are still at work whether at its extreme or somewhere approaching it. And for a good illustration of animation picture the wave as it is sucked back to the sea. There is overlap as the main body of water (primary action) rushes back down the slope, while the shallow foam-studded tip remains a moment longer (secondary action). Some of the foam will even go beyond the water's extreme, for a little follow through. The elastic-like action causes the circular or oblong foam patterns to stretch into long linear shapes that are stretched to the breaking point, all the while defining the shape of the beach.

Meanwhile, back at the studio, I confiscated a few drawings from the last drawing session to illustrate some points. *In all cases* there is the first consideration — story. Then the use of balance and counterbalance, weight distribution, and muscular tensions. And because of these things you automatically get an outline — you get silhouette, negative space, squash and stretch, etc. In the first drawing I interrupted the artist because I felt he was preoccupied with parts such as clothing bulges, folds, and an arm with a hand on it. And I could not tell what was taking place. What should have been taking place was that this person is aghast at something that was said to her on the telephone. She draws away from it in disgust and holds the phone at an "I don't believe what I just heard" distance. In my sketch, however crude, can you see the balance and counterbalance, the weight distribution, the tensions?

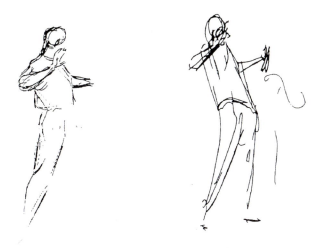

The next drawing, too, was begun minus a story. A very fine artist did this. She would have made a nice drawing of it, but I interrupted to plead for concentrating on the story first. The model was in a listening attitude, requiring that she lean forward with interest (weight distribution). The extended arm on the left counterbalances the extended elbow on the right. Muscular tension is used to stretch the upper body from the buttocks to the shoulder. Dropping the head down accents that stretch. Like the wave forming itself to the shore (its story), the figure forms itself to the "mold" of that gesture (its story). Any surface details on the figure would work like the patterns of foam on the wave.

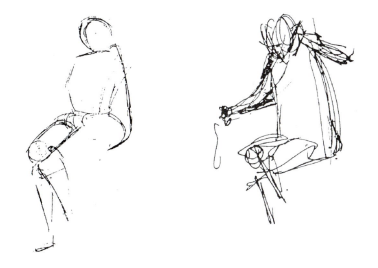

The next pose offers an excellent opportunity to use counterbalance. This is a large doll the model is holding (our own Carole Holliday — she was great). And whether it is heavy or just bulky, the natural thing to do is thrust out your hip or belly to form a resting "shelf" for it. This requires that you bend back at the waist, and counterbalance that by getting the feet back far enough so you won't fall over backwards. This, plus the shoulders held high to support the outstretched arms, shows that the doll is at least slightly cumbersome.

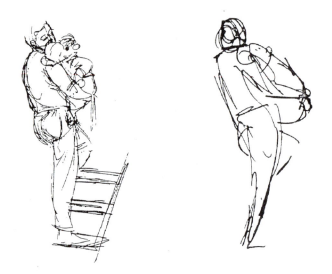

The last one is the same pose — different angle — same problem. I extended the right arm to show more bulk and thrust the left shoulder up to counterbalance. Also, since the weight is on the right leg, tilting the pelvis up on that side, the left buttocks will have dropped down. That forms a nice tension between that buttocks and the upraised shoulder.

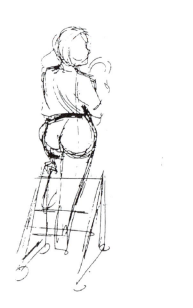
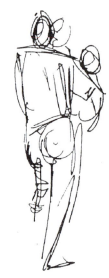

BONUS SECTION: The following are some of Ollie Johnston's drawings from *The Rescuers* that show Penny grappling with a similar problem (cleaned up incidentally by Walt Stanchfield). They read from right to left.

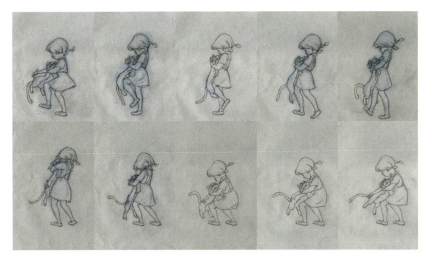

Again, I apologize for being so wordy but if you want to get the most out of your drawing, you're going to have to think like that. Once it becomes part of your "second" nature, it will happen unconsciously, but it's going to take some work to cut the groove first. It will not only make drawing more pleasurable, but will make it easier and faster to solve your problems by easing the pressure of those inevitable deadlines. As Ollie Johnston used to say, "It ain't easy."

119 A Meaningful Assembly

Drawing should reveal the structure of form and anatomy, but it must also reveal the structure of life and livingness. The structure of form and anatomy are some of the tools we use to build our drawings, but we must go beyond that to evoke the full range of the subject's feelings and gestures. It is possible to make a perfectly factual representation of a skeleton using all the proper parts in their proper proportion and position. Here are the parts.

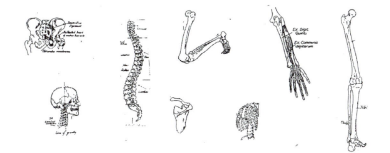

Here is the assembly.

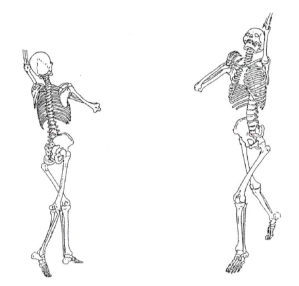

The mere assembling of parts, of course, results in a cold, lifeless diagram of a structure. Adding muscles and flesh would help to create an illusion of life to a certain extent, but it would need the infusion of a story to make it come to life. With the help of a story line, something to suggest life and livingness, even a skeleton can be brought to life. Look at what Edmund Sullivan has done with the skeleton in these illustrations for *Rubaiyat of Omar Khayyam*. Even without flesh, brain, blood, or nerves, the skeleton becomes a motivated being, acting out a part in a story:

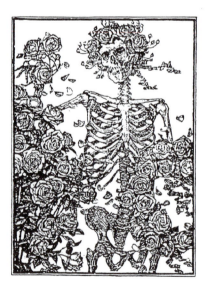
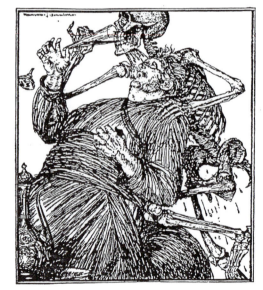

So, as you can see the parts in themselves mean nothing. Even if the parts were put together flawlessly, it would mean nothing. But give them a story to tell and they arouse the imagination of the artist and the interest of the viewer. The audience is captivated and becomes only too willing to allow themselves to be carried off into some other dimension. That's what story telling is all about. And whatever aura you may have been led to believe surrounds the "artist," the one you should consider and accept is that *the artist is a storyteller*.

Roger Chiasson, in his own way, has assembled the parts of model, Holly Brown, and given them meaning. Roger confessed that story was not foremost in his mind as he drew them. He first considered weight distribution then balance, proportion, and other principles of drawing to capture the gestures. Nevertheless, he has drawn the parts well, and has assembled them in a way that should inspire all of us to not only aspire to reach his enviable state of accomplishment, but to goad us into a self-improvement program that will ensure its realization.

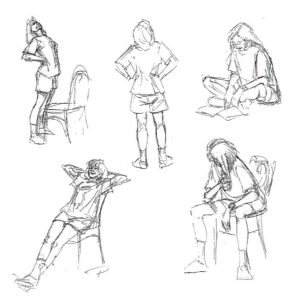

120 The Time has Come, The Walrus Said...

The time has come, the walrus said,
to talk of many things:
of shoes and ships and sealing wax
of cabbages and kings
and why the sea is boiling hot
and whether pigs have wings.

Well, I'm back from a two week-trip to Taos, New Mexico. It was an invigorating rut-breaker. You might think that being semi-retired would automatically set one free of ruts, but not so as some *Wizard of Id* characters so clearly point out.

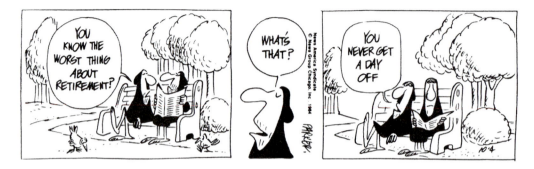

However, it's not always easy to get away like that (like to distant places), so one must look for substitutes closer to home. One of the best ways to escape life's tedium is closer to home than home, it is in the mind. Attitude, curiosity, interest, enthusiasm, discovery, awareness — those are all mental attributes that keep one alive and fresh and growing.

When my wife, Dee, and I go on a trip, she drives every inch of the way (she likes to) while I sketch (at 65 to 70mph — that will sharpen your senses); or I read short stories or positive thinking stuff aloud. New scenery is always invigorating. It's a first time experience that seems to reveal its contents in a flash. It's like revving up an engine to 75 mph to loosen the carbon collected there, and blowing it out the exhaust. First time experiences cleanse your senses. They break down habit plaque, clarifying seeing and thinking.

Well, when I got home, I looked around me and the people and the landscape were seen afresh as if I were traveling in foreign territory. So traveling is a major means of getting a soul massage. But what about those of us (meaning you) who have to go through long grueling periods of work and overtime. Diversity is hard to come by. And that's when it is needed most. One substitute is to travel vicariously. There're often excellent travel shows on television. Novels have a way of transporting us to distant places as if by magic. You can go to Fort Lauderdale, Florida, and then to far off places with Travis McGee as he carries out his Clint Eastwood type adventures in John D. MacDonald's exciting series. You can go to New Mexico via Tony Hillerman's books as his Navajo Indian cop takes you into the desert canyons in pursuit of the villain. They are sprinkled with Indian culture and legends.

Paintings, drawings, and cartoons have a renewing potion in them. If you feel the need of a new look at the world — study an artist you have neglected. Read up on him, research his methods, his way of life, his attitude toward life and art. Buy a newspaper or *The New Yorker* and study the cartoons. Don't just settle for laughs but study how different cartoonists have slanted their unique versions of life and humor. And of course, continue to watch animation and live action films always with a fresh view and purpose.

When I was in high school I took a class in motion picture study. In it I learned to judge and study films with four things in mind: story, direction, acting, and photography. There are many more ingredients in film making, but these things are basic (about all I could ever handle anyway). They gave purpose to my viewing pleasure. It sometimes led to boredom while others around me were enjoying a show, but I always figured that discrimination is an upward path. To settle for the mediocre is like dining at a fast food place. There's nothing wrong with being critical as long as it's for a constructive purpose. If we settle for mediocrity then mediocrity will find a welcome haven in our own work.

Reading, observing, analyzing, and studying new things are all good substitutes for traveling to new territories. They will help to blow the carbon out of your brains and keep your interest and curiosity always in sharp shape. Drift along, and ennui, arrested vision, stale thinking, and habit will envelop you. Tee Hee, that great teacher and lovable guy, advised: never drive home by the same route twice, but if you must, look at the surroundings anew each time. Get in the habit of treating every experience as a first time happening. Observe, observe, observe. Be like a sponge — suck up all the knowledge you can. William Mallack, on station KPFK, said the other day that "It's best to know a few things thoroughly than a lot of things in a shallow way." I disagree, partially. An artist has to be knowledgeable in many things: drawing (which is complicated enough in itself), acting, story, direction, physics, logics, music, drama, comedy, etc. Plus a sprinkling of philosophy and psychology to keep it all in reasonable balance. In your business you don't have to know all that stuff thoroughly, but you do have to have a smattering of it. Of course the clincher is this: There's not much you can do with any of that knowledge unless you can draw well enough to express it, which emboldens me to offer some advice: LEARN TO DRAW.

I would like to share one person's progress in learning to draw. Her training was in commercial art — rendering, lettering, layout, etc. – but she has decided to study drawing and animation. Her first attempts were matchstick figures. For starters, I encouraged her to use two matchsticks to show a thickness to the forms:

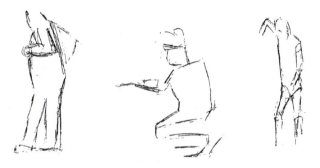

This encouraged her to think of the shapes as having volume. Then to simplify those bewildering complicated gestures, I suggested thinking of the torso as the base of the figure. It locates the figure on the paper, establishes the basic pose, and it establishes a place to attach the arms, legs, and neck. (It makes me almost weep to watch, night after night, artists attaching arms and legs onto a blank spot on the paper, then later having to draw the body to fit those connection points.)

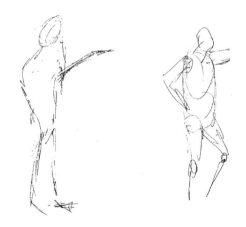

There were no long-standing bad habits to break. She very early began seeing in the round for she was introduced to thinking of foreshortened limbs as cylinders advancing into the picture plane. Right off, she was drawing her figures in space rather than copying the outline of the model. I won't venture to guess what the future holds for her, but I am impressed with her progress in the evening class to this point. Let's hear a round of applause for Wendy Werner, and a wish for continued growth. The following are some of her recent drawings.

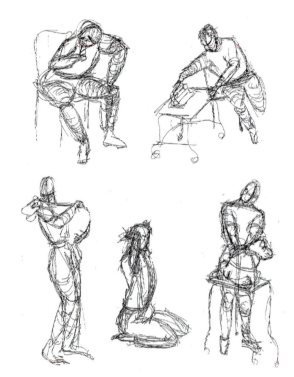

121 Clarity

Most of our daily activities could not be classified as spectacular. As a matter of fact most of our movements are rather confined. It's usually with a bit of self-consciousness that we flail our arms or act out some part of our dialog. Yet nothing is lost in our communication with others because they are "tuned in" to us auditorily. That is, they are in a listening mode. Sometimes someone will gesticulate with his hands while talking, which often pulls our attention away from the verbal attachment.

Drawing and animation are, in contrast, not auditory but visual. Therefore visual clarity is necessary. Oddly enough, verbalizing a pose or a gesture mentally before starting to draw will help to disengage any obstacles that might stand in the way of drawing the idea clearly. For instance, if you have a character looking at someone or something, verbalizing it by saying to yourself: "This guy is looking at something (how much clearer can you be than that?), so I will get every obstacle out of the way... like pulling back (in this case) the right shoulder. Then to show he is interested in what he is looking at, I'll have him lean forward. This can be done by bending him forward at the waist, and also by stretching his neck forward (still pretty simple and clear)." *Voila*! that gives me some squash and stretch, the salt and pepper of drawing and animation. And *voila* #2, I now have what Stanchfield calls the "first impression."

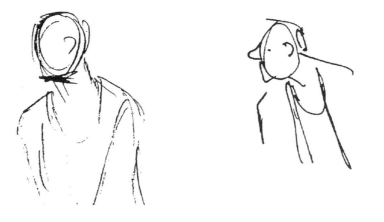

Here is another example. Maybe same pose with different artist, but same dialog.

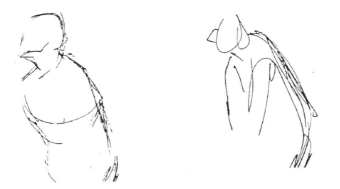

Run through some of our feature cartoons and notice how many scenes are just "looking" scenes. I would venture to guess 90% of them. (Not counting Sleeping Beauty and Rip Van Winkle) So it's not like we are talking about an action that just comes along every 100 feet or so, so why spend so much energy on it? Cartoons are not only mainly visual but the characters in them are visual – they look and see. Here's another example. This guy is not only looking at something, he is wondering about it also. What better way to show this than to have him bend forward. Note I simplified the bend by exposing his bent back. This allowed me to more clearly show the neck projecting forward from the back and upper chest. Then since he is bent forward, his garments in front can just hang down. That makes a nice use of straight (chest) against curve (back). And what better way to display bewilderment than to have a "sag" (the garments in front) somewhere in the drawing. The line of the bent back also helps to project the eye direction. The straight of the chest acts as a soundboard (sight board) for the look, like a ball bouncing off a handball court. All this came about through verbalizing what I wanted to make visual. It has nothing to do with highfalutin theory or complicated postulations. It is an act of simplification, a means of clarifying the "story" in my mind and how best to portray it (see the following illustration).

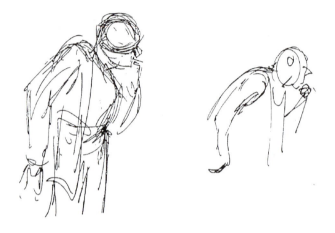

    Here is another pose that would be difficult to capture without some personal verbal guidance. The model had her left elbow stretched up a little higher than the right. "Stretched" was the clue word (verbal clue). So I turned that whole side into a stretch, using ziggy-zaggy lines on the other side for the squash. It may seem like an oversimplification of the problem, but if it's not clear in your mind, chances are it's not going to be clear in your drawing. The thing is it has to be clear in both places, for you can verbalize in your mind before making the drawing, but after the drawing is made you can't follow it around verbalizing an explanation to everyone who looks at it. Here are two artists' attempts at this pose plus my (possible) clarification.

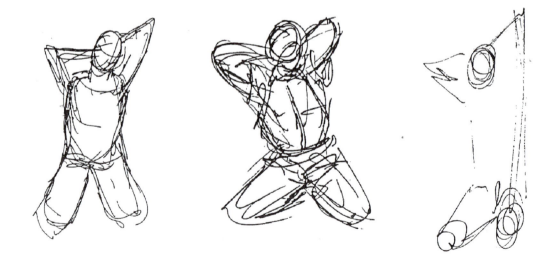

Awaken the storytelling capabilities in your mind and use whatever means you can to funnel it into your drawing. At this point I just don't know of another way than to rehearse it in your mind (verbalize) so you know what it is you are attempting to say like an actor who rehearses his lines and stage directions. If you can verbalize it, at least that means you are not sketching ghosts — you've something very tangible to work with.

I sometimes speak of logic in drawing. Here's a case in point. Stand up and try to bend from the waist to your right. Does your left hip want to protrude? It sure does. As a matter of fact it's almost painful to try to bend without that hip shooting out. If that knowledge isn't second nature to you yet, and if it's not real obvious on the model, then you're just going to have to have a friendly chat with yourself. Don't be embarrassed for having to instruct yourself on such simple matters, you'll be happy for it when you see the results. After all it's not pride your working for – it's results. Make the verbal advice clear and simple, say, "Hey, look man, when someone stands with their weight on the left leg — the left hip naturally protrudes. The whole hip tilts as a result, especially when the right knee is bent. It looks almost like the right knee is pulling the right side of the hip down. It adds movement and tension to the drawing." You sketch that. "Wow," you will probably say, "that's great," and will be encouraged to continue in that vein, "now, since the hips are tilted that way the shoulders would most likely tilt the other way for balance…," etc. Remember, clarity doesn't just happen — it's created.

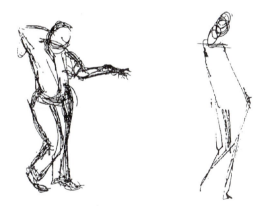

122   Action or Reaction?

Walt Disney said:

The story man must see clearly in his own mind how every piece of business in a story will be put over. He should feel every expression, every reaction. He should get far enough away from his story to take a second look at it … to see whether there is any dead phase… to see whether the personalities are going to be interesting and appealing to the audience. He should also try to see that the things that his characters are doing are of an interesting nature.

It's not my business to pass judgment on the story people, but I do feel strongly that they should be masters at the very things we are studying in the Tuesday and Wednesday evening classes; that is, gesture drawing (storytelling drawing). A story sketch should convey the complete message of all the combined efforts that have gone into the story boards up until the time they 're finally accepted (expand that word "efforts" to include the sweat, frustration, pain, and total involvement), When the story sketch is turned over to the animator, it should be a firm foundation for the scene's animation. The mood or atmosphere should be established so the animator understands what it is he is working for. Here is an example of Vance Gerry's beautifully conceived mood setting sketches that Ollie Johnston used (and clearly followed) to create a most sensitive bit of animation for the *The Rescuers*.

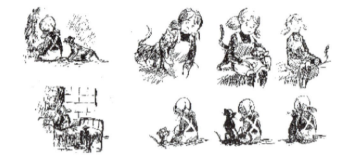

Here are some of Ollie's final drawings from that scene (cleaned up, by the way, by yours truly). Notice how Ollie was able to retain the feeling that Vance had created in his story sketches.

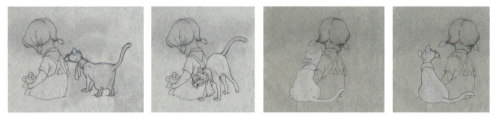

I'd like also to share a few of Ollie's ruff drawings to show how he didn't just draw the outline of Vance's drawings, but added his own vastly creative efforts to bring them to their ultimate fruition:

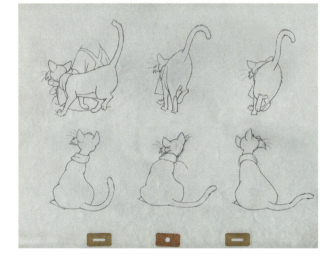

In one "handout" I spoke of assuming the role of a young child and "acting like" one to pry yourself out of the sedation that daily living inflicts on you. In another I suggested using an inner dialog to guide you into depicting the story behind the gesture. Here is another method you might consider — the figurative language of the poet.

1. A comparison likens two objects that belong to the same class; that is, you might say, "His nose looks like W.C. Field's nose." Such an association will help you hone in on a nose drawing problem, providing of course, you have done your nose investigation homework.
2. Simile. That is a comparison of things that are in different classes: "His nose looks like a light bulb." Sue… (sorry my memory fails me) thought I looked like a light bulb — here is her "How to draw Walt Stanchfield" classic.

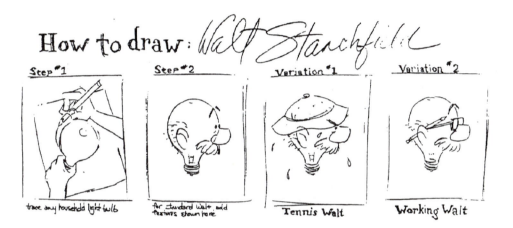

3. A metaphor is an implied comparison between objects of unlike classes. But instead of saying a thing looks like another, it says the thing *is* another: "His nose is a red light bulb."
4. Another more illusive and complicated one is analogy, where comparisons are made by attributes: "His nose is like a bat," because the nose hangs from the forehead like a bat hangs from a ceiling. Or "his nose is like an electrical wire." Not because it looks like a wire, but because something goes through both of them — air through the nose and electricity through the wire.

I'm not trying to make poets of you, but the mental pictures that aid them in writing can also aid you in drawing. And let me interject here the great benefits of reading, attending plays, movies, and sketching (studying people and wildlife), for as your input increases, so does your output. You need lots of background to form your comparisons.

Creativity begins with action. It ends with reaction. Let me explain that. If you simply *react* to your surroundings you will be a product created by your surroundings, but if you *act* on your own, your surroundings will be a creation of your own. So it is with drawing. If you simply copy the outline of the model, that is *reaction*; if you act, that is, use your intelligence to create a living gesture (with a story behind it) that is *action*.

Here are a couple of examples where action on the part of the artist could have led to a clearer portrayal of a piece of action. In the first example, the artist copied too much of what he saw, rather than match his drawing to the action that was to be depicted. The model was rather bent-backed and also portly in front. Trying to get both of those things in his drawing (reaction) the curved lines of the back and belly canceled out the feeling that the figure was bending forward slightly:

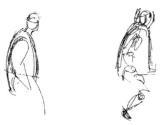

Here is another example where the artist reacted to the happenstance view he was "stuck" with and copied it in a submissive/reactive manner. I suggested since the sword was an important part of the story perhaps we could spread the legs more and adjust the angles of the arms, legs, and hands to get the sword out into the opening, also to get a feeling of movement by pulling up on the handle with the left hand and pushing down on the blade with the right hand.

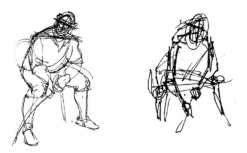

Here's another drawing that was more or less copied from the model. Live action can somehow get away with this kind of mincing acting, but drawing has to be caricatured. If you will glance back and forth from the student's drawing to mine you will see how I created a feeling of movement by projecting the face out beyond the hand. A good drawing should have that "tingly" feeling of life in it. Even though it's a still drawing, it has a suggestion of movement in it. Make it one of your thinking and drawing habits — ACTION, NOT REACTION.

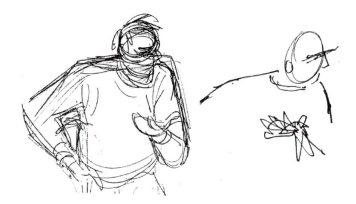

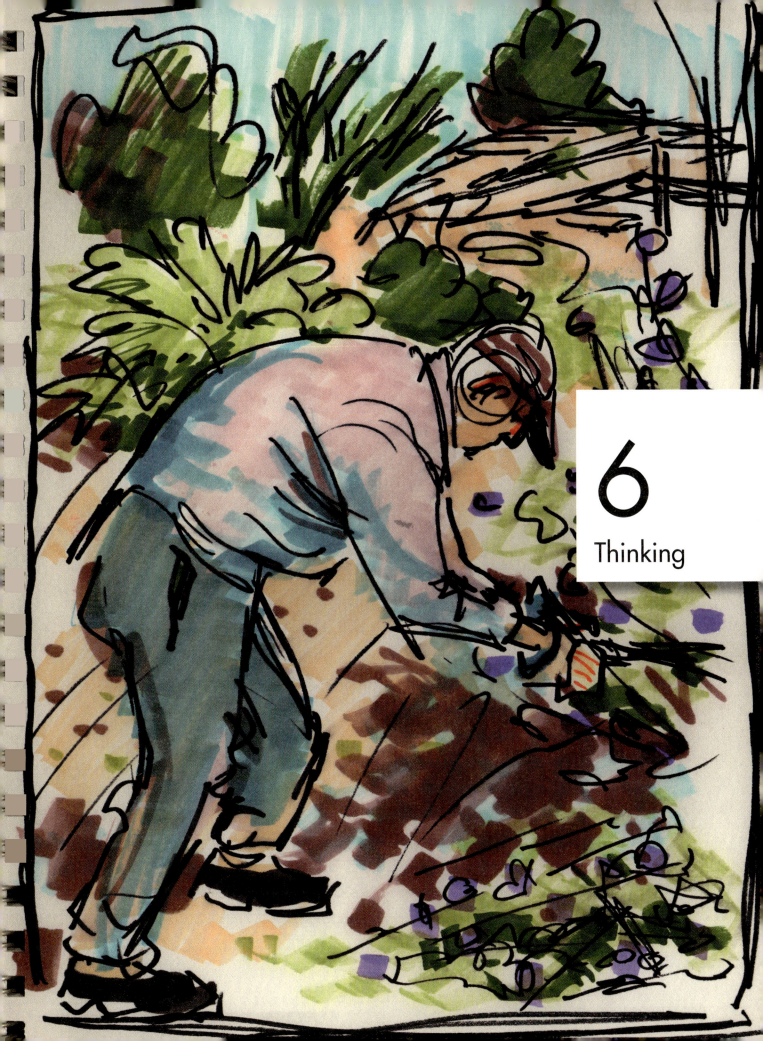

6

Thinking

123 Be Transformed

In an article in the *Christian Science Monitor*, I came upon the phrase, "the trance of non-renewal." It referred to organizations and communities that are satisfied with things as they are.

It is as though the system were asleep under a magic spell. A feature of the trance of non-renewal is that individuals can look straight at a flaw in the system and not see it as a flaw. Although the organization that is gravely in need of renewal may show many signs of its threatened condition, the signs cannot be seen by those who are under the spell.

It occurred to me that a variation of this kind of problem may be stalking some of you aspiring artists who may need to improve your drawing ability yet being under "the spell," are unable to see the flaw, or worse, look right at it and not see it as a flaw.

One reason I think this might be possible is that most of us are fairly private in developing our talents. Part of it is a downright reluctance to have someone else see our mistakes and shortcomings; part of it is that innate quality that says "I can do it myself." The isolation that this kind of philosophy leads to is a narrower and narrower view of the problem. Living with the sameness of our drawings and our drawing ability month after month is a trance former. The trance envelops us slowly so that we are eventually numbed into an inability to spot our defects.

If such is the case, there is a need to be trance-formed (transformed). But how to do this? Especially if you don't feel a need to improve, or if you do — don't feel you have the time and energy to act on it. There may also be that debilitating cult of "waiting for the light to come on." Believe me, the light isn't going to "come on" — you have to turn it on yourself. If you have neglected your drawing improvement badly, you may figuratively have to back up and do some rewiring so some electricity can get through. The longer you wait, the harder it will be to break the trance and the less time and energy you will have to do it.

Also you will have filled your life with other, albeit important, activities that become your lifestyle — your bag of habits. A friend once told me "You do what you are in the habit of doing." That statement has helped me greatly in avoiding habits that would eat into my valuable time. Once habits are formed they seem as natural as going to sleep and waking up. In time enough, habits will be formed to fill your days so you are entranced into saying, "I don't have time to study drawing." Perhaps only a few of you fit fully into that category, but still to some degree or other we're all a little bit "trancey."

I enjoy being critical. I'm being paid to criticize your drawings (of those who come to the evening classes), but only to search out a way to help improve your concept of drawing. I put it that way because drawing originates as a mental concept. In the evening classes I can spot evidences of trance malignancy. Most of it is caused by habit, the habit of approaching all drawings in the same way, but not always the best way. It's difficult to change a habit; especially if it's an old and comfortable one. I approach drawing instruction by trying to change one's method of seeing; that is, looking at a pose or gesture as a "story." This should encourage you to draw the idea behind the pose and not attempt to copy the model, line by line. Copying the outline and the details on the model remind me of a person working a crossword puzzle by blowing up the solution and pasting it on the blank puzzle, completely oblivious of the "story" or the meaning of the words.

Drawing should be fun. When I say drawing, I'm talking about grappling with a graphic depiction of some bit of story. I'm talking about digging down deep into your mental resources and coming up with a drawing that tells that story in a sensitive, exciting, and clear way; all the parts of it contributing to its efficacy; every line working in relation to every other line to compliment the whole. Nothing trance-like in that.

Artists are able to do that. They are an especially sensitive lot. Recently I was reviewing the book, *A Poetry Primer*, by Gerald Sanders.

In the first chapter he attempts to describe the "poet." In my mind I substituted the word "artist" wherever "poet" appeared and it seemed very apropos. Here is the passage with the word artist inserted:

In the first place, the artist has an exquisitely sensitive mind that makes him alive to nuances that escape the average person. He is aware of nice distinctions in both the inner and outer worlds — nature and the mind — and apprehends subtle influences that pass unheeded by prosaic folk. Bits of knowledge, inappreciable experiences, evanescent emotions of which a blunter consciousness is scarcely cognizant, he seizes upon and uses. Thus he is often able to trace more obscure causes and to perceive more distant effects than others usually do.

He also has a fine memory — not perhaps for names and telephone numbers, but for whatever he has experienced of action and emotion in the world around him or in his own mind. Wordsworth, for instance, says that drawing "takes its origin from emotion recollected in tranquility." But to the average person such experiences tend to recede with the passing of time and to become nebulous and indistinct. The artist, on the other hand, seems able long after the event to recall his experience and reproduce an emotion with the same acute consciousness as when they were new.

He has a wider and more varied experience than most men — the result, first, of his great sensitivity; secondly, of his ability to observe man and nature closely; and thirdly, of a deep sympathy, which enables him to enter easily into the experiences of others. Nothing seems too great or too small for his attention; further, he possesses in an extraordinary degree the ability to integrate his wide experience. By means of a powerful imagination, which acts upon the jumbled mass of information in his mind, he is able to create new experiences, to combine incongruous elements in such a way as to produce harmonious effects, and from old ideas to secure new connotations.

In addition he has the happy faculty of expressing his ideas and emotions in adequate images. This is one of his rarest attributes, for the expression of emotionalized experience in fitting graphic form is the culmination of man's ability to communicate, and in this the artist is supreme.

I'm afraid I've gone and gotten wordy again. So to win back your affection, here are some drawings to feast your eyes on. The first group was drawn by Pres Romanillos. These were done on a night when I badgered him to loosen up. He did, and the results are marvy. They are, on the Stanchfield scale of one to ten with ten being best — a ten. The second group is by Ash Brannon, who is no longer with us, but hopefully will return when he has completed his desired schooling.

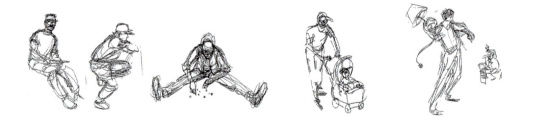

124 Be Relentless

I have been trying to pin down the difference in attitude that it takes to switch from copying the model (or model sheet) to creating from the model. At best, everything that has turned up has been either nebulous, arcane, or ethereal (to me it's all very concrete). But I am relentless. A couple of times I used the right and left-brain activities to clarify it. Simply put, the left brain loves to name the parts and place them in their proper places, which can be factual but sterile. On the other hand, the right brain is not interested in the parts per se (anatomy, for instance), only in so far as they can be assembled into some desired use; to bring meaning to them, or better yet, use them to create something meaningful. The left brain couldn't care less about telling a story. It only cares that the proper language was used or the parts are authentic. The right brain will gladly sacrifice scrupulous adherence to facts, as long as it can tell a story or describe a mood or gesture. To accomplish this the right brain will even stretch the facts, that is, caricature them.

True, as Glen Keane pointed out recently, knowing the parts well will help in many ways, especially in building confidence. This means if you know your anatomy well, you are free to manipulate it to your purposes. Whereas if you don't know your anatomy you are striving to capture it as you draw and deflecting your attention from what should be your goal — storytelling.

I continue to rack my brain for other ways to help you break away from copying. Here is another one prompted by the current persimmon season (I'm a persimmon addict). An unripe persimmon has all the physical parts of a respectable persimmon but will cause your mouth to pucker up if you bite into it. But when the fruit looks like it's ready to be thrown out, then a bite of it yields its true essence.

While we're on food, how about an apple pie. The apples, the sugar, the flour, and the printed recipe are certainly all factual ingredients but hardly say, "apple pie," as yet. It's a real expressive apple pie, though, when it comes out of the oven, warm and toasty looking, with that fresh baked apple and cinnamon odor wafting forth — that's apple pie!

Try this one. Consider the picture screen on your television. There are adjustments to manipulate when the picture is unclear. One knob controls the vertical hold, one the horizontal; one knob adjusts the color, one the hue, and one the intensity of the image. When all the knobs are adjusted properly, you get a clear picture. When drawing there are several "knobs" that need to be constantly adjusted — they clarify the image in a way that will help transfer it to paper. They are the principles of perspective. When any or all of them are off, you will have various combinations of flatness, tangents, parallels, direction-less lines, nebulous or missing parts necessary to tell the story, and the usual "snowy" veil of confusion (next you will find six of those principles of perspective in an ultra-simple form).

Maybe I'm stretching this whole thing too far, but I feel things like this when I draw. The essence is there — the ripeness, the proper combination of parts, angles, and shapes. It's a kind of shifting of gears (maybe shifting to the right brain mode) and going for the "ripe persimmon," or the full baked "apple pie," or the "sharp TV image."

You all know how putting on dark glasses brings out the clouds in a sky, cuts through the haze, and intensifies the lights and darks in a landscape. That is what should happen when you look at the model for your first impression. Try this experiment. Look at a scene with "naked" eyes, then alternately with dark glasses. You will notice that the glasses separate objects in space, almost as if they were 3D glasses. A more clarified reality is born. That is the kind of viewing you should be striving for while drawing. Not merely outlines, with their lateral predominance but rather three dimensionally, with depth employed to disentangle the shapes and lines, which in a two-dimensional drawing, try to occupy the same space, like a tree growing between two sheets of glass.

The scene you used for that experiment, of course, had light, shade, color, and aerial perspective to sculpt it. Drawing has but one thing — line. To get that same clarifying dark-glasses effect with line alone you have to incorporate these principles of perspective (or principles of drawing if you prefer).

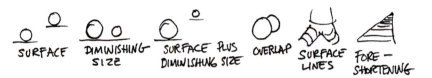

These may seem simple to the point of absurd, but believe me, every drawing you ever make will (or should) have all of these principles present.

I was fortunate to be able to Xerox some drawings from Glen Keane's sketchbooks from his recent trip to England and France. I want you to enjoy them for their excellence and beauty, but also to look at them critically; that is, analytically, especially with those rules of perspective in mind. I will break one of them down to get you started. (My apologies to Glen for performing vivisection on his drawings.)

Here is a quick sketch made in a park in London. See how he has created both a plane and depth by placing the feet higher than the hands (rules 1, 2, and 3). He meant to have the right hand higher and smaller (rules 1, 2, and 3), but when in his haste he realized the arm was already too low, he stopped drawing there. Finishing off the hand would have tipped the ground off kilter. Being a quick sketch he didn't bother to alter it. (Am I close, Glen?) How nicely the upper left leg overlaps (rule 4) the right leg, then the ankles cross over and the right foot then overlaps the left. Look how deftly the ear/or earring overlaps the subtle suggestion of a cheek. The knees, shorts cuffs, and blouse bottom display rule 5 surface lines. Foreshortening (rule 6) was acquired by making the legs diminish in size from the arms. Compare the leg size to the closest arm. Also he has made a very simple back bend whose curved line works so well with the straight arms. Compare the leg size to the closest arm. Also he has made a very simple back bend whose curved line works so well with the straight line of the right arm. Notice that since the shoulders are being forced to their maximum breadth by the posture, the cloth from the neck is stretched into a pull. Notice how the neck continues the stretch of the back. You can't see it but you feel a squash at the front of the neck, since she appears to be looking slightly down. Anatomy? It's there, but it's not an anatomical drawing. It's a drawing of a girl sitting on the grass in the park. The presence of all those principles of perspective have helped to make this an excellent drawing.

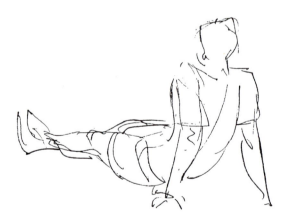

I'll spare you any further analysis (at this time) but I do hope you will study the rest of the drawings for the presence of these rules. I'm not inferring, by the way that Glen has ever heard of or seen these principles in the form I present them. But he has learned them somehow, and learned them well. When you are conscious of these rules, they are easier to incorporate into you drawing. Even as Glen said about anatomy, knowing them and how to use them will add to your confidence, and to your excellence in drawing. Be relentless in searching for ways to improve your drawings. Learn to apply these principles. Here are some of my favorites from Glen's sketchbooks.

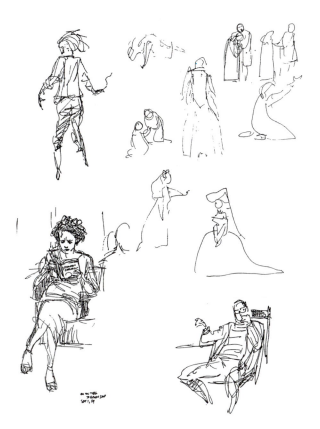
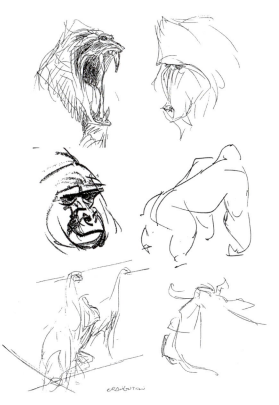

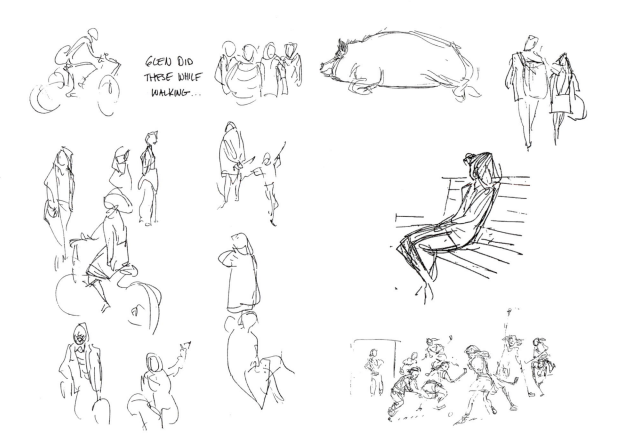

GLEN DID
THESE WHILE
WALKING...

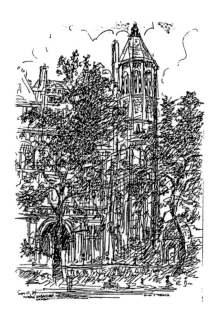

125 Adjust Your Crystal

While I am jotting down thoughts on drawing, I AM well aware that all who read them are at a different level of expertise. All I can do is pick my own brain and hope (sincerely, that is) that something will from time to time, pop up that you can incorporate into your psyche. Naturally, at this point, because the evening drawing class is almost my only contact with you, I base most of my criticism and analysis on what I observe in class. Some of you do not attend so there is no firsthand knowledge of either your problems or your skills. So I write on the assumption that drawing problems are at least partially universal. Even attitudes, in spite of that great verity individualism, are fairly universal. I am heartened by all that nebulous bit of assurance and move along. I am constantly encouraged by those who, week after week, comment on the handouts, remarking on how I had "hit home" on some problem.

I remember having very few brains to "pick" in my formative years. There was never anything as formal as a "handout." Occasionally someone would say something that hit home. I would dash back to my room, write it down, and tack it on my desk, hoping that in persistently reading it, it would somehow seep into my thick skull and become a part of me.

One of my big problems was not knowing the right questions to ask (or being ashamed to ask them). If you don't know something, even that it exists — what do you ask? How do you formulate a question about something you aren't even aware of? Even then, everyone is not able to communicate or verbalize the things they know and do. Even when you find someone who is verbally equipped to pass on his know-how, not everyone is equipped to sort it out and put it to use. Perhaps they are not on the same wavelength or of compatible "chemistry." A and B may be told something by C and afterwards A might have to explain to B the meaning of what C had said. Communication has a number of levels. A good teacher will be able to weave in and out of the possibilities of explaining something. I am reminded of the first radio my folks had.

It was a DeHoog crystal set. You had to move the point of a little wire around on a crystal to clarify the sound. That kind of adjustment between people is sometimes hard to manipulate.

Some people are "negative" by nature (or by upbringing or by self-choice) and so good chemistry is hard to come by. They may be wonderful people, desirous of learning and eager to do a good job, but often draw into a shell (of protection) because of repeated, non-productive attempts at communication.

Maybe it is because I was born in July, so being a "crab," I attack things sideways and from all angles. (Have you ever watched a crab running away from you at the beach? They run sideways, as if trying to fool you into thinking they're not really running in the direction they are running). One day, almost a half-century ago, during a discussion at coffee break, Hank Tanous, a very talented artist, said to me, "Walt, you're not broadminded, you're just wishy-washy." Well, I like the idea of being "wishy-washy." If I ever get "set in my ways," I want it to be in a flexible, "wishy-washy" way. I think everyone should practice "wishy-washyness" at least to the degree that they remain persuadable. There are ideas to be picked up all around us all on different levels. We must be willing to "adjust the wire on the crystal" to get in tune with them.

Smugness and self-satisfaction have no place in an artist's life. Not our kind of artists, anyway. Someday maybe you can retire and go to an attic and paint yourself into some narcissistic groove, but for now, everything should be OPERATION GATHER, with all levels of learning on GO.

RETRACTION DEPARTMENT Except this isn't a retraction but rather an explanation of something in the last handout. I wrote on a page of Glen Keane's drawings "Glen did these while walking." That wasn't really what I wanted to say about that page of drawings. I was in a hurry to wrap it all up and get it to the printer. Someone commented to me that they weren't impressed with his having done them while walking — as if it were some "acrobatic fete." I felt badly that it was taken that way, for what I really meant to say was that Glen is a relentless drawer, both in terms of learning and in practice. He's extremely enthusiastic about drawing, to the point where if he is on a sketching trip, he'll sketch out the window of a train or a hotel, or even sketch while walking. I admire that kind of attitude and devotion. I too am a walk-sketcher. While in England, I took some tours, and sketched all the way. We were approaching a castle once and I knew I wouldn't have a chance to stop (they'd have left me behind) so I sketched as I walked. I'm not saying this is or isn't a great sketch. That has nothing to do with it. What I'm saying is, the opportunity I had to sketch it was limited, but I made use of that opportunity. I'm proud of the sketch. I'm proud that I made it. I leave the judging of it to the "judges."

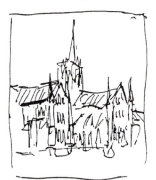

I have also sketched while sitting on snow, on wet rocks, and in freezing wind. I have done watercolor paintings standing in the cold wind and rain, holding an umbrella and a special drawing board I invented that strapped around my neck and leaned against my chest. (The spots on those paintings are real rain drops.) I never thought of them as "athletic fetes." There were things to sketch and my time to do it was limited to those particular moments. I am an inveterate lover of the Canadian 7, and Emily Carr, who trudged into the Canadian wilderness to sketch and paint Canada. They braved snow, freezing weather, mosquitoes the size of sparrows in numbers that rivaled the stars in the Milky Way, also grizzly bears that were a constant menace, and other countless hardships. Why?

Because they had an irresistible urge to sketch and paint what to them was the real Canada. No one in any sane way could interpret their activities as an "acrobatic fete." That was devotion to a cause that to me, is heroism, in all its glory. If you're called you go, if you're not called you stay home and prepare. You keep your crystal in good adjustment.

I was called to London to help out on the Roger Rabbit project. The first thing I did when I arrived in my office was to sketch the scene outside my window — the skyline of Camden Town:

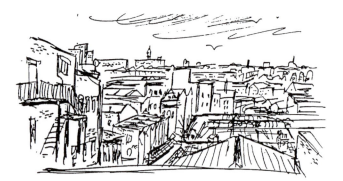

Also, I sketched out the windows of buses, trains, and the underground trains:

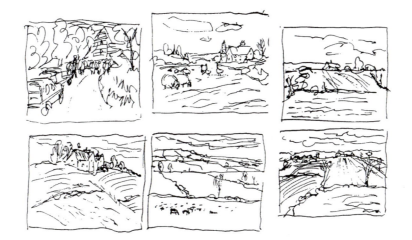

If you're an artist, you sketch period! Walk, run or fly, you sketch. Yes, I sketched out the window of the Delta flight to Orlando. Not because it was a fete but because it was an opportunity — you might say it was a necessity.

Incidentally, I admire people who keep on trying. There are a few people in the Tuesday and Wednesday class who are rank beginners. They come week after week and try and try and try. I pat them on the back not because they have made a Norman Rockwell-like drawing, but because there has been a little progress made. A lot of effort and a little progress. We may all be at different levels expertise-wise, but no matter what level we're on, we deserve credit for trying.

Sure, somewhere along the line there has to be some professionalism or the product will suffer. That's what these "handouts" are all about — to help in some small, large or whatever way. Me, I admire Glen for sketching while walking and I like the sketches, too. It was also suggested that if drawing while walking was such a special fete, maybe drawing while standing on one's head would be even more commendable. I won't argue with that. Betty Edwards, author of *Drawing on The Right Side of The Brain* (and other art teachers), have students draw the subjects upside down on their papers, and there seems to be some merit in that approach. I have beginners (and others) stop trying to draw, and let the pen do the work. Crazy? Perhaps, but it works wonders.

I don't mean for this to sound like a rebuke or a rebuttal, in any sense of the word. I just saw an opportunity to help broaden your view of this whole problem of drawing. Like a crab — learn to approach it from different angles. And above all, keep adjusting the crystal.

Now for something a little more tangible. Here is a drawing of the model holding a basket with her left hand on one side and by the forearm (half way between the wrist and the elbow) on the other side. She is looking into the basket opening. My sketch shows how she would thrust her hips out to make a "shelf" for the basket. Also since she was tilting the basket so she could look into it, she would have to raise her right arm and push down with her left hand. The tilt (angle) of her shoulders makes a nice foil for the neck and face angles and opens up a nice "stage" where her look into the basket is emphasized. Can you see how thinking these things out before you start to draw will help in getting the story down in a clear manner? Notice how all the angles and the whole stance point to the look at the basket opening, which is the story of this pose.

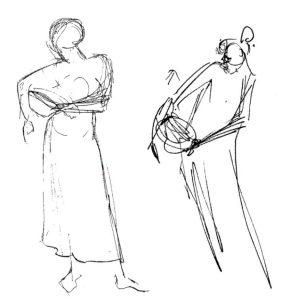

That's your critique for this week. Now here's your inspirational drawing — a very, very, very nice drawing by Lureline Weatherly. On the Stanchfield scale of one to ten, ten being best, this is a ten plus.

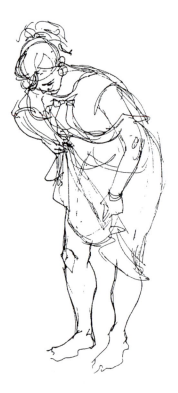

126 A Love for Drawing

A talent for drawing is not enough to be an artist. A deep love for all the aspects of drawing are what it takes to be an artist. One of the chief ingredients of that love is the determination to put your drawing endeavors in the forefront of your daily activities. There is no doubt — let's hope that you never thought there was — that developing and maintaining your drawing still makes real demands on your time and energy. But one thing is certain, if you truly love something, you never question the time it takes to nurture it be it marriage, hobby, pet, sports, religion, or whatever. It just, simply put, takes a great deal of searching and practice to translate emotions and impressions into visual images.

You nurture your drawing ability by drawing, sketching, and constantly studying drawing. Merely looking at what others have done has a strange psychological effect. True, it is beneficial to have good drawings around to view, but there is a vicarious experience that can't help but grab you. Unconsciously the feeling creates the impression that you have done something. You aren't always aware of it but there is a sympathetic kinesthetic feeling or reaction that takes place in your mind and body for nearly every experience you have. It's very obvious when someone yawns and you respond by yawning. Often when someone or something is about to be hit, on the screen or in real life, you flinch or dodge. While playing or watching sports, you lean forward to help the ball go where you want it to go, or twist and grunt to help a quarterback escape the clutches of a 290-lb tackle bearing down on him. For a moment or two you're right in the midst of the action. You have the feeling of having experienced it.

There is a similar reaction in the realm of observing drawings. As you look at a drawing (or painting), mentally you go through the motions of doing the drawing yourself. The process is a little more subtle than the physical urging you do while watching sports, but it's there. It's possible for you to do enough of that "inner drawing" to satisfy you, to make you feel you have accomplished something, drawn something.

Ultimately it will not be satisfying, for the fact that you have not actually produced a drawing yourself will be a source of great frustration and eventually lead to withdrawal and ennui.

That's one reason why I place such importance on sketching. It's fast, it's economical, and it's fun. It develops observation, it fosters awareness, and most of all you're not just observing — you're actually recording your observations. You're recording your impressions, which is a most important pursuit for an artist. Remember my formula:

IMPRESSION minus EXPRESSION equals DEPRESSION.

And, of course, the more you draw, the better you become, which gives you confidence, which emboldens you to expand your knowledge, which adds to the pleasure of drawing, which benefits all concerned. And your love for drawing is nurtured and grows. Getting vicarious thrills from looking at other artist's work is a poor substitute for vigorous self-involvement.

I have reproduced some of James Fujii's drawings for you; not so you can sit back, relax and feel that something has been done, but so they might inspire you to pursue your own talent with intensified energy. James has studied my suggestions zealously. He would come to class and work on one or two of them each night until he had relegated them to his subconscious, or as he put it, "they became second nature." On this particular night he worked on angles and on avoiding tangents and also the "story" of the pose. The mime, Ken Martin, modeled for us, and a model sheet of McLeach was taped to the drawing board.

I won't comment on these drawings — they speak for themselves. But I hope that you will not just enjoy them but will spend some time scrutinizing each of them to study *how* he avoided tangents and how he worked angle against angle to energize the gesture. Notice the angle of the hat against the face angle, and the shoulder angle; the angle of one arm against the angle of the other arm; the angle of one foot against the other; and the angle of the upper body against the lower. Check all angles against all others. They are very exciting, and provocative.

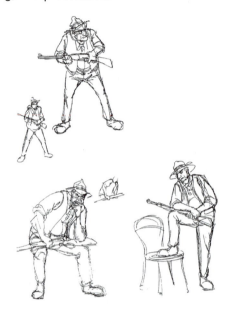

The small drawings are not my correction drawings, but are James' experimentation with alternate angles.

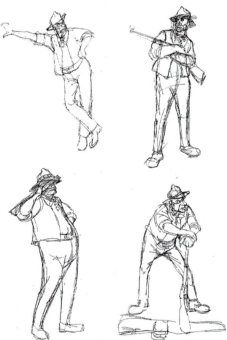

127 A New Slant on Drawing

I often speak of using angles in your drawings. Like so many other words, "angles" probably mean different things to different people. Some artists think of design as an important part of drawing, so when I mention angles, they may think of how an angle fits into the design. Some artists think of drawing as an anatomical depiction of a person or animal. Angle to them might refer to the proper angle of the clavicle from the sternum up to the shoulder (acromion part of the scapula), or how the angle of the forehead relates to the angle of the cheek. An artist who is involved in layout and composition might think of how the angles of the figure interact with the format of the borders or the background.

When I speak of angles, I am referring to gesture. In body language a slight change in the angle of the head, torso, arm, etc., can alter the meaning of the pose in sometimes subtle and sometimes blatant ways. For the purposes of animation (storytelling) we are interested in these graphic devices or tools. In comedy, even broad comedy, subtle nuances can be the difference between putting over a gag or story point in a laughable way or just a passable way.

The word angle has a kind of mechanical or geometrical intimation to it, but actually when they are used in gesturing they are more organic than mechanical. A very graceful person will sometimes use very acute angles to express a very dainty action or pose. Picture a petite, elderly lady drinking tea, with her back straight and at right angles to her legs; her hand and fingers that hold the cup are contorted into many acute angles, yet are the picture of delicacy. Take the cup out of her hand, turn the angle of the wrist inward instead of out, bend her forward, give her a cane and that same hand, with no more acute angles than when she held the tea cup, will conjure up images of arthritic pain.

The meaning of an angle of one part of the body will change as the angles of other parts of the body are altered. The relationships of angles can depict happiness, sadness, pain, fear, anger, etc. Yet many of the angles of the parts of the body are used in each of those emotions only in different combinations. The humor in a pose or action can be exploited by exaggeration or caricaturing those angles. As a matter of fact a slight bit of caricature is absolutely necessary in animation to keep the movements from looking stilted. You're probably all aware of how bland animation appears when photostats of live action are literally traced onto animation paper. Live action actors can get away with an amazingly minimal amount of movement. There can be two people talking for long periods with hardly more than eye blinks, but that goes over like a lead balloon in animation.

Take a moment to study yourself right now. Notice the angles of your arms, legs, feet, etc. Most likely none of them are doing the exact same thing; that is, twinning. Each angle is the way it is because it is expressing something. Every time you move you create a whole new set of angles.

One of the hardest things to "put over" in the Tuesday and Wednesday evening classes is to stop straightening up the pose. We are raised with this "thing" about straightening things up: "straighten up your room," "straighten that picture on the wall," "straighten out your affairs," "straighten up and fly right," etc. We can't stand men's ties that are askew, or wine glasses that lean, or cars that list as they travel down the highway. So you come to class. The models go to such trouble to contort themselves into expressive poses, and what do you do? Straighten everything up. It's okay to be neat — but not while drawing.

A study has shown that only seven percent of what is communicated between people is transmitted through the words themselves. Thirty-eight percent comes through the tone of voice. Fifty-five percent of communication, the largest part, is a result of physiology or body language. In the case of drawing from the model, *one hundred percent* of the communication is through body language. So it behooves us to slant things in the right direction, and get the whole one hundred percent out of the pose.

Well, have I straightened you out on this angle thing? I hope this gives you a new slant on drawing. Exploit those angles for all they're worth, and believe me, they're worth a lot.

Here is one of my corrections that exploits the angles of the hand, neck, back, hair, and hat brim, which I used to push his look to the object of his attention.

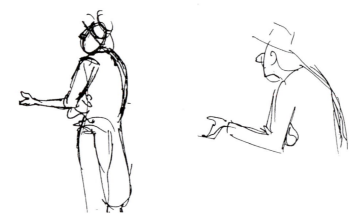

The angles of wrists and fingers are very expressive. A lot of times we gloss over them like they're just some kind of growth on the end of the arms. In drawing, hands are worth more than tongues.

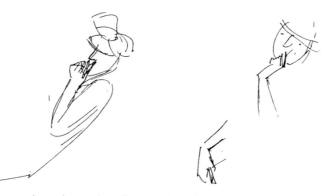

Angles plus a little squash and stretch will put a lot of nice tension, movement, and life into your drawings.

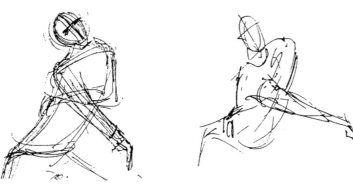

Intensifying the angles will get your audience to become more involved.

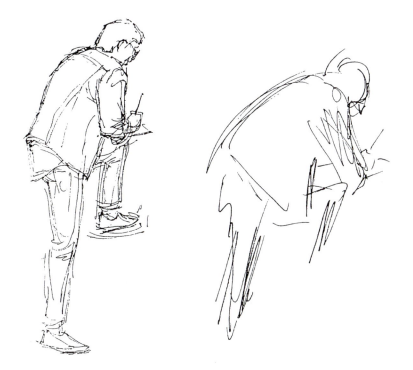

128 Think Gesture

In Alexander Dobkin's book *Principles of Figure Drawing*, there is a chapter on methods of drawing. He begins the chapter by suggesting that by experimenting with different ways of drawing, you will learn which way is best for you. He suggests, however, that no "good artist" abandons all other methods after choosing one particular way, for he may find different methods will be appropriate for different needs or problems. He also suggests that artists are always searching for a better way of saying what they mean. Dobkin lists four methods:

1. Contour drawing. It outlines the form in line. He says the beauty of this method is in its spontaneity. There are no erasures or renderings.
2. Rapid indication of form. I'm going to quote him in full here because it is my belief that this method is most suitable for animation. "Rapid indication of form involves a different kind of observation. Here the artist observes the main direction of a body and indicates it as completely as he can. He then goes back and finishes every part to his satisfaction, taking his time (well...not too much time), for

even if the model can no longer hold her pose or is no longer there, the lines of her movement have already been indicated." I interpret the "different kind of observation" to be the kind we are striving for in class — the ability to see action/gesture in our minds before we start to draw. In the drawing class, I call this "getting a good first impression." Most of my "handouts" and class suggestions have to do with this approach.

3. Finishing one part at a time. Here the artist usually starts with the head, finishing it before going on to another part of the body. He suggests, but I don't wish you to be tempted by this, that this is the best way to work from the model. However, he says, many artists feel this method teaches the artist to be careful and observant. So perhaps there is merit in it for study purposes.

Let me suggest, since you have to start somewhere, to start with the body, for the body is the foundation upon which all the appendages are attached and are dependent upon for positioning. If you locate the body, gesture-wise, you have somewhere to connect the neck, arms, and legs, eliminating the need to shift the foundation because you built the kitchen too far to the west.

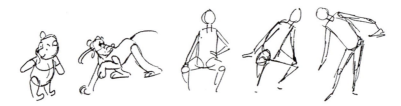

4. Trial-and error-method. This is enjoyed by the largest number of artists. But this is for the artist who does not have a prerequisite, an idea of what he wants to end up with. "The drawing glides along," Dobkin says, "and is conditioned partly by the artist's concept, which may be incompletely formulated, and partly by what he already has on the paper. Often the lines themselves will suggest an entirely different picture from the original conceived in one's mind....It's worth lies primarily in the possibilities it opens up for inventiveness and experimentation."

In working from the model (and I would add sketching) there is a danger of becoming dependent on it. Also it may stifle the imagination. On the other hand, the artist who refuses to "look at reality" is apt to formalize or stylize his way of seeing and drawing. The solution to that problem is to practice both methods. I think a judicial blend of all these methods will keep us "on our toes." But certainly, since in animation there is a preconceived story that you have to illustrate, you can't rely on a method that arrives at drawings through happenstance. Actually, I don't recommend getting too involved in methods of drawing. I think if you can form a good concept of what you want to portray then it will suggest the means to its accomplishment.

Here are some drawings from the last drawing class that may help us explore some of these points.

This is a drawing of an artist's concept of what a hat looks like on a man's head. It was a preconceived idea. He had seen hundreds of heads with hats on them and this is how he learned to see them. However, the model had pulled his hat lower down than "usual" or "normal" so that it became a gesture. The practice of drawing something the way you have learned to see it from past observation can sometimes be stifling. You may end up with an anatomy chart or a blueprint. That's okay for study purposes, but when drawing gesture you are in another element, one that transcends "normal" left-brain knowledge. You have to think gesture, think caricature, think exaggeration, think of manipulating the study chart into an expressive gesture.

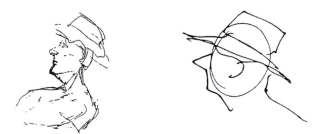

Here is another drawing where the artist is obviously intrigued with muscles and human structure. He was so enamored with the facts of anatomy that he neglected to interpret the pose. He may not be a person who goes around straightening pictures on walls, but he certainly straightened up this pose and made an anatomical chart out of it:

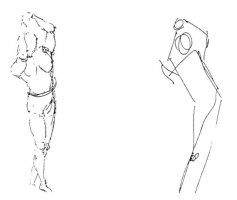

Here are two views of the same pose. Both artists seemed to have been more involved with the parts of the body than the gesture. Again, there is a tendency to straighten things up and a fear of using angles. I used very little so-called anatomy in my sketch but concentrated on having the figure lean on something. With that information, I can check the anatomy books later for details, if necessary, but there is not really enough gestural information in those other sketches to finish off the drawing at a later date.

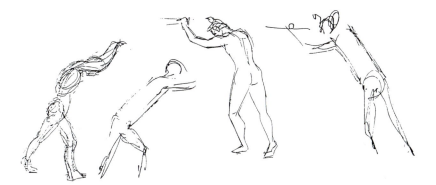

A gesture drawing should go all the way. You have to look for squashes and stretches, angles, tensions, balance, silhouette, overall shape, dramatics, and especially, directing attention to the center of interest.

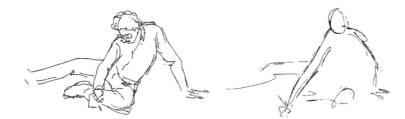

If you are going fishing, you'll have to get the hook and bait out where the fish are, no matter what shape you're in.

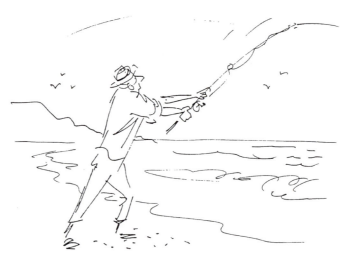

You won't catch any fish acting like an anatomy chart.

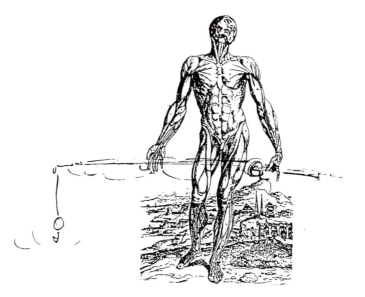

129 Precious Instruments

I've been aware of how you all treat your pencils and pens as if they were precious instruments through which your inmost thoughts may be expressed. You gently urge the image onto the paper with a tenderness that suggests a personal affection for the whole process of drawing. You see musicians display that kind of emotional attachment to their instruments. Classical guitarists hug their instruments and manipulate their fingers along the strings as if they were caressing them. Pianists do the same (except you can't hug a piano). I've seen them work their fingers on a key as if trying to get a vibrato out of the instrument like a violinist does. No way is this possible, but the feeling is there and that is an important part of playing the piano.

I have a piano instruction book with the delightful title, *Pumping Ivory*, by Robert Dumm. In its teaching and philosophy I see a parallel to that of drawing. I'll quote some passages as they appear in the book and ask you, as you read, to substitute drawing where music is meant.

Now start to think more personally about your instrument. The piano, like the guitar, is a "touchy" instrument. Touch it, and you both produce and color its tones, like a potter molding clay. Think of the keys, all gleaming white, as the "skin" of the piano; you can either please them or hurt them. Stroke them, and the sound will come out mellow and purring. Poke them, and the sound will either "bark" sharply or woodenly "thud."

Stop thinking of yourself as playing "on" or "at" the piano. Rather, think of the instrument as an extension of your own body. The French call the keys "le touches," or "touch-points" — as if the keys, not you, were doing the feeling.

Every musician wants to personalize his instrument. Take a look at the vocalist who hugs his guitar, or, without a guitar, woos his mike, or, without a mike, simply woos the audience! Every musician seeks to make his instrument an extension of his own body, the tool he or she needs to put across the strong feelings he has for the music.

Nadia Boulanger, one of the century's greatest teachers, put it best: "Don't speak to me of talent; speak to me of *desire*." It's what you want to say with the music that will create its own technique of expression.

Go to the piano not to reproduce a piece, but to experiment with your best way to bring out what is there. There is no one right way to play a piece — no matter how loudly some people protest there is. Artists, in fact, vary greatly, and audiences return again and again to hear the same piece, as played by pianist X or pianist Y. You simply cannot play a piece twice the same way. Try it! It's like a famous story that gets remade for the movies again and again. There's always a new twist: something you found the last time through that changes things.

Get closer to the composer. Help him "come through" to you. Sit quietly, upright and relaxed. (Are you still substituting drawing and story for instrument and music?) Hear the music in your head; hear it ideally; (first impression?) better than life. (Caricatured?). Sense its movement and pulse rolling through you (gesture?) turning and adjusting your own pulse. (Feeling it kinesthetically within your own body?) YOU are the prime "instrument" of this music — sitting there alert, tuned by silence, vibrating to its rhythm, lending it your own life entirely. As you feel the music filling you, heart and soul, you will know that it is getting ready to be born.

The late Glen Gould was very demonstrative at the piano. He would sometimes bend down close to the keys as if to get a more intimate sound out of the piano. He would even hum to the piano, much to the chagrin of the recording crews. Some of his recordings have been reprocessed in an attempt to eliminate the humming. Anyway, however you feel about all those "dramatics," his interpretations are beautiful, his technique was flawless, and his devotion to the piano was intense.

The next time you study your favorite artists, think not just of their knowledge and technique, but try to conjure up the emotional attachment to the medium they used and the subjects they drew.

In one sense it is a hazard to enjoy drawing so much, in that it can satisfy you into a sort of complacency, inbetweener and breakdown people especially. You push a pencil around the paper for several hours a day and it gives you a slight feeling that you have been drawing. You have a right to be satisfied for doing a good job, but may not have a right to feel you have improved your drawing ability. Time passes, lots and lots of time passes. Time has a bad habit of getting sucked into the past tense, and the resolves made to learn to draw and to animate somehow get all soft around the edges. The study-free way of life becomes a habit and seems normal, though your neglect may nag you at times. Old habits are sometimes hard to break and new ones are too easily put off and relegated to the "I don't have the time or the energy" file.

I don't practice the New Year's resolution tradition, but if you are so inclined, January 1 would be an opportune time to say "these things I resolve to do" and then make yourself a list of positive steps to take in your life as an artist, and specifically, a Disney artist.

I will certainly encourage you along that route — at least in the area of interpreting gestures and actions. Perhaps it is just being able to draw what you feel, rather than what you think you know or what you think you see. Let me try to explain that by illustration rather than by words alone.

Here's a carpenter with a panel. The student's version is what he knows are facts. The neck is in the right place, the arms are attached to the proper sockets, and it is fairly clear that he is looking up to where he might be going to place the panel. In my sketch I had the carpenter twist his upper body as if he had just picked it up from the floor or from his bench and has kept it, theatrically perhaps, off to the side, either to keep his path of vision clear or because he is standing too close to the wall to get it in front of him. In doing this it gave a better view of the panel, and the edges of the panel point to where he is looking. It allowed me to really stretch his neck to accent his looking up. It eliminated having the legs parallel each other. There is some nice tension, and a feeling of movement in the twist. I didn't invent all this. It was there in the pose — or at least the pose implied that this was or should be happening. I had what might he called an "out of body" experience. I went up there and stood in his space, like a sculptor pouring slip into a mold, so I could *feel* what he was doing. You might think of it as a director of a play showing an actor how he sees a gesture, then the actor taking it over from there.

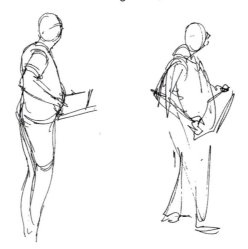

Here's a fairly nice drawing that rather blandly tells us that the carpenter is fitting the panel in place to see if it fits. I worked on just one area — the head. If he's looking up, his neck is going to stretch, the back of his head is going to depress into (or against) his upper back. He was looking slightly to his right so his left ear would swing around to the left. He was bending forward as if he were intensely interested in what he was doing, which required the artist to "take on" that interest and allow it to guide his choice of shapes and lines and tensions and pulls.

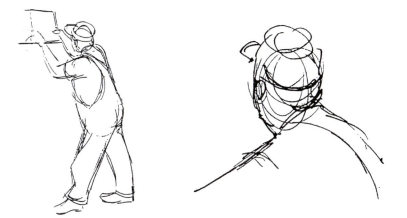

Here's a novice's attempt at having the carpenter study the panel. I suggested he not get too involved in the details such as the face and arms but rather to see a simple abstract of the whole happening, using simple shapes. Simple shapes are easier to manipulate. You can stretch them, angle them, squash them, and modify them at will. The details you can add after the gesture has been "bagged." Notice that even without eyes my carpenter appears to be looking at the panel.

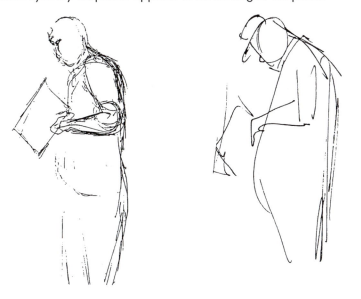

Here's a sketch by another relative beginner who again was drawing parts. My response was to abstract the pose into its basic elements: carpenter studying his blueprint for the next move. He was looking at the bottom of the print so he had his chin tucked into (or against) his chest. He appeared to be leaning forward. (There is that "what you think you see" again. Be wary, it may be some superficial bulge in the clothing. Take an "out of body" trip and feel what is taking place.) Actually he was in the attitude of drawing back so he could see the bottom of the plan. His humped back and shoulders made him appear to be bending forward. In thinking things through like this, you get a clearer, more direct gesture — one that spells it all out graphically, quickly, as in the snap of a finger.

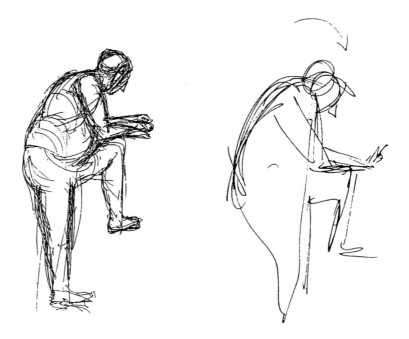

130 Gesture Drawing, Enthusiasm, and Stuff Like That

I can't resist the opportunity to comment on my recent ado in the hospital. Having access to the "press" I am taking it upon myself to give thanks for being associated with a group of such warm-hearted, caring, and loving people. The many calls I received and offers for help were truly heartening. Actually the multitude of phone calls and visits may be the things that cured me — I had to get better so I could go home and get a little rest.

I'm thinking that the quality of empathy is a needed ingredient in becoming a good animator or assistant animator. One needs to be sensitive to the feelings, emotions, and passions of others and to be able to portray those feelings to an audience in a sincere and often humorous way. All good art is brought about by feeling and sensitivity backed up by hard work and devotion to perfection. And all the above should be buoyed by enthusiasm. Hard work keeps you young. Enthusiasm keeps you young. Striving for perfection keeps you young. It keeps your eye on today and tomorrow not on the accomplishments of the past. Accomplishments are nice, but they should not be dwelt on too much. There's always plenty of exciting, life-giving new stuff to be conquered.

Let me tell you about a "new guy on the block" who has warmed my heart with his reaching out for a new accomplishment. His name is Dylan Kohler. Dylan is, for want of a better word, a "non-artist." He decided to come to the evening classes (usually both nights) and learn to draw. He came with no drawing background...so we're talking "scratch." According to my records he has been coming for exactly two months. In doing this I'm not trying to build Dylan up as a "whiz kid.'" nor am I plugging my part in it. What I mean to get at is that he is starting with a clean slate. No preconceived ideas of structure, technique, style, or details. He does not come to study anatomy or composition or any theories on drawing. He quickly picked up on the whole purpose of the class, which is to study gesture. You can almost hear his mind humming as he eagerly guides his pen toward that goal.

If he decides to continue his study of drawing, he will have to face up to the other aspects of drawing such as anatomy, foreshortening, perspective, etc. Most of us started with those subjects much to the neglect of the right brain's task of making sense of it all. The formal training and the need for emotional expression have to be brought together — blended into a usable form.

By "starting with a clean slate" he is not using a little Bridgman here, a little Perard there, no Hogarth, Michelangelo, Hopper, Inges, nor the host of other masters and teachers. You and I had to start somewhere and where better than in the presence of the former masters of drawing? But somewhere, sometime, there must be an apron string untying. All those artists had particular goals that guided them into the course for which they are famous. They were able to channel their formal training into their own unique expression. Your form of expression is one of storytelling. We're not sure Rembrandt or Hopper could fill that bill. You are filling it because you are training yourself for it. Animation! Storytelling (anatomy and gesture)! The ability to draw any character, from any viewpoint, in any kind of attitude, and in motion, all of this instantly readable by a general audience. So if you have spent too much time with Rembrandt, for instance, you may be trying to see the world through his eyes. I was re-reading my book, *The Group of Seven* (Canadian Artists), and this sentence struck me: "However, Thomson was a remarkably intuitive artist, often well ahead of his friends, who were probably more hindered than helped by their academic training." We need academic training, but we need also to be able to channel that kind of knowledge into our chosen use for it. Your uses are caricature, humor, pathos, violent action, subtleties, and all manner of physical activities like bombastic hustle and bustle. A variety no one would believe.

Anyway, Dylan neither has the help of those masters, nor does he have the hindrance of their influence to break away from. He just has himself, the model, and the gesture he's trying to capture. This is very refreshing. He reminds me of a western one-liner: "There was no training school for pioneers, you went out and you either was one or you wasn't."

I don't have his first tries, but here are some after a few sessions.

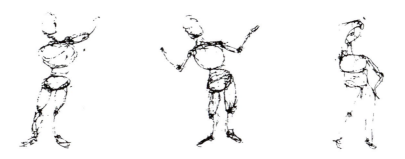

Here are some more recent ones. Look at them with the realization that he has not studied drawing and is going for the gesture in an unmixed, unalloyed, unadulterated, self-motivated way. They are quite remarkable.

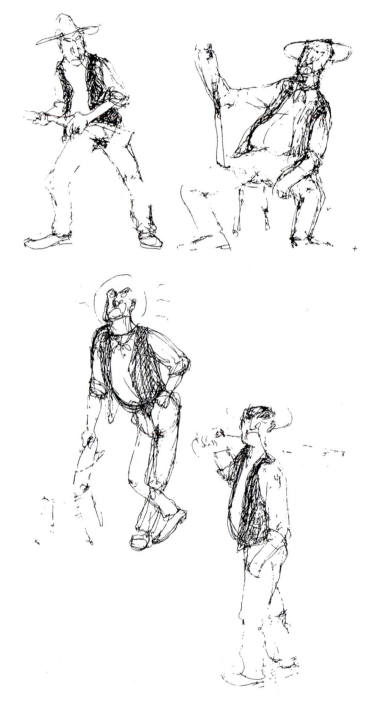

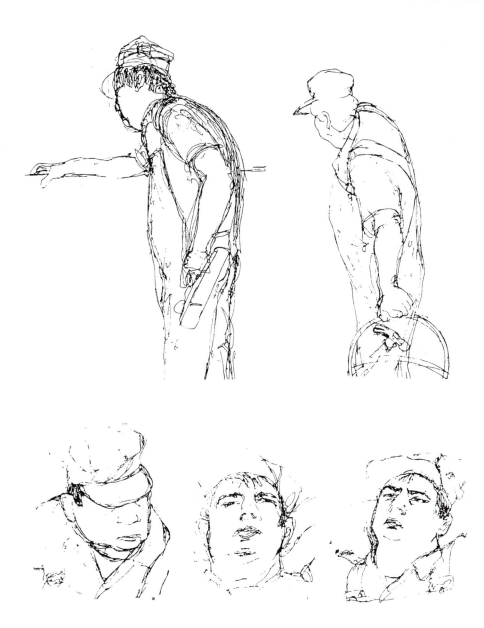

I came through the mill and had the chaff removed the hard way. When I started in animation in 1937 I was just 2 months out of high school. I didn't know art schools existed. And if I did, in my upbringing, there was no way I was going to get to one. At that time the character's heads were sometimes drawn in with a quarter or a half-dollar. I didn't even know how to study drawing. There were several excellent draftsmen at the studio (Mintz) but they were untouchable. We organized drawing sessions as time went on, but they were as much social affairs as learning experiences. I've always had a retention (or recall) problem so my life has been a treadmill of learn and re-learn, learn and re-learn. I'm not reminiscing; I'm just putting in a plug for all the opportunities of learning that surround you here at Disney studios. Bill Mathews has a research library that is enough to boggle the mind — if you need your mind boggled. In it are books, tapes, and lectures on animation pertinent subjects. Also there are many experienced animators and cleanup artists that are more than willing to help.

Now, taking the part of the fairy godfather, I wish you enthusiasm. Not just those exhilarating feelings that rush through you like small explosions, but a nice sustained, high-potency enthusiasm that will help you to accomplish the things you want to do. A real faithful, "on-call" enthusiasm that you can rely on when the need arises. You all have those feelings so you know the mechanism is working. With a little practice and some encouragement it can be enticed to stay around for longer periods of time. There is nothing like enthusiasm to see you through the more trying times, and there is nothing like enthusiasm to make your life a more joyful experience. So HAPPY NEW YEAR!

P.S. It somehow doesn't seem right not to include at least one critique. I'll tie this one in with what I said about starting out with a clean slate — no preconceived ideas, etc. Here's a nice clean, well-proportioned drawing of a head. You can see the "book learning" in every line. The artist's passion to reproduce the things he's learned was stronger than any desire to capture the pose, which in this case was a head turned away from us, no, that's too prosaic! Let's say he was thoughtfully staring at something in the corner of the room. That gets us involved in the story, and not in what the anatomy book says a head ought to look like.

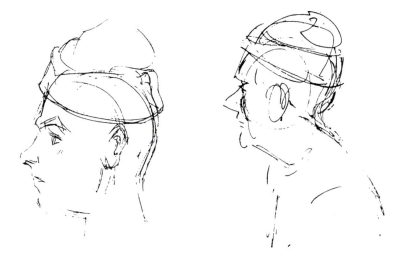

In *The Art Spirit*, Robert Henri says: "The wise draftsman brings forward what he can use most effectively to present his case. His case is his special interest — his special vision (gesture drawing) He does not repeat nature." In another place he states that "Every emotion has its expression throughout the body. The door opens, someone comes into the room. The look of the eye has its correspondence in every part of the body. The model sinks into reverie, every gesture of the body, externally and internally, records it." That kind of seeing makes drawing exciting, and animation effective. Sure, an artist needs to know anatomy and proportions, etc., but only as far as it helps him to capture the emotions and expressions of his characters. Remember your characters in animation will be either animals, caricatured humans, or out-and-out cartoons. The test of how convincing they will be in their roles will depend largely on how well *you* act out their parts, not on how they match up to Hogarth, Loomis, Bridgman, or Schider.

131 Shape — A Multi-Form Drawing Tool

If you do what you've always done, you'll get what you've always gotten.

Anonymous

Shapes have many functions to perform for you. One important function is to identify objects or parts of objects. Shapes, singly, are used to represent objects like a box or a banana, and collectively to distinguish complex structures like the human body.

Another important use for shape is to create feelings and to incite certain desired responses. We are constantly faced with symbols that evoke immediate responses. An arrow shape suggests direction. They are painted on street intersections to instruct us on which way we can turn, they are on lights outside elevators indicating up or down, and on crudely painted signs pointing to the garage sale down the street. Zigzag configurations suggest lightning or electricity. The weather reports on TV have them flashing on maps to indicate thunderstorms. Electrical companies incorporate them in their logos. Many such shape/symbols are an integral part of our culture.

Shapes also suggest movement. Streamlined cars and airplanes suggest speed.

A stairway suggests a kind of step by step progression.

A line on a graph suggests a steady progress over a longer period of time.

A curved line suggests movement in the direction of its bend.

A diagonal vertical line brings to mind a pendulum in movement.

Three such lines can suggest an increase in speed coming down or a decrease in speed going up (animators might think of it as slow-out and slow-in).

Several lines increasing in distance progressively appear to gain speed.

Using a bullet, and elongating the fastest ones increases the illusion of movement and speed.

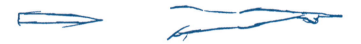

These are all things that either you are so familiar with, or are unaware of, that they are handled subconsciously. You respond blindly to their suggestions. As artists you should not allow them to go underground (into the subconscious), for they are powerful drawing tools. In drawing we can't use obvious symbols like arrows to suggest direction, but we can create movement, direction, and feeling by altering and juxtaposing the shapes in our drawings. For instance if you want to emphasize a person pointing at something, you can slightly elongate the arm and slightly narrow it down at the end (like the bullet going at high speed).

I can guess what some of you are thinking — DISTORTION! DEFORMITY! UNREAL! But remember these devices have been used by every animator in the business. A character is greatly squashed as he anticipates a jump, then at the peak of his leap stretches to his full length and *beyond*. A character like Roger Rabbit could conceivably stretch the full width of the field as he does a fast and frantic exit. Of course these things have to be done tastefully — but they must be done.

I often have a time getting the artist/students to take advantage of the basic shapes of the models. Some are of "average" build, while some are tall and thin and others short and thickset. That habit of straightening everything up and pulling everything back to "normal" is a strong one. Our model last week was Veronica Taft — tall, (6' 1") thin, with regal bearing. Still, most of the 18 or 19 artists in class brought her back down to a "normal 5' 9"" and used lots of curved lines and soft bulges. The quality of shape had lost its meaning. The shape of a person determines the uniqueness of their gestures. Disregard the shapes and the result becomes a watered-down version of an otherwise striking, or even extraordinary, pose.

The over concern for "getting it right"; that is, your desire to keep it somewhere in the "normal" range, is hard to break away from. It is as if striving for perfection is a narrowing down to a constricted point.

Actually perfection is a broadening concept that suggests an opening up.

In drawing, especially for animation, it means incorporating plenty of squash and stretch, elongation, caricatured movement, and shapes of all kinds; it means assuming a spirit of experimentation, daring, and a generous sprinkling of humor.

Everyone wants to make nice, pretty drawings. But there are times when your drawings need some bravado, humor, delicacy, or distortion, along with the hundreds of emotions that actors are called upon to portray. You can't just imagine they are in your drawings — you have to *put* them there. And by put, I don't mean trace or copy. I mean inject the appropriate action by graphic means, using those graphic tools mentioned above.

I can't conceive of anyone in the acting business not studying acting. Our business is interpreting a story line, whether it be comedy, tragedy, mystery, etc. If you were on the stage acting out the part of a strict militaristic parent scolding his child or a slapstick comedian in the hands of a ruthless gang of cut-throats, you'd have to "switch" characters. You couldn't go out on stage and "straighten" up the characters, pulling them back to "normal" people.

Sometimes I verbally describe a pose or gesture to the students. Some say "I wish I could think like that" or "Now that you point out what is going on — I can see it." You must work on developing your ability to see the dramatics of life. That is what separates you from your audience. *They love to be entertained.* You are on the other end of the camera — *you have to entertain.* It requires a sense of performing, pretending-to-be, representing another character — one in a story, making believe, fancy, mimicry, impersonation, invention, play-acting, fabrication.

You have to break away from the "norm" and concoct a variety of characters, each with their personal, distinctive style of gesture. You have to conjure up the feelings of comedy, tragedy, fright, happiness, smugness, and a multitude of emotions all in your drawings. You can't draw a "normal" human figure and try to fit it into all the characters.

You have to alter things — stretch things. Your everyday life may border on the routine, even humdrum, but in animation you'll have to act out some stuff that is foreign to you. You might have to rescue someone from the villain, fly an airplane, or fly to never-never land with pixie dust trailing behind you. Things that you've never experienced, but must convince your audience that you have — through your drawings.

A good way to start is to stop being so conventional and stop trying to "straighten" up the world. Learn to "bend" to the needs of your characters (or your model). Most of your audience already lives that "normal" life. They go to the movie to be transformed to another world. It's not just a matter of letting yourself go or being inspired, you have to force yourself into another person's suit or animal's skin — a realm you've not experienced first hand. You'll have to be someone you're not. You'll have to draw things you've never drawn before, express things that are foreign to your very nature. You'll have to be a bird, an animal, a girl, or a boy. Now is not the time to straighten pictures on the wall. Now is the time to step out of the "you" and into a world of transformation, modification into an alter ego, an other-likeness. You'll have to be a surrogate character, a stand-in, a pinch hitter, a proxy. This is no time for timidity. The acting ability of your character is on the line. You are responsible for it. You'll have to forget your dental appointments, your backaches, and your carburetors. This is the moment of demonstration. The journey begins when you are forming the first impression of what it is you have to draw. From then on it's goodbye John or Jane Doe, and your usual need to straighten things up. Your characters want, no, need to stretch those mundane limits. If you don't go beyond the world your audience lives in then what kind of a journey is it going to be for them?

It takes a lot of understanding, an affinity to alter-personalities, a lot of compassion and feeling. It will take some study. Lots of study, if you want to be good at it. Drawing is not just putting lines on a paper. It's all the above plus much more. Constant observation, interpretation, curiosity, involvement, and excitement; developing an eye for similarities, contrasts, subtleties…and being able to transpose all the above into line. All that into just line and shapes. Yeah! Lines and shapes that squash and stretch, and point, and that work with other lines and shapes to generate movement, mood, and the illusion of life.

Here are some drawings from the last class. They all demonstrate a need to "feel" the poses better. It's usually a matter of logic, which is, in a sense, what acting is. The first group are different artists' interpretation of similar poses — a girl bending over, head resting on hand, lots of weight on the elbow. Part of the problem seems to stem from an attempt to draw a *girl*, rather than the *action of bending over and preventing her head from falling into her lap by propping it up with her arm.*

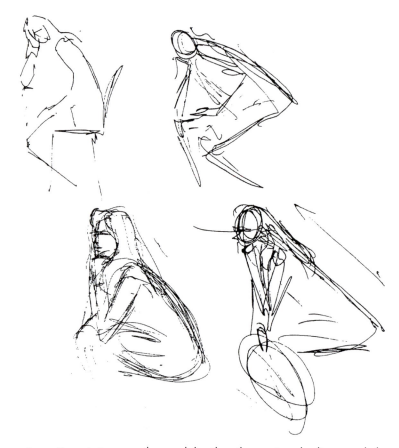

Here again are two attempts to copy the model rather than using the lines and shapes to tell a story. I can best explain it by having you bend forward and rest your head on your hand. Do you feel a cupping sensation as your chin fits nicely into your palm? Can you feel your jaw jut out and the front of your neck stretch? These are all separate shapes that work together to produce a gesture.

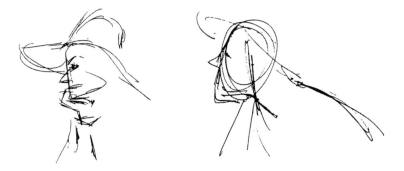

Here is a similar problem. Trying to copy lines from the model leads to trouble. Here the curved neck lacks feminine grace — it doesn't feel very comfortable either. Again, look up, feel your chin protrude, your neck stretch, the back of your head tuck into your upper back. You're dealing with three shapes here: the body, which is in a normal position; the head, which is looking up; and the neck, which is trying to keep some semblance of naturalness, gracefulness, and charm.

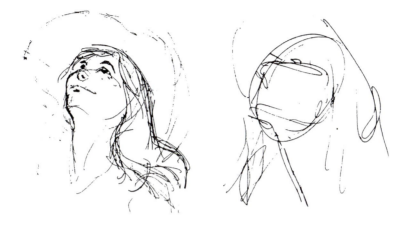

Darn, I was going to make this a short handout this week and get to my painting. I have some very exciting experiments I'm anxious to get at. Anyway, and finally, here is 6' 1" Veronica brought down to a 5' 9" "normal" gal. The student's sketch is about 6 1/2 heads tall, which is even below "normal." I overreacted in my sketch and made her 8 1/2 heads tall, which in my thinking better represents a tall, thin, 6' 1" woman. Also when there is confusion in a pose, it's probably best to avoid it. If the pose or gesture is nebulous, I think it's time to draw on your sense of logic. Pick the closest gesture you can and simplify it so it is easily readable. I'm not saying you shouldn't go for subtle nuances, but if they don't start coming off early in the sketch and the essence of the pose is in jeopardy, it's time to modify your nuance.

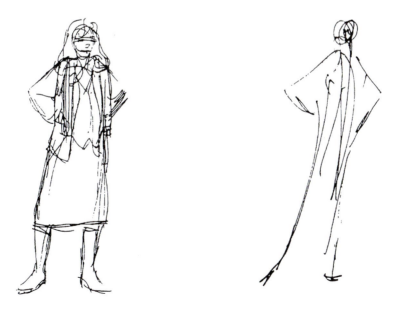

132 Deciphering and Defining Gestures

When I sit down to write these things my mind goes flitting about like a butterfly. There are so many different approaches to drawing. When you are drawing, your mind has to focus in and out of the many aspects of drawing. You have to keep your mind flexible so that you don't hone in on one or two of them and get stuck there, to the neglect or oversight of others, especially the story behind the drawing. Of course it's difficult enough to just isolate one thing and draw that well, let alone cover all bases. One our biggest enemies is habit. Do you recall what anonymous said in the last handout? He (or is it a she?) said: "If you do what you've always done, you'll get what you've always gotten."

Drawing is a constant back and forth, in and out process. Our minds have to weave in and out in a constant balancing act; that is, making sure we are using all the principles of drawing, of which, by the way, gesture is the very foundation. As a matter of fact, when we concentrate on the gesture, the rest of the drawing falls more easily into place.

Here are three tries at a pose by the same artist. He is still in the early student stage, but certainly not a beginner at habit. He realized he didn't "get it" with the first sketch, so he tried another. Again he was disappointed, so tried a third time — at which time I stopped him to make some suggestions. But can you see how his thinking habits bound him to that very same version three times in a row. I suggested if he wants the weight of the right arm and head to be leaning on the right knee, the guy will have to bend over more. And in bending over, the chin will be lower than the shoulders. Where his seat contacts the chair will be the anchor point from where the rest of his body leans forward.

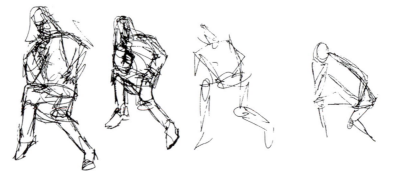

Usually a total, effective aggregation of all the elements of the pose is not possible by just copying the lines from the model. Especially if you don't have a definite goal (gesture) in mind then you could be enticed off into any number of unproductive directions. True, you might end up with a drawing; perhaps a handsome drawing, but the point is, in animation you can't just settle for whatever happens to evolve, you have a story to illustrate and your efforts plus your results must serve that purpose. It may be that during a rush period the animator has left the assistant animator (cleanup person) a rather roughly drawn scene to finalize. The cleanup person must gather all his interpretive powers to arrive at the most appropriate gesture. It is not unlike the problems we are facing in the gesture class — that of having to think through thoroughly the particular, physical attributes and the mental motivations for the pose, gesture, or action. That's the purpose of the gesture class and that's why I present these critiques. It's to encourage you to search out ways to get the most out of each action.

Here is a similar pose from a different angle. The head resting in the palm of the hand. What is the first thing you think of when considering a rest? Right! You lay your head down on a pillow or over onto the palm of your hand. A lot of nice things evolved in this drawing but what didn't evolve was the feeling that the head was leaning (or resting) on the hand. My sketch, crude as it may be, at least conveys that message:

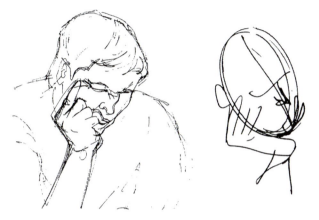

Here (and in the following drawings) are three sketches of the same pose from slightly different angles. You can see that one of the artists has featured the outstretched right arm. The others made a slight attempt to bend the upper body backward, which the model was doing, subtly. I pictured the guy addressing a crowd, saying "Hear me, ladies and gentlemen" or singing *Santa Lucia*. That gave me something to shoot for.

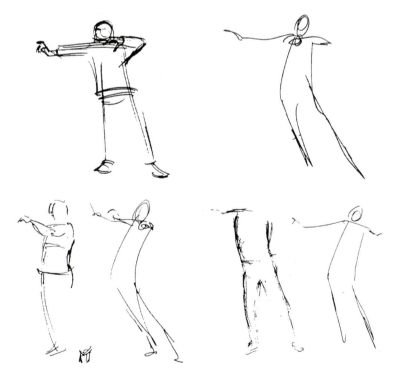

You may be thinking I have overexaggerated the gesture, but in the process of fitting him into the background, putting on his costume, and putting around, pulling him onto model, some of the extremity will be toned down. In this last example, the model was huffing on his glasses, maybe to blow off some lint or in preparation to clean them with a lens tissue. The student started out to draw *things* rather than a *story*. The glasses are there and the mouth is somewhat puckered up, but there is little connection between the two. In my sketch I attempted to show that the air was coming up from his lungs, through the neck — outstretched to emphasize the flow of air — out through his puckered lips to the glasses held in the path of the flow of air. Everything — the back, the neck, the ears, etc. — point to the glasses.

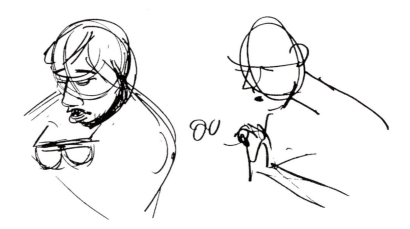

133   The Decisive Moment

You tell a joke, the listener explodes in laughter, and you enjoy that fleeting moment when their enjoyment is at its peak, not only for the fact that you've given some pleasure, but you also enjoy that extreme gesture.

You're watching your favorite sport on TV, or in person. A player seems to "hang in air" or snatch a ball that looks out of reach. It has taken a superhuman effort and you wish you could have a still photo of that extreme or perhaps be able to sketch it. If you were sketching, you would attempt to capture that "extreme" and of course would have to rely on a memorized "first impression" for the extreme only lasts for a split second.

Henri Cartier-Bresson, photojournalist and documentary photographer, was a master at capturing "the decisive moment." You've probably seen a collection of his photographs in a book by that title. Actually Cartier-Bresson started out as an artist. In the early 1930s he owned a brownie box camera and the results he got from the camera led him to switch to photography. "The camera was a quick way of drawing intuitively." He said the camera was his way of understanding what he sees: "The simultaneous recognition in a fraction of a second of the significance of an event, as well as the precise organization of forms that give that event its proper expression."

Well, does that not have a familiar ring to it? In your work as artists you have to "recognize in a fraction of a second the significance of an event," also "the precise organization of forms that give that event its proper expression." More than that, in animation you not only have to capture that "significance of the event," but you have to keep the drawings alive that are in-between those extremes. This is done through timing, anticipation, follow through, squash and stretch, and all the other tools of animation.

No wonder Cartier-Bresson switched to photography. All he had to do was push the little lever at the proper time — the "decisive moment."

In the gesture class we are attempting to discover what it is that makes up that decisive moment. If it isn't there in the model, we have to create it. The photographer has to rely on his subject to come up with a photogenic gesture. You as an artist have to rely on your own acumen. Sometimes when drawing from the model, and always when creating a scene of animation, you are required to draw on your ability to act or on your ability to mimic a gesture or an action, and certainly, always, your ability to caricature; that is, "organize the forms that give that event its proper expression."

I'm not putting down photography or Cartier-Bresson. He was a great photographer. I use him as an avenue to reveal some truths about yourselves as artists. For instance, here is a paragraph from *Current Biography*, 1976. In reprinting it I am not suggesting you all become Balzacs or Poussins, but in your way to "have an appetite for experience and a sense of form in rendering it."

Cartier-Bresson's ability to grasp and capture the essential is perhaps partly due to his early training in painting and composition and possibly also to his interest in Zen, but it is as much the result of a rare personal gift for seeking out and relishing life in all its manifold forms. It was in recognition of the multiple aspects of his art that Hilton Kramer, reviewing the 1968 Museum of Modern Art retrospective in the *New York Times* (July 7, 1968), commented that he is at once the Balzac and the Poussin of the modern camera, displaying both an extraordinary appetite for experience and a sublime sense of form in rendering it.

Last week we sketched Allen Chang, the martial arts model. As he went through some warm-up exercises, we discovered (or rediscovered) that when a subject is moving it is hard to retain in our mind any one position that we have chosen to sketch. When we do pick a pose, we have to lock it into our short-term memory just long enough to get it down on paper. It's like taking a mental photograph of the pose. If we keep staring at the subject as it moves — all those images start to blend together and we end up with a muddled montage in our minds. It would be better if we could isolate the chosen pose by momentarily looking at it intensely and then close our eyes or look away so that it doesn't become adulterated by subsequent movements.

That is just one of the many reasons why quick sketching is so important for us to keep up. It sharpens our hand-eye reflexes, which is a valuable thing for an artist/actor/animator. (A new word should be concocted that would encompass all three of those — one for you who are not yet animators, but are included because you are studying all three of those subjects. My wife Dee came up with "artactanim" but we decided that sounded too much like a dinosaur.)

A camera could record all of those subtle nuances of Allen Chang's warm-up exercises, but that isn't our business. We want to be able to draw them — and fast. The best suggestion I could come up with was to sketch in the body first. This gives you a center (a home base) on which to connect all extremities. It establishes in a split second where to connect the head, arms, and legs, which, if considered separately and independently, would lead to (especially when in a hurry) panic and confusion.

Also, when trying to record something in a hurry, we must stop trying to draw and start sketching. Most of you relied on your normal way of drawing sped up. It looked like one of those Keystone Cop movies where they cut out every other frame. The technique of keeping your pen or pencil on the paper most of the time as you sketch will be less taxing. Who cares if you end up with a few straggling lines wandering here and there? Your sketch will get done faster, with less effort, and it will be more organic; that is, it will be more like the living thing that you are sketching. And it will suggest movement, which is what you're after anyway.

So in your "mind photograph," you have already "named" the pose; that is, you have decided what is happening, spotted the over-all shape, the abstract, and in doing this you have picked the points which constitute and define the gesture. Those points will be the elbows and how they work with or against each other, likewise the shoulders, arms, hands, the knees and the feet. You connect those to the body and *voila*, a gesture drawing comes to life. Sound easy? Well, it is but you have to practice, practice, practice. So keep those sketchbooks within easy reach so you don't ever have to confess that you photograph more than you sketch.

I had some minor surgery recently that forced me to get some physical rest. So I forced myself to watch television at least a couple of hours a day. I chose some shows that lent themselves to sketching. When you do this you realize how heartless the directors and film-cutters are, for you no sooner decide to sketch a scene and what you were honing in on, suddenly is on the cutting room floor. Here are a few examples (mind you, I'm not trying to impress you with my quick-sketches, I'm only trying to encourage *you* to form the habit of sketching — constantly).

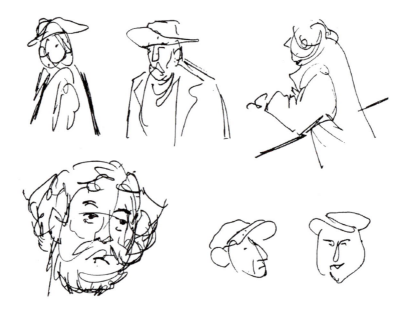

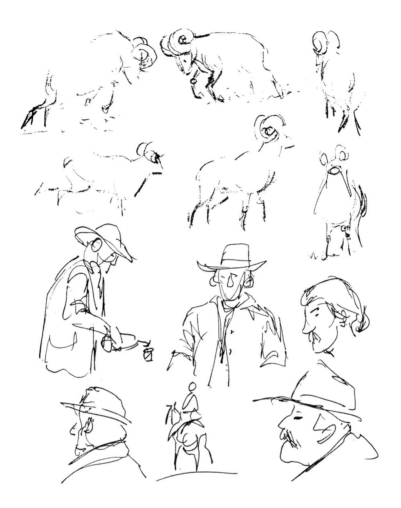

134   Relationship of Character to Prop

Too bad we can't have two models to work with in the evening class. It would give an opportunity to study relationships, which is something we have to deal with in animation. However, the next best thing is props and I try to incorporate them as much as possible. I am constantly imploring the students to build their gesture drawings around them because they tell what the pose is all about — what I call the "story" of the drawing. In animation you are dealing with the same thing. The only difference is the story has continuity to it. But the relationship between characters and props is exactly the same.

The prop could be an umbrella, which might suggest rain, or a parasol that might suggest an oppressive sun. A model using a telephone should spark some kind of a response in you; perhaps it's a call for help, or a social call, or an unwanted call from a former spouse, or a salesperson. Your mind should be free from the nitty-gritty of anatomy and other non-pertinent details to allow you to fabricate an imaginative story behind the pose. A simple prop like a hat can be used to shade the sun, hide a bald spot, or just spark up an outfit. Whatever the prop it ought to be considered in its relationship to the character that is using it. Disregard the proper use of a prop and you create a situation that can be disconcerting to your audience. Props have meaning and they deserve to be dealt with in a meaningful way.

Prop in theater jargon, is short for property. That means anything to do with the story, the action, or the role of the actor. It is even used attributively; meaning some part of a character's character. A stutter or some mannerism can be thought of as a prop. All characters have personalities that are identified by certain attributes. These have to be kept straight or the character becomes diluted or weakened. External props such as umbrellas or guns, etc., are no less important to a character. How she handles the prop reveals her character as applied to the plot or story.

Last week I modeled for the class, using an abundance of props to challenge everyone to make maximum use of them. The response was very gratifying. I confiscated some of the drawings for you to study in light of the magnificent way in which the props and the gestures were utilized. Here are some of Bill Berg's. He comes into the class with an air of confidence and eager anticipation that shows in his drawings. I've never timed these poses, but they're in the neighborhood of 8 to 10 minutes. Bill captures a lot in those 10 minutes.

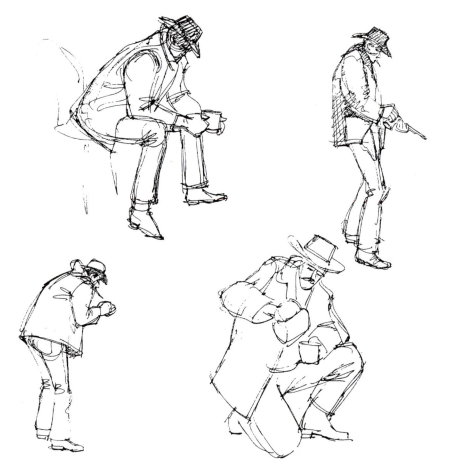

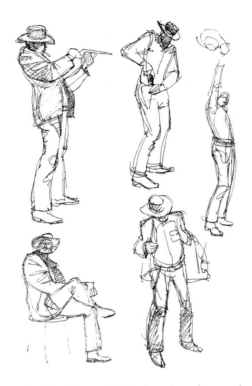

James Fujii, a "regular" at the Tuesday and Wednesday classes, has become quite proficient at going for the guts of the gesture. His drawings below are not photographic copies but are truly lifelike gesture drawings any animator would be proud of, had he made them.

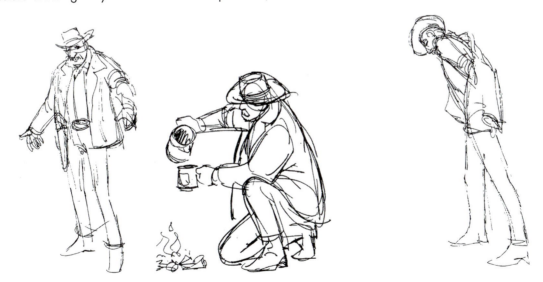

A while back I told you about Wendy Werner, who was new to drawing. She is still trying and succeeding. These drawings on the next page suggest that she is looking and seeing third dimensionally. The gestures are very clear.

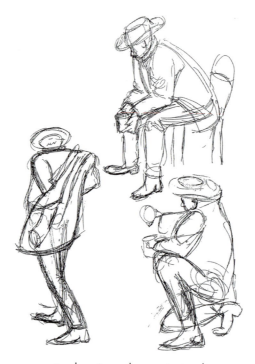

Dylan Kohler, another newcomer to drawing, demonstrates how one, without any formal training in anatomy or drawing, can, in spite of the seeming disadvantage, directs his attention to the important elements of a gesture drawing and come up with a convincing "story" drawing (just as in good English you should never construct that long a sentence — but my excuse is, it says what it has to say....).

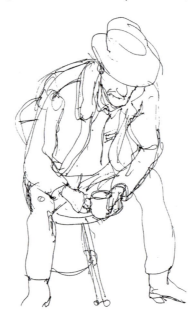

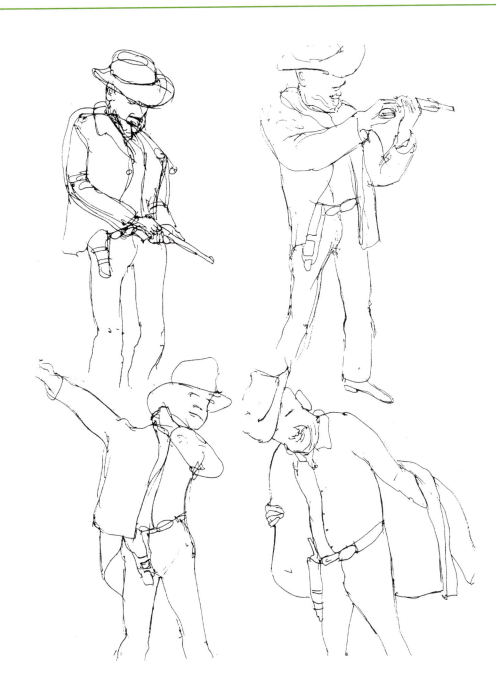

Dan Boulos is an energetic sketcher. He draws with great impetus, seemingly impatient to get to the gesture without all the humdrum of detail. But even without the fine-tuning of the details there is no doubt about what the props are and how they fit into the "story."

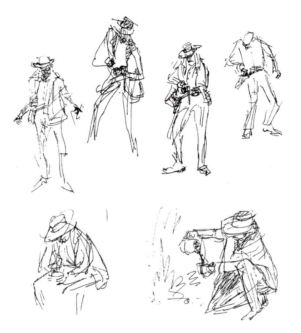

135 Drawing

A few weeks ago I touched on props and mannerisms and their importance in storytelling. I maintain that having a prop, a mannerism, or a story point to work with makes your drawing a lot easier (and more fun). Those things work for you like a tool works for you — a shovel, a drill, a vacuum cleaner, a spoon. When you have a job to do, the proper tool helps make the action complete. A prop (tool), be it a part of the body or its adornment or some story-related object, should be considered an integral and inherent part of any drawing. Look at the chapter on props again and notice how the first thing you see is not the anatomy or the details in those drawings, but rather the gesture — the appropriate use of the props.

Drawing is much like writing or communication by speaking. You have a story to tell and you choose only the most necessary and pertinent words to put over the idea. Detail is used only to add color and to solidify the image. Let's say your neighbor's house is on fire — you knock on his front door to see if he is aware of it — he opens the door and you say, "Great licks of flame dart into the sky. Glowing ashes are caught by the wind and drift into the surrounding brush. The trees in the back yard are bathed in an undulating orange glow, etc." That may all be "anatomically" factual, even colorful, but it's not communicating the proper story. Five well-chosen words would do the trick: YOUR HOUSE IS ON FIRE.

In drawing you can spend hours sketching in details like muscles, hairs, wrinkles, buckles, etc., and in so doing fail to tell the real story, or any kind of story at all. I say any kind of story for sometimes in class, the models don't give you enough clues as to what they are portraying (if anything). That is when your sense of story (and imagination) comes into play. Your first impression should supply you with all you need to make a "complete" drawing. You not only spot the overall body language, but you automatically attach that to some fabricated story point. Some time ago (actually many times), I encouraged everyone to read, read, read. Reading different kinds of writings like novels, fiction, biography, essays, etc., sharpens your sense of drama and humor. When you draw, it can be thought of as if you were an author creating a sentence or a paragraph in a novel. If you have chosen to do a dramatic drawing be serious; if you decide to draw a humorous drawing then be funny, comical, witty, droll, amusing, satirical, ludicrous, or sidesplitting — whatever the situation calls for.

Study anatomy, yes, and study inanimate things. But when actually drawing, tear yourself away from the mere tool and make the drawing complete by adding story. That's what gesture drawing is.

I have reproduced some of Milt Kahl's drawings in this week's "handout." I'm not selling Milt as someone to copy or even emulate. No one wants to be Milt. No one wants to repeat the things he did. But to grasp the freedom with which he handled the human anatomy for his purposes is what we are interested in. Solutions to your problems do not lie in what has been done, but in fresh thinking, honest investigation, and a personal dedication. If you learn anything from this group of drawings it should be that *knowledge of anatomy is imperative*, and a *creative use of the knowledge is even more imperative*.

So for your viewing pleasure and to illustrate how the use of story and props can transcend mediocrity, here are some of Milt's drawings from a scene in *Aristocrats* where Edgar, the butler, is smugly gloating over his guilt — his umbrella. As you glance from drawing to drawing, think of the hair, the cheeks, the eyebrows, the shoulders, etc., as props idiosyncratic of this particular character. He, like any human character, is built with the normal mixture of features (anatomy), but they go beyond what Bridgeman, Loomis, or Hogarth teach us the human male looks like. Humor, drama, and caricature have transformed them into the realm of gesture and fantasy. Milt was an excellent draftsman, but draftsmanship as applied here is not a photographic copy of a human character, it is the implementation of such knowledge to illustrate a story point as acted out by a particular character.

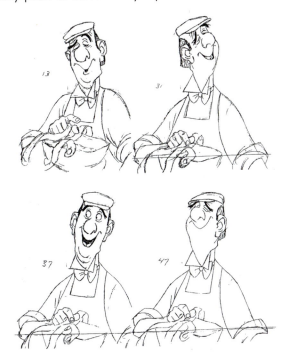

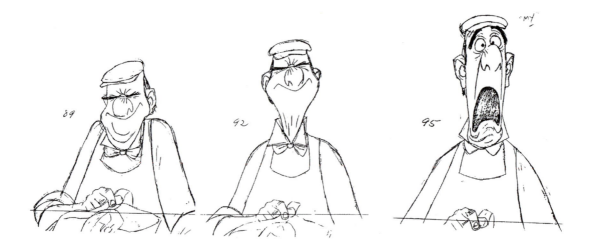

I encourage you artists who attend my drawing class to try to break away from a literal interpretation of the model's poses and to caricature them as if you were animating a scene. I'm not here to teach you how to draw like Rembrandt, Hogarth, or Milt Kahl, I'm here to help you form a creative attitude toward drawing. All of you are unique individuals. To develop that individuality or that uniqueness to its fullest, you'll need to study the tools of drawing and how to apply them in your own unique way to your work problems.

Resolve to make it an exciting quest, and in all ways it shall be.

136 Words That Help in Drawing

How important are words in drawing? In a sense we think with words, and communicate our thoughts in words. In animation the first stage of a cartoon is entirely in word form (the story). Then the story-sketch artists transpose those words into drawings in the form of storyboards (overly simplified version of the procedure, I agree), and then the animators carry it further into full animation. The dialog and descriptions that communicate the meaning of the story must be exact, simple (though often deep), explicit, and clear to all who are involved. Otherwise the picture might end up like one of comedian Gracie Allen's conversations.

Much of the material is open to interpretation by the director and/or animator. For instance, a scene description in *Aristocrats* goes: "Two shot — Marie and Berlioz still enjoying the situation." The situation — is that Berlioz had just called the butler, Edgar, an "Old pickle puss." The animator (Stanchfield) chose to make it a one-shot with Berlioz cracking up on the floor, rolling on his back in glee with Marie's dialog offstage. Here are three drawings from the scene.

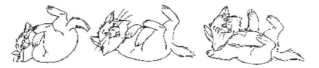

Without having a feeling for the situation and without first putting it all into words, like, "I'll make it a close-up of Berlioz rocking back and forth on his back," how could I have possibly made a drawing? Of course there were other considerations. I figured this would be clearer without Marie delivering the dialog on stage. Besides we saw her in last scene, and a close-up of Berlioz would be cute and add some pizzazz. Once I got those words settled in my mind the rest was easy.

What am I leading up to? I'm leading up to drawing from the model without selecting some appropriate words to describe the action or story you're about to interpret in your sketch. Without them your efforts are apt to be reduced to mere copying. The other night we were fortunate to have Craig Howell as our model. He is a living storyboard. He studies the label on a bottle, he holds a hot dish with his apron, and he twists a pepper mill so realistically that Roger Chaisson sneezed.

Here are some drawings from that session. The first correction was made essentially to get the artist to look for a simpler approach to drawing an action. Too many ruffles without a good basic abstract shape will interfere with the flow of action. In addition to a simpler shape, I had the character push down more with the pepper mill and strengthened the look as if he were willing the pepper to land in a particular place. You can almost see the ground pepper shooting out.

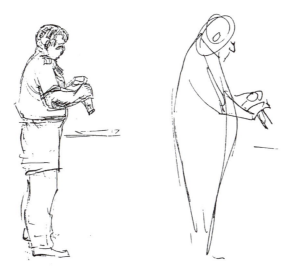

Here is another drawing where the model is so intent on smashing a cockroach it requires that he bend into the fray in a more aggressive manner — the key words being bend forward. As in tennis, you step into the ball, otherwise you get caught hitting the ball while backing up and off balance. (I knew you'd want to know that).

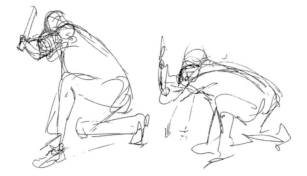

Here's a drawing that was hard to pin down in words, so I concentrated on the look — one of the most important actions in drawing. I tucked in the character's right shoulder and turned the other side into a bent back and this opened up a passage for the look to travel in. Notice how the right shoulder helps start the action and the left side helps to jettison the look on its way.

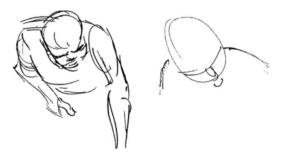

Here's another example of bending into the action. The artist tried to get a bend in the drawing but failed to bend at the waist. Actually, bending at the waist is hard to draw. Bending at the hips is simpler and clearer. Stand up and try it — your feet stay where they are, your rump goes out back yonder, your head goes forward, and everything is in balance. Now try to bend at the waist. It's not a clear move is it? When a character is doing something like this, I like to think of that area between his face and his hands, and between his two arms as a stage. That is where the story is taking place. I lowered the right elbow slightly to open up the stage and tipped the hands slightly to better show what is taking place there. In other words, I staged it so the action (story) was clearer.

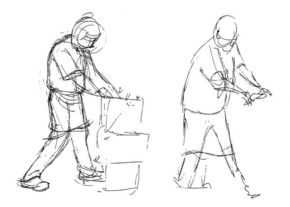

In this next correction I was suggesting that the artist concentrate on the action. Say to yourself "Guy standing there grinding out some pepper." Those are some words that suggest the simplest and most direct route to put over the idea. Actually, with words (and the ensuing word-picture), the drawing will more easily fall into place.

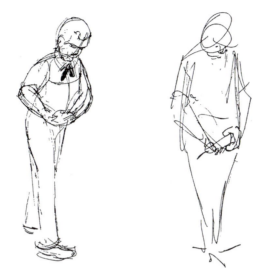

One more and I'll let you get back to work. Here we go again straightening things up, and consequently stiffening things up. Enter into the spirit of the thing and say "The guy's looking at something. I'll lower the near shoulder, twist the body toward me to open up that 'stage' (I mentioned earlier). Also I'll drop the knee of the right leg a little lower because of that leg's angle to the floor."

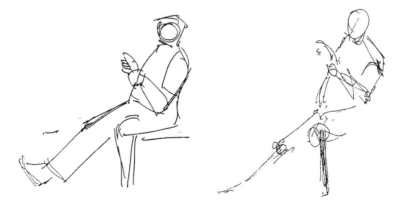

This all may sound like a cerebral and emotional nightmare, but not so. Thinking is only stressful when it has to do with income tax, divorces, and finding your keys. Figuring these things out in drawing is pure fun. Do you hear me? FUN.

Here are some of Mike Swofford's drawings. I had no suggestions on these for they are highly personal interpretations of the poses. At the beginning of the session he found himself copying the model, so he made a special effort to break away from that. Mike usually leans toward the cartoony side of drawing, so there is a delightfully whimsical quality to them.

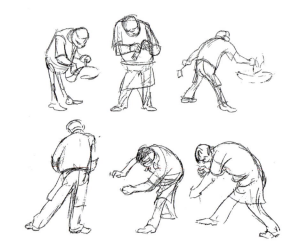

137 A Simple Approach to Drawing

For those in my class who have had little instruction or experience, I would suggest adopting a very simple approach to drawing. Even those who are experienced but have neglected working from a model can benefit from this. In animation, costumes may run from simple to complex in style, but they are all handled in a simple manner when it comes to folds and wrinkles. There is a kind of shorthand for drapery that is standardized for all characters. Most Disney characters only have wrinkles at the joints, and then only when there is pressure applied by bending or squeezing. So they'll occur at elbows and knees, and at the waist when seated. Women's clothes have wrinkles caused by pleats, gathers, puffed sleeves, etc., but you can always count them on two or three fingers. An excess of material will cause meaningless folds, bumps, and bulges.

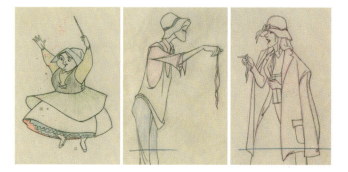

I have no control over what a model wears. I always ask them to wear something simple but often they come in some gaudy outfit with pleats, bulges, enormous jeweled belts, and abstract patterns and colors. All I can suggest is that it's not our job to copy all that stuff, but to cut through the confusion and come up with a simple drawing — one that might duplicate the style used in a feature cartoon. This class after all is not for drawing bulges in cloth, but how to be able to construct a figure with clothes on in multitudes of gestures. The most logical approach when faced with a model that is clothed in a complicated costume is to lay in the basic pose with some simple elemental shapes. First study the pose for the gesture — you may have to add a little of your own thespianism — then look for weight distribution and overall abstract shape (silhouette), ignoring all particulars like muscles or other detail, and go for the general, overall generic gesture. This gives you the opportunity also to concentrate on relative proportions. Proportions are important and you must develop a sensitivity to them — Mickey, Roger Rabbit, the Mermaid, Eric, Sebastian — all with distinct proportions.

Here are some suggestions for a simple approach. You'll not be encumbered or confused by a multitude of superfluous lines and puzzling shapes. Once you have the pose captured, the costume will be easier to put on. And using the known facts about wrinkles, you will be able to pick and choose the appropriate wrinkles from the model or make up some of your own. Let me suggest that in working out your "shorthand" body shape when the chest and hip are twisted, they can be handled as separate shapes. That way you can more easily draw them facing in different directions. When they are not twisting, the chest and hip areas can be treated as one shape.

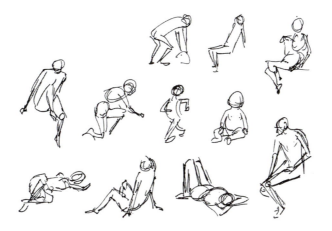

Here's a suggestion from Lariar's book, *Cartooning for Everyone*, on how to lay in a cartoon figure. He had no explanation for this illustration but you can see, he worked from the general to the specific.

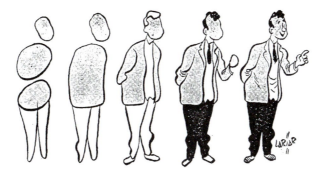

And here's one example from our last drawing session where the artist got trapped into trying to feature the complications of the costume. Actually it was a very austere pose. There was a lot of cloth but it was wrapped tightly around the model's body, making a simple but dramatic shape.

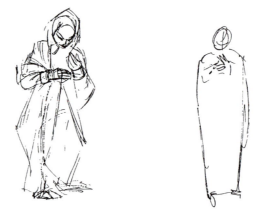

138 Vocalizing

With apologies to the "Nine Old Men," they were not what you could call actors. On paper, yes, but in the flesh, no. I used to watch Ollie, Frank, and Milt show each other how they intended to animate a scene. If their acting was any indication of how the scene was going to turn out, you would have worried about the future of Disney's animated features. But they did have a pretty good mental picture of what they wanted to depict, and of course, the drawing skill to get it down on paper. So if you feel awkward or clumsy at acting, don't let it worry you. But if you can't picture a gesture in your mind and draw it on paper, there is work to be done. This goes for story-sketch artists, animators, cleanup artists, and inbetweeners.

If a cartoon feature could be likened to a musical play, each scene is like a song, and each drawing is like a chord. Since the chord has to fit into the mood and individuality of the song, it is necessary that each chord be appropriate for the song. Likewise each drawing must be appropriate for the scene. There are comedies, tragedies, fables, etc., and there are multitudes of emotions to carry the audience along through such tales. And about the performers: What makes a Lawrence Olivier, a Sarah Bond, a Carol Channing? Certainly a complete ability to adapt to the role they are playing or the song they are singing, which, of course, was made possible by a substantial amount of training, practice, and discipline.

When I was younger (many, many years ago) I went around with some singers and musicians of sorts. They were, some of them, very accomplished musicians. I was struck with the fact that they never stopped studying. One day I was walking along a crowded street in Hollywood with an operatic tenor and this guy bursts out with some vocalizing. Amazed stares from the crowd didn't faze him. He suddenly felt the need to work on his voice — and so he did.

One day I was vocalizing in my car and while at a stop signal glanced over to the car next to mine and there was a gal staring at me like I'd lost my marbles, shooter and all. Even that kind of devotion didn't make a star of me, but at least I had learned how to get involved. That is why I so often encourage you to get involved in drawing by carrying a sketchbook and become emboldened to use it in public. When singers vocalize they are working on their diaphragm, voice placement, vowels or consonants (or consonance), or on their vocal range. When you sketch, it is like vocalizing. It is working on capturing attitudes, shapes, and poses that will aid you in the variety of acting and drawing problems you will face in your career and the dexterity with which to handle them. So reactivate those sketchbooks and start' "vocalizing."

Ron Westwood, who works on *Prince and Pauper*, "vocalizes" while watching TV. I raided his sketchbook for you in the hope that it might inspire you to do likewise. Sketching is a great loosen-upper. Most of you stare at ultra-clean, finished cleanup drawings day after day, and if you don't sketch, your drawings are apt to become stiff. Look at the looseness in these sketches — they seem to move around on the paper:

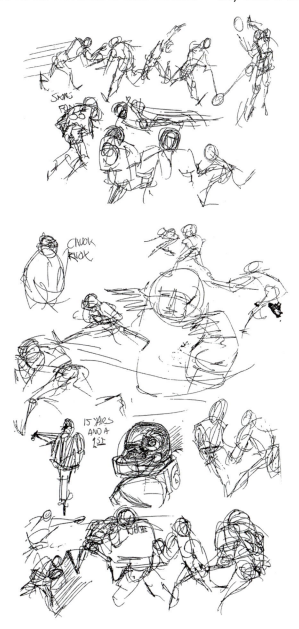

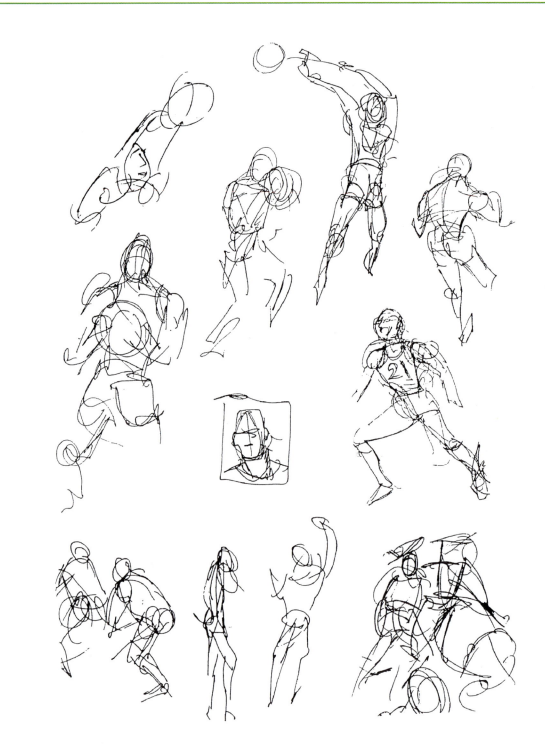

139 Abstracting the Essence

Last week I shared Ron Westwood's sketches with you. I was not advocating a style of drawing, only as far as a loose style allows you to study and practice drawing action — something that is hard to do if you try to make a cleaned up, finished drawing as you go. Here are some quick sketches done in class by Broose Johnson. They are simple in style and capture the essence of the pose with an economy of line, and as you might guess in a very few seconds.

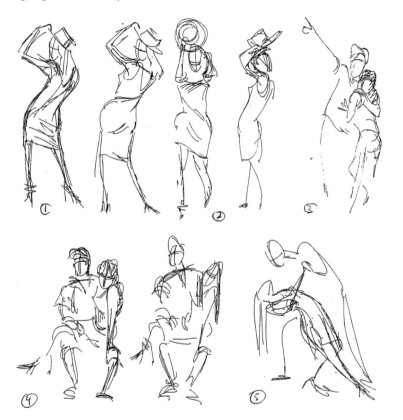

Notice how in group 1 Broose got more twist in the second try by opening up the armhole of the dress, bringing the breast into view, sending the V of the dress farther around, breaking the silhouette with the hair, and adding a wrinkle from the left hip to the right shoulder. In group 4 note how in the drawing on the right, the tension was increased between the heads and shoulders, causing a feeling of movement. A more acute angle on the girl's upper body allowed her hair to hang down — a nice touch. Note the improved negative space between the heads. That same area in the drawing on the left is slightly static — it repeats the perpendicular angles of the body and arm of the girl. I'm not trying to be esoteric. This kind of thinking will lead to more expressive drawing, especially in animation where body language is so important. It will aid you in capturing the essence of a gesture and, as with Broose's drawings, with and economy of lines. My philosophy is if you can draw it with 10 lines, why use 75. And who can argue with the philosophy of if you can draw it in 5 minutes, why take a half-hour.

I keep searching for a short cut to learning how to draw, but as Ollie Johnston used to say of drawing in general, "It ain't easy." Sometimes I try to get the students to look for the overall abstract shape. I'm not always sure I am explaining what is meant by "abstract." Last week (while driving home in my van) I sketched these abstracted shapes of some familiar (male) body types. If when drawing from life you can spot one of these shapes (or one of your own design) in the character you are drawing, it will save you the "agony" of searching for lines on the model to copy. If you know the overall abstract shape you are dealing with, it will be easier to apply that to the gesture.

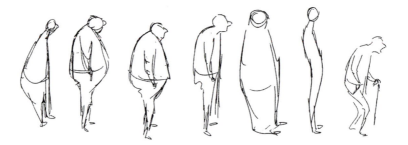

In addition to helping you depict general *body* characteristics, finding the abstract in the *gesture* itself will help, too. The word abstract, as I use it, means to summarize, to make an abstract of — a brief statement of the essential elements of a pose. So take a moment to study the type of body build, forming an abstract shape of it in your mind, then do the same with the overall pose. It simply means dropping 90% of the detail, and seeing only that 10%; that abstract of the pose, that essence of the pose.

A classic example was in a handout a couple of weeks ago. There was a beautiful, almost mysterious abstract shape in the pose. The artist got bogged down in the 90% (confusing) detail. In my sketch I attempted to deal only with that 10% essential stuff.

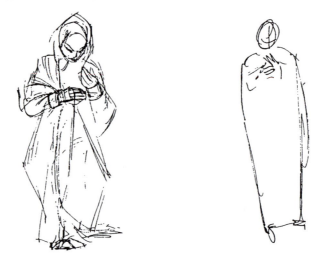

Here's another example where the artist was merely drawing things like heads, arms, legs, etc., just to get them all down. I looked for not only the abstract shapes of the bodies but also the abstract of the pose. (They were being "photographed" for the family album.) I used the man's straight, more youthful body as a kind of backboard for their attention to the camera, which is helped along by the older woman's bent forward shape.

Can you feel the movement going off to screen left where the camera is? Angles and negative shapes are involved also. Look from one drawing to the other and you will see what happens to the negative shapes and how they help to define and simplify the drawing. I made no attempt to draw a head, an arm, or a body. I looked for the abstract shapes and they defined the body parts for me.

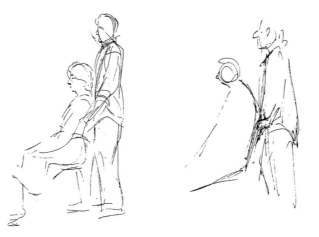

140 Common vs. Uncommon Gestures

My apologies to Ron Westlund for changing his name to Westwood in the last two "handouts." When my mind wanders it sometimes takes some strange byways. Years ago I did a paper with illustrations of Medusa, calling her Cruella deVil. That paper has been Xeroxed by numerous people in the business and sent to many parts of the world — too late to retract that one.

At times I may seem to get too involved in subtle and uncommon gestures. I defend the habit with the argument that you are doing uncommon films. If you were working on Bugs Bunny or the Road Runner, or heaven forbid, limited animation, you might get away with about a dozen common gestures: mad, surprised, scheming, a squash or stretch, anticipations, some crazy takes, a bombed-out pose with lots of smoke, and a fast run.

The stories you work on require a more diversified range of emotions and a much more sophisticated style for communicating them. The Disney style of animation goes beyond (in refinement) the "stock" variety. It often requires a little introspection — analyzing your own feelings to come up with an "uncommon" gesture. And at these times it would be a good thing if you knew the "principles" of drawing I so often speak of, so you could get the most out of what you are trying to express. That is also why I suggest reading a variety of writers who are able to describe that vast range of human emotions you as "actors" must deal with. Watching movies, not just for enjoyment, but also for study purposes is a must. The old silent movies are especially good because they were acted without the "crutch" of dialog to carry the story, or the gags. The gestures had to be caricatured with pinpoint accuracy. In these present times, good snappy dialog is "in" and very often substitutes for good acting or good pantomime.

In Disney feature cartoons mushy animation or weak gestures are not so readily acceptable. Even with good dialog to help, the acting has to be caricatured much like the old silent movies.

The style of drama and humor has changed, but the need for good visual portrayal is still needed.

If you neglect to update yourself through the study of good writing, movies, and plays, your sensitivity to these various emotions will surely atrophy. More important than just being able to recognize or picture in your mind the multitude of body gestures, you have to be able to draw them, and that is why I so often recommend sketching — constant sketching. That will keep your mind active and inquisitive, your eye sharp, and your drawing dexterity at "launch capability" at all times.

I "flip" when I get to peruse other artist's sketchbooks. It's like looking into their personal thinking. It's like observing their whole personality funneled into a series of drawings. It's like being shown "This is what I know, and how I draw it." Last week I had the privilege of Xeroxing these drawings from one of James Fujii's sketchbooks. I have been drumming angles and tensions and squash and stretch, etc., at James for many a month in the evening classes — he often attends both the Tuesday and the Wednesday night sessions — and I'd like to think that some of it has something to do with these delightful action sketches. Look hard at these drawings. Every part of each one is doing its bit to tell the story and to focus the eye or the mind on the idea behind the gesture, pose, or action. Each drawing, like a good actor or a highly skilled athlete, expresses the action with integrity and life-like meticulousness.

There was no time to do much planning or thinking while doing these sketches. It all happens pretty fast. The thinking was done in the months of study and preparation preceding their execution. At this point it was a matter of freeing his emotional energy and opening the adrenaline valve. I don't know about you, but I'm thoroughly impressed (and pleased).

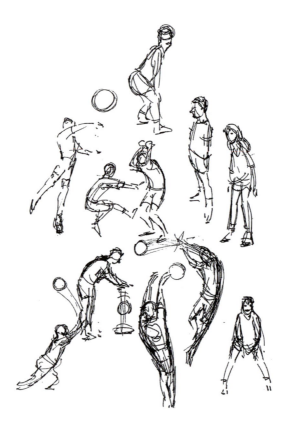

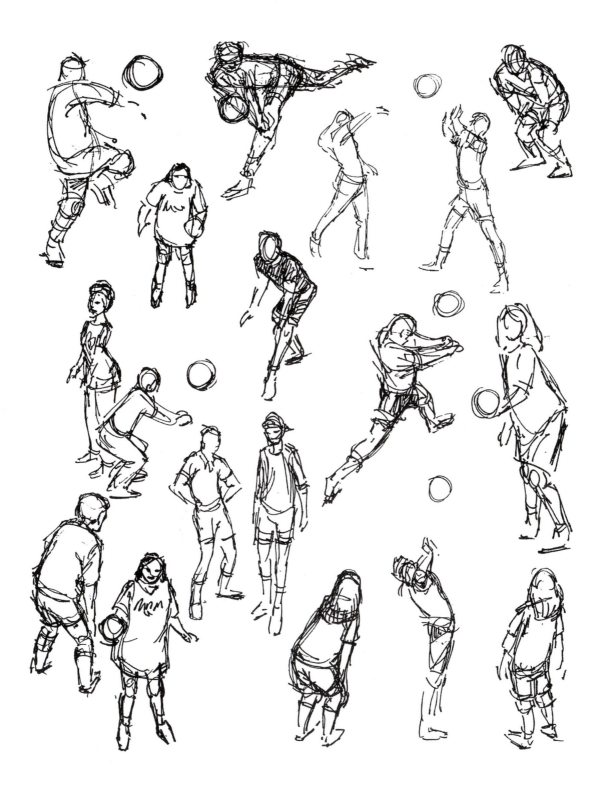

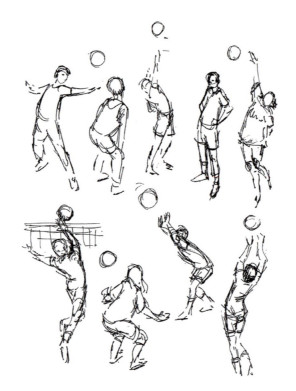

141   A Thinking Person's Art

I have often attempted to explain my approach to presenting the ideas in these "handouts." I have struggled to avoid referring to myself as a "teacher" and have used words like "suggestion" rather than "correction" when offering another version of a pose. I'm really here just to share my experience and it's your prerogative to treat it however you see fit. As for the suggestions, they are only to encourage you to see in new ways, to help you break any stultifying habits of "penny-pinching" seeing. I feel that the classes I conduct and the handouts, if nothing else, create a surge of group energy that you might tap for your own personal betterment.

A couple of weeks ago I said "These things I present are not esoteric concepts." But I was wrong — they are. They are things that only the chosen few absorb. It is the "chosen" few that lead the way and accomplish the "academy-award-worthy" animation and drawing. But it is my conviction that by earnest pursuit anyone can be of that group. It's just a matter of exposing oneself to some vehicle that will help one break the "sound barrier." (Actually, thought barrier, for drawing is a thinking person's art.)

"There's the rub." If you're not thinking about the story behind the pose or the action, you're just drawing lines. A storyboard will rarely call for a character to just stand there frozen in a do-nothing pose. The story will require the character to act or react in some story-related way: shake hands, walk toward the door, or something. Even just looking requires a drawing that expresses action.

So drawing requires thinking. Thinking, being in this case, synonymous with acting. I don't know how many hundreds, perhaps thousands of times I've watched artists use lines simply because that's how they appeared on the model or on the model sheet, or in the anatomy book. Many struggle so doggedly with the construction and the detail that they miss the gesture. Why are we so hesitant, so reluctant, or tentative to manipulate the character to suit the needs of the story? The human figure is extremely pliable, even capable of contortion. I'm not advocating contortion, but I am trying to promote thinking and acting.

We incorporate two models occasionally, in the class, to set up some relationships to draw. This complicates things because there are two separate characters that have to be woven into one pose. The desired result is not a dual action, but rather dual characters blended into one action. Here the lines and shapes used in each of the separate characters must relate to each other almost as if they were one character.

Here is a detail of one very successful duo pose. You feel an intensity of interest in both characters in whatever the man is pointing to.

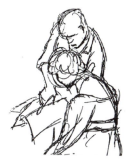

The very first stages of a drawing will tell where your thinking is. If you are thinking story then that will begin to emerge in the first few lines drawn. Many times in the evening class, artists will carry a drawing to an advanced stage yet have no clue as to what the story behind the pose is (the most important thing in a drawing). Here's a drawing that I intercepted at a stage where I thought the artist should have been well into the story. He has perhaps 75 lines drawn and you still can't tell what's going on. To make my point, I sketched in what was happening in about 10 lines.

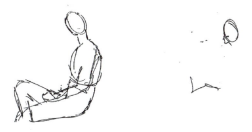

To arouse that sense of urgency to get the essence down, I often ask the class to imagine they are running to board a train that is about to leave the station. They see someone in a delightful pose that they have just got to sketch, so out comes the sketchbook. At that moment the conductor calls, "all aboard," and so they have just enough time to get the barest essence of the pose. If they get the essence down, then tomorrow it can be reconstructed, but if the essence is not there in the sketch — forget it.

Here is a nice little essence drawing. Just a few lines dashed off in bravura fashion. A common, everyday gesture told in a very delicate and expressive way. (This is a Dan Boulos sketch.)

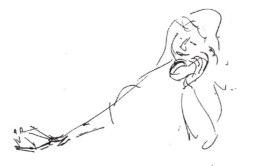

In an article about the author Reynolds Price, (*LA Times*, Wednesday, May 2) it stated that he "...has respect for the tradition of <u>storytelling</u>, which he ranks after food as <u>man's principle need</u> — sex and shelter being relatively expendable." I underlined the words I want you to remember, lest your attention be deflected by other thoughts in that sentence.

You, as animation cartoonists/artists, should acknowledge that *storytelling is also one of your principle needs*. Not only for your job but also for yourself. You should surrender to the delights of expressing yourself in drawing. If you don't feel that need now then you should expose yourself to more dramatizing, even if only in the form of books, movies, and plays, thus creating a desire to express those things. It's really quite a lot of fun coaxing a story (a gesture) out of a bunch of lines and shapes. And as I recently read somewhere, "It's okay to have fun."

Here's a two-model pose where one man was handing the other a telephone, saying "It's for you." I didn't have much room for my suggestion sketch, so the figures had to be done apart, but even so, you can see a definite action and reaction relationship. I reasoned that if you're handing someone a telephone you would bend forward a little to emphasize the "....for you." The other chap might react with, "Who, me? or "I wonder who it can be?" He is doing two things that comprise one gesture: reaching forward with his arms to take the phone, but rearing back in an, "I wonder who it is?" attitude.

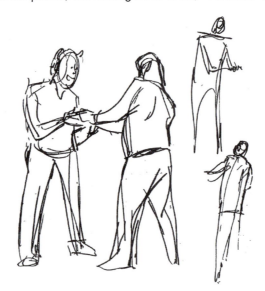

Here's another one. Two guys shaking hands. The one on the left is all excited because he hasn't seen his friend in ages. He is exuberantly pumping away, head tucked down, shoulders up — positively gushing. He is leaning forward at the waist, as if bowing. He is demonstrative but respectful. The other chap is a little more hesitant, saying, perhaps, "Oh, hi…" but thinking, "Do I know him?" The man on the left is the initiator of this action — the one on the right is reacting. He reaches out in involuntary response but the rest of him displays caution.

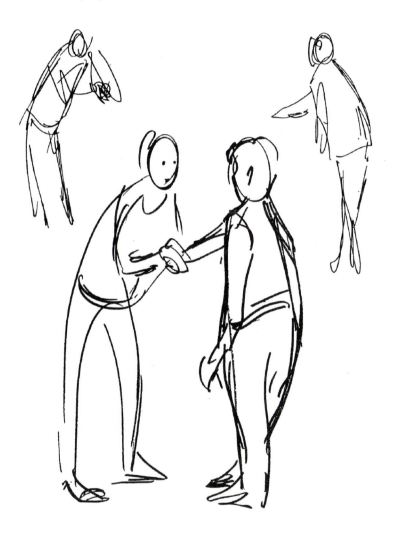

See what fun drawing can be. I'm a "frustrated actor" who has spent many an hour on the stage. But now I get my kicks by doing my acting/storytelling on paper or canvas. You don't have to be an actor, but you must develop their kind of thinking. I don't know how else you can make it happen. Surely you don't want to rely on chance. Even when reading, I picture the story in my mind. I become the stage designer, the director, and the actors. I am serious if it suits the story, or I can "ham it up." I require the actors to play their roles just like I did in those sketches above — acted out with heart and soul, and thinking.

P.S. What with all the trouble it is to learn how to draw and then the stress, struggle, and strain putting it to practical use, and then me saying it's fun reminds me of an episode of *Salt Chuck on the Rocks* by Chuck Sharman.

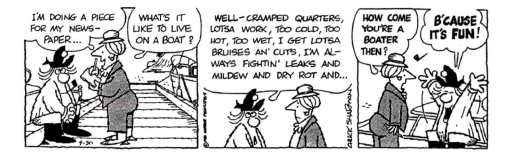

142 Lines, Lines, Lines

In your business (animation) line is one of the most important elements. With line you can create the wonder, humor and beauty of the Disney style cartoon feature. It all starts with a simple story line and progresses into a very complex and entertaining medium. Line is a very exciting discovery that man (artists) has developed to a phenomenal degree. Drawing in line can be a real adventure and when used skillfully can be a source of adventure for the millions of viewers who see your work on the screen. Line is not just a tracing tool — it is a living, organic thing, capable of describing just about anything you can dream up.

Last week as I was thinking about the next handout, I started to sketch some ideas on line. It soon veered off into some nonsensical ideas that, nevertheless, seemed playful, so I decided to pass them off as a handout.

There are many kinds of lines.

Short ones,

long ones,

curved lines,

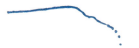

and some that get off to a good start but then seem to poop out.

You can do anything with lines. Years ago there was a silly gimmick that went like this: Do you know what this is?

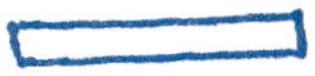

It's a TV screen for people who squint.
Know what this is?

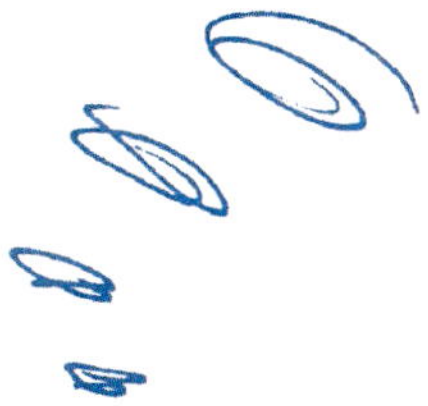

It's a tornado with the hiccups.
There are sturdy lines,

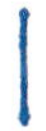

staggering lines,

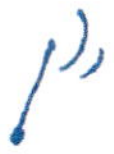

and lines that just can't seem to get off the ground.

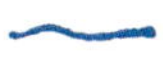

There are obsequious lines that always curtsy,

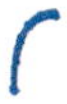

proud lines with chests out,

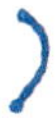

obese lines,

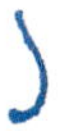

normal lines,

stretched lines,

and squashed lines.

There are graceful lines.

There are ugly lines,

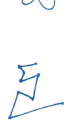

gregarious lines,

and loners.

There are choppy lines and

continuous lines.

There are lines that are the shortest distance between two points.

Lines make music possible (with the help of spaces).

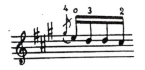

There are dotted lines to sign on,

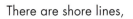

a line of bull,

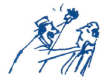

a skyline, and

invisible lines like the equator.

There are shore lines,

airlines,

scrimmage lines, and

fishing lines.

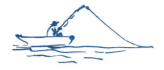

The moon, prima donna of the heavens,
in its proud fullness took
its place on the stage of night,
and performed its slow, graceful way
across the dark blue, speckled sky
in a costume of borrowed light.

Poetic lines on a page and the lines of old age,

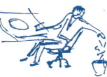

rebellious lines, lines that obey, leftover lines to be thrown away.
And if you are a theatre goer — lines in a play:

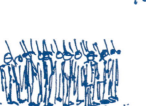

Lines that soldiers form while they're on duty, and last but not least, lines of wondrous beauty.

143 Feel, as Well as See, the Gesture

While working from a live model, I have found it is better to draw quickly and spontaneously, rather than slowly and overly careful. In the time it takes some artists to do one drawing (and that one often nowhere near completed) others have sketched in three or four tries. This encourages experimentation and looking for alternate interpretations of the gesture. Trying for variations of the pose will sharpen your observation and your hand–eye coordination, and help you to seek out subtle nuances of the gesture. After all, if you had to draw several of the Disney characters in the same pose you'd have to vary each one according to the personality of that character.

In the evening class, I try to get the artists to stop copying the model, especially in a ponderous fashion wherein the gesture is difficult to feel, and so often takes a back seat to the details. I encourage flexibility. Sketching quickly and loosely will help you to be more creative, inventive, and inspired and will train you to be more adaptable and versatile. (It'll be more fun, too.)

A couple of weeks ago we had the wonderful Bobby Ruth as our model. I think she's nearly as ancient as I am but she's just as energetic, and quite a talented actress. She did a clown for us (the night before that she did a sexy nightclub performer). The wonderful play-acting she did unearthed a typical clown-like character that was as distinctive as one of Red Skelton's characters, or Bob Newhart, or any other performer whose characteristic style is as memorable. If you saw Bobby in a supermarket checkout line, she might blend into the crowd, but while performing, she has that unique ability to carry us beyond the ordinary. She seems to transform herself into another realm — one of pure gesture. Bobby is not the only model who does this. Craig Howell, our carpenter, waiter, and gardener does it too. Our own people do it when we have them pose for us. They bring us marvelous bits of life to sketch (to capture). But it's not just the job of the model to do this — it's our goal too — to go beyond just making a drawing of arms and legs and clothes. We want to draw something that tells a story … like our models do.

Drawing is really your reaction to life — to the bits of life you are sketching. It is not merely a collection of parts being put down on paper. It's more like the colorful display of 4th of July fireworks after they have exploded in the sky, revealing their final "gesture." You can't see that gesture by just handling the physical thing called a Sky Fountain, or whatever they are called, it has to explode to reveal its beauty. So it is with a drawing. Handling the human parts of the body will reveal nothing but the means to the end. The end is when it assumes one of its story-packed gestures. As you draw, you *feel* as much as *see* the gesture as it comes to life on your paper. There is a kind of flush that grips you. If you are just seeing the parts, they will always remain parts, but if you go for the final "explosive" gesture, the parts will fall into place and the pose magnificent will emerge.

Here's a paragraph from *Drawing on the Artist Within* by Betty Edwards, which is quite apropos:

Gesture drawing is a technique of very rapid drawing, one drawing after another, perhaps fifteen scribbled drawings accomplished in fifteen minutes or less. It works, I believe to "set aside" the strong, verbal left-hemisphere mode, perhaps in the following way. L-mode, which prefers a rather slow (relatively speaking) step-by-step linear, sequential, analytic procedure for drawing, preferably using familiar namable forms, says, in effect, "First we'll draw the head, (let's see, that's sort of an oval); then the neck (two lines); then the shoulders (two slanty lines from the neck)…." But in gesture drawing, L-mode finds you drawing helter-skelter, all over the page, saying to yourself, "Just get it down! Faster! Faster!" And L-mode objects, "If you're going to draw that stupid way, count me out! I like to do things the sensible way — my way! One thing at a time, the way…we…always…do…"And L-mode bows out. Perfect! Just what we want!

Here are some drawings from that session with Bobby Ruth that I felt needed a little help. My "suggestions" were not attempts to make a Rembrandt-like drawing, after all, they were only ten-second sketches of Bobby's "play-acting." In her clown costume she was creating a charming clown-like character, and every move she made was typical clown.

For this first pose, I suggested that one of the many possible interpretations might be to let the principles of drawing permeate one's thinking — squash and stretch, angles, simplification, balance, tension, straight against curve, and perspective. Try to do it in about 10 or 15 seconds. Forget the details — that stuff is all on the "model sheets."

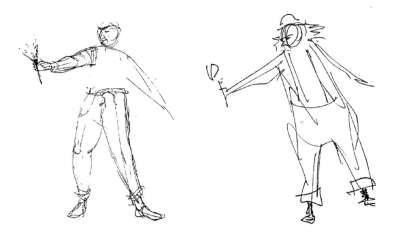

Here's one where you might line things up in an attempt to point her attention out to the "audience" she is entertaining. You might drop her right arm to get it out of the look's way, and curve her back to help send her communication with the audience forward. You might even have the little flower on her hat jump out at then (see the next drawings).

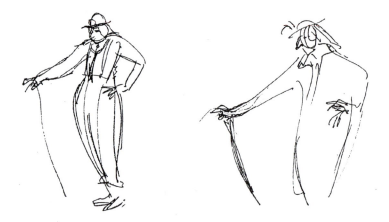

You know the pose — modest, bashful, shy — or better yet pretending to be shy. It's all in the shoving the hands into the pockets, the dragging of one foot and the tilt of the head, which tries to hide behind one of the shoulders.

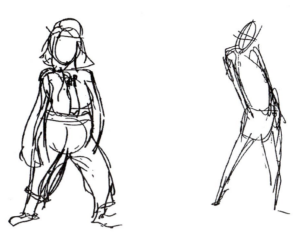

And when a clown leans on something, they LEAN. They exaggerate everything to the point of defying gravity.

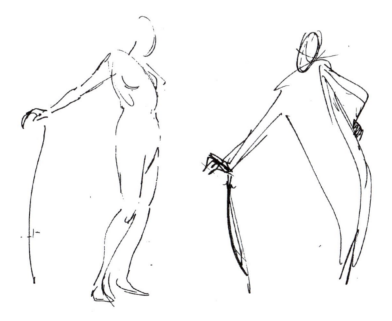

Here are two more. With the help of all those principles of drawing mentioned earlier, squash and stretch, etc., feel free to "push" these poses just a bit, allowing them to "explode" into what might be termed a caricature of the gesture. You might take it upon yourself in drawing sessions such as this to surpass the model, whoever it might be. After all, they have physical limitations, whereas on paper you have none (see the next drawings).

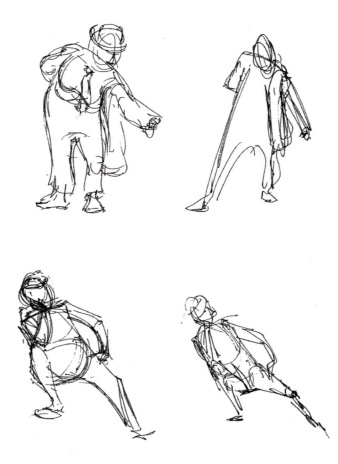

144 Savvy Sayin's

I have a delightful book called *Savvy Sayin's – Lean & Meaty One-liners*. It's a collection of old time western lore and art. It's full of wise and pithy sayings, and because of the clever "western" idiom, packs a special wallop. Funny how a lot of philosophy can be compacted into a simple colloquialism. Well, I thought, why can't something like this be directed to drawing? You know me — I'll try (almost) anything.

Here are a few excerpts from the book. Frederic Remington and Charles M. Russell illustrated the book.

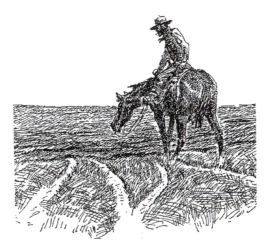

If you follow a new track,
there ain't no way of knowin'
If the man that made it
knew where he was goin.'

In between the illustrated one-liners are gems like these' ns/

Broke is what happens when you let your yearnin's get ahead of your earnin's.
Borrowin' is like scratchin'. It only feels good for a little while.
A string around the finger helps you remember. A rope around your neck helps you forget.
Lightning does the work; thunder takes the credit.
Drownin' your sorrows only irrigates 'em.

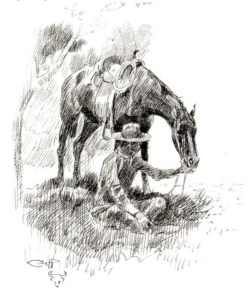

The good thing about talkin' to your horse is he don't talk back.

And here's my version. Let's call it Walt's Witty Wisdom, the Western Way, with illustrations by a local artist. (Or is that loco?)

If yer eyes is stuck on the model, yer mind is bein' left out.
It may take two hundert words to convince someone thet yer honest, but it only takes five lines in a drawin' ta prove you ain't.
In drawin', yer eyes and yer mind is pardners — yer eyes sees it first but yer mind has to correct what they seen.

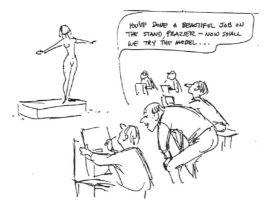

When you decide yer through with a drawin' — you've prob'ly gone too fer.
Life sometimes takes a heap of explainin', but a drawin' has gotta stand all by its self.

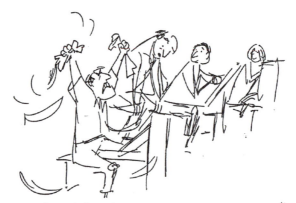

A model kin only go so fer — a drawin' has no limits.
It ain't th' number of lines in a drawin' — it's how they bin corralled.
Any details thet don't help the gesture 'll never be missed.
When drawin's takes tha place of talk — they gotta say jest as much.

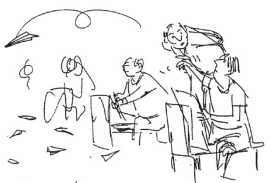

"JOHN, IF YOU'RE DISSATISFIED WITH YOUR DRAWINGS, PLEASE FIND SOME OTHER WAY TO DISPOSE OF THEM."

Lines used by artists is like a cowhands skill — if he cain't break a hoss, there ain't gonna be nothin' ta ride.

Lines is like members of a basketball team — if they don't work together, they ain't gonna be much slam-dunkin'.

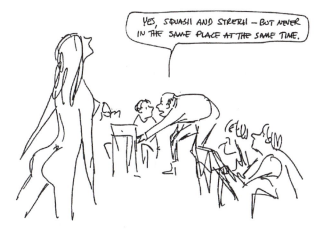

YES, SQUASH AND STRETH — BUT NEVER IN THE SAME PLACE AT THE SAME TIME.

Some well-chosen lines in a drawin' is like choosin' the right trail on the range.
They say a picture is worth a thousan' words, so with a little rationin', you could git a lot of drawin's out o' that many.
Drawin' is like buildin' a corral — ya gotta layout the overall shape first.
Like a good cup of strong coffee will git a cowboy goin' in the mornin', some good strong angles will get a drawin' off to a good start.
It takes a human a heap of years ta develop a set of gestures — artist's has gotta do it in a couple of minutes.
A model may strain to keep the pose, but a good drawin' looks fresh forever.
A good drawin' doesn't need dialogue ta say what it's got ta.
Many a poker hand is won by luck, but a good drawin' is got by skill.

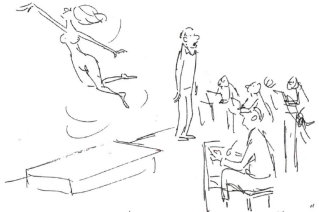

"HURRY CLASS, SHE WON'T BE ABLE TO HOLD THIS ONE VERY LONG."

Actually these cartoons were drawn in my motel room in Burbank in the evening. They were my way of relaxing after a day at the studio. Usually a night's batch would focus on one or two subjects. These happened to be on drawing. An average batch averaged around a dozen. Here are a few more.

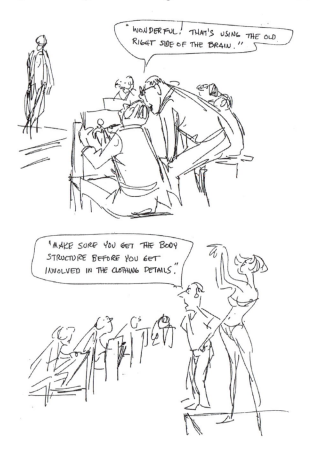

"WONDERFUL! THAT'S USING THE OLD RIGHT SIDE OF THE BRAIN."

"MAKE SURE YOU GET THE BODY STRUCTURE BEFORE YOU GET INVOLVED IN THE CLOTHING DETAILS."

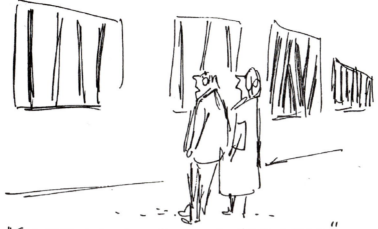

"I UNDERSTAND HE SPENT THE LAST TEN YEARS IN PRISON."

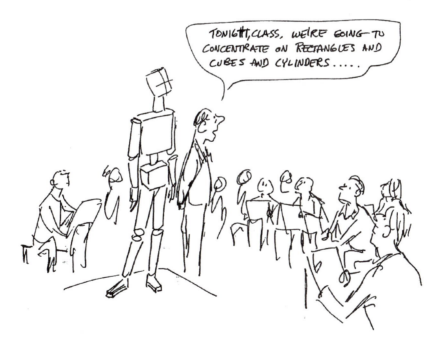

TONIGHT, CLASS, WE'RE GOING TO CONCENTRATE ON RECTANGLES AND CUBES AND CYLINDERS.....

145 The Inner Force

It is mighty tempting to go on making humorous handouts but I'm not getting paid to entertain you — I'm supposed to be broadcasting the good news about good drawing. However, here's a spin off from last week's handout. I didn't have room for this cartoon and someone who saw it said, "Hey, you could do a whole handout on tangents." I was tempted to try, but…well, here is the cartoon.

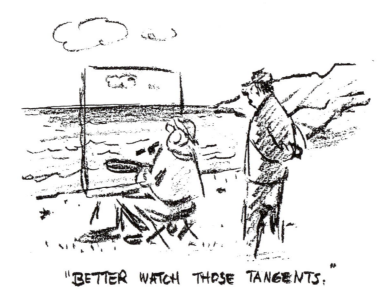

"BETTER WATCH THOSE TANGENTS."

The main thrust of my teaching is that you have to have a motive for drawing — a story to illustrate. Something to give you direction. And yet, here in one episode of a cartoon strip, *For the Birds*, which I did years ago, that notion is overruled.

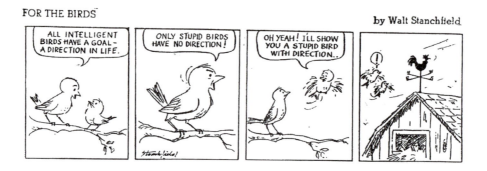

But I do believe we should be eternally flexible. We should never be so sure of ourselves that our minds are closed to new ideas:

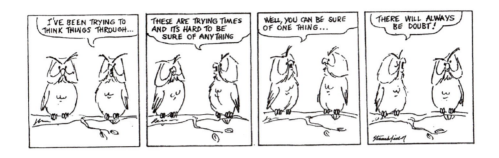

The best kind of learning is the kind that teaches you to think, that way you don't have to rely on anyone else, or on formulas.

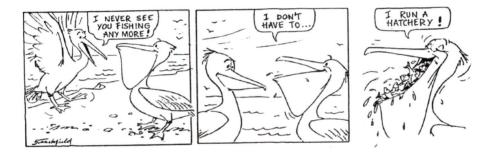

In the evening classes I try to make it clear that I am not "correcting" a person's work by using my version of how the drawing should look. I'm trying to help find better ways of seeing gestures and actions. As Don Graham used to say in a painting class at Chouinard's (Chouinard Art Institute which later became Cal Arts), after criticizing a painting, "So what! It could have been done a hundred different ways, and all of them could have been good." The idea was to open up the mind to possibilities and not to be satisfied with whatever happened to cone out, but to be able to consciously choose and guide the outcome.

Here is a student's drawing that is quite loose (something I encourage), but seems to lack the artist's wholehearted involvement in the gesture. An artist is "on stage" just like an actor in a play. He can't just "make a drawing"; that is, put down the proper number of legs and arms, etc. He has to make them "do" something …"act". He has to have a dramatic or a humorous point to put over, and must use all the principles of drawing at his command to put it over.

In this pose, Craig Howell was a gardener, probably cleaning the leaves out of his rake (I forget). The student's drawing seemed a bit passive, so I added a thrust of energy from his feet right up to the rake. The whole left side of his body became a stretch, causing the right side to be a squash. I dropped his left foot and the belt on the left side so they would pull away from the upraised shoulder. I got the hand out where *you* could see what it was doing and exposed the face so *he* could see what he was doing. I angled the whole body toward the center of interest, which was the rake:

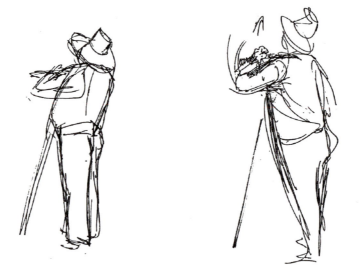

You've heard me speak over and over again about straightening things up. Here the student has straightened up the torso, the arms, and the hands. I suggested that the gardener would lean into whatever he was doing, bending forward from the waist. To guide the attention downward to the cutter, I lowered his left hand. See the triangle it creates between the two hands and the face. It sets up a downward movement in the direction of the cutters. His right hand's higher, which calls for the right elbow and shoulder to be higher, eliminating a sameness of angles, and sets up a tension as if he were pushing on the cutter handles.

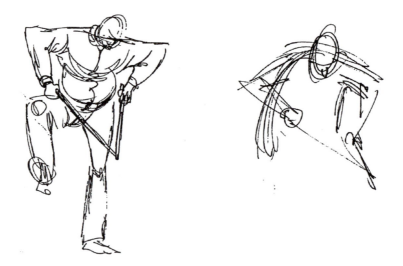

And speaking of straightening things up, here was a pose with lots of tension in it. The artist knows his anatomy; that is, how to draw arms, legs, waists, hips, etc., but failed to work those parts into what was a very expressive pose. Notice that he straightened up the body by making the hands, buttocks, knees, and feet horizontally parallel.

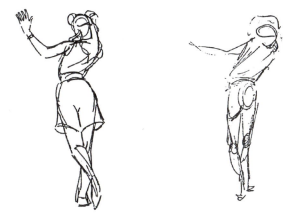

As you can see, anatomy is not the answer — acting is. If anatomy were the answer, an actor could go out on the stage and just stand there naked. The inner motivations that power a person's body to express body language is what it's all about. Anatomy is what is on the outside — motivation is the driving force within. That's what the gesture classes and these handouts are for. They're to whet your desire to go beyond just an anatomical drawing (or a copy of the model); to foment a life-long desire to express readable emotions in your drawings and to stimulate your inner forces to take over and rule the outer. May the INNER FORCE be with you!

To show what can be done through that inner seeing/feeling, here are some drawings by Dylan Kohler, who has never attended an anatomy class. There's no doubt about what's going on story-wise. (Mike Swofford gave us a whole evening of such great poses.) I have encouraged Dylan to learn anatomy but only to "tighten" up his drawing, but to be careful that it doesn't "stiffen" up his gestures. Incidentally, these are not timid attempts — they are an impressive seventeen inches high.

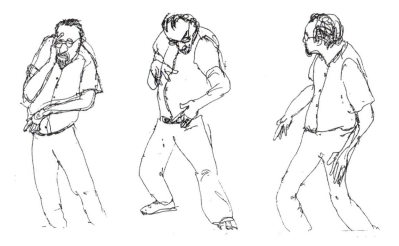

146 The Power of "mmm"

This may be a long one! It has been two weeks since I've written anything for you and since I wasn't interested in the movie on the plane to Orlando, Florida, I wrote, and wrote, and wrote. Several themes ran through my mind so I'm just going to put them all down the way they came to me.

Sometimes when I am trying to invent new approaches to thinking while drawing, I end up way out in "left field." But if you know anything about baseball, you'll agree that left field has a legitimate role to play in the game. Anyway, going home from the studio a couple of weeks ago, I stopped for a cheese-burger (I get mine on whole wheat toast at Denny's) and as I was eating it I noticed if I said "mmm" it made the burger taste better. This is nothing new, of course, I'm sure people all over the world say "mmm" when food delights them.

Then I remembered that I say "mmm" while drawing or painting. Not only when I see something good happen but even before I draw it. Students have heard me "mmm" over their drawings, especially when they try something I have suggested and it works. "Mmm" is a way of expressing admiration, relish, and recognition of worth. It expresses thanksgiving and the anticipation of something good about to happen, as well as something good that has just happened.

Here are a few "mmm" drawings that I confiscated so I could share them with you. I didn't pick them for their Norman Rockwell finesse, but rather because they seem to reveal the artist's thinking, his own inwardly felt participation in the gesture. They show that wonderful moment when all inhibitions are put aside and the "actor" comes out on stage to perform. The first four drawings are by Dan Boulos. The poses that night were very difficult. The model, who is into modern theater, gave us a lot of "far out" poses with no story behind them. Dan seemed to get the gist of it and came up with some beauties.

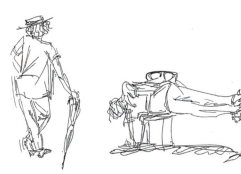
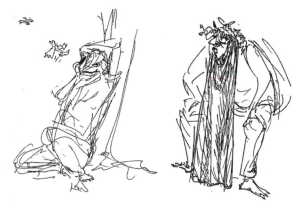

On the following pages are some drawings by Lureline Weatherly, James Fujii, Dave Woodman, Bill Perkins, and on the last drawings are an artist's work I can't at the moment identify (the hearing doesn't go first, the memory does). The name hopefully will turn up in next week's "Column Apologia." Incidentally, one of our best models, Mike Swofford, is represented in some of these following drawings.

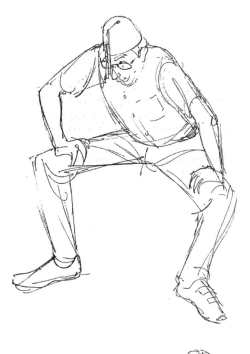

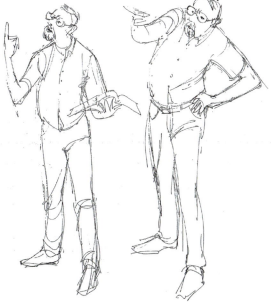

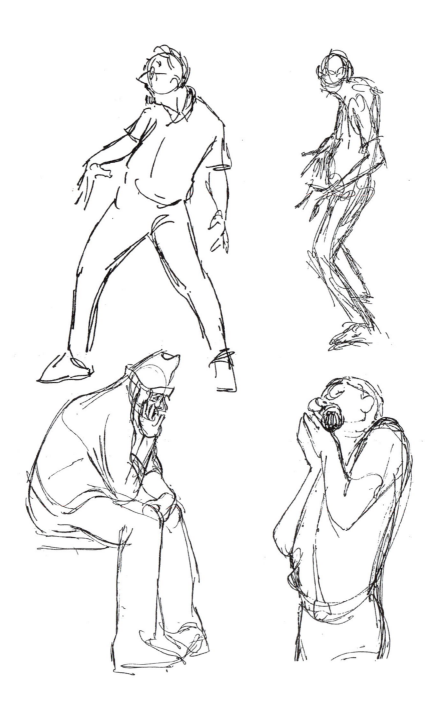

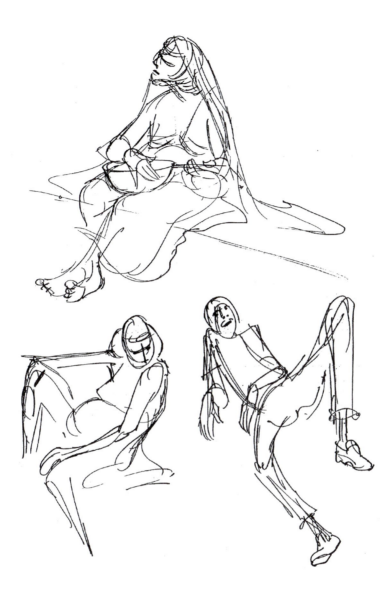

It takes courage to draw, to face a blank sheet of paper with only a pen or pencil and your inner thoughts that have to be grouped together to draw something that will induce a viewer or an audience to involuntarily say, "Mmm, that's nice," or "That's funny," or whatever you meant it to be.

If we keep in touch with our inner self, there will be less leakage of energy. If we know who we are and what we stand for, we are not buffeted by the hundreds of distractions and power tappers. Sometimes we feel like we're driving a car into a strong wind where we can almost see the gas gauge go down. When we sit down to draw, we want all the winds to cease. We want to save the fuel for the important things. Actually, man is a human dynamo. He is an energy-producing machine. Things that drain that energy, like confusion, indecision, doubt, negativity, etc., are soon put aside by enthusiasm, anticipation, positive thinking, etc. All of these things are the result of attitude. If we can control our attitude, our energy will be renewed and redirected. There is no shortage of energy — only occasionally a shortage of good attitudes.

I am back from a week with the artists at the Florida studio. It was only a couple of years ago that many of them went through the intern program here in Glendale. Now they are professionals, having recently completed Roller Coaster Rabbit, a real winner of a cartoon. Right alongside them, in the Florida studio, is a new group of aspirants struggling to understand the Disney way of life, the Disney style of animation, and all the many inroads necessary for a meaningful future. They know where they are — they are at the beginning. It's good to know where you are. It tells you what you have accomplished and what you need to do to accomplish more. Everyone is not on the same level of expertise. Even the number of years with the studio (or in the business) doesn't always indicate a person's capabilities, or his competence, or even his contribution.

When I started in the business in 1937 there weren't very many guidelines to follow. I didn't know where I was. I was only a couple of months out of high school with no art school, no anatomy lessons, no formal training at all. Not even a portfolio! Just a desire to get into animation.

Most of you have an art school background and are able to better judge where you are regarding your knowledge and potentiality. And there is an abundance of research material to draw on, plus interested fellow workers who are very willing to help. It's heartening when the more experienced artists freely share their knowledge with those younger artists who are new to the business. Maybe it's because in knowing who you are, you also remember where you were when you first came to the studio (or the business). Knowing where you are not only helps you to improve your abilities but helps you to sympathize with those who are still searching for solid footing.

Bill Matthews has done a fantastic job of instigating a training program at Disney. This was formerly unheard of. No other studio spends the time and effort and money to train people. But all of us are involved in the training program — not just with interns but with anyone that needs a helping hand. Working with artists less experienced than ourselves requires a great deal of interest and concern, both for the studio and for the one in need. It also requires that we maintain a huge "graveyard" wherein we can bury the mistakes and shortcomings of those who come to us for help. All of us are teachers in one way or another. And it is surprising how far and how fast our influence travels, be it positive or negative. Facts are not always what a novice needs. Sometimes he needs something as ephemeral as a little reassurance; perhaps a heartfelt "mmm" now and again.

147 Gestural Symbolism

When we draw, we in a sense, draw symbols. For instance when we draw a hand it is not a real hand, it is a symbol of a hand. To a viewer, though, it is a hand. Due to the standardized use of body language, most gestures have actually become symbols. As an example, by certain manipulations of the fingers you can create a symbol of prayer, obscenity, stop or go, stay or come, accusation, just a minute, shhhh, I'd like a ride, and many others.

In animation we make use of those facts. We not only move our characters around the stage, but we have them deliver their lines and their actions in symbolic ways. That is the fastest and surest way of communicating our story. There need be no worry that using these symbols will lead to a gutless and repetitious performance. The individualism of each artist plus the physiognomy and personality of each character will prevent that.

Gesture study is a period where we acquaint ourselves with these symbols. We learn how to manipulate the figure to evoke certain emotional or psychological responses. The variances are infinite within certain boundaries. When those boundaries are overstepped suddenly it becomes a different gesture — one that has its own symbolic meaning. Of course, the same gesture used in different settings can produce different symbols. In animation we have to develop a sensitivity to these gestural symbols so we can present the proper one for each particular story point, action, or emotion. So as we draw, we are symbolizing emotions, actions, movements, activities, adventures and humor by means of gestures.

Common everyday gesture is something that doesn't have to be learned. It is something we do all the time. It comes natural to us, we don't have to be trained to gesture. The reason drawing gestures is so difficult, is because we get caught up in the many problems of "drawing" that we lose sight of it. Reality is what we are trying to draw and reality is the first thing that fades from our minds as we begin to draw "things."

In the evening classes I have tried to get the students to stop "drawing" and with as few lines as possible, get the gesture down. Here are a few drawings that are indicative of that approach.

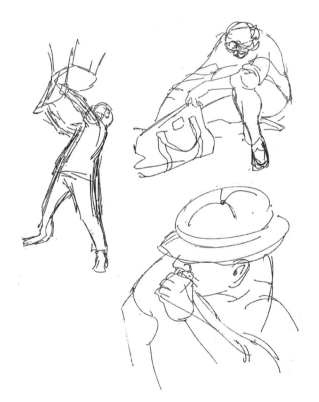

In my suggestion sketches, I try to point out how the parts of the body work to produce a certain gesture. Again, it's not something you have to learn — it is something you have to see, or remember, or feel, or if need be, create or fabricate. Creating a pose doesn't mean coming up with a never before seen pose, it merely means that you manipulate the body parts to express the gesture you want.

For instance, here is a pose where the guy is showing something in a magazine to a gal. Simple enough! Is the gal interested? I thought she should be, so I bent her forward a little more. As a result, the two heads together seem to gather energy. As you can see the first girl's head didn't go far enough so I pushed it a little farther. The heads the student drew, stacked one over the other, are rather static. In my book of drawing rules it says, "Don't stack two objects perpendicular to each other. Also don't have the upper arm perfectly horizontal and the lower arm perfectly perpendicular — those two angles are one half of a square, and as for squares, let me quote a paragraph from Thomas Berger's great tale, *Little Big Man*.

I got a choking sensation when I heard the news. There was already so many white men around Laramie you could hardly breathe, and I didn't sleep well in them rectangular barracks, on account of having been trained by the Cheyenne to favor the circular dwelling. I think I have mentioned their feeling about circles, the earth and so on. They was set against the ninety-degree angle, which brought continuity to a dead stop. Old Lodge Skins used to say: "There's no power in a square.

Also in my book of rules it says to create interest in the object of, the reason for, or the significance of the pose, which in this case is two people's engrossment in a magazine.

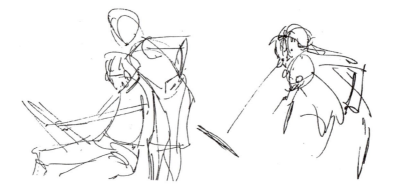

All athletes have certain goals in whatever game they play or feat they undertake. Each of them do certain exercises to strengthen the muscles they must use for the task. Most athletes train intensely with long hours of physical and mental preparation. Diet plays an important part also. Experimentation, inventiveness, resourcefulness, originality, imagination, ingenuity, creativity? Yes! The better trained an athlete is, the more innovative he can be during a contest, match, or tournament. Actually the best learning is acquired while performing. Ultimately the performance must take over where the preparation ends.

And so it is with an artist. There must be periods of study — anatomy, composition, perspective, design, etc. — but when drawing, (performing) those things are put behind, then acting and gesture guides the pencil or pen. I have tried to fashion the evening classes into a performance activity. One where all thoughts of "training" are put aside and we step out on stage and do the thing we have been training for, that is, to act on paper.

In Edward Dwight Easty's book, *On Method Acting*, he says:

There is a difference between the art of living one's part and merely representing or playing it. An actor must create a living human being on stage with all the complexities of the character: his behavior, thoughts, emotions, and their subsequent transitions. He must never settle for less.

Also from the chapter titled "On the Art of Acting" came this:

An actor's instrument is his whole self. It is his body, his mind and being, complete with thoughts, emotions, sensitivity, imagination, honesty, and awareness.

These are things that pertain to us as animation artists. We just happen to use a different medium. Easty goes on to say

The painter can paint until he alone is artistically satisfied; the musician and composer can work until their music is a part of them before scheduling a concert; the writer–author may write and rewrite over a period of years before he is satisfied. The actor, however, is more or less trapped in a Seine of time schedules centered around rehearsals in which he has to consciously create his art on time.

Sound like us? You bet it does! Like all movie actors, our work appears on film and is presented to audiences all over the world.
Let me continue quoting from the chapter "On the Art of Acting."

unlike other professions where an eight-hour day is deemed the normal amount of time to be devoted, acting requires a constant adherence to the profession itself. The actor's day should begin long before he reaches the theatre for the evening's performance. Whether he is working on a role or not, his day should begin as an actor when he awakens. Whether it be personal introspection, surveillance of life around him, appreciation of nature and her laws; awareness of people and their problems, or trying to wake up in the morning as the character he is playing, the actor must continually strive for perceptivity. For by seeing deeper than the surface aspects of life, he is able to broaden his own scope of any character he portrays. The depth of his art will depend greatly upon this perceptiveness.

Wow!
I'm tempted to go on but think I should shut up so you can use the time to reread some of that good stuff.

148 Some Left Over Thoughts

NO CONTEST: If a $5.00 bill is placed on a table, it can easily be read by passersby. But if $5.00 in assorted change is tossed on the table it could turn out to be a contest to see who could guess the proper amount. In drawing a gesture it should be recognized immediately and not turn out to be a contest.
CREATIVE ENERGY: There is a vital creative energy that builds up in an artist as he proceeds to draw. As he is caught up in the thrill of the project, his thinking is accelerated by each successful line he makes. It arouses all his faculties so that there is input from the farthermost parts of his

consciousness. Many of the observations he has made in the past come to the fore. He soon discovers himself beyond that line which convention has constrained him to stay behind. He is suddenly armed with all those sleeping genies that have been lying in wait for these special moments of intensification — these moments when the desire to perform wins over the mere half-hearted attempts to make a drawing.

GO WHOLE HOG ON ACTION AND POSES: Your action and gestures should be as broad as your audience is going to be. If you were a painter you might have patrons who like things painted a certain way, so you can direct all your expression to and for them. In cartooning your audience is not so narrow in their tastes (and perhaps discernment), so your expression has to be broad enough to gratify them all. Many of them need it all "spelled out," real clear like. Laughter is usually what you are after and if you deliver humor in a hesitant way, your audience will be hesitant to laugh at it.

STRETCH YOUR TALENTS: Keep reading and observing to increase your range of understanding. By so doing, you will be better able to adjust to the variety of stories and characters; and better able to work with the various directors and their particular approaches to story interpretation.

Having your talents guided and influenced by the directors and/or the story people, doesn't mean giving up your individuality — it does mean using your creative ability in a broader sense. So the broader your "world view," the more all-encompassing will be your contribution.

BREAK THE CHAINS OF CONFORMITY: Most of my criticism in the evening drawing classes has to do with the artists straightening things up. We are raised in a society where things must be orderly: "straighten up your room," "trim the hedge," "straighten your tie," "stay in your lane," and "walk the straight and narrow." It takes a conscious effort to break away from this kind of inflicted thinking, which, in an artist's life, becomes a straitjacket for the imagination.

ADD TENSION TO YOUR DRAWINGS: In our daily lives we avoid tension. Tension, of sorts, enervates us and saps our enthusiasm. Actually, tension is an indication that life exists. Just to stand up creates physical tension in the body. And when people want to put a little spice in their gestures they add more tension, stress, or torque. Symmetry in architecture may give you a feeling of stability, but in drawing and in humor, symmetry becomes lifeless. Tension, in a sense, forces the gesture out of the body by means of opposing force, altered balance, or augmented energy through the use of angles, squash and stretch, and greater emphasis on the action.

KEEP YOUR THOUGHTS STIRRED UP: When I recommend reading, attending good movies, and observing life around you (preferably with a sketch book in hand), I don't mean just doing it as a means of passing time. It's a way of keeping that constant stream of thoughts — that inner dialog we all engage in — stirred up and cross-indexed.

A good writer will use what I always advocate in drawing — verbs. A friend of John Muir's, a missionary named S. Hale Young, had a way of making the landscape come alive in his writing. After accompanying Muir on a trip into Alaska, he described the icebergs as, "Charging down upon us like an army, spreading out in loose formation, and then gathering into a barrier." I underlined the verbs to emphasize how he made a lot of frozen ice seem alive, active, and in a sense, gesturing.

The writer whose article I got this from is just as colorful. He says of their trip:

Yosemite-like canyons still in the making yawned on either side. Awesome rivers of ice ended in avalanches. Whale-size ice chunks plunged seaward, breeding huge waves and swells, and endless fleets of icebergs streamed out to sea. The slowly receding glaciers left in their wake a land totally wild and newborn, scraped clean of vegetation.

That kind of descriptiveness should be present in your drawings. Not just a lot of frozen lines that form an outline of something, but active, living lines that describe your character as doing things, and doing them in a descriptive way.

Comedians arouse a different kind of picture in your mind. They use a sort of twist that shocks you out of your normal state or realism. Like Groucho Marx saying "I would horsewhip you if I had a horse." Or like the other day someone made a remark about another person of questionable intelligence, saying, "He acts like he doesn't have both oars in the water."

Humor isn't always wisecracks, buffoonery, and silly drawings. Good humor often contains some real good common sense like these strips of *Salt Chuck on the Rocks!* by Chuck Sharman.

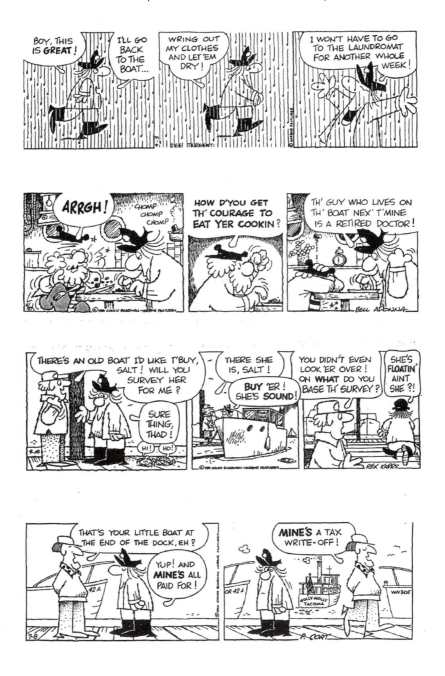

149 The Right Way?

I am often asked what is the right way to draw this or that, and of course, I am always hard pressed for an answer. So many things depend on what you have to work with and what it is you want to say.

In a dialog practice scene for the between pictures "jobless," it is impossible to pick a right way to solve the problem. There is merit in the practice and its intention was to make the artists think about it rather than just do straight inbetweens. One would need to hear the dialog recording and see the dialog reading on the exposure sheet to be sure. Using the simple principles of animation such as squash and stretch, anticipation, and timing will help in doing dialogue. Simply inbetweening the extremes would cause an undesirable mushiness. Dialog usually has a snap to it, in animation that snap even has to be accented. Also, in real life we rarely form every vowel and consonant with our mouth. We group similarly shaped sounds and words into phrases, saving the broad accents for dramatic effect. For instance, if you were delivering the line, "What do you think I should do with the rest of this stuff?," you more than likely would move only your tongue until you got to the word "rest" and would probably accent that word. Try it. Notice there is very little lip and jaw movement. Try it again accentuating every syllable using the lips and jaw. It feels silly doesn't it? Overdoing dialog in animation destroys credibility.

Let's say the character is saying "fly." Ideally there would be time for a squeezed up "f" with a drawing before or after to show it either forming or unforming. By that I mean a soft "f" that is not yet squeezed tight; that way you see the "f" happening and have enough of its shape on the screen to see it. Just one or two frames is hardly enough time to register, and if the adjoining mouths are similar in shape and position you will have something like this.

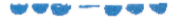

That closed mouth will "flash" on the screen because in among several frames of inside mouth color you will have one closed mouth surrounded by flesh color, and possibly two white teeth flashing like a strobe light.

A lot depends on how the "f" is spoken and how much time you have to spend on it as to whether you will show the upper teeth, turn down the corners of the lips, raise the cheeks, narrow down the eyes, or wrinkle the nose. The "right way?" Well, those diagrams of mouth action in various animation books are a good place to start, but into that stir a little common sense and logic and you will likely get something that works. So you can see why I am wishy-washy when it comes to coming up with an answer to the question: "What's the right way…?"

Drawing from the model is fraught with many similar problems. How to draw something always depends on what you (or your character) are trying to say. (I'm not speaking about dialog here.) But anyway, are you drawing the part where the character is saying "What do you think I should do with the…" or the accented, "…rest…" You have to have that in mind or your drawing will just lie there and say nothing at all. The most horrible fate any drawing can be subjected to is to have nothing to say. That is why I encourage everyone to form a story in their minds as they draw, so they will have a direction in which to go. Most drawing problems are solved by the answer to, "What is it doing?"

Following are some drawings that were made in one of the drawing classes. In my accompanying sketches I try to demonstrate the importance of having the figure doing something — anything! If the model's pose is unclear and you want to clarify it, or if you want to plus the pose or even change it, or if you want to change the character to Mickey or Ariel, do it. It has to be doing something, saying something, telling a story ... in a word, acting.

I try to have the models pose in a costume — a waiter, sailor, hula-dancer, carpenter, etc. I think it's as important to analyze how a carpenter saws a board as it is to search for the best way to animate an "f".

This all may seem rather involved to some of you, but I think it can make the difference between a *Doonesbury* or a *Kathy* drawing and a scene from *Bambi*.

Analyzing a gesture doesn't take a long time, nor does it use up a lot of energy (actually it's quite invigorating). All you have to do is decide what you want your character to do (that should take but a split second) and, then without getting sidetracked by fascinating and eye-catching details, get it down on paper. For instance, here's a student's sketch of a character supposedly leaning on the back of a chair, in a somewhat reflective attitude. His head says "reflective mood" but cover up the head with your fingertip and then name the pose. In my sketch (and this only took about ten or fifteen seconds) he is leaning back on the chair, his left hip is jutting out because all the weight is on his left leg, and the arm is relaxed along the left side with the hand dangling free. Between the support he gets from leaning on the chair and the placement of the weight on the left leg, he can relax and reflect to his heart's desire:

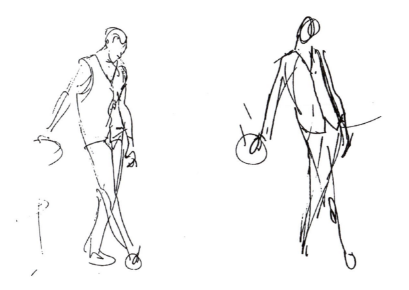

Here is another pose where the character is sitting in the chair, leaning on the back of the chair, again, in a reflective attitude. As you can see the student was struggling with how to draw the various parts of the body rather than having concentrated on the desired gesture and going for that. Notice in my sketch I made no effort to draw anything. I was drawing just the gesture — the parts seemed to fall into place. I concentrated on leaning him forward so the weight of the head and shoulders was on the chair back. That made the right arm look more like it was dangling out beyond (helping the attitude). Since he is seated backwards in the chair, I spread his legs apart (around the chair back) and in doing so brought his left leg out toward us, while the far leg appears to be going away from us, creating a feeling of third dimension. As you can see in the student's drawing both legs (and both arms) are profile, flat, and parallel to the picture plane.

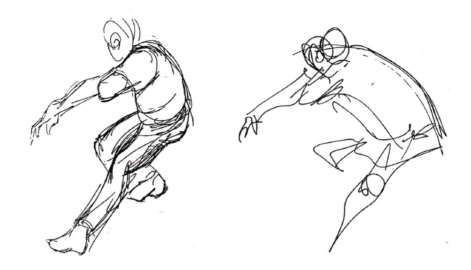

While parallels are fresh in our minds, here is another student's drawing where the arms are both profiles. Nothing will flatten your drawing better than parallel lines, shapes, and directions. Blatant verticals and horizontals are also undesirable. Add them to your unwelcome list. In my sketch I brought the left elbow forward to overcome that problem and to create some third dimensional space in the drawing.

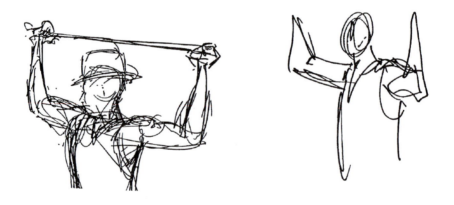

In this last example the pose was a complicated one. The model planted his knees on the floor in one direction and then twisted his body and head progressively to his right. In the student's drawing nearly everything is pointed in the same direction, obviating any twist.

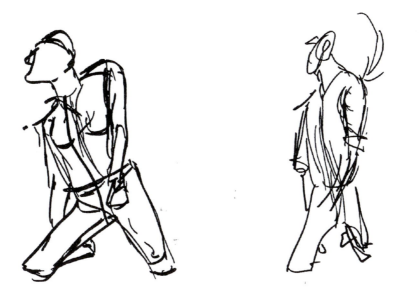

Due to an overwhelming desire to go to Yosemite for a couple of days to kick (autumn) leaves, and the need to build an addition to our (covered) patio to protect our ever growing accumulation of plants from the soon-to-come killer frosts, I am taking a two-week vacation. Consequently, there will be no Stanchfield drawing classes nor Stanchfield handouts during this time. Eat your hearts out!

If in that interim you decide you are better off without me, give me a call and I'll retire for the fifth time.

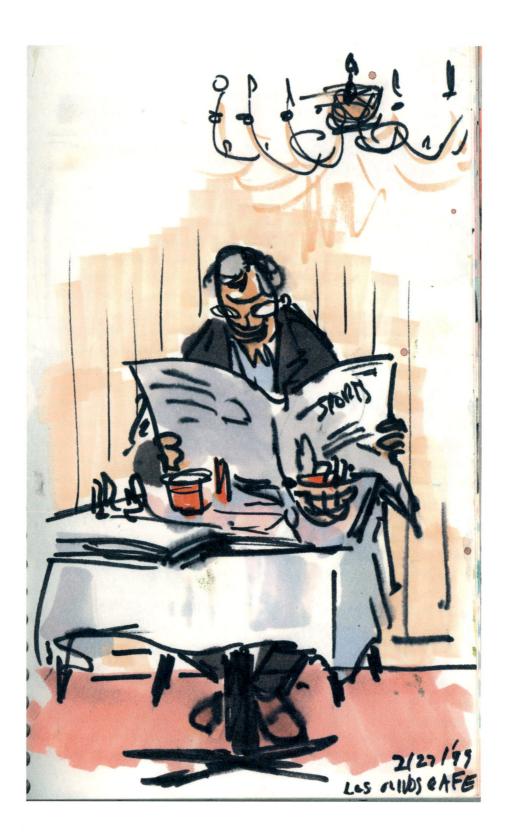

Credits — Volume I